How to TEPS

하우투 텝스

시크릿 독해편

How to TEPS 시크릿 독해편

지은이 정성수
펴낸이 안용백
펴낸곳 (주)넥서스

초판 1쇄 발행 2010년 9월 15일
초판 7쇄 발행 2014년 2월 15일

출판신고 1992년 4월 3일 제311-2002-2호
121-840 서울시 마포구 서교동 394-2
Tel (02)330-5500 Fax (02)330-5555
ISBN 978-89-6000-915-8 18740

www.nexusbook.com

유형별로 텝스 독해를 **공략**한다

How to TEPS

하우투 텝스

시크릿 독해편

정성수 지음

넥서스

머리말

I know all your tricks!

이 말은 전설적인 무술가이자 영화배우였던 이소룡(브루스 리)의 일대기를 그린 〈드래곤〉이라는 영화에서 이소룡에 도전했던 한 남자의 대사입니다.

대한민국에서 시행되는 영어 시험 중 최고 난이도를 자랑하는 TEPS 시험에서 수험생들이 최고등급 1+등급을 얻기는 매우 어렵습니다. 하지만, 저는 TEPS 시험에 호랑이가 토끼 한 마리를 잡을 때도 최선을 다하는 마음으로 수십 차례 응시, 2010년 8월 기준 TEPS 최고등급 1+급을 34번 획득하였습니다. 더불어, 수험생들을 좌절시키는 TEPS tricks에 대해 수험생들에게 실질적 도움이 되는 know-how에 대하여 연구해 왔습니다. 이 책은 TEPS 독해에 대한 제 노력의 최종 결과물입니다. 'I know all your tricks!'라고 외치며 무술의 대가 이소룡에게 도전한 한 남자처럼 이 책으로 공부한 수험생들이 시험장에서 'I know all TEPS tricks!'라고 외치며 자신감에 충만하여 문제를 술술 풀어내기를 바랍니다.

이 책의 구체적 특징들은 다음과 같습니다.

1. 과학적으로 출제되는 TEPS 독해 문제들을 꿰뚫는 초과학적 풀이 기법들을 간결하면서도 명확히 재정립했습니다.

2. 매달 TEPS시험 응시에서 나오는 경험을 바탕으로 실제 TEPS 독해 출제 원리와 tricks를 낱낱이 파헤쳐 모든 문제에 충실히 반영, 한 문제를 풀더라도 TEPS 독해 점수 향상과 깨달음을 얻을 수 있도록 했습니다.

3. 대부분의 교재들은 기출 변형으로 이미 접한 문제들을 복습하는 데 그치지만 수험생들이 정말로 원하는 실제 TEPS 독해 출제 원리를 100% 구현한 새로운 문제들을 다소 어렵게 출제해서 새로운 문제들에 대한 목마름을 채우고 동시에 고득점의 열쇠인 고난도 문제들에 대한 풀이 능력도 키울 수 있도록 했습니다.

갚을 수 없는 은혜를 베풀어 주시는 부모님, 항상 사랑 가득한 인생의 든든한 동반자인 아내 그리고 세세한 부분까지 챙겨 주시면서 계속 감동을 주는 사려 깊은 넥서스 임준현 사장님을 비롯, 다양하게 저를 밀어주고 끌어주는 넥서스 관계자 분들께 진심으로 감사합니다.

앞으로도 인터넷 칼럼, 강의, 교재 등을 통해 찾아뵐 것을 약속드리며 이 나라와 이 민족을 위해 참다운 인재가 될 수많은 TEPS 수험생들이 이 책을 통해 TEPS와 영어라는 탈을 쓰고 찾아오는 모든 어려움에 당당히 'I know all your tricks!'를 외칠 수 있을 것으로 믿습니다.

마지막으로 2009년 3월 8일, 세상의 빛을 처음 본 사랑하는 나의 딸 정수민과 지혜 주시는 이 책의 공저자이신 하나님께 이 책을 바칩니다!

"If you really have to be afraid, that would be only when you are sorry because you didn't do what you truly wanted to."

저자 정 성 수

목차

TEPS 독해
핵심 정보

TEPS 독해 특징

TEPS 독해에서 눈에 띄는 가장 큰 특징은 일지문 일문항이라는 점이다. 이는 문항 간의 연계성을 바탕으로 정답을 추측하는 것을 방지하기 위해서라고 한다. 이외에 수험생이 알아야 하는 특징은 다음과 같다.

1 속독

TEPS 독해는 지문수가 40개로 타 시험의 독해에 비해 많은 편이다. 또한 주어진 45분이라는 시간도 그리 넉넉한 시간은 아니기에 '속독'은 필수적이다. 따라서 '속독'에 대한 이해를 재정립해 보고자 한다.

대부분의 경우 빨리 읽는 것이 속독의 전부라고 생각하기 쉽다. 그러나 아무리 빨리 읽어도 내용을 이해하지 못한다면 소용없음은 당연하다. 읽는 속도가 다소 느리더라도 어떤 문장이든 한 번만 읽고 70%정도 이해하는 것이 속독의 시작이다. 특히 시험과 같이 제한된 시간에 많은 양의 글을 읽어야 할 때 단순히 속도가 문제가 아니라, 같은 문장을 반복적으로 읽는 횟수를 줄일 수 있느냐가 진정 필요하다. 한 번만 읽고 이해할 수 있느냐가 속독의 핵심!

2 Paraphrasing(바꿔 쓰기)

독해를 제대로 했다면 이해한 내용을 다른 표현으로 제대로 나타낼 수 있어야 하며 paraphrasing은 이런 능력을 측정하기 위함이다. 가령 어떤 지문을 다 이해했고 문제에 대한 정답은 a인데 b라고 생각했다고 하자. 물론 a, b, c, d 4개의 선택지 모두 다 읽었을 것이다. 그럼에도 불구하고 오답 b를 선택한 것이다. 물론 지문을 다 이해했기 때문에 이는 단순히 이해의 문제가 아니라는 것을 알 것이다. 근본적인 원인은 이해한 내용을 정답 a와 같이 가공해서 표현할 능력이 없기 때문이다. 즉, 여러분의 표현력이 출제자의 수준과 차이가 많이 날수록 고난도 문제로 느껴지는 것이다. paraphrasing은 듣기와 읽기를 통한 표현 능력의 간접 측정이라는 이론적 모델의 구현이다!

3 지문 길이

간단히 TOEFL iBT 독해와 비교해 보면 TEPS 독해가 양이 많다. TOEFL iBT의 경우 최소 2,100단어에서 최대 3,500단어로 독해 영역이 구성된다. 그러나 TEPS는 평균 100단어 남짓한 지문이 40개 출제되므로 매번 4,000단어 이상으로 독해 영역이 구성된다. TEPS 독해는 지속적으로 많은 지문을 읽을 수 있는지 영어 독해 '체력'까지도 까다롭게 요구한다. 따라서 평소에 집중적이고 지속적인 독해 경험이 TEPS 독해 고득점에 대한 핵심이다!

4 지문 내용

TEPS 독해에는 거의 모든 분야의 내용이 등장하기 때문에 평소에 다소 관심 없는 주제의 글에도 익숙해질 필요가 있다. 그러나 문제 풀이 능력을 향상시키기 위해 굳이 배경 지식을 쌓을 필요는 없다. 배경 지식이 있으면 지문 읽는 것이 조금 편안하게 느껴질 뿐이지 정답을 찾는 데 결정적인 도움이 되진 않을뿐더러 동일한 지문은 출제되지 않는다.

정작 중요한 것은 어떤 내용이 나와도 머릿속에서 내용 분석과 정리를 잘할 수 있는 연습을 얼마나 많이 했는가이다.

 **TEPS 독해 고득점 전략**

TEPS 독해 고득점을 가능케 해주는 것이 '속독'이라고 볼 수 있지만, 눈에 들어오지 않는 것을 '속독' 한다고 문제가 풀리는 것은 아니다. 따라서 정독을 통한 내용 자체에 대한 이해력을 향상시키는 것이 우선 과제이고 이외에 수험생에게 실제적으로 필요한 전략은 다음과 같다.

1 정확한 문장 해석 능력

맞았다고 생각했는데 알고 보니 틀렸을 때에는 대부분 특정 문장의 해석이 잘못되어 틀린 경우가 많다. 많은 교재와 강의에서 "해석하면 시간이 오래 걸리니 해석하지 말라!"고 가르치고 있다. 그러나 나는 생각이 다르다. 정확히 말하면 해석하지 말라는 것은 지문 내용을 우리말로 옮긴 후에 이해하지 말라는 것이지 이해 자체를 하지 말라는 말은 아니다!

특히 평소 학습할 때 학습자가 이해했는지 알 수 있는 가장 쉽고 가장 확실한 방법으로 해석 말고 뭐가 있는가? 해석은 이해력 연습의 가장 기본적이고 가장 중요한 도구다. 따라서 평소 학습할 때 잘 이해가 가지 않는 문장은 반드시 정확하게 해석하고 넘어가야 한다!

많은 학습자들과 심지어 가르치시는 분들도 시험 볼 때의 방법이나 태도를 연습할 때도 적용하도록 지도하는 경우가 많다. 학습할 때 방법과 태도를 시험 볼 때와 확실히 구분해서 적용하자! 시험은 시험 보는 것처럼 보고, 공부는 공부하는 것처럼 해야 여러분이 정말로 원하는 '실력으로 고득점'이 가능해진다!

2 지문의 주제 파악

TEPS 독해에서 출제되는 유형은 빈칸 채우기, 대의 파악하기, 세부 사항 파악하기, 추론하기, 흐름에 어울리지 않는 문장 찾기 5가지로 구분되지만, 실제로는 유형과 상관없이 심지어 세부 사항 파악 문제들과 추론하기 문제도 지문 주제를 정확히 파악하면 접근하기 편한 문제가 상당히 많다. 따라서 평소 학습 시, 단순히 문제를 푸는 것에 급급하기 보다는 지문의 주제를 정확히 파악하는 것을 우선 시하길 바란다.

문제 해결은 찍어서라도 할 수 있지만 지문의 주제를 파악하는 것은 그렇지 않다. 실력이 절대적으로 필요한 TEPS에 대한 진정한 대비는 단순히 문제를 해결하는 행위에 있는 것이 아니라 문제의 본질, 즉 지문의 주제를 확실히 파악하는 것이다!

3 질문과 선택지의 중요성

지문 자체 독해만 신경 쓰고 질문이나 선택지를 주의 깊게 읽지 않아 틀리는 경우를 조심해야 한다. 특히 몇몇 세부 사항 파악 문제는 질문을 잘 봐야 한다. 단순히 지문 내용에 맞는 것이 아닌 지문의 특정 내용만을 묻는 형태의 질문도 나오기 때문이다.

선택지를 지문보다 먼저 읽게 되면 당연히 정답보다는 오답에 대한 정보가 머릿속에 미리 많이 들어가 있게 되어 지문에서 제시된 정보를 올바르게 처리하는 데 어려움을 겪을 수 있다. 또한 일부분만 옳은 선택지, 정답이 되기에는 부족한 내용의 선택지, 지문에 없는 내용의 선택지, 지문 내용을 교묘하게 섞어 놓은 선택지를 조심해야 한다.

특히 정답이 잘 안 보일 때 선택지의 활용은 매우 중요하다. 가령 어떤 문제에 대한 정답이 잘 안 보일 때 지문을 다시 보는 경우가 많지만 항상 느꼈고 갈망했으나 지금껏 속 시원하게 누구 하나 말해주지 못했던 것은 일단 자신만의 논리에 빠지면 지문을 여러 번 읽어도 정답이 잘 보이지 않는다는 점이다. 이때는 새로운 논리의 출발점이 될 수 있는 오답이라고 생각했거나 자세히 보지 않은 선택지를 주의 깊게 읽고 이를 바탕으로 지문을 다시 읽어야 보이지 않았던 내용이 보여 문제에 대한 실마리를 잡을 수 있다는 것이다!

빈칸 채우기

유형 파악

빈칸 채우기는 TEPS 독해 1번부터 16번까지 (15, 16번은 적절한 접속어 넣기) 출제되고 빈 칸이 있는 문장만 놓고 볼 때 선택지 4개 모두 그럴듯한 경우가 많다. 따라서 정답을 찾기 위해서는 단순히 빈칸 주변만 잘 보기 보다는 지문 흐름까지도 정확히 읽는 것이 매우 중요 하다.

의외로 빈칸 채우기를 어려워하는 수험생들이 제법 되는데, 기존의 대부분의 영어시험은 질문이 제시되어 질문에 포커스를 맞춰서 풀면 됐지만 빈칸 채우기는 지문의 흐름을 읽어 야 하고, 말 그대로 빈칸을 채워야 하는 작문 능력도 간접적으로 측정하는 객관식 형태의 주관식이기 때문이다.

핵심 전략

빈칸 위치에 따라 접근하다가 정답이 잘 안 보이면 그때서야 지문의 다른 부분을 읽는 경우 가 있는데 이렇게 되면 결국에는 지문을 두 번 읽게 되는 거나 마찬가지이므로 처음부터 가 급적이면 끝까지 읽어가면서 푸는 것이 결과적으로 정확도와 속도를 높인다. 특히 지문을 다 읽었음에도 선택지에서 헷갈릴 때는 지문의 주제를 제대로 파악하지 못하거나 파악했더 라도 세부 내용에 지나치게 집착해서 지문의 주제를 순간 망각하거나 혹은 특정 문장이 제 대로 해석되지 않는 경우가 대부분이다. 따라서 주제를 파악하고 문제를 푸는 내내 주제를 잊지 말고 정확하게 해석해야 한다!

사실 잘 생각해보면 소위 말하는 독해 요령이나 기법들은 읽고 푸는 것이 아니라 '어떻게 하면 덜 읽고 풀까?'에 대한 고민의 결과로 '읽고 푸는' 독해와는 근본적으로 대치되는 것 이다. 엄청난 아이러니가 아닌가? 이런 점을 특히 최신 TEPS 출제자들이 잘 이용하고 있고 특히 어려운 문제들이 이런 경향이 심하다. 어떻게 하면 잘 '읽고' 풀까에 대한 고민이 최우 선임을 명심하자!

Reading Drills

A number of variables determine the equilibrium state of a system of constant composition. Any change in these variables will change the nature of the equilibrium state of our system. We can _____ by deciding what variations imposed from the surroundings are of major significance in natural situations.

(a) have a balanced view of the system
(b) greatly simplify our problem
(c) learn about what keeps the state stable
(d) organize things in our life

A research study showed that white-collar workers were described as very concerned about the impression their dress made on their superiors. Even though blue-collar workers _____ that they might be judged by their dress, they recognized that any departure from the accepted pattern of clothing would evoke ridicule from their co-workers.

(a) did not like the idea
(b) were against the fact
(c) were less aware
(d) did not believe

The omnipresent significance of water makes it _____. It makes water a major factor in the food industry, so much so that food preservation will be improved steadily thanks to the understanding of the ways water behaves and interacts with proteins.

(a) an axis around which the wheel of biological study should be built
(b) one of the ways to contribute to the improvement of the economy
(c) what every human being needs for his/ her survival
(d) of use to many kinds of industry and the examples are as follows

① 비법

지문 두 번째 문장에서 변수들의 변화가 우리 체계의 평형 상태의 본질에 변화를 일으킬 것이라고 했으므로 뭔가 변화되는 의미를 담고 있는 (b)가 정답이다.

variable 변수 **equilibrium state** 평형 상태 **composition** 조성 **simplify** 단순화하다

번역

많은 변수가 항존하는 조직 체계의 평형 상태를 결정지어 준다. 이들 변수에 있어서 작은 변화도 우리 체계의 평형 상태의 본질에 변화를 일으킬 것이다. 우리는 환경으로부터 가해지는 변화 중에 어떤 것이 자연적인 상황에서 매우 중요한가를 결정함으로써 우리의 문제를 크게 단순화시킬 수 있다.

(a) 조직 체계에 균형 잡힌 시각을 가질 수 있다
(b) 우리의 문제를 크게 단순화시킬 수 있다
(c) 무엇이 조직 체계를 안정적으로 해주는지 알 수 있다
(d) 삶의 여러 일들을 조직화할 수 있다

② 비법

지문은 복장에 대해 사무직 노동자들과 육체 노동자들의 다른 생각을 비교하고 있으므로 비교급의 (c)가 정답이다.

white-collar 사무직의 **impression** 인상 **superior** 상관, 상급자 **departure** 출발, 이탈, 탈선 **evoke** (감정 따위를) 일으키다, 자아내다 **ridicule** 비웃음; 비웃다

번역

한 연구 조사의 결과는 사무직 노동자들은 자신의 옷이 상급자들에게 주는 인상에 대해 무척 신경 쓰고 있다는 것을 보여줬다. 육체 노동자들은 자신이 옷에 의해 판단되지나 않을까 하는 것을 덜 의식하지만 그들은 일반적으로 받아들여지고 있는 옷의 양식으로부터 벗어나는 것이 동료 친구들로부터 비웃음을 사리라는 것은 알고 있었다.

(a) 그런 생각을 좋아하지 않았지만
(b) 그런 사실에 반대했지만
(c) 덜 의식하지만
(d) 믿지 않았지만

③ 비법

지문 두 번째 문장에서 물은 고유 성질과 단백질과의 상호 작용에 대한 지식이 식량 보존의 착실한 개선을 가져올 만큼 식품 산업에 있어 중요한 요인이 된다고 했으므로 물이 생물학적 연구의 중심이라는 (a)가 정답이다. (d)는 선택지의 many kinds에 해당하는 내용이 지문에 없다.

omnipresent 도처에 있는 **significance** 중요성 **factor** 요인 **preservation** 보존 **interact** 상호 작용하다 **axis** 축, 중심 **of use** 유용한

번역

물은 생물학적 연구의 중심이 될 정도로 널리 알려져 있다. 이런 연구를 통해 얻어낸 물의 성질과 단백질과의 상호 작용에 대한 이해 덕분에 식량 보존이 착실히 될 만큼 식품 산업에 있어 주요 요인이 된다.

(a) 생물학적 연구의 중심이 되다
(b) 경제 개선에 도움되는 방법들 중 하나이다
(c) 생존을 위해 모든 인간이 필요로 하는 것이다
(d) 많은 종류의 산업들에 의해 사용되고 그런 예들은 다음과 같다

 # Model Test

TOPIC 합성물

Materials can often be improved by putting two of them together, so that each makes up for the deficiencies of the other. In this way several excellent, inexpensive materials have been created that make better products available at lower cost. Composites are usually made from pairs of materials that have opposite properties. One is often in the form of strands or fibers, which, though _____, are too floppy to stand up to being compressed. The other material can then be something that will simply stick the fibers together. Often this second material is quite weak or brittle.

(a) strong in tension
(b) sometimes breakable
(c) stable yet light
(d) chemically simple

TOPIC 네버스가 새 일터에서 일하게 된 것과 루 씨의 일정

Mr. Nevers,

Congratulations on your appointment to the new Summit Grain office in Halifax, Nova Scotia. Ms. Lou has told me that you are the perfect person to manage the office, and she looks forward to seeing good things from you there. I am writing to inform you that Ms. Lou will not be able to attend the kick-off meeting at the Halifax office on Tuesday. Summit Grain's board members have called a meeting in Marseille that same day, _____. I will be staying at the Highcrest Halifax on Morton Street while in Halifax. You are welcome to call me at the hotel to set up our meeting.

Cordially,
Jannette Choi

(a) but she cannot make it to the meeting
(b) and it looks like you should be there, too
(c) but she might be available later that day
(d) and apparently her presence is required

TOPIC 이성 친구나 배우자 선택 시 남자와 여자의 차이

In recent research on college students' dating habits, studies found that _____ when it comes to choosing a partner for a casual date. What is intriguing is the explanation given by an evolutionary psychologist: For eons, it's been in the man's interest to spread his seed as widely and indiscriminately as possible, thus preserving the species. On the other hand, it's unwise for a woman to monkey around with just any suitor; her genetically inferior offspring could be at a disadvantage in attracting a mate and doing their part for civilization.

(a) how they look does not matter as much as it did
(b) men are less discriminating than women
(c) their parental influence is not important
(d) women are more picky than men

TOPIC 어린 아이들의 사회적 역할 학습

Children quickly realize what roles society expects them to play. Researcher Douglas Hofstadter tells this story: ten boys and ten girls visited a hospital on a school trip. At the end of the visit, hospital staff gave each child a hat: doctors' hats for the boys, nurses' hats for the girls. The parents complained, saying it was an example of stereotyping. The hospital director supported them and promised this would change. The next year, at the end of a similar trip, the parents again found out that all the boys had doctors' hats and all the girls had nurses' hats! They went to the hospital director. This time he said, "_____."

(a) It was totally unexpected to see that happen
(b) We didn't have anything but hats for the children
(c) The children chose which hats they wanted
(d) I promise you we will teach them the principle of equality

TEPS Reading Practice

Part I **Questions 1—10** Read the passage. Then choose the option that best completes the passage.

1. Shunning the somber hues and heavy shadows of earlier styles, the impressionists sought to paint on canvas what the eye sees in an instant. _____, they portrayed unposed subjects from unexpected angles. These artists also believed that the secret to visual impression is light. To emphasize the flickers of light reflected in the ever-changing scenes, impressionist painters daubed brilliant patches of color on the canvas with quick brush strokes.

(a) Being least attentive
(b) Trying to be prolific
(c) Breaking with tradition
(d) Creating natural looks

2. Clayton's educational fund budget is projected to be smaller than last year even though the district is continuing to grow. _____, and the district will have to hire more teachers. District officials point out, however, that over the past year many teachers have retired and, in most cases, have been replaced by younger, less experienced teachers. That keeps costs down because salaries are figured by seniority. Also, $680,000 was saved from the supply fund, which buys everything from rubber bands to construction paper. And a second look at the fund that pays for utility fees found that energy-saving efforts in schools will allow $250,000 to be spent elsewhere.

(a) Clayton has been growing for the last couple of years
(b) About 32,879 students are expected to enroll in the fall
(c) Education is regarded most highly in Clayton
(d) Efforts are being made to provide an inexpensive education

One day my brother Vincent had a minor pain in his hip. In an attempt to save both time and money, he tracked down his doctor on the phone. Seeking free advice, he described the pain. His doctor carefully said that he couldn't provide a diagnosis without a proper examination but obligingly suggested Vincent eat a good meal, take some paracetamol, and apply moist heat to his hip. "Hey, Doc," Vincent urged, "could it be arthritis?" "Hey, Vincent," the doctor asked, "_____?" Vincent got the point.

(a) do you need a prescription
(b) what do you think of the tie I'm wearing
(c) did I sound too serious
(d) why don't you come see me in person

Architects _____ to design modern buildings. Usually after first spending time with the clients who want to build the structure, they draw some pen-and-paper sketches of buildings that might accommodate their clients' needs. Next, they usually use wooden blocks, much like the ones children play with, to build rough but easily altered models. They make it easy to determine the client's size requirements. In the next step, they build a series of scale models; the final one is a perfect miniature version of the full-size structure. Finally, they use the model to enter all of the building's measurements into a computer program that figures out the total costs for all of the necessary materials.

(a) work with computer graphic designers
(b) use a combination of high-tech and low-tech procedures
(c) spend a large amount of time with their clients
(d) go through six steps involving different skills

Your life is often ruled by rituals or beliefs that have no basis in fact. While this behavior is anxiety driven, the cause of the actual anxiety is your fundamental feeling of not being in control of your life. If you were in control of your life, you would see examples of your actions producing specific results. Without this control, you lose the ability to distinguish between things that happen to you and those that you make happen. This _____ rituals. You need to have some sense of control, so you draw your own correlation between an event and a behavior. After all, your actions give you the illusion of control.

(a) leads you to know about
(b) makes you a virtual slave to
(c) is the basic meaning of
(d) cannot be solved only by

A new labor union representing child care employees is starting to be organized to try to improve wages and welfare for one of the nation's lowest-paying professions. According to the U.S. Bureau of Labor Statistics, child care workers make an average of $7.86 an hour, less than animal caretakers, and _____. With low wages and little welfare, the turnover rate in child care jobs is 30 to 50 percent a year. "It's necessary to make a national union of child care workers to improve the quality of these jobs," said Denise Dowell, taking charge of organizing the United Child Care Union.

(a) their employees aren't making money
(b) it doesn't reflect the difficulty of the job
(c) this amount is expected to decrease soon
(d) many work without health care insurance

Dear Editor,

I noted with disappointment that, in an otherwise outstanding issue on the artists of the 20th century, your magazine failed to mention, arguably, the most distinguished figure of the century. The emergence of George Harris in 1982 was significant in that _____. Although his career eventually collapsed, it reflected a watershed in popular culture's debate on what an artist should pursue.

(a) it effectively changed the preconceived ideas of the public about art
(b) that was when styles of painting kept appearing and disappearing
(c) no other artists could produce the proper works of modern art
(d) he contributed to the development of new theories of art

In this age of prospering commerce, one can be tempted to use the national wealth as a yardstick to decide how civilized a nation is. But could we call a nation which has all the gold of Peru but a vast majority of its people starving on the street a civilized nation? For me, being civilized is to develop the good sides of our human nature. That is to say, we should have compassion, pity, and understanding for people who are not like us. Thus, such terrible conditions for the poor _____.

(a) are not present in most civilized nations
(b) need nothing but our good will to improve
(c) can be found even in wealthy nations
(d) is a true mark of an uncivilized nation

We can't really afford to ignore the results from a recent survey. This survey was based on interviews conducted with senior managers in 300 corporations to find out what type of managers reach senior management positions. About 35% of the group of managers _____ reached senior management positions. On the other hand, 65% of the more individualistic managers who are decisive, dynamic, and able to make decisions on their own achieved senior management status. So, I think the conclusion is self-evident. If you want to reach the top of private-sector corporations, you have a much better chance if you adopt a fairly autocratic, top-down approach to management.

(a) who tend to depend on other people for important decisions
(b) with abundant field experience rather than high education
(c) who do what they have to do without gaining attention
(d) classified as participative in their management style

It all began with a mysterious and seemingly innocent postcard, which changed the life of Bantock, a solitary artist living in Ireland. His logical world got turned upside down by Shiella, a strangely exotic woman living on an island in the South Pacific. This stunning original novel unfolds in a series of postcards and letters, all fascinatingly illustrated with whimsical designs, bizarre creatures, and darkly imagined landscapes. Inside the book, Bantock and Shiella's letters are to be found nestling in their envelopes, permitting the reader to _____.

(a) learn about some good examples of love letters for a lasting relationship
(b) keep so interested in the story that he/ she feels that it is a good book
(c) examine the intimate correspondence of these inexplicably linked strangers
(d) understand the different ways of thinking and living between the two characters

접속어

유형 파악

접속어 문제는 15, 16번에서 출제되고 한 문제는 쉽게, 나머지 한 문제는 다소 어렵게 출제되는 것이 일반적인 출제 패턴이다.

최근에는 예전에 비해 However와 같은 역접 문제의 출제 빈도가 다소 줄었고, 보다 다양한 접속어가 선택지로 등장하고 있다. 지문 전체 흐름을 파악해야 하는 문제와 더불어 특히 지문 내용은 쉽지만 미묘한 차이가 있는 선택지들로 인해 풀기 어려운 문제도 출제되는 것이 최신 경향이다!

자주 출제되는 접속어들은 다음과 같다.

대조	but, yet, however, instead, rather, while, whereas, in contrast, conversely, on the other hand, on the contrary, in effect, in fact (강조 의미로 쓰일 때도 있음)
양보	still, despite, in spite of, nevertheless, nonetheless, notwithstanding
첨가	in addition, besides, furthermore, moreover, what is more, on top of
유사	similarly, likewise
예시	for example, for instance
이유, 결과	as a result, for this reason, consequently, subsequently
결론	thus, hence, therefore, eventually, overall, that is, in short, in sum, in conclusion

핵심 전략

표에서 제시된 자주 출제되는 접속어들의 의미를 정확히 알고 있어야 하고 빈칸 앞뒤 문장의 의미를 자연스럽게 이어주는 것을 고르면 되는데, 특히 비중은 낮지만 가끔 등장해서 괴롭히는 지문 전체 흐름을 파악해야 하는 문제를 주의해야 한다. 그래서 어떤 유형의 문제라도 글쓴이가 가장 전하고 싶은 내용이 무엇인지 정확히 파악하는 것이 중요하다.

또한 최근에 자주 출제되고 있는 의미가 비슷한 접속어 문제에 대비해서 이런 접속어들이 지문에서 어떤 논리 흐름으로 쓰이는지 눈여겨 봐야 한다. 가령 첨가와 유사, 결과와 결론은 자칫 혼동하기 쉬운데 유사는 근본 내용은 같지만 다른 예 같은 것이 나오고 결과는 적절한 원인이 선행되는 논리 흐름에서 사용된다. 따라서 이렇게 의미가 비슷한 접속어들을 개별적으로 학습하지 말고 실제 지문에서 어떤 논리 흐름으로 쓰이는지 살펴봐야 한다.

Reading Drills

Caesarian deliveries have risen so dramatically in the last decade that the procedure has stirred a nationwide medical controversy. Consumer groups charge that many C-sections are unnecessary and done to fit the convenience of the obstetrician's schedule. _____, physicians argue that wider use of caesarians has helped lower maternal and infant death rates in high-risk pregnancies.

(a) In other words
(b) As a matter of fact
(c) Furthermore
(d) Meanwhile

Neurofibromatosis is caused by a single dominant gene that is either inherited or produced by a spontaneous mutation. _____, an affected person has a 50-50 chance of passing the condition on to his or her offspring. Doctors cannot diagnose the disease prenatally, and many victims have firmly decided not to have children.

(a) At any rate
(b) No matter what
(c) In the former case
(d) In either instance

Pablo Picasso's period of powerful expression climaxed in the mural *Guernica*, a dramatic response to the agonies of the Spanish Civil War. _____, he continued to produce paintings and sculptures, working as always in many styles. Much of his later output was in pottery.

(a) Nevertheless
(b) Likewise
(c) Moreover
(d) Simultaneously

1 비법

빈칸 앞뒤 문장이 역접의 흐름이므로 (d)가 정답이다. As a matter of fact는 강조나 역접의 흐름일 때 사용하지만 둘 중 어느 경우든지 주관적인 내용이 아닌 객관적 사실이 와야 하는데 지문의 빈칸 다음 내용은 객관적 사실이라기 보다는 의사들의 주관적인 주장이다.

caesarian 제왕 절개의　**delivery** 분만
stir 자극하다　**controversy** 논란　**charge** 탓하다, 책망하다　**C-section** 제왕 절개
obstetrician 산부인과 의사　**physician** 의사
maternal 임산부의

번역

지난 10년 동안 제왕 절개에 의한 분만이 지나치게 많이 증가하여 전국적인 의학 논쟁으로 번지기까지 했다. 수요자 측에서는 제왕 절개 수술 중 상당수가 불필요한 수술이며 단지 산부인과 의사의 편의를 위해 행해지고 있다고 주장한다. 한편 의사들은 그 동안 제왕 절개 수술로 인해 위험도가 높은 임신의 경우에 산모나 태아의 사망률을 줄이는 데 기여해 왔다고 주장하고 있다.

(a) 즉
(b) 사실
(c) 게다가
(d) 한편

2 비법

지문 첫 문장의 신경원섬유증은 유전되거나 자생 돌연변이에 의해 발생된 우성 유전 인자에 의해 생긴다는 내용과 빈칸 뒤의 이 병에 걸린 사람이 그 자손에게 병을 유전시킬 확률이 50대 50이라는 내용을 보면 유전이든 자생 돌연변이든 어떤 경우라도 병에 걸린 사람이 그렇다는 흐름이므로 (d)가 정답이다.

neurofibromatosis 신경원섬유증　**dominant gene** 우성 유전 인자　**inherit** 물려받다
spontaneous 자발적인, 자생의　**mutation** 돌연변이　**offspring** 자손　**diagnose** 진단하다
prenatal 태아기, 태어나기 전

번역

신경원섬유증은 유전되거나 자생 돌연변이에 의해 발생된 우성 유전 인자에 의해 생긴다. 둘 중 어떤 경우라도 이 병에 걸린 사람이 그 자손에게 병을 유전시킬 확률은 50대 50이다. 이 질병은 태아기에는 진단할 수 없기에 이 병의 피해를 보고 있는 많은 사람들은 아이를 갖지 않겠다는 굳은 결심을 하고 만다.

(a) 어쨌든
(b) 무슨 일이 있더라도
(c) 전자의 경우에
(d) 둘 중 어떤 경우라도

3 비법

〈게르니카〉 벽화와 회화, 조각품은 서로 종류가 다르고 빈칸 뒤 문장의 항상 그렇듯이 많은 양식에 손을 댔다는 내용을 보면 (d)가 정답이다. (c)는 피카소의 박력 있는 표현 기법 시대나 〈게르니카〉 벽화에 대한 추가적인 내용이 나와야 한다.

period 시대　**climax** 절정에 이르다　**mural** 벽화　**agony** 고뇌, 고통　**sculpture** 조각품
civil war 내란　**simultaneous** 동시에 일어나는

번역

파블로 피카소의 박력 있는 표현 기법 시대의 결정판은 스페인 내란의 고통을 극적으로 표현해낸 〈게르니카〉 벽화라고 할 수 있다. 이와 동시에 그는 계속해서 회화와 조각품을 내놓았는데 항상 그렇듯이 많은 양식에 손을 댔다. 후기에는 주로 도자기 작업을 했다.

(a) 그럼에도 불구하고
(b) 마찬가지로
(c) 게다가
(d) 동시에

Model Test

Part I   **Questions 1—4** Read the passage. Then choose the option that best completes the passage.

1   **TOPIC** 혼다 광고에 대한 여성들의 반응

The commercial for the Honda Accord wagon begins with one cog rolling down and touching another. And then, many other parts—tires, ball bearings, springs, windows, and cams—are sequentially triggered into action. One hundred and twenty seconds later, the wagon rolls down, spreading a banner with the Accord logo. Then, a low voice speaks: "Isn't it nice when things just work?" But two minutes is too long for a TV ad, and a lot of machine-indifferent women will tune out the last 1:45. _____, the ad seems to require that unnecessary complexity to accomplish the simple task of just showing their logo, so it might be more or less opposite to Honda's brand promise of dependable machines.

(a) Furthermore
(b) Resultantly
(c) In fact
(d) Thus

2   **TOPIC** 소비자들이 물건을 사게 만드는 슈퍼마켓업자들의 계획

The modern supermarket is a scientifically designed human mousetrap. And you, the customer, are the mouse. If you don't believe that, consider this fact: average supermarket shoppers, even armed with a full shopping list, will buy an extra forty cents of goods for every one dollar they had originally intended to spend. If you asked them why they picked up the extra products, they would say something like, "Oh, I just happened to see something that caught my fancy." Do you think they came across them by chance? Certainly not. The truth is they didn't just "happen" to see that extra item—the supermarket carefully planned it that way. _____, the human mice fell into the trap.

(a) Namely
(b) Similarly
(c) Surprisingly
(d) Moreover

三 **TOPIC** 병에 걸려 누웠을 때 겪는 일

When nature hospitalizes an individual, whether he goes to bed in a hospital or in his own home, she takes him out of action so that she may use all of his energies for self-restoration purposes. Also, she gives the individual a much needed rest to discover the power of his own mind, as well as energy in meditation and thought regarding the cause of his pain. _____, he may discover that the cause came from a variety of sins which he might have avoided if he had listened to the voice of pain.

(a) For instance
(b) Ironically
(c) Thus
(d) Yet

너 **TOPIC** 교양 있는 영어 원어민들의 영어 사용

There are at large among us today a considerable number of people who make it their business to correct the speech and writings of others. When Winston Churchill says, "It's me," in a radio address, they murmur "It's I," and sit down to write bitter letters to some leading newspaper about "What is Happening to the English Language." Reading "I only had five dollars," they circle only and move it to the right of had with a profound sense of morality. If these people were all retired school teachers of English, their weight in the community would be negligible; but unfortunately they are not. They are authors, businessmen, librarians; _____, they are to be found wherever educated people read and write English.

(a) nevertheless
(b) indeed
(c) even so
(d) thus

TEPS Reading Practice

Strong and resilient, polyurethane foam is now the most widely used filling for lift-out seat and back cushions. Because it is quite firm, it's most comfortable when wrapped with another material, such as down or polyester batting. To test the quality of a polyurethane-foam cushion, pick one up. If it is very light, it may be made of poor-quality material. _____, an 8-inch cushion that measures 2x3 feet shouldn't weigh less than 3 pounds.

(a) However
(b) In general
(c) Alternatively
(d) Most of all

First of all, if we used Chinese characters officially, traditional culture would be better understood, as most ancient Korean documents are written in Chinese characters. _____, wider use of Chinese characters would help expedite exchanges with Japan, China, and other Asian countries using Chinese characters. So, I think the Ministry has good reason to promote the use of Chinese characters in government papers and on street signs.

(a) In addition
(b) For example
(c) Undoubtedly
(d) For this reason

When both parents have professional careers that are on the fast-track, their children can often be very anxious and competitive, and feel a lot of pressure to be as successful as their parents. They also show a lot of the problems that children of divorced parents show. _____, just like children who come from broken homes, they don't get enough parental supervision, nor attention.

(a) Obviously
(b) Hence
(c) Similarly
(d) Or

In this century, livestock is undergoing a dramatic change. You are still able to buy a steak at your local meat counter, but it comes from animals produced by new high-tech methods of farming. For example, the steers here are cloned: identical copies produced from the genes of one genetically superior animal. Bred to grow faster, with less fat, and needing less feed. But meat has an inherent problem—cholesterol. _____, numerous meat substitutes are being developed.

(a) Instead
(b) In conclusion
(c) For all that
(d) Consequently

When we settled in the Upper East Side, it was filled with galleries. Its variety of cultural attractions reminded us of Mexico City, where we had grown up. But we were beginning to get tired of the neighborhood's party atmosphere. _____, when we were expecting our first baby, suddenly our apartment on the third floor of a brownstone didn't seem like the best place to live. It didn't have a second bedroom, and it posed the problem of stairs, which are intimidating with a baby in one arm and a stroller in the other.

(a) Furthermore
(b) Apart from that
(c) Worst of all
(d) Strangely

The investigating commission announced on Saturday that preliminary findings showed that the Kursk was involved in a collision with an object near the surface weighing 8,000 tons or more. The Russian government said it was possible that such an object could have been a ship or an old mine. _____, some unknown chain of events could have set off an explosion aboard the submarine. Whatever the case, Russian officials say most of the crew died in the first two minutes after the explosion, including all the officers on the bridge.

(a) Besides
(b) If so
(c) Alternatively
(d) By contrast

Computers are too clever to ignore but too stupid to be trusted entirely. For over 35 years researchers have been struggling to build a computer in man's image. They are not even close to doing so. Although scientists have succeeded in giving machines all sorts of human skills, the goal of creating a machine as clever as a person seems to recede all the time. _____, this failure may eventually change the way in which people work and live more comprehensively than if scientists had succeeded in getting a computer to sit up and say, "Mother!"

(a) Indeed
(b) Resultantly
(c) Additionally
(d) Ironically

Financial experts admit they are puzzled by the market's strange behavior during the previous day's trading. Although all the economic signs indicated that the market would rise, the market nosedived instead and lost over 5% of its value in the first three hours of trading. Experts stated there was no logical reason for this. Some economists insisted that investors were merely involved in profit taking. Experts stated that the market was due for a slight negative correction. _____, a large majority of brokers are high on the market and don't expect today's losses to reoccur any time in the near future.

(a) Unbelievably
(b) Nevertheless
(c) Eventually
(d) Meanwhile

For their existence and comfort, men depend on certain products of the earth. These cannot be used in common, however, without certain disputes arising, nor do natural products suffice unless they are improved by human labor. Yet no one works unless he will receive some benefits to himself. Therefore, certain rules arise implying a mutual recognition of rights and the institution of private property. _____, such is a general utilitarian account of the origin of the ideal of justice and of its relation to human interests.

(a) Even so
(b) Yet
(c) Briefly
(d) Accordingly

Hamlet is possibly Shakespeare's—and the English language's—most famous play. Though it was written as a play, numerous film versions have also been produced since the early 1900s. Most notable of these are probably the 1948, 1990, and 1996 versions. Sir Laurence Olivier both directed and starred in the title role of the 1948 version. Olivier worked hard to change the play visually from a production intended for the stage to one for the movie screen. Interestingly, Olivier was 41 when he made his film. Hamlet is supposed to be 30. _____, the actress who played Hamlet's mother was in her late 20s when the movie was filmed! Nevertheless, Olivier's efforts won him Best Film and Best Actor Oscars.

(a) Likewise
(b) Furthermore
(c) Unfortunately
(d) On the other hand

대의 파악 – 구 중심

유형 파악

대의 파악하기는 17번부터 22번에 걸쳐 비교적 쉽게 풀 수 있는 문제들이 출제되므로 빈칸 채우기를 풀다가 어려운 문제가 나오면 바로 17번부터 푸는 것이 시간 관리에 도움된다는 점을 실전에서 반드시 기억하도록 한다. 그러나 지문 전체를 읽어야만 정답을 고를 수 있는 다소 시간이 걸리는 문제도 간간히 출제되는 것이 최신 경향이므로 TEPS 독해 고득점은 얼마나 많은 부분을 정확하고 신속하게 읽을 줄 아느냐에 달려 있다!

또한 다른 유형들에 비해 질문의 형태가 다양하고 형태에 따라 선택지가 구 혹은 문장 형태로 나뉘는 것이 특징이다. 여기서는 구 형태의 선택지가 제시되는 문제들을 살펴보자.

핵심 전략

대의 파악하기 문제를 풀 때 가장 중요한 것은 지문 내용과 일치하는 세부 내용을 담고 있거나 지문에 없는 내용을 담고 있는 선택지를 조심하면서 글쓴이가 가장 하고 싶은 말이 뭔지를 문제 푸는 내내 생각하는 것이다. 이것은 대의 파악하기 문제에서 헷갈릴 때 가장 유용한 방법이다!

대개 지문 핵심 내용을 다른 말로 paraphrasing한 선택지를 고르면 되는데 But, However, Although, Though, Even though와 같이 지문의 흐름이 반전되는 부분이 있을 경우 그 부분 이후로 지문 핵심 내용이 나오는 경우가 많기 때문에 특히 잘 읽어볼 필요가 있다.

또한 최근에는 단순히 지문 앞이나 마지막 부분에 단서가 있기 보다는 지문 전체를 아우르는 선택지가 정답이 되는 문제도 간간이 출제되므로 평소에 정확하고 빠르게 지문 전체를 읽는 습관을 들여야 한다.

* 질문 유형

① What is the passage (mainly) about?

② What is the main topic/ focus of the passage?

③ What is the best title/ purpose of the passage?

④ Why…?

Reading Drills

Part II   Questions 1—3 Read the passage and the question. Then choose the option that best answers the question.

A critic of politics finds himself driven to deprecate the power of words, while using them copiously in warning against their influence. It is indeed in politics that their influence is most dangerous, so that one is almost tempted to wish that they did not exist and that society might be managed silently, by instinct, habit, and ocular perception, without this supervening babel of reports, arguments, and slogans.

Q: What is the passage mainly about?
(a) Negative aspects of words best reflected in politics
(b) Politics most influenced by words in various forms
(c) Words in politics often used in a confusing manner
(d) Something else to replace words in politics

One of the most common causes of emotional difficulty is conflict. Conflict arises when we have a need or wish to do something, but the taboos of society or conscience prevent us from doing it. Frequently, we repress our conflicts, thrusting them out of consciousness because they are too unpleasant, or because we feel guilty about them. They remain in the subconscious, however, and may then cause continual trouble.

Q: What is the topic of the passage?
(a) Conflict as a major cause of emotional problems
(b) Emotional difficulty rooted in the subconscious
(c) How people usually cope with emotional conflicts
(d) The remaining possibility of emotional trouble

It is wholesome to see our own beliefs as one stage in the long progression of beliefs in human history. It shows that there is nothing which has been believed always, everywhere, and by everybody; and that whatever has been believed by everybody in a certain stage of culture has seemed to everybody in the next stage nothing more than an absurdity.

Q: What is the best title of the passage?
(a) Historical Proofs That Things Change
(b) Nothing Absolute in Human History
(c) Stages of Culture People Go Through
(d) Broad View on Human History

해설 및 정답 : 뒤로 ➡

1️⃣ 비법

글쓴이가 가장 하고픈 말은 말의 영향이 가장 위험한 분야가 바로 정치라는 것으로 (a)가 정답이다. (b)는 지문에 말이 정치에 끼치는 부정적인 영향에 대한 내용만 있어 오답이고, (c)는 지문 마지막 부분의 babel(소란한 말소리)을 이용했으며, (d)는 막연한 Something else와 지문의 silently, by instinct, habit and ocular perception과 같은 구체적인 대안들이 서로 맞지 않다.

deprecate 비난하다 **copiously** 매우 많이, 풍부하게 **tempt** ~할 생각이 나게 하다 **ocular** 눈의, 시각적인 **supervene** 잇따라 일어나다, 부수되다

번역

정치 비평가는 말의 위력을 비난하는 처지에 처해서 말의 영향력에 대한 경고를 하면서도 정작 말을 지나치게 많이 사용하는 자신을 발견하게 된다. 말의 영향이 가장 위험하게 작용하는 곳이 바로 정치 분야로, 때론 세상을 뒤집는 각종 문서, 논쟁과 구호 같은 것 없이 본능, 습관, 눈으로 보이는 것만으로 사회가 유지되었으면 좋겠다는 생각과 함께 심지어 차라리 말이라는 것이 존재하지 않았으면 하고 바랄 지경에 이르기도 한다.

(a) 정치에 가장 잘 반영된 말의 부정적인 면들
(b) 다양한 형태로 말의 영향을 가장 많이 받는 정치
(c) 종종 헷갈리게 사용되는 정치계의 말들
(d) 정치계의 말들을 대체하기 위한 다른 어떤 것

2️⃣ 비법

지문 전반적으로 갈등에 대해 이야기하고 있으므로 (a)가 정답이다. (b), (c), (d)는 지문 일부 내용만 반영된 오답들이다.

conflict 충돌, 대립, 갈등 **taboo** 금기 **conscience** 양심 **repress** 억누르다, 억제하다 **thrust** 밀다 **subconscious** 무의식

번역

정서 장애의 원인들 중 가장 흔한 것이 갈등이다. 어떤 일을 해야 하거나 하고 싶은데 사회나 양심의 금기가 이를 가로막을 때 갈등이 일어난다. 갈등이 매우 불쾌하게 느껴지거나 우리가 죄책감을 느끼기 때문에 갈등을 억제하고 의식 밖으로 내던져 버리는 일이 종종 일어난다. 그러나 여전히 우리의 잠재 의식에 남아서 끊임없이 말썽을 부릴지도 모른다.

(a) 정서 문제들의 주요한 원인으로서의 갈등
(b) 무의식에 뿌리를 둔 정서 장애
(c) 사람들이 정서 갈등에 대처하는 법
(d) 정서 문제가 다시 생길 수 있는 가능성

3️⃣ 비법

지문 두 번째 문장이 핵심 내용이므로 (b)가 정답이다. (a)는 Proofs에 대한 내용이 지문에 없고 (d)는 주제로 보기에는 범위가 너무 넓다.

wholesome 유익한 **progression** 전진, 진행 **absurdity** 불합리함

번역

우리는 우리 자신의 믿음도 인류 역사상 연쇄적으로 끝없이 길게 이어져 온 인간의 다양한 믿음 중 하나라고 생각하는 것이 정신 건강에 좋다. 역사는 언제 어디서나 모든 사람이 공유해 온 믿음은 하나도 없다는 것을 보여준다. 게다가 어느 문화의 어느 단계에서 모든 사람이 믿었던 것이 그 다음 단계에 가면 모든 사람에게 불합리한 것으로밖에 보이지 않게 되는 것도 알 수 있다.

(a) 만물이 변한다는 역사적 증거들
(b) 절대적인 것은 없는 인간 역사
(c) 사람들이 겪는 문화의 단계
(d) 인간 역사에 대한 거시적 견해

Model Test

Questions 1—4 Read the passage and the question. Then choose the option that best answers the question.

1 **TOPIC** 에트루리아 제국

The Etruscans lived in a part of Italy that is called Tuscany today. They were good sailors, and after about 700 B.C. they were known in the Mediterranean area both as merchants and as pirates. An Etruscan empire began to spread throughout Italy and the surrounding lands. About 616 B.C., Rome, which was a very small village, was conquered without difficulty by the Etruscans. Under the Etruscans a great construction period turned Rome into a large, powerful city for the first time. Then, in 510 B.C., the Etruscan king was driven into exile, and Rome became an independent republic.

Q: What is the passage mainly about?
(a) The rise and fall of the Etruscan empire
(b) The Etruscans' construction technology
(c) The emergence of the Roman Empire
(d) The Etruscan influence on Rome

2 **TOPIC** 양치류 서식지

Many ferns grow in the rich soils of forests, but some seem to be growing out of rocks. These ferns can't grow in a place with rich soil. They only grow in rocky areas. They live in just a little bit of soil that is found in the cracks in rocks. That soil is different from soil that is on the ground. It takes many years for the soil to form there. Some of it is washed down into the rocks, and some is blown in by the wind. Part is made by plants that die on the rock, and part is made by frost, which causes tiny pieces of the rock to split off. The soil has the right combination of ingredients to support the life of a fern.

Q: What is the passage mainly about?
(a) Two kinds of soil for ferns
(b) Ferns growing in rocky areas
(c) Formation of soil in rocks that supports some ferns
(d) Factors that make rocks crack for ferns to live in

3 **TOPIC** 앰브로스 번사이드 장군과 구레나룻

Ambrose Burnside would have preferred to be known as a war hero. Instead, his name makes us think of whiskers. Burnside was an army general. He fought for the Union Army in the Civil War. Unlike many men of the time, Burnside had no beard. But he did grow short whiskers down the sides of his face. The whiskers covered part of his cheeks. Other men began to imitate Burnside's unique whiskers. At first they called them "burnside," after the general. After a time, though, the name was changed to sideburns, possibly because they are grown on the sides of the face. If it doesn't seem to make much sense, think about this—it's better than naming them after the general by calling them Ambroses.

Q: What is the main topic of the passage?
(a) How whiskers had another name
(b) How "burnside" changed to "sideburns"
(c) Why whiskers are not called Ambroses
(d) Who first grew whiskers in history

4 **TOPIC** 미국과 일본의 칡

The kudzu plant is considered an uncontrollable nuisance in the southern United States. Kudzu, introduced to the U.S. from Japan in 1876, is a spreading vine that moved into 18 American states stretching from Alabama to Massachusetts. In the south, kudzu plants can grow as much as a foot per day with root systems stretching 12 feet. The irony is that while kudzu is seen as an unwanted nuisance in the U.S., it is in demand in Japan where it is used to make starch and certain food products. Because of this, officials from Alabama cities traveled to Tokyo to discuss selling their surplus of kudzu to Japanese companies. They were interested and agreed to finance a kudzu farm in Alabama.

Q: What is the best title of the passage?
(a) The Past and Future of Kudzu
(b) Kudzu, America's New Business
(c) What's Good and Bad about Kudzu
(d) Popularity of Kudzu in Japan

TEPS Reading Practice

Infants are not self-conscious about cameras. They do not know what the camera is for, and this innocence allows us to capture their native actions. But the child learns very quickly, and by the age of five or six he may not be able to stand in front of a camera without frowning and feeling ill at ease. In most cases, this feeling is gradually brought under the control of an adjusting response which is a pose. Studying how poses change with time, in different social classes, in different cultures, and through the growth and maturation of the individual, is a first-class research problem.

Q: What is the passage mainly about?
(a) Infants becoming conscious of their surroundings
(b) The importance of studying what makes poses change
(c) Poses made by babies from different backgrounds
(d) Studying poses to take better pictures of infants

Mathematics is a highly effective thinking system made even more effective by our invention of the computer. Thanks to mathematics we can perform such unthinkable operations as landing men on the moon, letting them drive round on the surface, hearing and watching them do it, and then bringing them safely back to earth. But getting to the moon is easier than solving social poverty, juvenile offense, or a simple strike. On the earth, most situations are interrelated, subjective, and vague, changing in value and dependent on human impulse. If we could translate every situation into definite relationships and symbols, we should never need to look beyond mathematics for our thinking.

Q: What is the passage mainly about?
(a) The necessity of creating a new mathematical thinking system
(b) Mathematical applications in astronomy and social science
(c) Computers as one of the greatest mathematical inventions to solve problems
(d) The usefulness and limitations of mathematics as a thinking system

Dear Sirs,

Upon examination of the received order, we found that 12 SO 305 lenses had been sent by mistake in place of the ordered SO 307's. In view of the fact that this is not the first time such a mistake has been made and that we have to satisfy our customers immediately, we would appreciate it if you would send us the SO 307's by the quickest possible means at your expense. To simplify the handling of the SO 305's, we would be happy to take them off your hands at a 20% discount in order to save you the expense of having to pay for the return postage.
We look forward to your dealing with this matter without delay.

Very truly yours,
Bob Tracer

Q: What did Bob Tracer write the letter mainly for?
(a) To report a wrong delivery of SO 305 lenses
(b) To have a problem solved right after it's being recognized
(c) To order SO 307 lenses again at a discounted price
(d) To complain about a repeated mistake

The stripes stay striped in striped toothpaste because they get striped at the last minute. The red stripe color is stored in the cone-shaped part at the top of the tube. It surrounds an inner, slotted tube that extends part of the way into the main tube. The white paste fills the rest of the main tube. When it is squeezed up, the white paste presses on the red color. That forces the red color out through the slots in the small tube. And because the white paste has to pass through that same small tube, the two pastes meet. Therefore, just before they leave the main tube, the red color and the white paste join up to make big, bold stripes.

Q: What is the main topic of the passage?
(a) How to mix different kinds of toothpaste
(b) How striped toothpaste comes out striped
(c) What makes striped toothpaste popular
(d) What is in striped toothpaste

The game birds' play with the wind consists of practiced movements which are simply enjoyed for their own sake. These are not instinctive actions, but are carefully learned. Their accomplishments—use of the wind, amazing judgment of distances, and understanding of wind conditions—are all acquired skills. They play with the wind like cats play with mice. They let the wind throw them into the air. Then with a wave of wings, they turn themselves over and dive downward. Another snap of the wings returns them to their normal position. They playfully shoot away to the west to annoy the invisible monster that tries to drive them eastward.

Q: What is the main focus of the passage?
(a) Game birds flying against the wind
(b) Game birds teaching their young to fly
(c) Game birds using the wind for no reason
(d) Game birds practicing with the wind to have fun

When Cortez and his Spanish soldiers first met the Aztecs in 1520, they were greeted with a drink normally reserved for the god-king only—hot chocolate. However, it was quite a different drink from the cheery cocoa enjoyed today. It was really hot. The Aztecs served hot chocolate laced with ground chili peppers instead of sugar. Needless to say, the Spaniards weren't very impressed with the drink. The cocoa plant was very important to the Aztecs, however. They used the tree's flowers to cure apathy and timidity, its bark for stomach trouble, and its butter for burns. They even used the beans as currency.

Q: What is the best title of the passage?
(a) History of Chocolate
(b) The Aztec's Use of the Cocoa Plant
(c) How the Aztecs Treated Spanish Visitors
(d) How Chocolate was Used in the 1500s

Forging strong partnerships with strategic local partners and investors in new markets is crucial to rapid, successful expansion. As one of the largest real estate companies in Asia, Captaland has garnered strong core competencies in real estate development and management of residential, retail, and commercial properties as well as serviced residences and real estate financial services. Through our strategic alliances, we have gained footholds in new markets and broken frontiers in existing ones, giving rise to our ever-growing presence in Asia Pacific, Europe, and the Middle East, with more than 100 cities in over 20 countries.

Q: What is the purpose of the passage?
(a) To encourage readers to be interested in Captaland
(b) To introduce what Captaland can do internationally
(c) To attract potential employees to Captaland to expand its business
(d) To discuss the importance of partnerships in new real estate markets

Suspension bridges are magnificent pieces of architecture. They can be found in many major cities that have bays and rivers that are crossed regularly by commuters. Most suspension bridges have tolls. Sometimes these tolls are extraordinarily high. Considering it takes less than 3 minutes to cross over most, a fee of $5.00 seems exorbitant! Suspension bridges generally only allow motor vehicles but some actually take foot traffic. The famous Golden Gate Bridge in San Francisco is one such bridge. You can see runners, walkers, and bicyclists going right along with drivers and enjoying the beautiful California weather way up high.

Q: What is the best title of the passage?
(a) Expensive Suspension Bridges to Cross
(b) People Crossing Urban Architectural Wonders
(c) Where Suspension Bridges are Found
(d) How Golden Gate Bridge is Different

Dear Mr. Chow,

We were pleased to receive your letter, and also remember fondly the few days you spent with us, as well as the interesting conversations we had. We are just now beginning to enjoy the fruits of your suggestions concerning improvements to our packing and labeling. We are happy to let you have copies of our annual reports for the current year and the previous two years. However, the full reports are published in Chinese and Thai only, although we do issue much-abridged versions of the reports in English. I am enclosing a copy of each publication, and would be glad to hear which version you would like to receive in the future.

Sincerely,

Ben McCameron

Q: Why did Ben McCameron write this letter?
(a) To thank Mr. Chow for his suggestions
(b) To reply to a request from a business partner
(c) To know what language Mr. Chow speaks
(d) To offer suggestions regarding packing and labeling

For people who can and will provide advanced care for their pets, a whole new scientific era has been born. It has been a technological explosion. Take a surgical robot. It can cut into and maneuver inside bones far more accurately than any human being ever could. The problem? The robot costs around 400,000 dollars. Pet owner Steve Ryan, however, says that he wouldn't mind the unavoidably high cost of the extremely advanced surgery using this robot as long as his dog can get back the quality of life he'd like him to have.

Q: What is the passage mainly about?
(a) The next scientific advancement for sick pets
(b) Pet owners' unreasonable concern for their pets
(c) The development of technology for pet lovers
(d) What is good and bad about surgical robots

Unit 04

대의 파악 – 문장 중심

선택지가 문장 형태이므로 구 형태의 선택지보다는 많은 정보가 제시되어 있기 때문에 읽었던 지문 내용을 혼동할 수 있다. 따라서 일단 구 형태의 문제보다 선택지를 보다 꼼꼼하고 정확히 읽어야 한다.

선택지가 문장으로 나오는 대의 파악하기 문제는 평균 1문제 정도 출제된다.

핵심 전략

지엽적인 세부 내용을 정답으로 착각하는 경우를 가장 조심해야 하고, 특히 헷갈릴 때는 글쓴이가 정말 전하고자 하는 내용이 무엇인지 지문을 읽고 문제를 푸는 내내 자문하면서 항상 지문의 '나무'가 아닌 '숲'을 봐야 한다. 또한 선택지가 문장 형태이다 보니 선택지를 해석하는 데 다소 시간이 걸리고 잘못 해석할 수 있으니 한 번만 읽고 정확히 파악하도록 노력해야 한다.

* 질문 유형

① What is the main idea of the passage?

② Which of the following best summarizes the passage?

Part II **Questions 1—3** Read the passage and the question. Then choose the option that best answers the question.

African resistance to European penetration in the sixteenth century was considerable. The Black continent, unlike Brazil, did not open up to the Portuguese without defending itself. The European might, however, have persisted in his invasion if he had not been halted at the coasts by diseases. Fever, dysentery, phthisis, and dropsy, as well as numerous parasites, took a heavy toll. European advance was frustrated owing to the bravery of the warlike tribes and disease.

Q: What is the main idea of the passage?
(a) It was difficult for European invaders to advance into interior Africa.
(b) African resistance to European invaders was very intense.
(c) Portugal tried to take over Africa only to fail.
(d) African tribes were constitutionally different from Europeans.

Because it has failed to engage itself with the problems that dog us during our working days and haunt our dreams at night, politics has not engaged the best of us, or at least the best in us; existing political systems have only evaded and confused the real issues rather than sharpening or resolving them. If people seem complacent or inert, the cause may lie less in people than in the political system.

Q: What is the main idea of the passage?
(a) Politics is important in addressing the issues we are faced with.
(b) Political ideas do not properly reflect what people want.
(c) Politics means how we are made to feel about our life.
(d) Political systems fail to work out solutions to our problems.

Somewhat unconsciously, men were developing a tendency to believe that if you could explain motion on the earth, this would help to explain also the movements in the sky. In other words, they were tending to depart from the older view that everything in the heavens was composed of a special kind of matter subject to its own peculiar laws.

Q: What is the main idea of the passage?
(a) The belief that things are mutually connected existed.
(b) Men have realized what the heavens truly comprise.
(c) People thought that everything works in its own way.
(d) The idea about the world changed in an inexplicit manner.

해설 및 정답 : 뒤로 ⤶

1 비법

지문 두 번째 문장과 마지막 문장을 보면 포르투갈의 아프리카 침략 시도가 결국 좌절된 것이 지문 주요 내용임을 알 수 있어 (c)가 정답이다. (a), (b), (d)는 지문 전체를 아우르지 못한다.

penetration 침략, 침투 **considerable** 상당한
halt 정지하다, 정지시키다 **dysentery** 이질
phthisis 폐결핵 **dropsy** 수종 **parasite** 기생충 **take (a) toll** ~으로 희생자를 내다
frustrate 꺾다, 헛되게 하다

번역

16세기 유럽인의 침투에 대한 아프리카인의 저항은 대단했다. 검은 대륙은 브라질과는 달리 저항 없이 포르투갈인들에게 문호를 개방하지 않았다. 그러나 질병 때문에 해안지역에서 길이 막히지 않았더라면 유럽인의 침략은 계속되었을 것이다. 많은 기생충은 물론 열병, 이질, 폐결핵, 수종 등의 질병은 많은 희생자를 냈다. 유럽인의 진격은 호전적인 원주민들의 용맹과 질병 때문에 좌절되었다.

(a) 유럽인 침략자들이 아프리카를 정복하기 어려웠다.
(b) 유럽인 침략자들에 대한 아프리카의 저항은 매우 강했다.
(c) 포르투갈은 아프리카를 정복하려 했으나 결국 실패했다.
(d) 아프리카 부족들은 체질적으로 유럽인들과 달랐다.

2 비법

정치 제도가 현실 문제를 파헤치고 해명하기보다는 오히려 이들을 회피하고 혼동시켜 왔을 뿐이라는 것이 지문 주요 내용으로 (d)가 정답이다.

engage A with B A와 B를 관계시키다
dog 따라다니다 **haunt** 자주 나타나다
engage 보증하다 **evade** 피하다, 당혹케 하다
complacent 만족한 **inert** 무기력한 **lie in** ~에 있다

번역

근무 중인 낮에도 우리를 괴롭히며 따라다니고 밤중에는 꿈에 나타나서 우리를 시달리게 하는 문제들을 다루지 못해 왔기 때문에 정치는 선한 사람들의 관심을 끌지 못했을 뿐만 아니라, 사람들 안의 선함을 끄집어 내지도 못했다. 현존하는 정치 제도는 현실 문제들을 예리하게 파헤치고 해명하기보다는 오히려 이들을 회피하고 혼동시켜 왔을 뿐이다. 만약 국민들이 현실에 안주하는 것으로 보이거나 무기력해 보인다면 그 원인은 아마도 국민 자신에게보다는 정치 제도 쪽에 더 많을 것이다.

(a) 정치는 우리가 직면한 문제들을 다루는 데 중요하다.
(b) 정치 사상들은 사람들이 원하는 것을 적절히 반영하지 않는다.
(c) 정치학은 인생에 대해 우리가 어떻게 느끼도록 되어 있는지를 의미한다.
(d) 정치 제도들은 우리 문제들에 대한 해결책을 내놓는 데 실패했다.

3 비법

우주의 모든 물체는 서로 관련되어 (지상에서 움직임을 설명할 수 있다면 하늘에서 움직임도 설명할 수 있을 것) 각자의 고유 법칙에 지배받는 특별한 물질로 구성되지 않았다는 과거 사람들의 생각이 지문 주요 내용이므로 (a)가 정답이다.

unconsciously 무의식적으로 **subject to** ~의 지배를 받는, ~의 영향을 받기 쉬운
peculiar 독특한, 고유의, 묘한

번역

다소 무의식적으로 사람들은 만약 지상에서 움직임을 설명할 수 있다면 하늘에서의 움직임도 설명할 수 있을 것이라고 믿으려는 경향이 생기고 있었다. 즉, 우주의 모든 물체는 각자의 고유 법칙에 지배받는 특별한 종류의 물질로 구성되어 있다는 기존의 견해에서 벗어나려는 경향을 보인 것이다.

(a) 만물이 서로 연결되어 있다는 믿음이 존재했다.
(b) 인간이 우주가 진정 무엇으로 구성되어 있는지 깨달았다.
(c) 사람들은 만물이 각자의 방식으로 작용한다고 생각했다.
(d) 세상에 대한 생각이 애매한 방식으로 변했다.

Model Test

TOPIC 로마 제국의 쇠퇴와 몰락

The search for a logical explanation for the decline and fall of the Roman Empire has been more diligent than that in any other field of history. This is the only known instance of the decay of a more or less universal civilization, which might serve as something of an object lesson to our own; accordingly it has been very thoroughly studied, and the attempt to explain it has engaged some of the ablest historians who ever wrote about it. Almost any orator or politician can tell you why Rome fell, but the men who know most about it are not so ready with glib explanation. Even they must admit at critical moments the decisive interposition of chance.

Q: What is the main idea of the passage?
(a) The late history of the Roman Empire cannot be explained completely logically.
(b) The decline of the Roman Empire needs to be studied further.
(c) The collapse of the Roman Empire is a popular historical study subject.
(d) The fall of the Roman Empire came about unexpectedly.

TOPIC 적당한 일과 휴식

The knowledge that you are punctual gives a feeling of calm security. But if you are always racing to catch up with your schedule, you are in a constant state of excitement; you are incapable of getting any enjoyment out of the present moment. The only moment you have to live is this one. Being urgent is not a virtue. It is merely a sign of bad management. A well-planned daily schedule has a few empty spaces, moments in which you can relax and think at ease about the problems at hand. Every day should have some pleasure, whether small or great. To rob yourself of that enjoyment because you are too busy is to miss the whole point of living.

Q: What is the main idea of the passage?
(a) Leading a busy life is not as beneficial as being urgent.
(b) Setting up a daily schedule helps understand life.
(c) Staying balanced between work and play is important in life.
(d) Planning an everyday schedule should be pleasant.

해설집 : P23

TOPIC 머큐리 우주 프로그램 프로젝트

Project Mercury placed the first Americans into space. The pioneering project was organized to orbit a manned spacecraft, investigate man's reaction to and abilities in space flight, and recover both man and spacecraft. Project Mercury experiments demonstrated that the high-gravity forces of launch and atmospheric entry as well as weightlessness in orbit for as much as 34 hours do not impair man's ability to control a spacecraft. It proved that man can not only augment the reliability of spacecraft controls, but also can conduct scientific observations and experiments that expand and clarify information from instruments.

Q: Which of the following best summarizes the passage?
(a) America was the first nation to put a manned spacecraft into orbit.
(b) Project Mercury experiments produced unexpected results.
(c) Project Mercury was the first project to send people to space.
(d) Project Mercury helped gain knowledge about space flight.

TOPIC 안정의 정도

It is often said that one of man's most distinct needs is for security, but too much security can be boring. No one likes to be treated like a child. A man in bed in a hospital is pretty secure, but when he ceases to be sick, he soon becomes bored. The fact is that most people do not want to have security provided so much as to be in a position to create their own security. Man has a need to run his own life, to make his own decisions, which we may call the need for self-determination. Thus, just as we can have too much food or too much love, we can have too much security.

Q: Which of the following best summarizes the passage?
(a) Man should avoid having too much security in life.
(b) Man can have just as much security as he wants.
(c) Security, food, and love are man's most distinct needs.
(d) Those with too much security want to be adventurous.

TEPS Reading Practice

Although many countries around the world have banned whaling, these gentle sea mammals are still at risk. Whales are still being hunted, and more than 10,000 have been killed since 1986. Some are hunted for scientific purposes; others are killed by "pirates." Endangered species include blue whales, sperm whales, and northern right whales. Because whales have very low rates of reproduction, marine biologists believe that some of these species may never recover from the damage that whale hunting has caused.

Q: What is the main idea of the passage?
(a) Whaling continues to the point where it is dangerous.
(b) Whales are being hunted for a variety of reasons.
(c) Ways to make whales more reproductive are needed.
(d) Whale hunting should be banned more strictly.

When a child fails, simply drawing her or his attention to the failure is unlikely to improve that performance. No doubt the child already knows she cannot read, or spell, or multiply. Her performance is more likely to benefit if she is shown that, just as she can control her breathing by panting, breathing deeply, or holding her breath, so too can she control her thinking. The child needs to understand that there are specific strategies for specific tasks and that the generation and use of these strategies is something she can do for herself.

Q: What is the main idea of the passage?
(a) Children are born to think and learn without any assistance.
(b) Pointing out failures that children make does not benefit them.
(c) Teaching how to control thinking matters when educating children.
(d) We should let children know that they are in charge of their thinking.

The right to vote is a key benefit of a democratic system. Citizens in the U.S. have many opportunities to participate in the political life of their communities and the nation. They can participate by voting, by expressing their views to elected officials, and by voicing their opinions in newspapers and on radio and television. Unfortunately, many citizens don't take advantage of their rights. Fewer than fifty percent of all eligible voters have participated in recent national elections. Many citizens' groups, such as the League of Women Voters, work hard to encourage voters to participate, so that more and more citizens will exercise this important privilege.

Q: What is the main idea of the passage?
(a) More than 50% of the U.S. population should vote.
(b) Americans are less interested in politics than before.
(c) The right to vote is not exercised as much as it should be.
(d) Democracy is mainly characterized by people's voting power.

It is widely believed that the "hot dog" began on a cold day in New York's Polo Grounds in 1901, when a salesman began selling sausages in long buns. Sports cartoonist T. A. Dorgan captured the event in a drawing, depicting the sausages as dachshunds and calling them "hot dogs" because he couldn't spell "dachshunds." Nice story, but it's just nonsense. Jokes about dachshunds looking like sausages have been around for hundreds of years. The term "hot dog" was current at Yale in the fall of 1894, when sausages in a bun were sold at the dormitories. By the time T. A. Dorgan was "inventing" the term, "hot dog" was already replacing the other names for a sausage on a bun.

Q: What is the main idea of the passage?
(a) Nobody knows exactly who first created "hot dog."
(b) People disagree on when "hot dog" first came into use.
(c) The 20th century's explanation for the origin of "hot dog" is wrong.
(d) "Hot dog" is an example of replacing old words with new ones.

It's true that we love technology, but the time will never come when we lose real person-to-person interaction. What with cell phones, computer games, and robots, the situation might seem troubling, but not all of us young people are socially withdrawn. I do not need super high-tech devices to kill time. Machines won't replace my friends. People of my generation don't have that much craving for technology, since we've grown up with it. We never needed to dream of having high-tech gadgets, because they have always been within reach.

Q: What is the main idea of the passage?
(a) Technology will not necessarily breed a total dependency.
(b) Different generations have different tastes for technology.
(c) Technology does not affect our social life as much as it appears to.
(d) Friends will not be replaced by machines for young people of this age.

According to the FBI, bombing incidents have almost tripled in the United States in the last 10 years. Last year alone, 2,577 explosives killed 193 people and caused over $105 million in property damage. Motives range from political terrorism to personal grudges to sheer thrill-seeking. In addition to real bombs, there are many false alarms and hoaxes. Each has to be treated seriously by expert technicians and professionals on bomb squads. A package from a jilted lover, a plain box found in an underground courthouse parking lot, a briefcase left under a table in a McDonald's—all are possible threats.

Q: Which of the following best summarizes the passage?
(a) Various potential causes of bombings account for increased bombing incidents.
(b) The increasing frequency of bombings has alerted the world to all bomb threats.
(c) False alarms and hoaxes remain serious until they are investigated by authorities.
(d) Three main reasons have been identified over the last decade for bomb threats.

Let's assume that we can learn to speak someone else's language—not just a few polite phrases, but really learn to speak it fluently. We know that speaking a language fluently will certainly improve our communication with other speakers of that language, but something else happens as well. I think that learning another language can fundamentally change us as individuals—can change our worldview and even our personalities. For example, if we speak French fluently, we can form grammatically correct sentences, of course, but we can also begin to see the world in a way that is typically French.

Q: Which of the following best summarizes the passage?
(a) Studying grammar rules is part of learning a foreign language.
(b) Language skills mean more than simply the mastery of a foreign language.
(c) Learning another language improves communication and ways of thinking.
(d) Understanding a foreign culture helps one master a foreign language.

When you consider the enormous range of fitted units and elaborate accessories available today, it's difficult to believe that the kitchen has only recently been considered a suitable area for decoration. Although this room has always been extremely important, until the start of the First World War no sensible household would spend unnecessary time and effort on it since it was essentially the domain of servants, and even ordinary families had at least one maid whose responsibilities included the preparation of meals. Besides, cooking involved greasy work and thick smoke with soot made so that unnecessary units and accessories meant nothing but extra nuisances.

Q: Which of the following best summarizes the passage?
(a) World War I changed the postwar image of the kitchen.
(b) The kitchen was not decorated with units and accessories until lately.
(c) Not all the households were interested in the kitchen.
(d) People's view on the kitchen is a far cry from that of the past.

If you were standing in a river, you would think the left bank would be the one to your left. But what if you were facing the other way? It seems as though the left and right banks of a river depend on where you are standing. However, there's a way to determine which is the left or right bank of a river no matter where you're standing. First, find the way the river flows. Now, face downstream. This means you're facing the same way the water is flowing. The left bank is now on your left. When people talk about the left and right banks of a river, they mean the left and right of the direction of flow.

Q: Which of the following best summarizes the passage?
(a) The direction of river flow has been confusing.
(b) How you face a river lets you know where it flows.
(c) Where a river flows decides its left and right orientation.
(d) One can tell left from right in a river by only one way.

When change is slow, the new is gradually assimilated, and only after a number of generations is it noticeable that the world is really different. In our century enormous changes in the circumstances of our lives and in our knowledge have occurred rapidly. It is not at all surprising that our intellectual, our social, and our political processes have failed to keep abreast of contemporary problems. It is not surprising that we become confused in the choice of our goals and the paths which we must take to reach them.

Q: Which of the following best summarizes the passage?
(a) Since the beginning of the century, things have been uncontrollable.
(b) These days, people find it more difficult to realize their goals.
(c) New things have become too difficult for our generation to catch up with.
(d) Recent changes have occurred at such a pace that they cannot be followed.

Unit 05

세부 내용 파악 – 일반 유형

유형 파악

세부 사항 파악하기는 23번부터 32번까지 출제되고, 시간이 다소 걸리기 때문에 중급 이상으로 여기는 경향이 있지만, 핵심 풀이 기법만 알면 가장 빨리 풀어 독해 점수를 올릴 수 있다. 참고로 2010년 상반기부터 세부 사항 파악 문제들의 몇몇 질문 형태가 Which of the following is stated about…?, Which of the following is supported by the passage?, Which of the following claims is made about…?으로 바뀌어 출제되면서 LC Part IV 세부 사항 파악 문제들의 질문 형태도 다소 영향을 받는 경향이나, Which of the following is correct about…?으로 생각하고 풀면 되고, 앞으로 꾸준히 등장할 질문 형태로 예상된다.

핵심 전략

지문을 3분의 1 정도 읽고 정답을 찾거나, 정답이 보이지 않으면 나머지 부분을 읽으면서 같은 과정을 반복한다. 이로써 지문 전체를 다 읽지 않고 풀 수 있는 문제들을 풀 수 있다. 실제 시험을 볼 때는 긴장할 수 있으므로 선택지에서 틀린 부분을 반드시 표시하면서 풀고 지문과 선택지에 나오는 정보에 교묘한 차이를 둬서 혼란을 유발하는 경우가 종종 있으므로 선택지에 대한 연구가 중요하다.

① 일부분만 옳거나 정답이 되기에 부족한 내용의 선택지

   가장 일반적으로 주의해야 할 경우로 선택지 일부분만 읽고 성급하게 판단하지 말고 틀리거나 빠진 내용이 없나 주의 깊게 확인하라!

② 지문 내용을 잘못 해석한 내용의 선택지

   언뜻 보면 정답 같은 교묘한 오답에 빠지게 하는 주 원인이다. 세부 사항 파악하기는 정답과 오답을 명확히 규명하려면 지문의 해당 문장을 정확하게 해석할 줄 알아야 한다.

③ 일반적·상식적인 내용의 선택지

   지문을 제대로 읽지 않고 찍는 수험생들을 노린 함정으로 이런 선택지가 나오면 일단 조심하는 것이 좋다.

④ all, must, never, only 등 극단적인 내용의 선택지

   대부분의 경우 오답으로 나오나 가끔 정답으로 나오는 경우가 있으므로 주의를 요한다.

⑤ 질문에서 요구하는 내용은 아니나 지문과 일치하는 내용의 선택지

   특히 공부 좀 했다는 수험생들이 문제 번호에 따라 질문 유형을 미리 파악하고 있는 경우가 많아 질문을 제대로 읽지 않고 틀리기 때문에 정말 주의해야 한다.

Reading Drills

An unstated assumption is something that a speaker presumes to be true but does not actually say. For example, suppose someone claims: "Jane finally got a job. Now she can buy that car she has wanted for so long." The claim that Jane can buy the car is partly based on the unstated assumption that she will have the job long enough to earn the necessary money. So you need to identify this assumption and judge its accuracy before accepting what the author has actually stated as true.

Q: Which of the following is correct according to the passage?

(a) A statement may not be true based on an unstated assumption.

(b) An unstated assumption is based on what will definitely happen.

(c) Some truths are not told but everyone knows that they exist.

(d) Every statement should be verified to be accepted as valid.

Many consider an increased knowledge of hygiene and a larger number of health-related products as factors that have lessened the overall risk of disease. While this seems true and logical, those same factors have also contributed to the rise of extremely dangerous agents like drug-resistant bacteria. Drug-resistant bacteria are strains of common bacteria that have been exposed to an antibacterial agent of some sort, such as antibacterial soap. Additionally, commonly used antibiotics like penicillin and amoxicillin are becoming increasingly ineffective, largely because of over-prescription and misuse.

Q: Which of the following is correct according to the passage?

(a) Medical advancements have as many negative aspects as they have positive ones.

(b) Knowledge of hygiene has not prevented as many diseases as it should have.

(c) Some popular antibiotics have been used for purposes other than for which they are made.

(d) New antibiotics are being developed to fight against drug-resistant bacteria.

해설 및 정답 : 뒤로 ➡

1 비법

작가가 말한 것을 사실이라고 받아들이기 전에 그 이면의 가정들을 알아내고, 정확성을 판단할 필요가 있다고 했으므로 그런 가정의 정확성에 따라 어떤 진술은 사실이 아닐 수 있어 (a)가 정답이다. (b)는 선택지의 definitely에 대한 근거가 지문에 없고, (d)는 선택지의 Every가 맞지 않다.

assumption 추정 **presume** 가정하다

번역

진술되지 않은 추정이란 화자가 사실로 가정은 하지만 직접 말로는 표현하지 않는 내용이다. 예를 들어 어떤 사람이 "제인은 마침내 취업을 했어. 이제 드디어 그렇게 오랫동안 갖고 싶어 하던 차를 살 수 있겠다"라고 말했다고 하자. 제인이 차를 살 수 있을 거라는 내용의 일부는 그녀가 필요한 돈을 벌 때까지 충분히 오랫동안 직장에 다닐 것이라는 진술되지 않은 추정에 기초해 있는 것이다. 그러므로 작가가 실제로 쓴 내용이 사실이라고 받아들이기 전에 그 배경에 깔려 있는 가정들을 찾아내고 정확성을 판단할 필요가 있다.

(a) 진술되지 않은 가정에 따라 진술은 사실이 아닐지도 모른다.
(b) 진술되지 않은 가정은 반드시 벌어질 일에 토대를 두고 있다.
(c) 어떤 진실들은 진술되지는 않지만 존재한다는 것을 모든 사람들이 안다.
(d) 모든 진술은 타당하다고 받아들이기 전에 검증되어야 한다.

2 비법

지문 마지막 문장에서 페니실린이나 아목시실린과 같은 항생제들의 효과는 점점 떨어지고 있는데 이는 주로 약물 오남용 때문이라고 했으므로 (c)가 정답이다. (a), (b)는 선택지의 동등 비교에 대한 근거가 지문에 없고, (d)는 지문에서 확인할 수 없다.

hygiene 위생 **lessen** 줄다 **contribute to** ~의 원인이 되다 **drug-resistant** 약재 내성의, 약물 저항성의 **strain** 변종(變種) **over-prescription** 과잉 처방

번역

많은 사람들은 위생 관련 지식과 건강 관련 제품의 증가가 질병의 위험을 전반적으로 줄어들게 한 요인이라고 생각한다. 이 주장이 사실이고 논리적인 것처럼 보이지만, 그와 같은 요인들이 내성균과 같은 매우 위험한 병원(病原)들을 만들어내는 데 일조하기도 했다. 내성균은 일반 세균의 변종으로 항균 비누와 같은 항균 물질에 노출되면서 생긴 것이다. 게다가 주로 과잉 처방과 오남용으로 인해 페니실린이나 아목시실린과 같이 흔히 사용되는 항생제들의 효과도 점점 더 떨어지고 있다.

(a) 의학 진보에는 긍정적인 면만큼 부정적인 면도 따른다.
(b) 위생 관련 지식이 기대만큼 많은 질병을 예방하지는 못했다.
(c) 잘 알려진 몇몇 항생제들은 원래 목적과는 달리 쓰여왔다.
(d) 내성균에 대처하기 위한 새로운 항생제들이 개발 중이다.

Model Test

TOPIC 어업으로 파괴된 필리핀 산호초

The Philippine Islands have some of the richest coral reefs in the world. However, scientists are concerned that fishermen are destroying the reefs. One common practice used to catch a large number of fish is to throw explosives into the water. This kills many fish and destroys the reef where they live. Another practice is used to catch certain fish for use in aquariums overseas. Fishermen throw poison into the water around the reef. The poison stuns the fish, which float to the surface and are easily caught. The poison destroys the reef and kills the fish by poisoning them slowly. A result of these practices is the eventual loss of one of nature's most lovely works of art.

Q: Which of the following is correct according to the passage?
(a) The Philippine Islands boast the most beautiful coral reefs.
(b) Coral reefs make it hard for fishermen to increase their catch.
(c) Some of the world's coral reefs are being destroyed for fishing.
(d) Philippine fishermen are not interested in environmental issues.

TOPIC 음성으로 작동되는 기능을 갖춘 자동차

Our Concept Auto, which will be on the market within five years, is different from any car ever made. Most of the features in the car are voice activated, so you won't have to take your hands off the wheel or your eyes off the road. Instead of reaching down to turn on the radio, the driver only has to say "radio on." Furthermore, the Concept Auto will be extremely lightweight, yet strong enough to stand up in accidents with the same performance as the cars we know today. Because of the weight, the car will use less energy. Any way you look at it, this car is an exciting prospect for the future.

Q: How will the car advertised interest potential buyers?
(a) Most of its features will be automatic.
(b) It will be able to use a special kind of fuel.
(c) It will be lighter and stronger than its competitors.
(d) It will be able to carry out its driver's oral instructions.

3 **TOPIC** 터너가 브룩사이드 정원에 한 일

Turner was a quiet but determined woman. She, a retired government officer, enjoyed going to antique auctions. She also loved gardens, especially Brookside Garden. She made up her mind to do something for the Garden. In 1986, she asked to see Els Benjamin, then the director of the Garden. The public garden, with its museum and lakeside jogging course, is a 50-acre oasis. Turner found solace there and wanted to leave something for others to remember her. She asked Benjamin for a list of items Brookside might want. The list included some paintings and a piece of sculpture for the garden. Benjamin thought Turner would leave as much as $10,000, but her donation reached $800,000 when she died in 1990.

Q: Which of the following is correct about Turner?
(a) She saved money for Brookside Garden for about 4 years.
(b) She once didn't know what to do for Brookside Garden.
(c) She felt that something about Brookside Garden was worth sharing.
(d) She wanted Brookside Garden to have some artworks.

4 **TOPIC** 평소와 다른 구매 패턴을 보인 신용 카드 소지자에게 보내는 편지

Dear Mr. Cousen,

We are writing to notify you that the Everycard credit card you hold with our company has been showing usage, including online and in-store locations, that is not characteristic of past purchasing patterns. We are writing to make sure that you are in possession of your card ending in the digits 3248 and that you are in fact making the purchases being charged to your card. Please contact us by phone or e-mail as soon as possible to confirm that your card or identity has not been stolen and is not being abused. We hope that you will understand that this is a necessary step to protect your credit, your money, and your identity.

Chris Wilkens
Everycard
Customer Service

Q: Which of the following is supported by the letter?
(a) Mr. Cousen's Everycard credit card has more than 4 digits.
(b) Mr. Cousen will call Chris Wilkens right after reading the mail.
(c) Mr. Cousen's Everycard credit card is being used by another person.
(d) There are two ways for Chris Wilkens to contact Mr. Cousen.

TEPS Reading Practice

Part II   **Questions 1—10** Read the passage and the question. Then choose the option that best answers the question.

Most of the world's largest cities have existed for centuries, over the course of which they have grown and evolved to meet the ever-changing needs of their populaces. This process must continue today, particularly through the removal of old, run-down buildings that currently take up space in many metropolitan areas. While many individuals favor a system of urban revitalization that attempts to renovate and modernize old buildings, that process is simply not efficient and does not do enough to solve problems faced by expanding and modernizing cities.

Q: Which of the following is correct according to the passage?
(a) The number of needs of city residents has multiplied.
(b) The growth of the world's largest cities must continue.
(c) Much land in large cities is occupied by centuries-old buildings.
(d) Some old buildings in the world's largest cities have collapsed.

iBridge is the standard software for connecting digital cameras and printers of different manufacturers and printing out pictures directly. By connecting the camera to an iBridge-compatible printer with the USB cable, you can print out recorded pictures directly. With the camera connected to the printer, select the pictures you want to print and the number of prints on the camera's monitor. It is also possible to print out pictures using the print reservation data. All printers that support iBridge have standard print settings. If [STANDARD] is selected on the settings screens, images are printed according to these settings. Refer to the instruction manual for its standard settings or contact the manufacturer.

Q: Which of the following is correct according to the passage?
(a) iBridge-compatible printers can print out pictures in different settings.
(b) iBridge is a software that can be installed using a USB cable.
(c) Both printers and cameras should have iBridge installed to print out pictures.
(d) The print settings can change the number of pictures to print out.

해설집 : P32

Top designer Clay Depp, 38, is pleased to announce that he will show his latest line of evening clothes starting this Saturday. The exhibition of the new collection will be held at So Chic Gallery in Manhattan, located at 2745 W. 74th Ave. The world famous designer, who grew up on a farm in Kansas, first became prominent in 1992 in Paris, at the Le Chateau Noir, the stylishly modern street shop, where he sold his first line of women's clothing and startled the world with wild colors, ragged hemlines, and flaring sleeves. "My newest line mixes raw urban emotion with romantic sophistication," said Depp, speaking by phone from his New York City penthouse apartment, near the new exhibition.

Q: Which of the following is correct about Clay Depp?
(a) He was once involved in farming.
(b) He became internationally renowned in 1992.
(c) He made a phone call at his house to be interviewed.
(d) He lived in Paris before coming to Kansas.

Pirates would take the combs of all the people on board the ships they robbed. Earlier combs, from around nine hundred years ago, were made of bone. They had animal shapes carved on them. Unlike plastic combs used today, these combs could last longer. Later, combs made of gold were used in church. It was a custom of the Greek Church to comb the priest's hair. The combing was a part of the service. Today, the Japanese place more value on combs than do people in the West. Japanese women always combed their hair neatly, and some Japanese people feel that to throw away a comb brings bad luck. But, to get one as a parting gift is good luck. The comb is supposed to make all future paths straight. That is because the comb makes the hair straight.

Q: Which of the following is correct about combs?
(a) They are sometimes used for religious purposes.
(b) They are believed to mean shortcuts to future goals.
(c) They were first made about 900 years ago.
(d) They were sometimes not paid for when taken.

The finch is found throughout most grassland areas of the world. It is believed that finches were caught in Australia and taken to England in the early 1800s, where they soon became popular due to their quiet song and wonderful coloration. The wild finch is grey, but captive breeding programs have produced more than 100 variations such as blue, silver, white, black, etc. Finches are social birds and should not be kept in small cages as a solitary bird. As they are not usually aggressive to other birds, they may be kept with some other species. Finches are quite cheap to purchase and easy to breed. So they are ideal for novices.

Q: Which of the following is correct according to the passage?
(a) The world has more than 100 kinds of finch.
(b) Although finches sing, they often stay quiet.
(c) Finches are aggressive to each other.
(d) Australians took finches to England.

Aircraft, of course, impact not only the environment but the passengers who fly them and the companies that operate them. So the challenge is to design jets so that everyone wins—creating models that are fuel-efficient, emissions-friendly, comfortable, and cost-effective. With its groundbreaking new aircraft, the A380, Airworld shows that these goals can be achieved. The Airworld A380—the most technically advanced civil aircraft in operation—sets new standards for environmental performance. By building roughly 25% of the A380 out of lightweight carbon fiber composite materials, Airworld was able to decrease the weight of the aircraft. Lower weight means less fuel is required, which means fewer emissions.

Q: What is Airworld?
(a) It is a newly developed plane.
(b) It is an award given to the best aircraft.
(c) It is a company that makes products.
(d) It is a group that improves air traffic.

The Tunguska Event occurred in 1908 over a remote region of Russia. Locals observed a bright light moving across the sky, followed by an enormous explosion and earthquake. Thanks to modern-day research and study, we can conclusively say that the explosion of a comet fragment caused the Tunguska Event. The results of this massive explosion can still be viewed, as trees were felled and burned in an area of roughly 50 square kilometers. The lack of an impact crater suggests that the object completely vaporized in midair. This supports the conclusion that the event was caused by a piece of comet, which became superheated upon atmospheric entry and exploded 5-10 kilometers above the earth's surface.

Q: Which of the following is stated about the passage?
(a) The Tunguska Forest has not been fully restored.
(b) The cause of the event was not studied until recently.
(c) The comet did not complete its course to impact the earth.
(d) The comet was not large enough to resist heat upon atmospheric entry.

In the event of Lessee being transferred other than temporarily by his present employer to a location for work so distant from the country, as to render it impractical for Lessee to maintain residence in the country while performing such work, Lessee may terminate this lease by providing Lessor with a statement in writing from both Lessee and Lessee's employer setting forth the fact of the transfer, the place to which Lessee is to be transferred, and in general the nature of the work Lessee will perform when transferred. Upon receipt of both such statements, the Lease will terminate as of the first day of the first full calendar month which is more than thirty (30) days after the date of receipt by Lessor of the two required statements.

Q: Which of the following claims is made about the passage?
(a) An employer should prove his or her relocation by providing written statements.
(b) Lessee should submit the written reason for stopping paying the rent in time.
(c) Lessee must provide the documents by the first day of a month.
(d) A transferring employee should inform the employer of the new location.

Low literacy rates are common in the United States: a decade ago, 40 million adult Americans scored on the lowest of five levels (level 1) of the National Adult Literacy Survey (NALS). This low literacy level corresponds to having trouble finding pieces of information or numbers in a lengthy text, integrating multiple pieces of information in a document, or finding two or more numbers in a chart and performing a calculation. Consequently, it may damage functioning in the health care environment, affect patient-physician communication relation, and unintentionally lead to poor quality of medical care. It is related to the fact that people poorly understand medical advice in a written or spoken form so that their health is adversely affected.

Q: Which of the following is supported by the passage?
(a) U.S. medical care is negatively influenced by low illiteracy rate.
(b) Some patients cannot understand properly doctors' advice to get well.
(c) NALS surveys the literacy rate in the U.S. every 10 years.
(d) About 40 million of the U.S. population turned out to be illiterate.

The pawnshop industry has been in decline in most parts of the world. In the United States, however, the pawnshop business actually grew during the same time period, from under 2,000 to more than 7,000 today. One of the reasons for the growth of pawnshops is that many states have relaxed their restrictions on the maximum interest rates that can be charged. Pawnshops in these states can now legally charge the high rates needed to stay in business. Further, the percentage of U.S. citizens classified as low-income has risen in recent decades. These individuals cannot get loans from mainstream financial institutions, such as banks and savings and loan associations, and so must turn to alternatives, one of which is the pawnshop.

Q: Why did the pawnshop business grow in the United States?
(a) There have been changes to restrictions on pawnshops.
(b) The U.S. economy has been impacted by the world economy.
(c) The most recent decades have seen the increased patronage of pawnshops.
(d) The pawnshops have become more competitive than mainstream financial institutions.

세부 내용 파악 – 연계 유형

유형 파악

매월 출제되는 TEPS 시험 자료를 분석한 결과, 지문의 두 부분 이상을 연계해야만 정답을 찾을 수 있는 문제가 출제되고 있고, 이에 대해 제대로 다루는 유일한 책이 바로 이 책이다! 왜 연계 유형이 출제되는 것일까?

우선 제한된 시간 안에 지문의 더 많은 부분을 정확하면서도 신속하게 읽고 이해할 수 있는 지를 보기 위해서이고, 더불어 paraphrasing된 정답 선택지 이해 여부를 통해 지문 내용을 능동적으로 분석, 처리하면서 새로운 형태로 표현할 수 있는 본격적인 독해 능력, 즉 '능동적인 독해력'을 측정하기 위함이다.

핵심 전략

세부 내용 파악(일반 유형)의 핵심 전략을 바탕으로 접근하되, 정답이 잘 안 보이거나 읽었던 내용을 망각할 수 있으므로 지문에 표시를 해두면서 읽어야 나중에 정답을 찾는 데 필요한 부분들을 보다 쉽게 연계할 수 있다.

Reading Drills

Hemingway's short story *Big Two-Hearted River* is a beautiful fishing story, based on his experience. But I was surprised at the explanation by Kinsbury—I mean, about why Hemingway chose *Big Two-Hearted River* as the title of his story instead of the Fox River, where he actually fished. Like any other self-respecting fisherman, Hemingway was protecting "his spot" with a clever device that fooled even his own son.

Q: Which of the following is correct according to the passage?
(a) Hemmingway took his son on a fishing trip to Big Two-Hearted River.
(b) *Big Two-Hearted River* is one of Hemmingway's many fishing stories.
(c) The writer of the passage read *Big Two-Hearted River* after Kinsbury did.
(d) Hemingway did not want to tell readers about the Fox River where he fished.

To escape religious persecution in Germany, the ancestors of the Amana colonies emigrated to the U.S. in 1800. They pooled their money and resources and established a communal religious society that built eight villages and acquired seven thousand acres of farm and timberland. The colonies prospered and became well-known for their delicious food and wine and their industrial products. In 1931, members of the society voted to end communal ownership, and all property reverted to private hands.

Q: Which of the following is correct according to the passage?
(a) It took more than a century for the emigrants to settle in the U.S.
(b) Some villages of the society had wineries which produced tasty wine.
(c) The ancestors agreed to share things once owned by communities.
(d) Germany knew about the industrial products made by the colonies.

On the Acropolis, overlooking the city of Athens, stand the ruins of what many consider the most splendid building ever constructed: the Parthenon. The Parthenon was erected in the fifth century B.C. as a temple to the goddess Athena, patroness of the city. The religion associated with the Parthenon, however, was not confined to worship of a deity. In ancient Greece, veneration of the gods was closely related to the political and social ideals of a city-state that celebrated its own greatness.

Q: Which of the following is supported by the passage?
(a) People in Greece gathered at the Parthenon to pray for Athens to prosper.
(b) The Parthenon is still believed to be the oldest structure to admire.
(c) Greek god worshipers in the fifth century B.C. were proud of their nation.
(d) The Parthenon collapsed in the fifth century B.C. and stopped attracting worshipers.

🔒 비법

폭스 강 대신 빅 투 하티드 강을 소설 제목으로 선택했는지에 놀라지 않을 수 없었다는 내용과 다른 낚시꾼처럼 헤밍웨이도 '자신만의 영역'을 지켰다는 내용을 연계해 보면 (d)가 정답이다. (a), (c)는 지문에 없는 내용이고, (b)는 지문에 다른 낚시 이야기가 없다.

self-respecting 자존심 있는

🗨 번역

헤밍웨이의 단편 소설 〈빅 투 하티드 강〉은 그의 경험을 바탕으로 한 아름다운 낚시 이야기이다. 그러나 나는 킨스버리의 설명, 즉 헤밍웨이가 왜 실제로 낚시하던 폭스 강 대신 빅 투 하티드 강을 소설 제목으로 선택했는지에 놀랐다. 자존심 있는 다른 낚시꾼처럼 헤밍웨이는 자신의 아들까지 속일 정도로 재치 있는 방법으로 '자신만의 영역'을 지켰던 것이다.

(a) 헤밍웨이는 빅 투 하티드 강 낚시 여행에 아들을 데리고 갔다.
(b) 〈두 개의 심장을 가진 큰 강〉은 헤밍웨이의 여러 낚시 이야기들 중 하나다.
(c) 지문을 쓴 사람은 킨스버리가 읽은 후에 〈두 개의 심장을 가진 큰 강〉을 읽었다.
(d) 헤밍웨이는 독자들에게 그가 실제로 낚시를 했던 폭스 강에 대해 말하길 원하지 않았다.

🔒 비법

여덟 개의 마을을 세웠다는 내용과 맛있는 음식과 와인, 산업 제품으로 유명해졌다는 내용을 연계해 보면 (b)가 정답이다. (a)는 정착하기까지 걸린 시간이 지문에 없고, (c)는 ancestors가 아니라 1931년에 해당한다. (d)는 지문에 없는 내용이다.

persecution 박해 **ancestor** 조상 **colony** 식민지 **emigrate** 이주하다 **pool** 공동 출자하다 **communal** 공동의 **timberland** 삼림지 **prosper** 번영하다 **revert** 되돌아가다

🗨 번역

아마나 식민지의 조상들은 종교적 박해를 벗어나기 위해 1800년 독일에서 미국으로 이주했다. 그들은 돈과 자원을 공동 출자해 종교 공동체를 설립하여 여덟 개의 마을을 세우고 7,000에이커의 농장과 삼림지를 얻었다. 식민지는 번성했고 그들이 생산한 맛있는 음식과 와인, 공산품으로 유명해졌다. 1931년 회원들은 투표를 통해 공동 소유제를 중단하기로 했고 모든 재산은 각 개인에게 되돌아갔다.

(a) 이민자들이 미국에 정착하는 데 1세기 이상 걸렸다.
(b) 공동체의 몇몇 마을에는 맛있는 포도주를 만들던 양조장들이 있었다.
(c) 조상들은 한때 공동체가 소유했던 것들을 나누기로 동의했다.
(d) 독일은 식민지들이 만든 공산품에 대해 알고 있었다.

🔒 비법

파르테논이 기원전 5세기에 세워졌다는 내용과 고대 그리스에서 신들을 경배하는 일이 스스로의 위대함을 자축했던 도시국가의 정치적, 사회적 이상과 밀접하게 연관되어 있었다는 내용을 연계해 보면 (c)가 정답이다. (a)는 지문에 없고, (b)는 선택지의 oldest가 맞지 않으며, (d)는 선택지의 collapsed in the fifth century B.C.에 대한 내용이 지문에 없다.

overlook 내려다보다 **ruins** 잔해 **splendid** 훌륭한 **erect** 세우다 **goddess** 여신 **patroness** 수호여신 **confine** 한정하다 **deity** 신(성) **veneration** 존경, 숭배 **city-state** 도시국가

🗨 번역

아테네 시가 내려다보이는 아크로폴리스에는 많은 사람들이 가장 훌륭한 건물로 여기는 파르테논의 잔해가 서 있다. 파르테논은 기원전 5세기에 아테네 시의 수호신인 아테네 여신의 신전으로 세워졌다. 그러나 파르테논과 연관된 종교는 신성을 숭배하는 것에 한정되지 않았다. 고대 그리스에서 신들을 경배하는 일은 스스로의 위대함을 자축했던 도시국가의 정치적, 사회적 이상과 밀접하게 연관되어 있었다.

(a) 그리스 사람들이 아테네가 번성하도록 기도하기 위해 파르테논에 모였다.
(b) 사람들은 파르테논이 감탄할 만한 가장 오래된 건물이라고 여전히 믿고 있다.
(c) 기원전 5세기 그리스의 신 숭배자들은 그들의 국가를 자랑스러워했다.
(d) 파르테논은 기원전 5세기에 무너져서 숭배자들이 더 이상 오지 않았다.

Model Test

Part II   Questions 1—4 Read the passage and the question. Then choose the option that best answers the question.

1 TOPIC 전통 한국 회화의 종류

Traditional Korean painting can be divided into two distinct categories. The first is the Confucian style which was first introduced by China in the 14th century. These paintings originally imitated the style of the Chinese scholar-gentry artists, but soon developed many characteristics which were distinctly Korean. Most of these paintings are of pastoral settings—landscapes, birds, and flowers. The other tradition of Korean painting is the folk painting, which is not bound by Confucian restrictions, but instead reflects Korea's shamanistic and spiritual heritage. These delightful pictures depict tigers, mountain spirits, and household gods. Most Buddhist temples are gaily decorated with pictures of this type.

Q: Which of the following is correct about traditional Korean painting?
(a) It began around the 14th century.
(b) It was greatly influenced by Chinese artists.
(c) It did not have its own restrictions.
(d) Its Confucian style is not seen at temples.

2 TOPIC 네즈퍼스 인디언들과 미국 군인들과의 전투

For centuries the Nez Perce Indians lived among the grassy hills and plateaus of the area that is now part of Washington, Idaho, and Oregon. In 1877 the people, under the leadership of Chief Joseph, were told that they would have to leave the area within 30 days. Several battles followed in which the Indians were victorious under the leadership of their great war chief. Finally, the Nez Perce were defeated. Joseph chose to retreat rather than surrender. This was one of the most skillfully planned and performed retreats in American military history. The Indians traveled over 2,500 kilometers and were stopped just before reaching the Canadian border, where they would have been safe from U.S. soldiers.

Q: Which of the following is correct according to the passage?
(a) The Nez Perce Indians lost only one battle against U.S. soldiers.
(b) U.S. soldiers and the Nez Perce Indians fought each other for a month.
(c) Chief Joseph provided military training to his people.
(d) The Nez Perce Indians wanted to cross the Canadian border.

해설집 : P37

TOPIC 노숙이 생긴 세 가지 원인

Homelessness has arisen from at least three social forces. One is the increased shortage of inexpensive housing for poor families and poor unattached persons because of diminishing government subsidization of such housing. Another social force is the decreasing demand for unskilled labor that has occurred since the 1980s, which has resulted in extremely high unemployment among young men in general and African Americans in particular. A third social force is the erosion of the public welfare benefits that has occurred over the last two decades. These three social forces enlarged the ranks of the extremely poor, thereby increasing the chances of these people becoming homeless.

Q: Which of the following is supported by the passage?
(a) The government will increase public housing subsidization in the future.
(b) African Americans have been affected most by the three social forces.
(c) Homelessness and unemployment among young men have become more serious.
(d) There has been little demand for unskilled labor since the 1980s.

TOPIC 경찰차와 승용차 충돌 사고

A Whitesville police officer, responding to an incident call in his private car near Port Ericsson, crashed into another vehicle around 2:40 p.m. Sunday, killing its driver, according to Whitesville State Highway Patrol reports. Patrick T. Houston, 32, an assistant inspector of the Port Ericsson Police Department, remains hospitalized in moderate condition at the Cooper County Regional Medical Center, according to the hospital authority, while Debora Hammersmith, 58, the assistant principal of Port Ericsson Industrial High School, was confirmed dead at the center. A witness said Houston was driving a 2005 Toyokuni 3000 convertible westbound when he entered the intersection and struck Hammersimth's 1999 ABM SUV traveling from downtown.

Q: Which of the following is NOT correct?
(a) Patrick is not on duty temporarily.
(b) Debora's car was manufactured before Patrick's.
(c) The incident in Port Ericsson was not taken care of.
(d) Patrick and Debora were driving toward different directions.

The United States' forest management policy for much of the mid-20th century advocated preventing and extinguishing fires. This practice led to a buildup of dead timber, brush, and other combustible material on the forest floor. After years of drought, that debris dried into volatile tinder that fed inordinately large and hot fires beginning in the late '90s and recurring every summer. Because of the unnatural amount of fuel in forests that had not been allowed to burn for decades, fires that should have been moderate became massive raging infernos that engulfed everything in their paths.

Q: Which of the following is correct according to the passage?
(a) Forest fire extinguishing operations have often failed for some years.
(b) The U.S. forest management policy seemed to work for about 50 years.
(c) Droughts are severest in summer with many forests being burned out.
(d) The buildup of dead timber was not cleared until the late 1990s.

The most practical method of employing hydrogen as a widespread source of power is through the use of fuel cells. In such devices, hydrogen is combined with oxygen in the presence of an electrolyte, creating energy. Just as importantly, the process releases only water vapor and heat as waste products, neither of which is truly harmful. Hydrogen fuel cells come in a variety of sizes, and can be joined together in circuits to yield higher voltage and stronger current. Thus, they can provide power for a wide variety of industrial and personal applications without harming the environment.

Q: Which of the following is correct according to the passage?
(a) Hydrogen is being used for different industrial and personal applications.
(b) Hydrogen fuel cells are replacing some popular types of energy.
(c) Hydrogen must be mixed with oxygen to produce energy.
(d) Hydrogen fuel cells cause no environmental problems.

Dear Mr. Henry,

We extend our gratitude for your special attention to our company the other day. With your detailed presentation, we learned a lot about propane and propane accessories. We have known propane as barbecue grill fuel but did not know it could be efficient and environmentally friendly as well. We were also impressed by the propane-powered refrigerator. We came to realize that propane is ideal for our business operation. We are planning to make an infrastructural building project next month, and are happy to tell you that we will revise our business practices to use this natural resource soon. Before we launch this project, we would like you to visit us once again and help us implement propane accessories safely. We are looking forward to hearing from you at your earliest convenience.

Sincerely,

Lola William

Q: Which of the following is correct about Lola William?

(a) She gave a presentation about propane and its accessories.

(b) She thought that she knew everything about propane.

(c) She wants Mr. Henry to help her with a building project.

(d) She has ordered propane from Mr. Henry before.

The "1421 hypothesis," based on ideas proposed in the book *1421: The Year China Discovered the World*, by Gavin Menzies, suggests that Chinese sailors actually reached the Americas by sailing across the Indian Ocean, around the southern tip of Africa, and across the Atlantic Ocean roughly 70 years before Columbus made his famous journey. The evidence for the "1421 hypothesis" is fairly scattered, as it has to be pulled from what remains today, almost six centuries later. Three categories can be used to organize the supporting evidence: maps, Chinese records, and assorted historical oddities. Menzies uses maps to bolster his revolutionary contentions, which seem to show that the Chinese had an outstanding understating of world geography prior to Columbus.

Q: Which of the following claims is made about the passage?

(a) Evidence shows that the Chinese knew how to get to the Americas.

(b) Chinese sailors discovered the Americas in the early 14th century.

(c) The Chinese made maps to the Americas that were first found by Menzies.

(d) Menzies does not believe that Columbus discovered the Americas.

Paleontology is the branch of science focused on the study of prehistoric life, which is accomplished through careful examination of the fossilized remains those creatures have left behind. It is closely related to two other specialties: archaeology, which studies past human cultures, and paleoanthropology, which studies prehistoric human ancestors. Paleontology, however, is confined to the study of prehistoric animals. Even though the organisms studied by paleontologists have been extinct for thousands or millions of years, they still provide substantial scientific evidence for close research and discovery. Fossils provide an intriguing glimpse into the wildlife that roamed the earth long before humans became the dominant life form on the planet.

Q: Which of the following is stated about the passage?
(a) Paleontology is also studied by archaeologists and paleoanthropologists.
(b) Scientists study carefully the animals that died millions of years ago.
(c) The creatures that roamed the earth have been found by paleontologists.
(d) Paleontologists examine the fossils of the animals that took over the world.

In the 19th century, people began to recognize that clearing breeding grounds for mosquitoes was supremely effective at curbing malaria's spread and effects. Scientists started to understand that just as rats propagated the bubonic plague, mosquitoes carry and transmit malaria. This critical fact ultimately proved paramount in purging malaria from the U.S. As settlers moved into the Upper Mississippi Valley during the 18th and 19th centuries, outbreaks of malaria were triggered by land use habits. Because the Anopheles mosquitoes dislike shade, coolness, and dryness, the settlers' efforts to clear land and irrigate created perfect mosquito breeding grounds. Thus, through their efforts to make land more productive for their use, early settlers also inadvertently improved mosquito habitat.

Q: Which of the following is supported by the passage?
(a) Most Mississippi settlers died of malaria carried by mosquitoes.
(b) The Upper Mississippi Valley was developed by settlers.
(c) Scientists found out that malaria is actually spread by humans.
(d) Settlers did not know that their efforts could damage the land.

추론 – 일반 유형

🔬 유형 파악

추론하기는 33번부터 37번까지 출제되는데 가장 어려운 유형이라 실제로 평균 정답률도 가장 낮다. 그러나 다음에 소개할 핵심 전략을 연습하면 생각보다 쉽게 접근할 수 있다.

🎓 핵심 전략

수험생들이 추론하기를 유난히 어려워하는 가장 큰 이유는 '추론'이란 말에 너무 집착한 나머지 지문에 없는 내용의 오답을 선택하기 때문이다. 추론하기는 지문의 주제를 정확히 파악하고 지문에서 제시된 내용만 갖고 옳은 것을 고르면 되는데, 좀 더 구체적으로 말하자면 주제 파악하기 혹은 세부 사항 파악하기 문제를 푸는 방식으로 풀면 된다. 급할 때는 지문에 없는 단어들이 가장 많이 쓰인 선택지를 고르는 것이 도움이 될 수 있다.

또한 선택지와 관련해서 다음과 같은 사항들을 주의해야 한다.

① 지문에 없는 내용의 선택지

　추론하기에서 가장 주의해야 하는 경우로, 주관적인 판단이나 논리의 비약을 교묘하게 유도해서 틀리게 만든다. 따라서 지문에 나온 내용만으로 정확하게 판단해야 한다!

② 일부분만 옳거나 정답이 되기에는 부족한 내용의 선택지

　언뜻 보면 답이 2개로 보이는 주 원인이다. 선택지 일부분만 읽고 성급하게 판단하지 말고 틀리거나 빠진 내용이 없나 주의 깊게 확인하라!

③ 일반적, 상식적인 내용의 선택지

　지문을 제대로 읽지 않고 찍는 수험생들을 위한 특별한 함정으로 이런 내용의 선택지가 나오면 일단 조심하는 것이 좋다.

④ all, must, never, only 등 극단적인 내용의 선택지

　극단적인 내용의 선택지는 보통 오답이 되는데 그렇지 않은 경우도 출제되므로 주의를 요한다.

⑤ 다음에 할 일과 관련된 선택지

　이 경우에 조심해야 하는 것은 '바로' 다음에 할 일을 고르는 것이다. 즉, 답이 두 개인 것 같은 경우에는 둘 중에서 보다 먼저 할 일을 고르는 것으로, TEPS 청해 Part 3, 4에도 적용되는 사항이다!

Reading Drills

Stanford University anthropologist John Blake confronts the skull of an African man exhumed from the 17th-century African Burial Ground, found during the construction of a federal building in lower Manhattan. Blake's five-year study of the remains of 299 people shows that nearly half died by age 12. All lived hard lives; 70 percent of the men and 60 percent of the women had telltale evidence of torn muscles or fracture caused by carrying heavy loads. One child had two such fractures, dental defects indicating malnutrition or disease, and signs of anemia.

Q: What can be inferred from the passage?

(a) Many African people were mobilized to build massive structures.

(b) African women had to work just as hard as African men did.

(c) African children were physically exploited about 400 years ago.

(d) In the 17th century, about 300 people lived in what is now Manhattan.

The failure of Latin American democracies and the rise of repressive military governments led some Latin Americans to choose a more radical means of bringing about change. During the 1960s, left-wing revolutionary guerilla movements sprang up throughout Latin America. Many Latin Americans were inspired by the success of Castro's revolution in Cuba and the gains made there in health care, housing, literacy, and other social reforms. Revolutionaries were willing to postpone democratic reforms such as free elections and a free press until basic social reforms had been achieved.

Q: What can be inferred from the passage?

(a) Some social reforms were so important that they could not be given up.

(b) Latin American democracies did not recover until the end of the 1960s.

(c) No newspapers were in circulation until Castro finalized his revolution.

(d) Castro helped Latin Americans overthrow their governments.

3 비법

유해의 거의 절반이 12세 이전에 죽은 것이었고 무거운 짐을 져서 생긴 근육 손상과 골절, 그리고 영양실조와 질병이 있었다는 내용을 통해 (c)가 정답이다. (a)는 선택지의 build massive structures가 맞지 않고, (b)는 선택지의 just as hard as가 맞지 않으며, (d)는 지문에 나온 299명이라는 숫자가 아프리카 흑인만 해당하고 그것도 맨해튼 남단 지역에만 해당하므로 맞지 않다.

anthropologist 인류학자 confront 직면하다, 맞서다 exhume 발굴하다 telltale 숨길 수 없는 fracture 골절 malnutrition 영양실조 anemia 빈혈

번역

스탠퍼드 대학의 인류학자인 존 블레이크는 맨해튼 남단에 연방 건물 하나를 건설하는 도중에 17세기 아프리카인 묘지에서 발굴된 아프리카인 남성의 두개골을 연구하게 된다. 블레이크가 299구의 유해를 5년에 걸쳐 연구한 결과 그 중 거의 절반이 12세 이전에 죽은 것으로 나타났다. 모두가 거칠고 고단한 삶을 살았다. 남자의 70%, 여자의 60%가 무거운 짐을 져서 생긴 근육 손상과 골절의 증거가 역력했다. 한 아이의 유골은 이와 같은 골절 두 군데, 영양실조를 보이는 치아 손상, 그리고 빈혈의 징후를 보였다.

(a) 많은 아프리카인들이 거대한 건축물들을 짓는 데 동원됐다.
(b) 아프리카 여성은 아프리카 남성만큼이나 열심히 일해야 했다.
(c) 약 400년 전에 아프리카 아이들은 육체적으로 학대받았다.
(d) 17세기에 약 300명의 사람들이 지금의 맨해튼에 살았다.

4 비법

혁명가들은 기본적인 사회 개혁이 이루어질 때까지 자유 선거와 언론의 자유와 같은 민주 개혁들을 기꺼이 지연하려고 했으므로 (a)가 정답이다. (c)는 카스트로보다는 라틴 아메리카에 대한 내용이라고 봐야 한다.

repressive 억압적인 radical 과격한 bring about 야기하다 spring up 생기다, 발생하다 postpone 연기하다, 지연하다

번역

라틴 아메리카의 민주주의가 붕괴되고 억압적인 군정부가 들어서면서 몇몇 라틴 아메리카인들은 변화를 가져올 좀 더 과격한 수단을 선택하기에 이르렀다. 1960년대에는 좌익혁명 게릴라 운동이 전 라틴 아메리카에 걸쳐 일어났다. 많은 라틴 아메리카인들은 쿠바에서 일어난 카스트로 혁명의 성공과 그것으로 인한 의료, 주거, 탈문맹, 그리고 다른 사회 제도의 개혁에 고무되었다. 혁명가들은 기본적인 사회 개혁이 이루어질 때까지 자유 선거와 언론의 자유와 같은 민주 개혁들을 기꺼이 지연하려고 했다.

(a) 사회의 몇몇 개혁은 너무 중요해서 포기할 수 없었다.
(b) 라틴 아메리카 국가의 민주주의는 1960년대 말까지 회복되지 않았다.
(c) 카스트로가 그의 혁명을 완결하고 나서야 신문들이 유통됐다.
(d) 카스트로는 라틴 아메리카인들이 그들의 정부를 전복하도록 도와줬다.

Model Test

Part II   **Questions 1—4** Read the passage and the question. Then choose the option that best answers the question.

1   **TOPIC** 투자 정보 제공 회사 샤힐 & 선스

As part of our commitment to serving your investment needs, we are striving to ensure that you receive timely information from the fund company in which you are investing. The enclosed information is from New Century Funds and the Paulson Investment Group. If you prefer not to receive this sort of information material from fund companies, please return the enclosed card. We will remove your name from future correspondence. Of course, there are legally required fund materials, such as prospectuses and reports, which we will continue to send you. We thank you for investing through Shahill & Sons and hope you will continue to take advantage of our low-cost, wide selection of investing services.

Q: What can be inferred from the passage?
(a) Shahill & Sons works with investment companies.
(b) Shahill & Sons sent the requested information.
(c) Shahill & Sons provides special information.
(d) Shahill & Sons has a list of financial aid seekers.

2   **TOPIC** 코페르니쿠스적 혁명에 대한 견해

It has become usual to refer to the revolution that occurred in the seventeenth century—the revolution in ways of knowing that led to the establishment of science as the ultimate authority about material reality—as the Copernican Revolution. But this, I think, is unjust. Copernicus, if in fact he desired to bring about a major change in thinking about the world, was afraid to produce it in his lifetime. He may never have had any such idea. Furthermore, his proposal that the earth revolves around the sun was not a revolutionary idea at all. Six ancient Greeks said the same thing before he did.

Q: Which of the following would the writer of the passage most likely agree with?
(a) Copernicus was given astronomical teachings in Greece.
(b) A revolutionist should stand up against a popular belief.
(c) The 17th century is marked most by the Copernican Revolution.
(d) Ancient Greek astrology did not develop much until the 17th century.

3 TOPIC 물질적 진보와 여가 시간 증가

Actually, the practical result of all material progress ought to be increase of leisure, but too often new activities are born of the old, not all of which are beneficial, so leisure is decreased rather than increased. Life was so strenuous for a primitive man that his whole time, or very nearly his whole time, was taken up in providing for the necessities of life. To work for his very existence, to eat, and to sleep were all he could do in the twenty-four hours of each day. Now we have, or ought to have, ample leisure for all sorts of other activities, and indeed the insistence on the eight-hour working day as the standard ensures that we do have this leisure.

Q: What can be inferred from the passage?
(a) The meaning of leisure changes with time.
(b) The amount of leisure time changes with time.
(c) More leisure is not always beneficial.
(d) Some primitive leisure activities do not live on.

4 TOPIC 물가 상승에 따른 제품 가격 상승

Dear Mr. Brockman,

As you no doubt know, commodity prices have increased dramatically over the past several months. Not surprisingly, our costs have increased as well. In this difficult business climate, we have had to acknowledge the impossibility of maintaining our prices at their past levels while continuing to provide the superior quality and service that you have come to expect from us. As a result, we have revised our price list. The enclosed list shows the prices that apply to all purchases effective the first of the month.

On behalf of Faremont Foods, I would personally like to thank you for your past purchases and continuing support.

Sincerely,
Brian Weiss
Account Representative

Q: What will Mr. Brockman do after reading the letter?
(a) Decrease the current order volume
(b) Check the prices
(c) Look for another food company
(d) Contact Brian for a new product catalog

Part II　**Questions 1—10** Read the passage and the question. Then choose the option that best answers the question.

The film preview for *Atlantic News* readers will be a special screening of *Happy Days*, Francis Kitano's film of Arthur Nelson's long-running musical. It is nominated for seven Oscars including best film. The screening will take place at 11:00 a.m. on Saturday, February 10th, at the Atlantic Club. The film runs for two and a half hours. To obtain a free ticket, present this coupon from 9:00 a.m. next Monday at the Atlantic News office in the Central building. Tickets will be given to the first 100 applicants. Only one coupon per person will be accepted. This film will resonate better with those who have speculated on the meaning of happiness.

Q: What can be inferred from the passage?
(a) The movie is even for those who have not pondered happiness.
(b) The ticket holders will have to skip their lunch to see the whole film.
(c) February 5 is the first day to use the coupons for the tickets.
(d) 100 coupons have been issued for *Atlantic News* readers.

Some people say that it is bad to read old-fashioned fairy tales to little children because they make them afraid. But, like very primitive people, they already live in a world that they cannot begin to understand. Fairy tales could do for small children, and indeed did for many years, what myth, ritual, and religion did for primitive people—give their fears a name and an identity, a handle to take hold of and perhaps to cast them out by. A child who can channel his fear of the unknown into a fear of ghosts, witches, giants, and the like, may be able to rid himself of much of that fear when he finds that such things do not exist.

Q: What can be inferred about fairy tales?
(a) They help children understand what scares them.
(b) They are as old as primitive people.
(c) They secretly reveal how primitive people lived.
(d) They teach children how to solve problems.

This year, as every year, the Annual Ventriloquist Convention will be held the last weekend in June at Fort Mitchell, Kentucky. For four days and nights, men, women, and dummies will converse, debate, argue, and generally enjoy themselves. Ventriloquism is the art of speaking in such a way that the voice seems to come from some source other than the speaker. When watching ventriloquists perform, it is clear that they have a very close relationship with their dummies. Some people speculate that this is because often ventriloquists were lonely as children and invented an alter ego, a separate personality, that followed them around and kept them company.

Q: What can be inferred from the passage?
(a) Ventriloquists do not have as many friends as others do.
(b) The convention is more than two years old.
(c) The convention is open to members only.
(d) Part of ventriloquism is imitating other people.

Fast readers cannot understand completely the whole meaning of a book. It's because they just skim and guess the meaning of it. But there seems to be one person who can read about 20,000 words a minute with near-perfect comprehension. His name is Kim Peek and he has the ability to read two pages simultaneously, one with each eye, with 98% comprehension. It's not clear how it works for him, but he didn't have a corpus callosum upon his birth. However, others born without it couldn't show such reading or comprehension abilities. He was partly the model for the idiot savant in the movie *Rain Man*.

Q: What can be inferred from the passage?
(a) Kim Peek wanted to teach others how they should read.
(b) Some people born without a corpus callosum were studied.
(c) *Rain Man* is partly about how Kim Peek influenced educators.
(d) Other fast readers do not know as many words as Kim Peek does.

The number of people taking cruises continues to rise, and so does the number of complaints about cruise lines. A prime concern that has arisen with the proliferation of cruise-line mergers—as it did with airline consolidation—is the apparent decline in staff courtesy, service, and cuisine. One reader reported "less than coffee-shop quality." Another writes that food "was never hot." Travel arrangements like fly/cruise programs, late port arrival, and confusing disembarkation procedures were also criticized. When asked about these irregularities, industry spokespeople say they are trying to improve their service and ask that the public report dissatisfaction to the appropriate management.

Q: What can be inferred from the passage?
(a) Cruise lines have not made their service better.
(b) Coffees provided by cruise lines were cheap.
(c) Cruise lines are trying to cancel mergers.
(d) Complaints about the service were not heard.

Many people say that the statue called *The Thinker* shows a man in deep thought over a serious topic. That makes sense because this statue was designed to be placed over a set of great doors which would show the things that happened to people in hell. Both *The Thinker* and the doors were designed by Auguste Rodin, an artist who lived and worked in France around the same time as the painter Claude Monet. Like Monet, Rodin was much criticized for his non-traditional style. In the 1800s there was a strict standard for realistic sculpture. Some people thought a smooth finish was one of the essential marks of fine sculpture. However, the surface of *The Thinker* is wrinkled and rippled.

Q: What can be inferred from the passage?
(a) *The Thinker* was liked by many people for a long time.
(b) Auguste Rodin was inspired by Claude Monet.
(c) Auguste Rodin and Claude Monet taught each other.
(d) Most sculptures in the 19th century shared something similar.

Among the Crowell Museum's collections is the world-famous glass flower exhibit, featuring over one hundred delicate hand-blown replicas of actual floral species. The glass flower display was donated by a benefactor who was the force behind the museum in its early years, the nephew of the enigmatic Elberth Crowell, founder of the museum. The collection is part of the museum's permanent display of collections. It is a curious fact that although Elberth Crowell founded the museum when only forty-three, he never visited it or inquired as to the collections it housed. The collection is housed in the West Gallery and may be visited weekdays from 9:00 AM to 5:00 PM.

Q: What can be inferred from the passage?
(a) Elberth Crowell founded the museum for his nephew.
(b) The display was donated when Elberth Crowell was forty-three.
(c) Elberth Crowell did not create the glass flowers.
(d) West Gallery is owned by Elberth Crowell's nephew.

Dear Mr. Washburn,

Thank you for your payment of $543.78. We are removing the penalty based on your explanation of why you paid your tax late. We charge interest on any unpaid tax, however, regardless of whether you had a reasonable cause. If you have already paid the penalty and you have no other outstanding balances, you will receive a refund of the penalty amount you paid within six to eight weeks from the date of this letter.

If your tax return is selected for examination later, the examiner may review this decision about the penalty and ask for your explanation or additional information about it. If you have any questions, please call our Taxpayer Customer Service area telephone number.

Sincerely yours,
Rodney Foxfield
Accounts Representative

Q: What can be inferred from the letter?
(a) Washburn has paid interest for paying tax late.
(b) Washburn did not tell Rodney whether he paid the penalty.
(c) Washburn's tax return will be selected for examination.
(d) Washburn will call Taxpayer Customer Service.

The early colonists in the United States did not build in stone. In the southern and Dutch colonies, the important buildings were mostly of brick, but for other buildings, wood was most commonly used. Wood frequently determined the form and style, but there was not much architectural elegance until the influence of Sir Christopher Wren's work had some effect on the middle and southern colonies in the eighteenth century. Williamsburg Town Hall in Williamsburg, Virginia, and St. Michael's Church in Charleston, South Carolina, were attributed to Wren, but they had no special architectural elegance, although they were of simple and pleasing design.

Q: What can be inferred from the passage?
(a) Wood is most frequently used as a building material in the U.S.
(b) Brick buildings in the southern colonies were not architecturally elegant.
(c) St. Michael's Church in Charleston, South Carolina, was built during the 1900s.
(d) Sir Christopher Wren supposedly designed only two buildings in the 18th century.

Refreshment stands can be found everywhere. These concession stands give the "small guy" a chance to make really good money and be his own boss at the same time. There are a variety of stands. Some are permanent. Others are actually moving vehicles that can be parked anywhere. Concession owners usually have to pay license fees to be able to set up in particular places. Their wares range from Coke made from syrup and seltzer water to homemade baked goods to organic health food smoothies. A concession stand is a welcome sight in extreme weather conditions: an ice cream stand in the sweltering heat or a place to get a cup of hot chocolate by an ice rink!

Q: What can be inferred from the passage?
(a) Concession owners pay license fees instead of taxes.
(b) Seltzer water is one of the wares that concession owners sell.
(c) Weather decides where refreshment stands are set up.
(d) There are two main kinds of refreshment stands.

추론 – 연계 유형

유형 파악

추론하기에서도 연계해서 푸는 문제가 출제되지만, 세부 사항 파악하기보다는 비중이 다소 낮고, 이것이 출제되는 이유는 능동적인 독해력을 보다 심도 있게 측정하기 위함이다. 또한 지문의 보다 많은 부분을 읽어서 제한된 시간 안에 얼마나 많이 읽고 정확히 판단할 수 있는지, 즉 전체적인 속독 능력을 측정하기 위함이다. 지문의 길이를 늘리지 않고 읽어야 할 부분을 늘려 난이도 높은 문제를 출제하는 것이 최신 TEPS 독해의 특징이다! 여기에 지문 내용을 새로운 형태로 가공해서 표현할 줄도 알아야 하므로 적절한 paraphrasing 능력도 필요하다!

핵심 전략

추론하기(일반 유형)의 핵심 전략을 바탕으로 접근하되 정답이 잘 안 보이거나 읽었던 내용을 망각하는 경우도 있으므로 지문에 표시를 해두면서 읽어야 나중에 정답을 찾는 데 필요한 부분들을 보다 쉽게 연계할 수 있다.

Reading Drills

Part II **Questions 1 and 2** Read the passage and the question. Then choose the option that best answers the question.

Naples in Italy stretches around the Bay of Naples and lies at the foot of Mount Vesuvius. As a reminder of the force of the great volcano, the unearthed ruins of Pompeii and Herculaneum pay tribute to the destruction Vesuvius has brought to southern Italy, and are just a short trip from the capital city of Campania. The city of Naples is blessed by great beauty and history but the harsh conditions of modern life stand in stark contrast to the scenic grandeur of this coastal region.

Q: What can be inferred from the passage?

(a) Naples is located next to the capital city of Campania.

(b) Mount Vesuvius is a dormant volcano.

(c) Many archaeological discoveries are made in Naples.

(d) Naples' economy mostly depends on tourism.

The quest motif is certainly important in American literature. Benjamin Franklin's quest in his *Autobiography*, for example, is for material comfort and outward success. His quest may be considered an explicit one, because he announces clearly what he is trying to do: perfect a systematic approach for living long and happily. The whole *Autobiography* is a road map intended for other people to use as a guide; Franklin apparently meant rather literally for people to imitate his methods.

Q: What can be inferred from the passage?

(a) Material success is a typical subject for American writers.

(b) Benjamin Franklin's autobiography was widely read.

(c) Books written by Benjamin Franklin are easy to understand.

(d) Benjamin Franklin wanted people to live to a great age.

해설 및 정답 : 뒤로 ➦

1 비법

나폴리아가 베수비오 산 발치에 자리잡고 있다는 내용과 거대한 화산의 위력을 상기시켜 주듯이라는 내용을 연계해 보면 (b)가 정답이다. (a)는 선택지의 Naples is가 The unearthed ruins of Pompeii and Herculaneum are가 돼야 하고, (c)는 선택지의 are가 were가 돼야 하며, (d)는 선택지의 mostly에 대한 근거가 지문에 없다.

stretch 뻗다 **bay** 만 **lie** 놓여 있다 **unearth** 발굴하다 **ruin** 잔해 **pay tribute to** ~에 경의를 표하다 **bless** 축복하다 **harsh** 혹독한 **stark** 현저한 **scenic** 경치의 **grandeur** 웅장 **archaeological** 고고학의 **tourism** 관광 사업

번역

이탈리아의 나폴리는 나폴리 만을 따라 길게 뻗은 모양으로 베수비오 산 발치에 자리잡고 있다. 거대한 화산의 위력을 상기시켜 주듯이, 발굴된 폼페이와 허큘레니엄의 잔해들이 베수비오 화산이 남부 이탈리아를 덮쳤던 파괴력에 경의를 표하고 있으며 수도인 캄파니아에서 멀지 않은 거리에 위치하고 있다. 나폴리는 훌륭한 풍경과 역사의 축복을 입고 있으나 현대의 삶이 가진 혹독한 조건들은 해안 지역 경치의 웅장함과 현저한 대조를 이룬다.

(a) 나폴리는 수도 캄파니아 근처에 있다.
(b) 베수비오 산은 휴화산이다.
(c) 많은 고고학적 발견이 나폴리에서 이루어진다.
(d) 나폴리의 경제는 대부분 관광 사업에 의존한다.

2 비법

벤저민 프랭클린 자신이 하고자 하는 것이 행복한 장수를 위한 체계적인 접근을 완벽하게 만들어 놓는 것이라는 내용과 그의 의도는 말 그대로 사람들이 자신의 방법을 모방하도록 하는 것이었다는 내용을 연계하면 (d)가 정답이다. (b)는 선택지의 widely에 대한 근거가 지문에 없다.

quest 추구 **motif** 주제 **autobiography** 자서전 **material comfort** 물질적 풍요 **outward** 외면상의 **explicit** 뚜렷한 **systematic** 체계적인

번역

미국 문학에서 추구라는 주제는 상당히 중요하다. 예를 들어 벤저민 프랭클린이 그의 〈자서전〉에서 추구하는 것은 물질적 풍요와 외면적 성공이다. 그가 추구한 것은 뚜렷하다고 간주해도 좋은 것이, 자신의 의도를 명확하게 밝히기 때문이다. 행복하게 장수하는 체계적인 접근법 완전 정복이 그것이다. 그의 〈자서전〉은 사람들에게 안내를 해주는 지침서 역할을 할 의도로 쓰였다. 프랭클린의 의도는 말 그대로 자신의 방법을 모방하도록 하는 것임이 분명한 것 같다.

(a) 물질적인 성공은 미국 작가들의 전형적인 주제이다.
(b) 벤저민 프랭클린의 자서전은 널리 읽혔다.
(c) 벤저민 프랭클린이 쓴 책들은 이해하기 쉽다.
(d) 벤저민 프랭클린은 사람들이 장수하길 바랐다.

Model Test

1   TOPIC 아시안 항공이 제공하는 2일짜리 무료 휴가

To refresh yourself and get rid of the boredom of everyday life, fly from America to Southeast Asia with the extras you'll need for a free 2-night luxury holiday. We invite you to relax at the first-class hotel. We also give you a chance to play a free round of golf on the championship course. You can also choose from four other free options: Car hire for two days. A half-day city tour in a private, chauffeur-driven car. A Jungle Safari with dinner. Or a voucher worth $120 to spend at the Duty Free shop. To accept our offer, fly First or Business Class with Asianlines between America and Southeast Asia before June 17.

Q: What can be inferred from the passage?
(a) Qualified Asianlines passengers can visit a jungle in a Southeast Asia.
(b) Car rental provided by Asianlines in a travel destination is $60 per day.
(c) Asianlines passengers are eligible for a free hotel stay before June 17.
(d) A free golf lesson is provided to First or Business Class passengers.

2   TOPIC 결혼이 늦어지는 원인과 결과

Many changes in cultural attitudes and social values are responsible for the increased later marriages. There is the growing acceptance of cohabitation in which adults live together in a sexual relationship without being married. Cohabitation has increased rapidly since the 1970s. This change in marriage patterns has various implications. One of them is smaller family size because couples marry later and have a shorter time when they can have children. Another is the increasing number of older parents; people getting married and having a child in their 30s means they will be in their 50s as the child graduates from high school. No matter how late people marry, marriage, in one form or another, is functional in so many ways that it keeps existing in every society.

Q: What can be inferred from the passage?
(a) Birth rates have been on the decline since the 1970s.
(b) People getting married in their 20s will retire in their 50s.
(c) The meaning of marriage is different in every society.
(d) Certain social attitudes are responsible for illegal activities.

TOPIC 도하니 스트리트 유대 교회의 과거와 현재

It may bear the scars of past abandonment, but the Dohany Street Synagogue, here on the edge of what was once Budapest's Jewish ghetto, has finally triumphed over the successive onslaughts of the Holocaust and Communism. During World War II, as much of its congregation perished at the hands of the Nazis, this imposing Moorish-style temple, which is one of Europe's largest with a seating capacity of almost 3,000, was completely neglected. For nearly half a century its twin turrets and elaborate mosaic floors deteriorated. Then in the early 1990s the newly democratic Hungarian government, working in concert with private donors from abroad, began restoring this magnificent 137-year-old synagogue.

Q: What can be inferred from the passage?
(a) Hungary had to be democratic to be aided in repairing the synagogue.
(b) The synagogue had been used for about 87 years following its construction.
(c) Hungarian and foreign architects will work together to restore the synagogue.
(d) People who stayed in the synagogue survived World War II.

TOPIC 양치류 잎 무늬 가구의 과거와 현재

Inspired by the popularity of ferns during the Victorian period, cast iron fern-leaf furniture was first introduced in Great Britain in the 1870s. Now, more than a century later, it thrives again, thanks to Marbletown Craftsmen, Ltd., which in cooperation with the Appleton Institution has issued heavy cast aluminum versions of licensed adaptations of the historic leafy-design furniture. Although Garden White is the most popular color, the replica furniture is also available in Appleton Green, Baltimore Blue, and Federal City Yellow.

Q: What can be inferred from the passage?
(a) Leafy-design furniture was not popular in the middle of the 20th century.
(b) Original leafy-design furniture of the 1870s was made in Garden White.
(c) Fern-leaf furniture is made by two independent manufacturers.
(d) Adapting the old furniture is regulated by law in Great Britain.

TEPS Reading Practice

Part II   **Questions 1—10** Read the passage and the question. Then choose the option that best answers the question.

American artist Georgia O'Keefe attracted much attention when the first of her many floral scenes was exhibited. Everything about these paintings—their color, size, point of view, and style—overwhelmed the viewer's senses, just as their creator had intended. In one of her familiar poppies, O'Keefe directed the viewer's eye down into the poppy's center, much as the flower naturally attracts an insect for reproduction purposes. By contrasting the light tints of the outer ring of petals with the darkness of the poppy's center, the viewer's eye is pulled beelike into the heart of the flower. The overwhelming size and detailed interiors of O'Keefe's flowers give an effect similar to the photographer's close-up camera angle.

Q: What can be inferred from the passage?

(a) The viewers appreciated Georgia O'Keefe's works as photographers would.

(b) Georgia O'Keefe's first exhibition of poppies was a success.

(c) The subject of the exhibit was what Georgia O'Keefe often worked on.

(d) Georgia O'Keefe was also interested in photography.

The Department of Linguistics at Stanford University invites applications for the tenure-track position of assistant professor of phonetics to begin in fall next year. Responsibilities will include teaching courses in phonetics; directing the master's and doctorate programs; engaging in an active program of research and publication; and rendering service at the departmental, college, and university levels. Candidates must have a Ph.D. in phonetics, or other appropriate discipline. Please send a letter of application, a CV, and three letters of recommendation. Salary commensurate with qualifications and experience. Minority and women candidates are encouraged to apply.

Q: What can be inferred from the passage?

(a) Phonetics classes can be taught by an inexperienced professor.

(b) Foreign applicants are not to apply for the position.

(c) One of the phonetics professors left Stanford University.

(d) Applications must be submitted by next fall at the latest.

해설집 : P53

Most people have no idea how much effort is devoted to influencing their eating habits by large-scale food corporations and lobbyist groups. From creating food to putting products on shelves and advertising, almost every aspect of most food is overseen by some large companies. Such firms want people to eat more of the foods and products bearing their name regardless of health consequences, and will go to great lengths to enhance and protect those products' images. Considering this, rather than wasting time combating such staggering lobbying and advertising powerhouses, health crusaders would be wise to focus their efforts on giving healthy foods similar exposure and treatment.

Q: What can be inferred from the passage?
(a) Some popular foods have been proved unhealthy by health-concerned groups.
(b) Minor food companies produce more healthy foods than major ones do.
(c) Healthy foods should gain as much public attention as those of large companies.
(d) People's eating habits will change with healthy foods being consumed more.

A small island in central Caribbean Bay was once called Treasure Island because of the riches pearl cultivation brought to its residents. In 1992, a deadly red tide of poisonous plankton struck the bay. The mortality rate of oysters increased from about 40 percent to more than 55 percent. In 1996, a more threatening scourge hit the oysters. The mystery disease rapidly spread to other pearl-cultivating sites. In the case of red tide, oysters can be moved to a safe place. At some point in the season, growers usually clean the oysters to remove any attachments from the shells. But the new disease makes the shells so fragile that cleaning is impossible.

Q: What can be inferred from the passage?
(a) Economic difficulties began to emerge on the island in 1992.
(b) Between 1993 and 1996, no cases of red tide were reported.
(c) Red tide made the mystery disease spread on the island.
(d) The mortality rate of oysters jumped by about 15% in 1996.

The Opium War, though often considered a conflict centered simply on the smuggling of contraband opium into China by British merchants, effectively made China's resources a massive source of British commerce. It was less a war about drugs, and more one about British imperialist designs. When declaring war, British officials acknowledged that its citizens had been breaking Chinese law by importing opium into China. However, England's Prime Minister argued that the Chinese government had mistreated those issues because the laws applied only to foreigners. In short, the British felt wronged at being subject to laws that the Chinese themselves did not obey. So, England enacted a naval blockade of Chinese ports in 1840, beginning the Opium War.

Q: What can be inferred from the passage?
(a) England's Prime Minister thought that importing opium was not against international law.
(b) After the Opium War, the Chinese government illegalized domestic opium sale.
(c) The Chinese government did not try to apply its laws to its citizens.
(d) Before 1840, England did not have access to China's resources.

All middle class families would like a larger living space. Doesn't this then mean that the proliferation of the middle class and economic success will eventually lead to the mass production of children who, proudly armed with individuality, show no consideration whatsoever toward other people? Many studies indicate that personal space affects the formation of one's personality and values. The residential space of the poor is structured in such a way that they have to interact with one another, whereas the living space of the upper class is secluded enough to ensure privacy, completely blocking public access.

Q: What can be inferred from the passage?
(a) Changing living conditions is important for middle class families.
(b) Most of today's living spaces have little educational value for children.
(c) Middle class families became richer and want privacy more than the poor.
(d) The children of the rich should interact with family members in their house.

The Marxist theory of history as a series of class struggles has had powerful consequences for what many people believe about the world. Many of the political and social conflicts around the world involve people acting on or acting against this vision of human organization. In a less dramatic way, this theory has had a serious impact on the study of history, politics, economics, sociology, and even art and literature. The far-reaching effect of Marxism demonstrates forcibly that theories are not just empty abstractions, with little relation to reality.

Q: What can be inferred about the Marxist theory according to the passage?
(a) It changed every field of study profoundly.
(b) World views did not change until its introduction.
(c) It turned out to be more real than any other theory.
(d) It produced literary works that supported class struggle.

Columbus's personal life turned out to be an abject failure despite his astounding success as a greatly mistaken but even more greatly fortunate navigator. A magnificent seaman, he was an abysmal administrator. Ferdinand and Isabella soon saw this. They had made him promises, and they never ceased to be generous and affectionate toward this strange, mad, wonderful man who had made them almost as famous as he was. But they could not endure his autocratic claim that he was the king of the Western World, and they merely the Spanish viceroys.

Q: What can be inferred from the passage?
(a) Ferdinand and Isabella helped Columbus rule the Western World.
(b) Columbus stepped down after all those years as an administrator.
(c) Columbus's belief about himself was different from his actual status.
(d) Ferdinand and Isabella were not as good as their word with Columbus.

Well known throughout the world, black powder was invented by the Chinese. This invention opened the first era of human utilization of explosives—the black powder era. As early as 220 B.C., the Chinese laboring people already had primary knowledge of it. Around the 11th to 12th centuries, it began to spread to Arabian countries, and then to Europe. In about 1627, black powder was used for mining. Compared to the original method of breaking rock by fire, it proved to be more effective to blast rock by black powder. It remained in use as the world's only explosive until the mid-1870s.

Q: What can be inferred from the passage?
(a) Black powder was used exclusively in China for more than a millennium.
(b) People stopped using black power from the mid-1870s.
(c) China was the first to use black powder for mining.
(d) Nations around the world shared the knowledge of explosives.

After Alexander the Great died in 323 B.C., the rule of Egypt passed to one of his generals, the Macedonian Ptolemy. In 305 B.C., Ptolemy became king of Egypt, and moved his capital to Alexandria on the Mediterranean coast, and it became a great center of trade and scholarship. From 285 B.C., he ruled jointly with his son, Ptolemy II, who went on, after his father's death in 282 B.C., to further strengthen the country's commerce. Ptolemy III continued to consolidate the power of the dynasty, but his successors were weak. The Ptolemaic dynasty ended when a joint Egyptian and Roman fleet under Mark Antony was defeated by Octavian, Caesar's heir, at the Battle of Actium in 31 B.C.

Q: What can be inferred from the passage?
(a) Ptolemy gave financial help to poor students.
(b) The Ptolemaic dynasty lasted for about 270 years.
(c) Mark Antony was against the Ptolemaic dynasty.
(d) Caesar was involved in battles in Alexandria.

Unit 09 문맥 흐름

유형 파악

흐름에 어울리지 않는 문장 찾기는 독해 마지막 파트로 38번에서 40번까지 출제된다. 지금까지는 배점이 높기 때문에 먼저 푸는 것이 좋다고 알려져 있다. 그러나 TEPS 채점 방식인 IRT(Item Response Theory) 이론에 의해 이 3문제를 맞췄다 하더라도 다른 쉬운 문제를 틀리면 찍어서 맞췄다고 보고 감점하기 때문에 마찬가지이다.

어쨌거나 가장 먼저는 아니더라도 가장 나중에 푸는 것은 좋지 않다. 왜냐하면 이 3문제 중 보통 2문제 정도는 그리 어렵지 않게 출제되기 때문이다.

핵심 전략

독해 Part 3은 일단 첫 문장은 선택지 (a)로 나오지 않는 출제 원칙이 있고, 이런 이유로 첫 문장에 지문 주제가 대부분 들어 있다. 따라서 지문 첫 문장을 잘 읽고 몇몇 단어들만 보고 지문 전체 흐름에 어울린다고 착각하지 않도록 주의하면서 주제에 벗어나는 문장을 고르는 것이 핵심 공략법이다!

가령 피카소 그림 전시회를 알리는 지문이 나왔을 때 In fact, the extent to which Picasso paintings have influenced geometry is minimal(사실 피카소 그림이 기하학에 영향을 준 정도는 미미하다)과 같이 Picasso paintings라는 말은 있으나 내용상 전시회와 기하학은 연결되지 않는 식이다.

또한 접속어, 대명사, 지시형용사, 동의어, 반의어가 앞 문장과는 연결되나 지문 전체 흐름과는 연결되지 않는 선택지 등 오답을 정답처럼 보이게 하는 함정들이 등장하는 것이 최신 경향이므로 더욱 주의를 요한다!

Reading Drills

Part III   Questions 1—3 Read the passage. Then identify the option that does NOT belong.

It is difficult to comprehend the immense proportions of the blue whale, the largest animal ever to inhabit the earth. (a) At 25 to 30 meters in length, this marine mammal is longer than three railroad cars and bigger than any dinosaur that ever walked on land. (b) It weighs more than 25 elephants or 1,600 fans at a basketball game. (c) Its heart is the size of a beetle—a Volkswagen beetle—and its tongue that of a grown elephant. (d) This giant creature is still caught in large numbers around the coasts of some countries.

In the 17th and 18th centuries, the human senses generally provided a major source of scientific information. (a) However, from the beginning of the century they began to play a relatively secondary role. (b) In their place, scientific instruments began to supply the primary data of science. (c) During the 17th century, it is true, relatively simple instruments, such as the microscope and the telescope, could still be regarded as extensions of the eye. (d) But today scientific instruments have grown to such complexity that observations are more and more remote from immediate sense perception.

The FAA (Federal Aviation Administration) proposed depriving Georgia Airlines of its authority to perform heavy maintenance. (a) The FAA has been closely watching several airlines since the crash of Flight 361 in April, in which 91 people died. (b) The government agency's inspections found 125 instances where heavy maintenance work had been carried out, but not documented correctly. (c) According to the agency, lack of documentation means poor attention to detail. (d) The airline has two weeks to show it has taken measures to keep it from losing its authority for heavy maintenance.

📽 비법

흰긴수염고래의 크기가 주요 내용으로, 고래잡이에 대한 내용을 담고 있는 (d)가 지문 흐름에 어긋난다.

comprehend 파악하다 **proportion** 크기
marine mammal 해양 포유류

💬 **번역** 지금까지 지구에 서식한 가장 거대한 동물인 흰긴수염고래의 거대한 크기를 파악하는 것은 어려운 일이다. (a) 길이가 25내지 30미터에 해당하는 이 해양 포유류는 3대의 열차 객실을 이은 길이보다 길고 지구상에 발을 디딘 어떤 공룡보다도 크다. (b) 흰긴수염고래는 25마리의 코끼리를 합한 것보다, 또는 농구장 관중 1,600명을 합한 것보다 무게가 더 많이 나간다. (c) 흰긴수염고래의 심장은 그 크기가 비틀, 즉 폭스바겐의 소형차만하고 혀는 다 큰 코끼리 한 마리의 크기와 같다. (d) 이 거대한 동물은 여전히 몇몇 나라들 해안가에서 다량으로 잡힌다.

📽 비법

(a)의 from the beginning of the century의 the century가 앞의 17과 18세기 중에서 몇 세기를 의미하는지 불분명하므로 지문 흐름에 어긋난다.

source 출처 **secondary** 부차적인
scientific instrument 과학기구
microscope 현미경 **telescope** 망원경
remote 먼, 동떨어진

💬 **번역** 17세기와 18세기에는 인간의 감각이 일반적으로 과학적 정보의 주된 출처였다. (a) 그러나, 이것은 세기 초기부터 비교적 부차적인 역할을 하기 시작했다. (b) 대신 과학기구들이 과학의 일차적 정보들을 제공하기 시작했다. (c) 17세기에는 현미경이나 망원경처럼 비교적 간단한 기구들이 인간의 눈의 연장이라고 여전히 간주될 수 있었다. (d) 그러나 오늘날 과학기구들은 대단히 복잡하고 정교해져서 직접적인 감각과는 점점 더 동떨어진 것이 되어가고 있다.

📽 비법

조지아 항공의 과다한 정비 업무에 대해 연방 항공국이 제재를 가하는 내용의 지문으로, 조지아 항공이 아닌 몇몇 항공사들 이야기가 나온 (a)가 지문 흐름에 어긋난다.

aviation 항공 **deprive** 빼앗다
maintenance 유지, 정비 **inspection** 조사
carry out 행하다 **document** 기록하다
take measures 조치를 취하다

💬 **번역** 연방 항공국은 조지아 항공의 중장비 정비 권한을 박탈할 것을 건의했다. (a) 연방 항공국은 지난 4월 91명이 사망한 361기 추락 사고 이래 몇몇 항공사들을 예의 주시해 왔다. (b) 정부 당국의 조사에 의해 중장비 정비를 시행하고도 제대로 기록하지 않은 경우를 125건 찾아냈다. (c) 당국에 따르면 증거 자료 부족은 세부 사항 부주의를 의미한다고 한다. (d) 조지아 항공은 중장비 정비 권한을 상실하지 않기 위해 그동안 필요한 조치를 취했다는 사실을 2주 내로 입증해야 한다.

Model Test

Part III   Questions 1—4 Read the passage. Then identify the option that does NOT belong.

1   **TOPIC** 통근과 건강의 관계

Ray Novaco has been observing commuters since the late 1980s. (a) His research shows that a stressful car trip can cause astounding physical effects. (b) He found, for example, that the number of times a person commutes seemed to increase the individual's risk of getting the flu or a cold. (c) Novaco links his research finding to the "deleterious effects of stress on the immune system," adding that commuters who encountered a lot of traffic jams also took sick days more frequently than those with a relatively hassle-free route to work. (d) Novaco also found out that blood pressure goes up in proportion to how far commuting distance is.

2   **TOPIC** 영국 숙박 시설 B & B

The bed and breakfast, or B&B, is a form of holiday accommodation for which Britain is world-famous. (a) It gives you the opportunity to learn how British villagers used to live. (b) And you can have the chance to make friends and see some of the most attractive and less well-known parts of the country, ranging from John O'Groats to Land's End. (c) Generally, it will be run by the owner of the premises, and you will be treated like a royal guest. (d) The welcome will be friendly and warm, but you can have all your meals in a separate dining room for your privacy.

TOPIC 인간의 모든 역할의 보여지는 부분과 보여지지 않는 부분

Every role we play in life has an onstage and backstage area; in one we're on our best behavior, and in the other we can be more relaxed. (a) For example, in the dining room, a waiter is onstage. (b) No matter how rushed he is or how annoyed he feels, a waiter is expected to be polite and helpful to his customers. (c) Once he returns to the kitchen, however, he is backstage and can let his true feelings show. (d) In the kitchen, the waiter can take it easy for a minute and get ready for another round of serving.

TOPIC 남미 국가들의 금융 시장 자유화

The governments of several South American nations, including Brazil and Argentina, jointly announced a number of changes in their monetary exchange policies. (a) Long considered some of the most stringent in the world, the liberalization of their financial markets was applauded by economists throughout the region. (b) A number of recessions have plagued Brazil and Argentina, and implementing monetary reform has long been cited as one way to cure their economic ills. (c) The major change announced was that the transfer of capital from one country to another would become a quicker, more efficient process. (d) This should help encourage investment in the region and spur the economies of South America to future success.

Part III **Questions 1—10** Read the passage. Then identify the option that does NOT belong.

Much has been said about the need for industrialization as the quickest and most effective way to raise the income and the level of living of underdeveloped countries. (a) But they cannot industrialize successfully with a substantial improvement in their food and human efficiency. (b) This depends primarily on the improvement of their agriculture and utilization of food. (c) In these countries 60 to 80 percent of the people are engaged in farming, but their productivity is so low that it falls far short of feeding the population. (d) Unless they improve their food-producing efficiency, any efforts of turning their working force to industry will only make their food problem more hopeless.

In a dry climate like that of Egypt, papyrus is stable, but storage in humid conditions can result in destroying the material. (a) By 800 AD the use of vellum had replaced it in many areas, though it continued to be used in Egypt until it was replaced by cheaper paper introduced by the Arabs. (b) The reasons for this switch result from the fact that it was quite expensive to make paper using papyrus. (c) People gradually began not to use sheets of papyrus, and the latest certain date for the use of it is 1057. (d) Although it was used as late as the 12th century in the Byzantine Empire, there remain no known surviving examples.

Tonight the whole park had become a small forest of blossoming cherry trees. (a) Under the calm cloudy sky the blossoms formed a mass of solid whiteness. (b) The paper lanterns that hung from wires between the trees had been put out; in their place electric light bulbs, red, yellow, and green, shone dully beneath the blossoms. (c) It was well past ten o'clock with most of the flower viewers having gone home and all the lights had been turned off. (d) As passers-by strolled through the park, they would kick aside empty bottles or crush waste paper beneath their feet.

Truth as ultimate reality, if it is actually in existence, must be eternal, imperishable, unchanging. (a) But that infinite, eternal, and unchanging truth cannot be apprehended in the fullness of it by the finite mind of man. (b) It is natural that the mind of man can only grasp, at most, some small aspect of it, limited by time and space and by the state of development of that mind. (c) As the mind develops and enlarges the scope of it, new aspects of it come to light. (d) Not to mention, the fact that the core of truth may yet be the same doesn't need to be reconfirmed.

The quartet, consisting of the United States, the European Union, the United Nations, and Russia, has invented a plan for Israeli-Palestinian peace, a "Road Map." (a) However, this new peace plan contains more questions than answers. (b) It is so lacking in important details that even the most experienced navigators will have to find or create their own trail markers in order not to get lost on the way. (c) Therefore, the quartet doesn't welcome the peace plan. (d) But they agree that despite all its many flaws, it is the only game in town for the present.

Now is the time to subscribe to the *Dunhill Networker*. (a) To add your name to the *Dunhill Networker* mailing list, just detach, fill out, and mail the postpaid card below. (b) We will be sure each quarterly issue of the *Dunhill Networker* is addressed to you by name—no guesswork for your mailroom or administrative staff. (c) The *Dunhill Networker* is a quarterly publication prepared by Dunhill International particularly for managers dealing with the complexities of human resources. (d) If you would like to forward any comments, reactions, questions, or suggestions related to the Dunhill International, please write to the *Dunhill Networker*.

Today's top story is on an extreme daring that has baffled senior detectives nationwide. (a) In this morning's early hours it appears that several robbers managed to enter the palace grounds, bypassing guard dogs, a sensor-activated alarm system, and electric fencing before making their way inside the building. (b) Once inside, they stole four original paintings by Goya, a diamond necklace, three Persian rugs, and a bronze statue. (c) They are believed to have then made their getaway in a hijacked taxi cab that was recovered later, in a wood in Essex. (d) The royal family are currently staying at their Greek holiday home while the palace security system is being fixed.

Korean food begins to tickle the world's taste buds. (a) Many food manufacturers are continuously working on various kinds of Korean food to make them appeal to foreigners' tastes and their efforts bear fruit. (b) A bowl of rice topped with Kimchi has become very popular among many European gourmets or food-lovers. (c) In Russia, many people enjoy Korean soy sauce instead of salt, and they are also known to be big fans of Korean dumplings. (d) In addition, "Hot & Joy," a red pepper paste sauce, is also made from many different ingredients, including Korean pepper.

Dr. Carlo Bellieni, a pediatrician at the University of Siena in Italy, announced that TV can be helpful for numbing pain. (a) The study involved 50 children, ages 5 to 12, who were separated into three groups and told to rate their pain on a numerical scale when they were poked with a needle. (b) Those watching TV cartoons were soothed by a parent but reported the full pain. (c) However, when compared to children who just sat in a hospital with mothers who didn't try to soothe them, the TV watchers recorded one-third the pain. (d) Dr. Bellieni has found that TV can be a great aid for children going through painful medical procedures.

The funny word "couch-potato" was created because many people usually eat snacks like potato chips while watching TV on a couch. (a) And now a fresh new word, "mouse-potato," has been coined to refer to those who spend time surfing the Internet all day. (b) Researchers from the University of Glasgow in Scotland said that the number of these mouse-potatoes is increasing rapidly among teenagers. (c) For 6 to 16-year-olds in the U.K., the average time for exercising is only 25 minutes a day. (d) These habits cause severe child obesity, and 16% of them are now classed to be too fat.

ACTUAL TEST 1

READING COMPREHENSION

Part I   Questions 1—16

Read the passage. Then choose the option that best completes the passage.

1. Each year malaria kills about one million people, most of whom are African children under the age of 5. The Gates Foundation donates more than 30% of the world's malaria-research funds, and _____. Artemisinin, the most effective medicine for the disease, is in very short supply. But the scientists funded by the foundation made an announcement last month that they succeeded with development of the technology to create artemisinin in the laboratory. They expect the cost of artemisinin to drop from $2.40 to 25 cents within the next 5 years.

(a) the number of patients is decreasing
(b) it appears to be paying off
(c) improved treatments will be available
(d) the percentage is expected to increase

2. The first thing to remember about an angry customer is that, while his/ her behavior is directed at you, _____. The person is usually angry with you not as a person but as an employee of an organization that is perceived as cold, unfeeling, and unhelpful. Since it is difficult to yell at or abuse an entire organization, he/ she will direct the anger towards you. It is important to know that angry people want a chance to express their anger and want to have their voice heard. If you fail to acknowledge their anger and act too fast to try to work out the problem, you will probably make them angrier.

(a) you should first listen, not ask what the problem is
(b) he/ she is actually talking to a whole company
(c) the real source of his/ her anger is elsewhere
(d) your proper explanation should be made in no time

3. Of all the natural forces, gravity is the most implacable and controls our lives from birth to death. No wonder that, conscious of their earth-bound slavery, men have always _____. Mysterious as it may seem, most of the creatures on this planet are hardly aware that gravity exists. Dominant as it is over all the lives of large land animals to anything much smaller than a mouse, it is seldom more than a mild inconvenience. To the insects it is not even that; flies are so light and fragile that the air buoys them up, and gravity bothers them no more than it does a fish.

(a) pictured the sky as the abode of the gods

(b) looked for ways to free themselves from gravity

(c) went about looking for suitable places to settle

(d) wondered about invisible natural forces including gravity

4. Six senior citizens aged between 60 and 80 died in a car accident on the coast in Hawaii Saturday. At about 5 P.M., their vehicle _____ and crashed into a fish farm 1.5 meters below the main street, killing all passengers onboard, police said. According to the investigation authorities, they were on their way back home after having spent the afternoon at a nearby beach, which opened that day. Although the case is still under investigation, police authorities say the accident was most likely caused by the driver's inability to control the vehicle as the road forked to the right just prior to the scene of the accident.

(a) ran into a dead end sign

(b) skidded on the road

(c) broke the speed limit

(d) veered off the road

5. If not cared for by some other human being, a child _____. This kind of helplessness is in distinct contrast with the ability of many newly born animals to get to their feet within minutes of birth and to run with the herd within a few hours. This long period of vulnerability would seem to be the price that mankind has to pay for the long learning process which fits man for survival as a species. It is during this very long period in which the human infant is totally dependent on others that it reveals the feature which it shares with all other human infants: a capacity to learn a language.

(a) cannot stay healthy enough

(b) will be slow to learn to speak

(c) may have a hard time walking

(d) is not likely to survive

6. Acne has been plaguing mankind for thousands of years. Although acne is often called "teenage acne," this is wrong because it is not evidence of maturation. While more than 80 percent of teenagers develop some kind of acne, almost 95 percent of the population will suffer from acne at some time in their adulthood. As a matter of fact, acne is a disease that some people never outgrow. Besides, some people become adults before they suffer from acne. The _____ doesn't make any difference in treating acne.

(a) prominent symptom
(b) age of onset
(c) long history of the disease
(d) best-known treatment

7.

Dear Editor,

The author of the editorial piece "What about the Children?" that appeared in last Sunday's paper is uninformed and has his facts completely wrong. Additionally, he is not looking at the big picture of what is happening in the field of medicine. The Ministry of Health has enacted several new requirements for doctors who treat children. The Association of Health Care Professionals is currently involved in a legal battle with the Ministry on the grounds that, with the current workload, most doctors cannot meet the requirements. Infant vaccination and nutrition education are extremely important for the proper development of our youth, but the Ministry itself should be following through with its commitment _____. Your readers should understand the background of all the issues before blaming hard-working medical professionals.

(a) instead of putting the responsibility on overwhelmed physicians
(b) to develop new vaccines to help sick children in underdeveloped countries
(c) and realize once again what is going on in the field of medicine
(d) to publish journals that provide reliable medical information to readers

8.   William Jesperson, 47, bit his neighbor's dog in a dispute about her garden fence yesterday. Mrs. Carol Ramsey complained to the police and her dog had to be stitched four times. The argument between the two started when Mrs. Ramsey took down the fence between their two backyards. She told her neighbor she was going to replace it with a newer one, but she has not yet done so because, she claims, she cannot afford to. When the fence was removed, Mrs. Ramsey's dog used Mr. Jesperson's yard to play in, on one occasion frightening his two-year-old son. Despite repeated complaints, Mrs. Ramsey did nothing, and when the dog chased Mr. Jesperson's pet rabbit, _____.

(a) Mr. Jesperson was arguing with Mrs. Ramsey

(b) the man decided to complain about the dog

(c) the angry father and pet-lover took action

(d) Mrs. Ramsey ran after them to stop the chase

9.   Music has always influenced fashion, especially among teenagers and young adults. In the late 1980s and early 1990s, Seattle, Washington, was home to a new sound—grunge—that came out of garages and small clubs. Rock music by bands like Nirvana, Pearl Jam, and Soundgarden became the rage. The Seattle sound was loud, and the look was down-to-earth, affordable, and not at all flashy. As the music became more popular, so did copying the style of the musicians. This translated to fashion that mixes work clothes like flannel shirts and long johns with vintage clothes. Fashion designers are often influenced by pop culture, so _____.

(a) the designers at that time were very knowledgeable about rock music

(b) music, a form of pop culture, can be said to be influenced by fashion

(c) it didn't take long for the grunge look to make it to the runaway

(d) the fashion industry began to reflect various cultural factors

10. The Employment Opinion Survey is an excellent communication and feedback tool that can provide management with crucial organizational improvement information. It can be used to build trust, confidence, and mutual respect between the management and the workforce as it demonstrates management's interest in learning about employees' concerns, opinions, and suggestions. It is a great way to help establish the foundation and communication process necessary for _____. It is suitable for all organizational levels and requires only twenty-five to thirty minutes to administer. Easy scoring instructions show you how to calculate the percentage of employees positively responding to survey issues.

(a) total quality performance
(b) organization-wide management
(c) quick results to share and show
(d) better supervision of employees

11. Determinism, which means that every event has natural causes, has been hypothesized as a natural law _____. According to scientific laws, a certain set of conditions will undoubtedly bring about a predetermined outcome. However, studies in physics have shown that the speed and location of tiny particles such as electrons are the results of irregular behaviors rather than predictable results determined by previously existing conditions. These studies made Werner Heisenberg formulate the principle of indeterminacy in 1925. From a philosophical viewpoint, those who regard human beings as creature with free will show the greatest opposition toward the principle.

(a) but it needs to be studied further in physics and philosophy
(b) to help people accept what they go through in their lives
(c) and it still applies to every cause and effect in nature
(d) yet is under criticism in other fields of study

12. The decade of prosperity that the stock market crash of 1929 ended had been dazzling. In 1919, the First World War was over and the nation had turned its attention to making money. It succeeded beyond its wildest dreams. With a friendly Republican government in Washington fully committed to business growth, United States industry mushroomed. Mechanization, electrification, and the spread of assembly-line techniques led to a manufacturing output increase of 64 percent between 1919 and 1929. Wages and real earnings rose, but _____.

(a) they did not affect the number of job seekers

(b) profits rose far higher

(c) demand dwindled

(d) the stock market did not rebound

13. The signs of math anxiety vary: students sometimes get in a bad mood when it's time for math class, ignore low grades by saying they didn't try, or simply complain that they hate the subject. _____; scientific research has shown that these feelings can have negative effects on students' ability to do math. What happens is that anxious thoughts crowd the brain and occupy memory that would otherwise be dedicated to computation. Experts believe that teachers can help relieve the anxiety. The first step is to acknowledge that a student's anxiety is real but fixable. Then they go back over the curriculum to figure out where the student started getting lost.

(a) This kind of anxiety, in most cases, influences students for a long time

(b) The culprit of the trouble is not clearly understood by teachers

(c) These students are tired of working to reverse the situation

(d) The anxiousness at the root of such behavior isn't an emotional matter

14. You know that modern organizations must continuously improve to thrive. _____. There is no shortage of people offering to help deliver high performance. Yet recent research shows that there is room for improvement. 49% of business executives believe that consultants put forward solutions that cannot be sustained in the short to medium term, let alone the longer term. Ernst&Young's Performance Improvement services are different because we recognize that you are. So we focus on helping you achieve sustained improvement by developing an approach that draws on our considerable experience in performance improvement.

(a) Employees are also required to be more competitive than ever

(b) Success today should be matched tomorrow

(c) They, however, do not know how to make that possible

(d) Some of them have been more successful than others

15. Culture evolves naturally, but we need "education and training" to make it become part of our chemistry. And to do so, we need to develop various programs for people to participate in cultural club activities as families and develop a system of funding to reward exemplary cases. _____, we should establish a social environment in which a person's experience in cultural activities can be counted into his/ her resume. Let us now say goodbye to our old, wasteful, uniform culture of the adults and develop cultures for workplaces, families, and couples instead.

   (a) For example
   (b) As a result
   (c) Above all
   (d) Hence

16. Will widespread disapproval or resentment of the English language have any significant impact on its use? It seems that many non-native speakers around the world have a love-hate relation with English. Whether it is reflected in wearing baseball caps or eating fast food, the habit of imitating American culture seems inescapable, especially among the young and even among those who disapprove of American politics. _____, using English is a desirable habit to be acquired and imitated around the world, even among those who dislike English for the role it plays in spreading Western values and for its effect on other languages.

   (a) Similarly
   (b) In fact
   (c) Relatively
   (d) Hence

Read the passage and the question. Then choose the option that best answers the question.

17.   Because power over people is shown in forcing them do what they don't want to do, the person who acts upon the love of power is more likely to inflict pain than to allow pleasure. If you ask your boss for leave of absence from the workplace on some reasonable occasion, his/ her love of power will bring more satisfaction from a refusal than from approval. If you need a building permit, the narrow-minded official in charge will obviously feel more pleasure from saying "No" than from saying "Yes." It is this kind of thing which makes the love of power a very dangerous motive.

Q: What is the best title of the passage?
(a) Who Should Gain Power?
(b) Results Made by Power
(c) Ways Power Makes People Satisfied
(d) What Is a Power Lover Like?

18.   The rise of circulating libraries helped literature expand. At a time when the prices of books were very high in relation to the purchasing power of the great number of the population, the libraries were a meaningful social invention. They furnished those who had acquired a taste for reading with access to books otherwise out of their reach. They helped reduce the gap between interest in reading and purchasing power. The first circulating library was opened to the public in London in 1740. Rivals quickly sprang up in London and in the provinces as well. By the end of the century, about 1,000 libraries dotted the country. Their quick success attested to the growing interest in reading.

Q: What is the main topic of the passage?
(a) The different kinds of circulating libraries
(b) The influence of circulating libraries
(c) The reason for the success of circulating libraries
(d) The beginning of circulating libraries

19. You may think that some books will be too difficult for you to understand because you don't have any previous knowledge of the subjects. But knowledge is not as necessary for understanding as you suppose. You will not become a better reader if you read books always within your ability. You must read books that are beyond you, books that will make you work to understand them, and unless you work, you will not learn. Each time you read books beyond you, you will discover something new. You should keep in mind that the mind has no limit to growth and development, unlike the body.

Q: What is the passage mainly about?
(a) Books beyond one's understanding
(b) The doubt about the benefit of previous knowledge
(c) How to gain new knowledge through reading
(d) The necessity of reading difficult materials

20. For about 700 years, Japan was officially ruled by an emperor, while the real power was in the hands of the shogun. Under the shogun came the daimyo, provincial governors. Society was like a rigidly controlled pyramid, with the peasant at the bottom. The glue that held that structure together was the military caste that served the daimyo: the samurai. That system began to come apart in 1854, when the U.S. Navy forced Japan to join the modern world—at gunpoint. Japanese leaders decided that they needed a modern army equipped with the most up-to-date weapons and trained by the best officers of the day. Suddenly, 2 million samurai found themselves unqualified for careers that had once been theirs alone.

Q: Which of the following best summarizes the passage?
(a) The Japanese imperial army was aided in being reorganized.
(b) The samurai helped the shogun to rule Japan for 700 years.
(c) The U.S. intervened in Japan's internal affairs in 1854.
(d) The samurai suddenly became obsolete in the mid-nineteenth century.

21. Fifty years ago there was a general, though vague, belief that it was the duty of grammarians to lay down rules for the correct use of the language, and the duty of everybody else to obey them. This belief has not entirely disappeared, but it is no longer respectable. Today's linguists generally believe that grammar is dependent on usage and that a grammarian cannot say how people should talk just like a chemist defines how molecules should act upon each other. The laws of grammar are similar to those of any other science, merely general statements about what happens, not directions about what should happen—and they can change as soon as any new evidence is suggested.

Q: What is the main idea of the passage?

(a) Grammar changes through linguistic studies.

(b) Grammar is based on usage rather than rules.

(c) Grammar describes how a language is used.

(d) Grammar is less important than it used to be.

22. Even though you see beautiful people in ads drinking together, alcohol itself doesn't make you beautiful or guarantee you'll meet a great guy. Alcohol slows down your central nervous system by blocking messages to your brain. So, even when you drink small amounts, your responses to everything are slower. Also, because your head is not clear, you can make bad judgments like drunk driving. If you drink too much, you may vomit because alcohol is toxic and vomiting is the body's way of getting rid of an unwanted poison. If you consume large amounts of alcohol in a very short time, you can get alcohol poisoning.

Q: What is the best title of the passage?

(a) What Drinking Does to Our Brain

(b) Untold Truths about Drinking

(c) How Our Body Reacts to Alcohol

(d) Effects of Alcohol Poisoning

23. Based on a new survey on the cost of living in the world's major cities, Tokyo is the most expensive place for expatriate business people or diplomats to live. Prices in the Japanese capital are more than double those in New York. Western Europe is also relatively pricey—lunch in Zurich or Paris will cost over 20% more than in New York. Moscow is becoming an increasingly expensive place to live; last year the Russian capital was already 4% more expensive than New York; this year the difference is 10%. Moscow is now about as expensive as Hong Kong. The cost-conscious would do well to stay in Central Europe; life in Prague is half as expensive as in New York.

Q: Which of the following is correct according to the passage?

(a) Prices in Hong Kong stayed the same as last year.

(b) Prices in Prague are less than 25% of those in Tokyo.

(c) Prices in Paris are less than 20% of those in New York.

(d) Prices in Moscow have more than doubled since last year.

24. A truck carrying electronics valued at over $200,000 was hijacked yesterday morning. The truck belonged to the Ruby Star Company, and the driver, Nicolas Estrella, was making deliveries to the customers in the Bedford section. This is the eleventh truck hijacking in the first five months of this year. Over the last four years there have been 38 hijackings in the metropolitan area. The hijackers target trucks carrying cargoes that can be sold fast for cash. Drivers have been warned to lock their doors and not to pick up hitchhikers. But some insurance investigators believe that as many as one-third of these cases are not hijackings at all. They believe that some drivers steal their own cargoes.

Q: Which of the following is correct according to the passage?
(a) Nicolas Estrella is believed to have stolen his cargo.
(b) This year's 11th truck hijacking happened yesterday.
(c) The electronics stolen yesterday were sold for cash.
(d) Up to 30% of all the hijackings have been investigated.

25. Researchers at TechnoGear reported on Tuesday that they had succeeded in developing an affordable type of portable reading device that could revolutionize the way books are consumed. The team of researchers produced a bendable, portable, waterproof reading device that is 90 percent cheaper than similar devices produced using other technologies developed so far. The device is tentatively called E-BookPlus. The technology is also capable of displaying moving images and generating sounds. This raises the possibility that in the future this medium could be used for enjoying movies as well as music. Apart from this, TechnoGear officials said they are looking at other ways to differentiate their product in the marketplace.

Q: Which of the following is correct about E-BookPlus?
(a) It was developed using technology that already existed.
(b) It should be used in water.
(c) It might have its name changed.
(d) It is being purchased by cost-conscious buyers.

26. The paramecium is larger than the amoeba. Like an amoeba, it also is only one cell in size and can move. It can be found in ponds. It is rounded at one end and pointed at the other. It is covered with microscopic hairs that make it move. These hairs are referred to as cilia. The paramecium can move in every direction with its cilia. It eats minuscule algae, plants, and so on. The cilia thrusts the food into a small opening in the middle of the paramecium. Then, the food is pushed down a gullet which looks like a little tube. The food is held in the food vacuole. There is an opening called an anal pore near the pointed end of the paramecium.

Q: Which of the following is correct about the paramecium?
(a) It does not have a symmetrical figure in any way.
(b) It uses its cilia to eat tiny algae or plants.
(c) It is one of the smallest creatures living in ponds.
(d) It has its mouth in the middle of its back.

27.

Dear Mr. Johnson,

I am writing to inquire about the possibility of procuring parts for a 1995 Magenta 323 RX coupe. I was referred to your company by Mike Ward of Performance Auto here in Madison. He thought you might be able to help me locate the parts I need to rebuild the turbocharger. I acquired the car recently and the turbo gave out almost immediately. If you have any of the necessary parts, please contact me at (608) 661-3457. I am willing to pay shipping and handling on all parts if you can find them within the next two weeks. I have an interested buyer and must get the car in working order by the 29th of this month. If you can help me out in this regard, please let me know.

Sincerely,
Micky Smith

Q: Which of the following is NOT correct?
(a) Mr. Johnson has parts for a 1995 Magenta 323 RX coupe.
(b) Micky Smith wants to sell his car.
(c) Micky Smith is not worried about the shipping and handling costs.
(d) Mike Ward knows Micky Smith.

28. For all Bert Snelling fans, you're in for a real treat with his latest book, *Through the Sands of Time*, a historical novel set in ancient Egypt. As with his previous publications, this one will please history buffs as it is well-researched and true to the time period in every detail. Readers who like less history and more intrigue will also be satisfied with Snelling's fast-paced plot and fascinating characters. The story opens with the beautiful but headstrong heroine, Serafina, daughter of the ruling Pharaoh. She uncovers a secret plot to dethrone her father, devised by his most trusted advisor, Artemis. Her courageous and inventive plan to reveal the king's enemies is successful, but comes at a high price for her.

Q: Which of the following is correct about *Through the Sands of Time*?
(a) It is about the rise and fall of an Egyptian king.
(b) One of its characters, Serafina, gets killed eventually.
(c) It was written by a historian as an addition to a series.
(d) Its audience will be wider than that of the other books of its kind.

29. The National Bird Watchers' Association is now accepting nominations for the Person of the Year, or POY Award. This prize was founded in 2002 with the intention of raising interest, appreciation, and concern for the birds on our planet. The nomination form is two pages long and has to be sent with at least one letter specifying why the nominee deserves consideration for the award. The names of the five finalists will be released by October 31 with their nominations and summaries of their activities posted on our website. The winner will be announced at the NBWA's annual convention and receive 10,000 dollars with 5,000 dollars to be donated to his or her favorite charity.

Q: Which of the following is correct according to the passage?
(a) The POY Award has been given in October since 2002.
(b) The winner will take only part of the prize money.
(c) The NBWA was established by bird watchers from all over the world.
(d) The winner will be announced on the NBWA's website as well.

30.   Americans used to eating hamburgers will soon be trying Asian fast food. Thailand's government is planning to open about 1,000 new Thai restaurants in the U.S. Many of them will be fast-food places called Elephant Jump. These restaurants, which probably would be jointly funded by private investors and the Thai government, would compete with other leading fast-food chains. In addition, Jollibee, a Filipino fast-food chain with restaurants across Asia, recently opened its first U.S. store. Japanese food is hitting the American fast-food market, too. Yoshinoya, a Japanese chain specializing in beef and rice dishes, already has over 75 restaurants in North America, and is planning an expansion. Yoshinoya reports that by 2014 it hopes to have over 2,000 restaurants outside Japan.

Q: Which of the following is correct according to the passage?
(a) Thailand has the greatest fast-food market share in North America.
(b) Yoshinoya will add more than 2,000 restaurants in the U.S.
(c) Competition in the fast-food market in America is getting stiffer.
(d) Americans used to have more hamburgers than Asian fast food.

31.   The sounding line, the navigator's first instrument, was created because of dangerous hidden rocks and sandbanks. It had a lead weight at its end and had knots that marked distance along its length. People considered the sounding line such an important tool in early navigation that ships kept back in port for not paying taxes, or for other reasons, had their sounding lines taken away by the police. This practice continued even when ships carried more modern tools like compasses. Samuel Clemens chose Mark Twain as his pen name on the basis of the sailors' custom of employing the sounding line on board going down the Mississippi River in the 19th century.

Q: Which of the following is correct according to the passage?
(a) Samuel Clemens changed his name.
(b) Compasses were not used when they were first introduced.
(c) Sounding lines were made for safety and tax collection.
(d) Some sounding lines were taken away for an official reason.

32. Today, chamber music has evolved into small ensemble music in which each performer in the ensemble plays an individual part. The compositions written for this type of performance can easily be classified into three distinct periods. In the earliest period (1450-1650), the violin and other instrumental families developed considerably, and instrumental music took its first steps toward equal footing with vocal music. In the second period (1650-1750), trio sonatas dominated. These ensemble compositions were often written for two violins and a cello; the harpsichord was also featured in various compositions of this period. In the modern period (after 1750), the preponderance of chamber music was written for the string quartet, an ensemble composed of two violins, a viola, and a cello.

Q: Which of the following is supported by the passage?
(a) The harpsichord began to disappear in the middle of the 1700s.
(b) Chamber music is characterized by the periods of its development.
(c) Chamber music got its name because only a few people enjoyed it.
(d) The earliest period of chamber music is the longest.

33. Thomas Osborne was a millionaire who hailed from Auburn, New York. Twice he held the post of town mayor. Later he became a banker and newspaper owner. Then, in 1913, Thomas Osborne became Convict 3333X. Osborne went to prison even though he had not committed a crime. Why did a leading citizen like Osborne go to jail? He wanted to help the governor of New York. The governor had asked Osborne to suggest the best way to improve life in the state's prisons. Osborne decided that the best way to learn about prisons was to become a prisoner himself. He spent one week in Auburn Prison. He found many things that shocked and angered him. Prisoners and guards were afraid of each other.

Q: What can be inferred from the passage?
(a) The governor was asked to improve conditions in prisons.
(b) Thomas Osborne wanted to stay in Auburn Prison a week ago.
(c) Thomas Osborne's idea about what it is like in prisons changed.
(d) Thomas Osborne was not afraid of prisoners and guards.

34. When unidentified thieves took $4,000 worth of musical equipment from the Two Tones musical duo on Wednesday, the two performers were forced to cancel all their fall bookings—and plans for a December wedding. Joyce Benedict, 25, and Donald Jarvis, 27, both of Albany, were planning to help pay for their December 20 wedding with money earned from performances here over the next four days. The couple arrived at the Stagecoach Hotel in South Merrick about 3:00 P.M. Wednesday for their first appearance. When Jarvis went to their car at about 4:30 P.M., he found a broken window and their speakers, microphones, and other sound equipment missing. The equipment was not insured and there is little hope of recovering it.

Q: What can be inferred from the passage?
(a) The couple did not take their musical equipment into the hotel.
(b) The couple was supposed to get married at the end of December.
(c) The couple had their musical instruments stolen in the morning.
(d) The couple had to have part of the performances canceled.

35.

Dear Mr. Gupta,

It has come to our attention here at Oleander Ltd. that your magazine has been publishing unfavorable reviews of our products. We take pride in producing the best cosmetics and creams from all-natural products. Your assertion that we use "questionable production practices" to make our New You line of facial creams is unfounded. I assure you that we do not, as you reported, pay our workers in Southeast Asia "slave wages" but rather have them all on a rate that is higher than the local average. I invite you to investigate our company further and more thoroughly. You will find that we produce high-quality products with a heart.

Q: What can be inferred from the letter?
(a) Mr. Gupta will respond to the letter before he visits Oleander Ltd.
(b) Oleander Ltd. is doing business in Southeast Asia.
(c) Oleander Ltd. just began to produce a new line of facial creams.
(d) The employees of Oleander Ltd. can speak more than one language.

36. Play is an almost universal activity of higher animals but one that is hard to define. In essence, it consists of two main ingredients: activity for its own sake and experimentation with types of behavior that will subsequently be carried out in earnest. In animals, both of these kinds of play are carried out by the young and are clearly a part of the learning process. The former aids in familiarizing the young animal with its capabilities. The latter provides practical training in skills which may be utilized later in life. In humans, play is important for what it can reveal about society. Forms of sport reflect the nature of society, as do forms of art, theater, and literature.

Q: What can be inferred from the passage?
(a) Play can be a subject of study in sociology.
(b) Some forms of art are based on play.
(c) People use play differently.
(d) Animals can be taught to play.

37. When we talk about development, we talk about human progress with its positive and negative consequences. On this occasion, we should not forget that development does not start with goods. Rather, as a scientist points out, it starts with people and their education, with organization, and with discipline. All these three require time and effort to succeed. However, even more important than development are the quality of life of the people and the strong social structure it provides. A good quality of life and a strong social structure, which depend as much on the spiritual as on the material, provide social welfare, the goal of every society. At the same time they provide the foundation on which to build as the society develops and prospers.

Q: What can be inferred from the passage?
(a) Quality of life is as important as a strong social structure.
(b) The goal of human progress is social welfare.
(c) The foundation of society is based on the quality of life.
(d) Human progress does not involve material development.

Part III   Questions 38 — 40

Read the passage. Then identify the option that does NOT belong.

38.   Gelufire announced Wednesday that their financial problems have gotten the best of them. (a) The hair and body care product manufacturer has seen profits fall into the red for the sixth month in a row and has declared bankruptcy. (b) There have been reports that Realmake has expressed interest in acquiring some parts of the company, but analysts expect that offer might only be extended to the profitable HairGlare line. (c) Realmake has indicated a desire to expand into hair care and this might be a good opportunity for them. (d) As yet, it is still unclear what will become of the company's facilities and employees.

39.   An accident at an air show in Colorado yesterday claimed the life of a pilot. (a) Captain Paul Morris was flying a Korean War era F-86 Saber Jet when he failed to pull out of a steep climb. (b) No one on the ground was hurt and investigators are blaming the crash on pilot error. (c) "The plane went straight up, did a loop, and then came straight down," said Jack Harvey, a spectator at the air show. (d) The crash was the first in the fifteen-year history of the Colorado Air Show.

40.   The basic things in life are the same no matter where you live. (a) A toothache feels just as miserable to an American in the United States as it does to a Korean in Korea. (b) Joy and pleasure are the same sensations whether their origin is in the Orient or on the other side of the world. (c) Then what is it that makes people who live in one part of the world so similar to people living in another part of the world? (d) They aren't really different at all, but the ways in which they express their sensations and sometimes the things from which they derive pleasure are different.

ACTUAL TEST 2

READING COMPREHENSION

Part I **Questions 1—16**

Read the passage. Then choose the option that best completes the passage.

1. The book, *Your Husband: Napoleon or Tsar Nicholas?* humorously compares spouses of various historical figures, emphasizing their negative and positive qualities. The author shows a good knowledge of history and provides interesting details of how each famous man got along with his wife. Unfortunately, the book offers the reader only vague sketches of each figure, and it becomes less and less funny as it gets longer. Ms. Francini seems to have either lost her focus or _____. I'm afraid I cannot recommend this book to buyers. My advice is that if you're really interested, wait for the paperback edition to come out in June.

    (a) been the victim of poor editing
    (b) seen her good days
    (c) failed to apply her new writing style
    (d) did not make more efforts than she had done before

2. Being a female concierge at a hotel, I've become adept at politely rebuking approaches from male guests. One evening there was a heavy rainstorm, which resulted in a long line at the hotel taxi stand. A customer asked me how much a limo would cost. I told him that _____. He decided to check the taxi queue. Moments later he was back. "I don't need the car now. I've got a taxi." Then he smiled, and asked, "Could I have your phone number?" Rather embarrassed, I explained it was against hotel policy to be friendly with the guests. "Young lady," he said, "I want the number of this place in case I need to call for a limo to get back."

    (a) I was afraid to tell him that the service was not available
    (b) it would be decided by how far his final destination was
    (c) it depended on whether it was a one-way or round-trip transfer
    (d) I would ask the hotel manager about that and let him know

3. Cystic fibrosis is a dangerous disease in which abnormally thick mucus builds up in many organs, including the lungs. The accumulation of mucus causes difficulty in breathing. Cystic fibrosis is caused by a wrong gene. In cystic fibrosis patients, the gene for making a protein that helps pump ions into and out of cells has the wrong instructions. Because the protein is not made correctly, the cells cannot pump ions into and out of cells. This eventually results in ions building up within cells. Like sponges, these cells soak up the surrounding water, _____.

(a) causing a diuretic effect on patients to make them dehydrate to death

(b) turning the fluid around the outside of the cells into thick mucus

(c) resulting in patients having difficulty in breathing

(d) mutating the gene responsible for producing a certain protein

4. You can hardly believe it, but within a few years, treating eye disease may be as simple as popping in a contact lens. Special contact lenses are being developed which _____. Today most eye medications are in the form of drops, but often they drain into the nose and enter the bloodstream and travel throughout the body. Only about five percent of the medication stays in the eye. But these amazing lenses will deliver the drug to where it's needed in a steady dose, and could potentially treat most eye disease, including glaucoma and many other eye infections.

(a) will be sold both online and offline to reach more buyers

(b) contain tiny particles of drugs that are slowly released into the eye

(c) eye doctors and patients have waited for to be available

(d) are different from other ophthalmics in many ways

5. According to museum officials, as many as 170,000 artifacts have been stolen. The cuneiform tablets of the Code of Hammurabi, one of the museum's most famous collections, are also missing. What were the U.S. troops doing? Instead of stopping the robbery, they seem to have sat back and watched it. Some people suspect that the United States may have had some bad political intention. The antiquities in the museum, which belong to one of the four major civilizations of mankind, are the property not only of the Iraqis but also of all people around the world. Therefore, _____.

(a) it is wrong to hold only the U.S. troops responsible for the robbery

(b) the Iraqi government should seek as much international help as possible

(c) we should let the Iraqi government know the whereabouts of the missing items

(d) the international community should focus their attention on restoring human civilization

6. The young minister was on the pulpit for the first time and he was a little nervous. He read the text; "Behold I come." The sermon was to follow immediately, but his mind went blank and he repeated the text; "Behold I come." hoping to remember the opening words of the sermon—but with no success. Trying to calm himself, he leaned forward _____. Under his weight the pulpit gave way and he landed in the lap of one of the elders. "I'm awfully sorry," he said, much embarrassed. "I really didn't expect this to happen." The man gave a kind smile and replied, "Oh, that's OK. I should have been prepared after your third warning."

(a) and lost his footing
(b) to reach for the glass of water on the pulpit
(c) to gain attention from the audience
(d) as he repeated the text for the third time

7.

Dear Mr. Cooper,

Thank you for your recent photographic submissions to our publication. Your experiences in Colorado and Wyoming were obviously quite interesting, and your photographs are vast and impressive. Unfortunately, the material for our magazine is supplied solely by our staff photographers and writers, and we are presently unable to accept contributions from outside sources. Please _____. If you would like to apply for a staff position, please send a cover letter and résumé to our Human Resources Director, Mr. Mark Hanlan. He would be happy to review your work and application. Good luck in your future endeavors.

Sincerely,

T. Simon Sinclair

Editor-in-Chief

(a) learn about our contribution policy
(b) try again with better photographs and text
(c) find enclosed your submissions
(d) understand the difficulty we are going through

8. People who want to work, to do something in the world, find an unfailing inspiration in Schubert. He is a continual example to get up and go on again. His little room was always littered with music manuscripts, much as a dressmaker's is with scraps after a busy project. He knew no rest; as soon as one thing was finished, he put it aside and began to work on another, as if this new work, be it song, or mass, or sonata, or opera, _____. It is idle to imagine what Schubert would have finally most excelled in had he lived to a good old age. He died when he was only thirty-one.

(a) were the only thing he had been born to do
(b) should be done as fast as possible
(c) couldn't be done anywhere but in his little room
(d) were something that he could do by himself

9. _____ over the past decades. This has, for many, been a sad occurrence in a land where the railroad was widely heralded as the key to expansion into the West, and where many cities achieved greatness as railroad hubs. Sadly gone are the days when the most famous neighborhood in Chicago was the Stockyards, made famous by the thousands of heads of cattle sent there daily for slaughter. Gone, too, are the days when a trip to California was a scenic ride on the rails. President Eisenhower's push to build the interstate highways system for national defense and the development of modern airliners rang the death bell for railroads.

(a) The operation of the railroad in the U.S. has become more expensive
(b) The decline of the railroad in the U.S. has been continual
(c) The development of the railroad in the U.S. has been slow
(d) The railroad in the U.S. has been replaced by other means of transportation

10. Outside of the Unites States, _____. For instance, in certain countries, African Americans are shown only as athletes, or criminals. The citizens of these countries receive very little or no exposure to the majority of African Americans, who are neither athletes, nor criminals. The Arab has also often been portrayed as either a wealthy merchant or a terrorist. However, in the United States, there are now citizen organizations that condemn and, therefore, influence the media when a group has been wrongly represented. This reaction to ethnic and cultural stereotypes is positive and healthy.

(a) it is difficult to learn about the status of foreigners living in the U.S.

(b) African Americans are treated only as a minority group

(c) there are not enough support groups for the rights of minorities

(d) the mass media does not always fairly portray American minority groups

11. During the summer of 1829, Mendelssohn took a vacation in Scotland. The excursion, including a visit to Edinburg and a trip through the Highlands, lasted less than three weeks. It no doubt produced pleasant memories, as witnessed in his letters and a few drawings he made of the scenery, but otherwise the trip was relatively insignificant. The present book gathers together Mendelssohn's drawings, reprints the letters, and provides a kind of commentary to the trip along with additional drawings, maps, and photographs. Except for a brief biographical sketch of Mendelssohn and a totally superficial discussion of his Scottish Symphony, this _____.

(a) is a recommendation for those interested in Mendelssohn's taste in travel

(b) provides very little information about how Mendelssohn lived in Scotland

(c) is easy to read and can be purchased at all the bookstores in town

(d) is essentially a travel book of exceptionally limited value

12. We are entitled to reconsider Aristotle's notion of the tragic flaw, if we find it incompatible with his central idea of the nature of tragedy, the indispensable feature of the literary form we have been able to study for ourselves. What Aristotle called catharsis is still as available for examination as in the fourth century before Christ. The examination we have so far been able to make does not suggest that a tragic flaw is a precondition of the phenomenon. It is true, _____, that this phenomenon is more difficult to examine than an egg, and that we are bound to look for validation or objection of our findings with some care.

(a) as admitted earlier

(b) like established literary theories

(c) whereas looked at metaphysically

(d) although discounted by some scholars

13. Bonfires haven't always been innocent fun. In the Middle Ages, many criminals were burned at the stake. Because their bones were the last body parts to burn, this form of execution became known as a "bone fire." When Henry VIII of England separated from the Roman Catholic Church in the 1530s, he ordered all materials connected with the church to be burned. The resultant blazes recalled the bone fires, and like them, they _____. Gradually, the name was shortened to bonfire, and large fires grew to be a festive part of some celebrations. Indeed, the only similarity between today's bonfires and the bone fires of old is that they are often at the center of onlookers.

(a) were not simply used to warm people

(b) burned things to be burned completely

(c) usually attracted a crowd of bystanders

(d) had much for historians to study

14. After the French Revolution, French people didn't want any remains of the tyranny. As a result, French playing cards underwent an interesting transformation. Before the Revolution, the French used cards that were the same as those used today. Each deck was divided into four suits, and each suit had three face cards representing the King, Queen, and Jack. After the Revolution, the royal figures disappeared from the cards. The Queen was replaced by symbols of liberty, the King became nature, and the Jack became virtue. However, the unusual French cards _____, although they were revolutionary.

(a) failed to spread gambling among the public

(b) were not as popular as expected

(c) only lasted for a short period

(d) did not help people forget the tyranny

15. "Surfacing Sadness," a collection of poems, essays, and short stories written by 37 Korean-American writers, is the first serious attempt to bring together the Korean-American literary experience. Most of the works in this volume are translations from the Korean language and there is no doubt that some of the original meaning and cadences have been lost in the process. _____, some of the translations are awkward enough to render the final product a piece to be endured rather than enjoyed. The editors acknowledge this shortcoming, but point out that despite the problems presented by translation, there must be jewels in the mud.

(a) Likewise
(b) In addition
(c) In fact
(d) Consequently

16. Scientists agree that we are at present treating the effects of drug abuse rather than the underlying psychological and social causes. Addicts often "come off" one type of drug, only to take up another type, and a recent study revealed that almost half the patients at various drug clinics continued in their use of "hard" drugs, even after treatment. _____, the situation is continually being made more complicated by the use of newer and newer drugs by the addicts, so that as methods are found to deal with one particular type, another one replaces it, and doctors must look forward to future problems with as yet undiscovered drugs.

(a) Thus
(b) For all that
(c) Particularly
(d) In the meantime

Part II Questions 17—37

Read the passage and the question. Then choose the option that best answers the question.

17. A Danish biotech company will use a genetically modified flower they have developed to find land mines. Currently, experts remove them by putting a stick into the ground to locate them, but it is very dangerous because they are still able to take away the life of the person who activates them. Despite their war purposes, many of the old mines are still influencing the lives of humans in negative ways. Thale Cress, a kind of flower, will be a less dangerous way to find explosives because it changes color when its roots are exposed to nitrogen-dioxide coming from explosives buried in the ground.

Q: What is the passage mainly about?
(a) The development of Danish biotechnology
(b) The purposes of land mines in the past and now
(c) Flowers that change color when in contact with nitrogen-dioxide
(d) A form of biotechnology application to detect underground explosives

18. Long before the white men set foot on the American Continent, the Native Americans were living there. When the Europeans started to arrive in the 16th and 17th century, they were welcomed by the Native Americans. They introduced many of the foods that are common today: corn, pumpkins, beans, chili peppers, pecans, cranberries, maple syrup, etc. It was the Native Americans who taught the colonists how to gather and use them. By the end of the 20th century, more than one third of all food produced in the U.S. originated from Native American crops. Much of what we take for granted comes directly from Native Americans. Perhaps we should learn how to say the Apache word for "thank you."

Q: What is the main idea of the passage?
(a) The Native Americans lived peacefully and helped the Europeans with farming.
(b) The traditional Apache Indian language is gaining popularity in the U.S.
(c) The American Indians helped the settlers live on a variety of foods.
(d) The contributions that the Native Americans made are not appreciated enough.

19. "No female can swim the English Channel," scoffed newspapers around the world. But Gertrude Ederle didn't pay any attention. On August 6, 1926, just over 14 hours after entering the waves off the coast of France, Ederle stepped onto the pages of sports history. The English Channel was to swimmers what Mount Everest was to climbers. Before Ederle's attempt, only five people had successfully crossed the Channel—all of them men. During her crossing, the waves were so violent that people on her guide boat were seasick. Fighting 20-foot waves, she sliced through the water with her brand new stroke, the crawl. Ederle not only became the first woman to swim the English Channel, but she also beat the men's record by almost two hours.

Q: What is the best title of the passage?
(a) World's Fastest Female Swimmer
(b) The Crawl, Ederle's New Stroke
(c) Ederle's Success Against the Waves
(d) How Female Swimmers Have Changed

20. In 1947, the AK-47, the automatic machine gun, won a Soviet competition for a submachine gun for the Red Army. It has been the primary weapon in most wars, causing 300,000 annual combat deaths in the wars of the last decade. As it were, it is the most successful killing machine. Even so, the inventor Mikhail Kalashnikov is proud of his creation. He takes no responsibility for the deaths it has caused. "I made it a mission of my life to protect the motherland. The weapon has been used successfully to complete that mission. I am not to blame for the fact that people die because of it. It is not because of the designer, but because of politics."

Q: What is the main topic of the passage?
(a) Why Mikhail Kalashnikov created the AK-47
(b) Mikhail Kalashnikov's success in protecting his nation
(c) Who should take responsibility for the deaths in wars
(d) Different views on how the AK-47 is used

21. The protein, calcium, and other vital minerals of milk are of great biological value for growing children, but they don't drink enough milk. How can parents persuade their children to drink such nutritious milk? Some scientists argue that making milk more like soda is the best way to get them to drink milk instead of soda. Soda is popular with so many of today's young people. Scientists in Illinois are mixing milk with carbon dioxide gas to make milk like soda. These scientists are even trying to add more flavors to milk. Perhaps within a few years, people will enjoy a bubbly glass of lemon- or orange-flavored milk on a hot summer day.

Q: What is the best title for the passage?

(a) Getting Children to Drink More Milk

(b) How to Make Milk More Popular

(c) Benefits of Soda Drinks

(d) Making Better Milk

22. Some medical researchers in the U.S. are developing a clear gel that can immediately stop a cut or wound from bleeding. The gel creates a barrier of peptides when it is placed on a wound. And this has proved to be helpful in facilitating faster blood clotting in tests in monkeys. The medical industry is saying that if it works on humans, it could prove to be a significant advance for ordinary people as well as surgeons. Although surgeons have devised ways to stop it, excessive bleeding remains a serious challenge during surgery. The researchers have announced that the miraculous gel will be released to the market in about three years.

Q: Which of the following best summarizes the passage?

(a) Monkeys are used to test the most advanced medical products.

(b) The gel has yet to prove to be a breakthrough for its purpose.

(c) The product will facilitate the secretion of peptides in the human body.

(d) The gel will not be used for medical operations in the near future.

23. John Barnes, manufacturer of ball bearings, agrees to supply Vitesse Automobile Company with 100 boxes of custom-designed ball bearings (Model CX-123) by March 31, 2012. If the ball bearings are delivered on or before 3/31/2012, Vitesse will pay Mr. Barnes $1,000 per box, or $100,000 for the order requested, plus a bonus of $5,000 for prompt delivery. However, for every day the order is past 3/31/2012, Mr. Barnes will pay Vitesse $2,000 per day as penalty. Also, because Vitesse designed and tested Model CX-123, Mr. Barnes must let Vitesse know that appropriate security measures will be offered to protect the design from being stolen. If both parties agree to the points, the contract will go into effect on January 1, 2012.

Q: Which of the following is correct according to the passage?

(a) Vitesse will pay $98,000 to John Barnes if the delivery is made before April 1, 2012.

(b) It will take about 3 months for John Barnes to make the ball bearings.

(c) John Barnes and Vitesse have to conclude the contract before January 1, 2012.

(d) Vitesse specified the type of ball bearings that they wanted for their products.

24. Each December, the World Elephant Polo Association tournament is held in Nepal. Elephant polo is quite similar to horse polo. Players wear traditional polo hats and use a polo ball. There are four players on each side. The largest elephant is always given to the referee because it gives him an excellent vantage point from which to watch the game. There are some special rules for this sport. Because one team trained a baby elephant to dribble the ball with its front foot, elephants are no longer allowed to touch the ball with their trunk or hind feet. Another team trained an elephant to lie down in front of the goal, which now draws a penalty.

Q: Which of the following is correct about Elephant polo?
(a) Its rules have changed recently.
(b) It is held every year with horse polo.
(c) Every match starts with nine elephants.
(d) Elephants will not be trained in front of the goal.

25. A blind boy is the subject of an unusual psychological experiment designed to speed up the learning process in blind children. Through the use of a sonar-type electronic device on his head, Dennis Daughters is learning to identify objects in the world around him by means of echoes. A transmitter emits an ultrasonic pulse that creates an 80-degree cone of sound at six feet. Echoes from objects within the cone are changed into audible signals fed into each ear. The signals vary in sound and pitch with the size and distance of the object. What remains to be determined is how well the device will help children as they venture further into their environment and must cope with more complicated surroundings.

Q: Which of the following is correct according to the passage?
(a) The echoes are changed into sound electronically.
(b) The device is not fully functional at the moment.
(c) The transmitter of the device imitates a cone of sound.
(d) The closer an object is, the louder the sound becomes.

26.

Dear Tucker,

Enclosed are some cases involving sewer rate increases. They are relevant to our case and for your reading interest. The scheduling hearing on August 9 affirmed the final hearing date for October 4 in the De Kalb County Magistrate Court and confirmed the need for a pre-trial order. Further, I need to provide opposing counsel and the court with a list of witnesses within the week. Since the hearing will only last a couple of hours, our witnesses should be limited to three to four, one being Mr. Greenwood. Do you also wish to spend money on finding an accountant who specializes in utility rates? If so, we must contact that person immediately.

Sincerely yours,
Ronald Glen Thomas
Enclosures

Q: Which of the following is correct according to the letter?
(a) The date for the final hearing was set in the magistrate court.
(b) Tucker and Ronald will contact an accountant before October 4.
(c) Tucker asked for cases regarding sewer rate increases.
(d) Mr. Greenwood will defend for Tucker.

27.   Without fruit bats, baobabs would be unable to get fruit and would die out as a species. Yet, fruit bats are detested by mango growers in East Africa who consider them to be crop pests. Mango growers set fire to the concentrated fruit bat colonies found in the few caves in the area, and threaten the species with extinction. Yet, fruit bats only eat ripe fruit, which is never picked by mango growers, who ship green fruit to market to prevent spoilage. Ripe mangos, when uneaten by fruit bats, usually fall to the ground and host fruit fly larvae. East African mango growers are risking not only their mango crops but the delicate balance of East African ecology.

Q: Which of the following is correct according to the passage?
(a) Baobabs are in danger of extinction because of fruit flies.
(b) Baobabs are dependent on fruit bats for pollination.
(c) Fruit bats do not eat ripe mangos fallen to the ground.
(d) Fruit bats in East Africa are almost extinct.

28. The seyah ythak is a beautiful ostrich-like creature which lives in the Sinai Peninsula, Israel, and on across into central India. They prefer semi-desert and desert regions and can withstand the high temperatures and low water availability which characterize these areas. As an adult, it stands approximately 75-80cm and weighs about 15-23kg. It has light, sandy colored feathers on its back and creamy white belly plumage. Its face is handsome, with the brown color running along its nose and the creamy white coloration along its cheeks. Peculiar among birds, it has horns which are about 10cm in length and protrude upward in a somewhat V-like shape, curving to the center as they terminate.

Q: Which of the following is correct about the seyah ythak?
(a) The length of its horns is equal to its height.
(b) It appears colorful.
(c) It can live without water.
(d) An adult standing about 80cm weighs about 23kg.

29.

Dear Kim,

Thank you for your participation in HUG's REFLECTIONS. The unique mirror that you are designing will be displayed for auction at the HUGS benefit, which will be held on Friday, June 2, from 7:00-10:00 P.M. at the home of Bob and Lori Bergman, 1620 Forest Park Boulevard. In appreciation of the generous donation of your time and talents to this project, HUGS would like to invite you to be our guest at the gala. You may order additional reservations by sending $75.00 per guest, with a check made out to Friends of HUGS. You may claim $30.00 as a tax deduction for each person.

We hope to see you at our fantastic REFLECTIONS.

Sincerely,
Camilla

Q: Which of the following is correct according to the letter?
(a) Camilla will be at a private residence this Friday.
(b) Kim showed his interest in HUG's REFLECTIONS.
(c) Bob and Lori Bergman want to invite Kim as a guest.
(d) Kim will get a $30.00 tax reduction.

30. Go did not become a genuinely popular game with everyone until the twentieth century. At first it was played only by the aristocracy and then gradually spread to the warrior class and the Buddhist clergy, these being the educated classes. There was some improvement in the game at this time, but perhaps the most significant development occurred in the 14th or 15th century, when the traditional practice of placing two white stones and two black stones on the corner star points prior to the game was abandoned. Up to that time fighting ability was most important, but without corner stones players began to develop opening strategies as well.

Q: Which of the following claims is made about the passage?
(a) Most of the changes to go were made in the 14th or 15th century.
(b) Go was not popular among the learned people for about 550 years.
(c) There were four corner star points on the original go board.
(d) A major go improvement involved the omission of pairs of stones.

31. The world's first subway system was put forward for London in 1843. After years of discussion, Parliament gave approval and work began in 1860. The line was open in 1863, using coal-burning steam locomotives and, in spite of the sulfurous fumes, it was a success from its inception. In 1886 the city started excavations for a tube railway. Two twin tunnels were driven deep in the London clay and consequently neither support of buildings nor disruption of traffic was required. The original plan called for the use of steel cables to haul the trains, but before the tunnels were completed electricity was substituted. In 1890, the London underground was opened, becoming the first underground electric railway.

Q: Which of the following claims is made about the passage?
(a) It took more than half a century to complete the London underground.
(b) The plan to build the world's first subway system went through a change.
(c) British people first became interested in a subway system in 1843.
(d) Coal-burning steam locomotives were replaced by underground trains in 1890.

32. After the birth of the baby rhino Athena last fall, the zoo's attendance soared to more than a million visitors for the seventh time in history. The number of zoo visitors jumped to 1,013,990—up 35,943 from the previous year. The all time attendance record of 1,211,100 was set in 1963, the year Trumpet the elephant was born. The zoo keeps having the highest attendance of all paid tourist attractions in Kansas. Only Pioneer Lodge and Muddy Falls, which are free tourist attractions, attract more yearly visitors. Attendance could jump to the record high once again this year thanks to the koala exhibit running through October, and the new Metropolitan rail station.

Q: Which of the following is supported by the passage?
(a) The zoo's attendance has reached one million seven times since 1963.
(b) Less than one million people visited the zoo two years ago.
(c) It is expected that 1963's attendance record will be broken this year.
(d) The zoo has the largest number of newborn animals of any in Kansas.

33. A glacier, simply put, is a slow-motion river of ice. It runs from high mountaintops through rough valleys, carrying off frozen snow that compacted over many years into a hard, slowly flowing ice stream. This ice is driven by gravity and the constantly mounting snows behind it and into an area called the accumulation zone. In Alaska only a few glaciers reach the sea, pushing out across the floor of a bay or seacoast. Several factors affect the actions of these great cascades of mountain-born ice, among them long-term atmospheric warming or sustained changes in precipitation patterns.

Q: What can be inferred from the passage?
(a) Only a few glaciers in Alaska melt away.
(b) There are many accumulation zones in Alaska.
(c) Four factors are involved in moving glaciers.
(d) Glaciers react slowly to environmental changes.

34. NFL officials announced today that they would begin random drug testing in all league training camps beginning this summer. This is in response to the recent wave of incidents involving some of the league's most well-known players. Owners were not available for comment on the league's action, but many players have expressed their displeasure with the announcement. In the past the player's union has opposed such tests on the grounds that they were often unreliable and that even players taking prescription medicines could test positive initially. Union officials have stated they might seek a court order that would delay putting this into effect until further studies could be done.

Q: What can be inferred from the passage?
(a) The NFL feels its announcement has been misunderstood.
(b) Players are considering suing NFL officials to nullify the decision.
(c) Drug testing has been done to players regularly.
(d) The NFL has developed a more reliable drug test.

35. What caused slavery? One factor that contributed to the rise of this social evil was Eli Whitney's invention of the cotton gin in 1793. The cotton gin was designed to separate the cotton plant's fibers from its seeds. Done by hand, this was a time-consuming task that made cotton farming costly, and as a result, not widely practiced. After the invention of the gin, however, cotton farming suddenly began to make economic sense, and legions of plantation owners quickly began to grow the crop. The need for hands to pick the cotton increased rapidly, and the best source of cheap labor, as far as the owners were concerned, was the slaves.

Q: What can be inferred from the passage?
(a) Eli Whitney was one of those who supported slavery.
(b) Cotton had not been picked by hand before the cotton gin.
(c) Cotton farming needed more slaves than any other industry did.
(d) Eli Whitney did a lot of business with plantation owners.

36. Guatemala's Indian tribes are as of yet an unassimilated group. The country has two cultures sharing the same land but not sharing the same cultural values. The Indian has distanced himself from Guatemalan society as is reflected in the differences in traditions, languages, dress, and attitudes toward social obligation. Some feel that Indians combine outward docility with an inward refusal to accept European ways, thus creating an environment in which they could be exploited by a social order that they elect not to join. For a country with such formidable social problems and separate cultures to achieve success as a nation will be a difficult task and a tough problem for Guatemala's fledgling democracy.

Q: What can be inferred from the passage?
(a) Indians do not comprise the entire population of Guatemala.
(b) Indians in Guatemala have lost their own ruling system.
(c) Guatemala's Indian tribes have to accept European ways.
(d) There is not an official language in Guatemala.

37. Many students study English as if they were jumping through hoops. They practice grammar exercises and memorize rules. They believe that when they learn all the rules, they have learned English. But English is more than a list of rules. English is a tool for thinking and communicating. In English-speaking countries, English classes do not emphasize grammar and language rules. These things are helpful, but they are secondary. The emphasis is on thinking and communicating. Students learn to organize ideas and information; build cogent arguments; tell the narratives of life and work; distill and interpret written materials; and communicate their thoughts, insights, and feelings to their readers.

Q: Which of the following would the writer most likely agree with?
(a) English rules can be ignored as long as speakers understand each other.
(b) Most students study English only when told to do so.
(c) Sharing outside classroom experience is part of learning English.
(d) Learning English is all about making oneself understood.

Part III Questions 38 — 40

Read the passage. Then identify the option that does NOT belong.

38. Norbert Rillieux was born in the United States; however he received his education in Paris, France. (a) At 24, he was teaching applied engineering at the Ecole Centrale; however, his interest in chemistry and steam engineering led him to a process that almost revolutionized the sugar industry. (b) In 1846, Rillieux made use of the reduced boiling point of a liquid under a vacuum evaporator. (c) This process produced a cheaper, better, and more automated method of crystallizing sugar. (d) The same concept is now used in the manufacture of condensed milk, soap, and glue.

39. There is no doubt that there are many tourist attractions in Prague. (a) But some visitors have complained of there not being enough light for them to walk around the streets at night. (b) Recently, the magnificent 600-year-old Prague Castle was equipped with a new lighting system, so it could be seen better at night. (c) The high-tech system was financed by the British rock group the Rolling Stones, and set up by the engineer who designs the lighting for their own rock performances. (d) The Rolling Stones' gift to Prague resulted from their friendship with the Czech President, but they made all the arrangements without his knowing of the plan.

40. The movie *X-Men* is a powerful reminder that many of us still abhor the idea of differences and hold strong bonds to things that are similar. (a) If we see *X-Men* only as entertainment, we miss so many precious messages in it. (b) W. H. Auden once said, "Many misunderstandings arise over a failure to recognize certain attitudes we all take, according to our upbringing, in such a way that we cannot imagine anybody taking any other one." (c) Yet, we are still avoiding the unfamiliar, out of groundless fear and prejudice. (d) This is why the movie is regarded as one of the best by psychologists.

TEPS

Test of English Proficiency
developed by
Seoul National University

TEPS

Test of English Proficiency
developed by
Seoul National University

청해 Listening Comprehension

문법 Grammar

어휘 Vocabulary

독해 Reading Comprehension

서약

본인은 필기구 및 기재오류와 답안지 훼손으로 인한 책임을 지고, 부정행위 처리규정을 준수할 것을 서약합니다.

수험번호 Registration No.

성명 한글
Name

한자

문제지번호 Test Booklet No.

감독관확인란

주민등록번호 National ID No.

수험번호 Registration No.

비밀번호 Password

좌석번호 Seat No.

고사실란 Room No.

답안작성시 유의사항

1. 답안 작성은 반드시 **컴퓨터용 싸인펜**을 사용해야 합니다.
2. 답안을 정정할 경우 수정테이프(수정액 불가)를 사용해야 합니다.
3. 본 답안지는 컴퓨터로 처리되므로 훼손해서는 안되며, 답안지 하단의 타이밍마크(▌▌▌)를 찢거나, 낙서 등으로 인한 훼손시 불이익이 발생할 수 있습니다.

4. 답안은 문항당 정답을 1개만 골라 아래와 같이 정확히 기재해야 하며, 필기구 오류나 본인의 부주의로 잘못 표기한 경우에는 답 관리위원회의 OMR판독기의 판독결과에 따르며, 그 결과는 본인이 책임집니다.

Good ●   Bad ◐ ◑ ⊗ ⊘

5. 감독관의 확인이 없는 답안지는 무효처리됩니다.

TEPS

Test of English Proficiency
developed by
Seoul National University

응시일자 : 20　　년　　월　　일

성명 | 영문
서명

단체 구분

학생 ○　　일반 ○

질문란

1. 귀하의 TEPS 응시목적은?
   - ⓐ 인사자료　ⓑ 인사정책
   - ⓒ 개인실력측정　ⓓ 입시
   - ⓔ 국가고시지원　ⓕ 기타

2. 귀하의 영어권 체류 경험은?
   - ⓐ 없다　ⓑ 6개월미만
   - ⓒ 6개월이상 1년미만　ⓓ 1년이상 2년미만
   - ⓔ 3년이상 5년미만　ⓕ 5년이상

3. 귀하께서 응시하고 계신 고사장에 대한 만족도는?
   - ⓐ 0점　ⓑ 1점
   - ⓒ 2점　ⓓ 3점
   - ⓔ 4점　ⓕ 5점

4. 최근 2년내 TEPS 응시횟수는?
   - ⓐ 없다　ⓑ 1회
   - ⓒ 2회　ⓓ 3회
   - ⓔ 4회　ⓕ 5회 이상

성명 (성·이름순으로 기재)

EX　HONG GIL DONG

（A〜Z 마킹란）

학력	전공	직업
(졸업 / 재학·휴학) 초등학교, 중학교, 고등학교, 전문대학, 대학, 대학원	인문, 사회과학·법학, 경제학·경영학, 자연과학, 이학·약학·간호학, 공학, 교육, 음악·미술·체육, 기타	공무원, 고시준비, 교사, 군인, 의료인, 자영업, 회사원, 학생, 주부, 기타

직	종	직책
고등학생, 전문직(과학·공학), 전문직(법·의), 전문직(법률·회계·금융), 기술직, 영업·판매직, 사무직, 생산·서비스직, 일반직, 주부, 자기개발, 구직	마케팅, 인사, 자금, 교육, 영업, 품질관리, 생산관리, 연구개발, 서비스, 기타	임원, 부장, 차장, 과장, 대리, 계장, 사원, 인턴, 기타

<부정행위 및 규정위반 처리규정>

1. 모든 부정행위 및 규정위반 적발 및 이에 대한 조치는 TEPS관리위 원회의 처리규정에 따라 이루어집니다.

2. 부정행위 및 규정위반 행위는 현장 적발 뿐만 아니라 사후에도 적발될 수 있으며 모두 동일한 조치가 취해 집니다.

3. 부정행위 적발 시 당해 성적은 무효 처리되며 사안에 따라 최대 5년까지 TEPS관리위원회에서 주관하는 모든 시험의 응시자격이 제한됩니다.

4. 문제지 이외에 메모를 하는 행위와 시험 문제를 일부 또는 전부를 유출 하거나 공개하는 경우 부정행위로 처리됩니다.

5. 각 파트별 시간을 준수하지 않거나, 시험 종료 후 답안 작성을 계속할 경우 규정위반으로 처리됩니다.

TEPS

Test of English Proficiency
developed by
Seoul National University

수험번호 Registration No.

성명 Name
한글
한자

문제지번호
Test Booklet No.

감독관확인란

청해 Listening Comprehension

문법 Grammar

어휘 Vocabulary

독해 Reading Comprehension

주민등록번호
National ID No.

수험번호
Registration No.

비밀번호
Password

고사실란
Room No.

좌석번호
Seat No.

서약

본인은 필기구 및 기재오류와 답안지 훼손으로 인한 책임을 지고, 부정행위 처리규정을 준수할 것을 서약합니다.

답안작성시
유의사항

1. 답안은 작성은 반드시 컴퓨터용 싸인펜을 사용해야 합니다.
2. 답안을 정정할 경우 수정테이프(수정액은 불가)를 사용해야 합니다.
3. 잘못 답안지는 컴퓨터로 처리되므로 훼손해서는 안되며, 답안지 하단의 타이밍마크(॥॥)를 찢거나, 낙서 등으로 인한 훼손시 불이익이 발생할 수 있습니다.

4. 답안은 문항당 정답을 1개만 골라 ● 와 같이 정확히 기재해야 하며, 필기구 오류나 본인의 부주의로 잘못 표기한 경우에는 답 관리위원회의 OMR판독기의 판독결과에 따르며, 그 결과는 본인이 책임집니다.

Good ● Bad ⊙ ◐ ⊗ ⊘

5. 감독관의 확인이 없는 답안지는 무효처리됩니다.

TEPS

Test of English Proficiency
developed by
Seoul National University

응시일자 : 20   년   월   일

	영문	성
	서명	명

성 명 (성·이름순으로 기재)

EX H O N G   G I L   D O N G

| | A | B | C | D | E | F | G | H | I | J | K | L | M | N | O | P | Q | R | S | T | U | V | W | X | Y | Z |

학력
| 학력 | 졸업 | | | | | | |
| 재학·휴학 | | | | | | | |

초등학교 / 중학교 / 고등학교 / 전문대학 / 대학교 / 대학원

전공
인문 / 사회과학·법학 / 경제학·경영학 / 어학·어학·건축학 / 공학 / 음악·미술·체육 / 기타

직업
공무원 / 교사·준비 / 교수 / 군인 / 의료인 / 자영업 / 학생 / 회사원 / 직장 / 기타

중직
무역 / 외환 / 금융 / 자금 / 영업 / 관리 / 품질관리 / 생산관리 / 설비·비서 / 기타

직책
임원 / 부장 / 차장 / 과장 / 대리 / 계장 / 주임 / 인턴 / 기타

직무
고위임원 / 전문직(과학·공학) / 전문직(법·의료) / 전문직(변호·회계금융) / 기술직 / 영업직 / 사무직 / 생산직 / 리·서비스 / 기타

단체 구분
학생 / 일반

질 문 란

1. 귀하의 TEPS 응시목적은?
a 입사시험 b 인사정책
c 개인실력측정 d 입시
e 국가고시 지원 f 기타

2. 귀하의 영어권 체류 경험은?
a 없다 b 6개월미만
c 6개월이상1년미만 d 1년이상2년미만
e 2년이상3년미만 f 3년이상

3. 귀하께서 응시하고 계신 고사장에 대한 만족도는?
a 0점 b 1점
c 2점 d 3점
e 4점 f 5점

4. 최근 2년내 TEPS 응시횟수는?
a 없다 b 1회
c 2회 d 3회
e 4회 f 5회 이상

〈부정행위 및 규정위반 처리규정〉

1. 모든 부정행위 및 규정위반 적발 및 이에 대한 조치는 TEPS관리위원회의 처리규정에 따라 이루어집니다.

2. 부정행위 및 규정위반 행위는 현장 적발 뿐만 아니라 사후에도 적발될 수 있으며 모두 동일한 조치가 취해집니다.

3. 부정행위 적발 시 당해 성적은 무효 처리되며 사안에 따라 최대 5년까지 TEPS관리위원회에서 주관하는 모든 시험의 응시자격이 제한됩니다.

4. 문제지 이외에 메모를 하는 행위와 시험 문제의 일부 또는 전부를 유출하거나 공개하는 경우 부정행위로 처리됩니다.

5. 각 파트별 시간을 준수하지 않거나, 시험 종료 후 답안 작성을 계속할 경우 규정위반으로 처리됩니다.

취업 전에도, 취업 후에도
Multi **TEPS!**

취업 전 입시, 편입, 졸업에서도!
취업 후 승진, 해외파견, 사내 커뮤니케이션에서도!
언제 어디서든 활용할 수 있는 TEPS로
모든 도전에 통(通)하라.

TEPS 공식페이스북

민간자격국가공인 영어능력평가
(제 2010-11호, 1+급, 1급, 2+급, 2급 해당)

TEPS	TEPS-Speaking	i-TEPS	SNULT
• 대기업, 의·치전원, 고시 등 다방면에서 활용되는 한국대표 영어시험	• 실전 영어말하기 능력평가! 대기업, 공기업 취업 및 주요대학 내 평가활용	• 듣기, 읽기, 말하기, 쓰기 통합 영어능력 측정! 공무원 국외장기훈련 파견 선발시험 등	• 제2외국어능력평가의 정확한 기준! 영어, 일어, 중어, 불어, 독어, 서어, 노어

서울대학교 TEPS관리위원회   Homepage: www.teps.or.kr   Tel: 02-886-3330

● 넥서스 수준별 TEPS 맞춤 학습 프로그램

서울대 기출문제

기출·독해

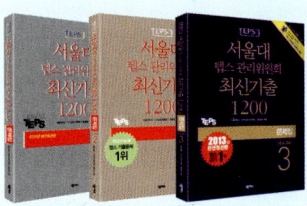

서울대 텝스 관리위원회 최신기출 1000 | 서울대학교 TEPS관리위원회 문제 제공·양준희 해설 | 628쪽 | 28,000원
서울대 텝스 관리위원회 최신기출 1200/SEASON 2~3 문제집 | 서울대학교 TEPS관리위원회 문제 제공 | 352쪽 | 19,500원
서울대 텝스 관리위원회 최신기출 1200/SEASON 2~3 해설집 | 서울대학교 TEPS관리위원회 문제 제공·넥서스 TEPS연구소 해설 | 472쪽 | 25,000원
서울대 텝스 관리위원회 최신기출 Listening | 서울대학교 TEPS관리위원회 문제 제공·넥서스 TEPS연구소 해설 | 320쪽 | 19,800원
서울대 텝스 관리위원회 최신기출 Reading | 서울대학교 TEPS관리위원회 문제 제공·넥서스 TEPS연구소 해설 | 568쪽 | 24,800원

실전 모의고사

실전·어휘

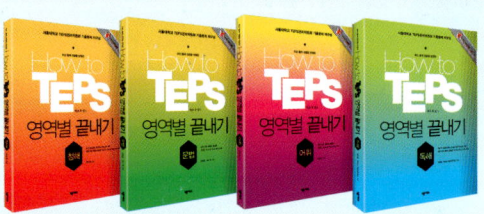

How to TEPS 영역별 끝내기 청해 | 테리 홍 지음 | 424쪽 | 19,800원
How to TEPS 영역별 끝내기 문법 | 장보금·써니 박 지음 | 260쪽 | 13,500원
How to TEPS 영역별 끝내기 어휘 | 양준희 지음 | 240쪽 | 13,500원
How to TEPS 영역별 끝내기 독해 | 김무룡·넥서스 TEPS연구소 지음 | 504쪽 | 25,000원

How to TEPS 시험 직전 리얼 청해 | 넥서스 TEPS연구소 지음 | 296쪽 | 19,500원
How to TEPS 시험 직전 리얼 문법 | 장보금·써니 박 지음 | 260쪽 | 14,000원
How to TEPS 시험 직전 리얼 어휘 | 양준희 지음 | 252쪽 | 14,000원
How to TEPS 시험 직전 리얼 독해 | 넥서스 TEPS연구소 지음 | 504쪽 | 25,000원

초급 (400~500점) / 중급 (600~700점)

영역별

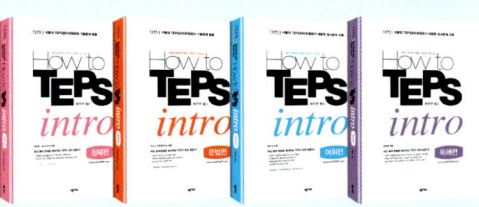

How to TEPS intro 청해편 | 강소영·Jane Kim 지음 | 444쪽 | 22,000원
How to TEPS intro 문법편 | 넥서스 TEPS연구소 지음 | 424쪽 | 19,000원
How to TEPS intro 어휘편 | 에릭 김 지음 | 368쪽 | 15,000원
How to TEPS intro 독해편 | 한정림 지음 | 392쪽 | 19,500원

How to TEPS 실전 600 어휘편·청해편·문법편·독해편 | 서울대학교 TEPS 관리위원회 문제 제공(어휘), 이기헌(청해), 장보금·써니 박(문법), 황수경·넥서스 TEPS연구소(독해) 지음 | 어휘: 15,000원, 청해: 19,800원, 문법: 17,500원, 독해: 19,000원
How to TEPS 실전 700 청해편·문법편·독해편 | 강소영·넥서스 TEPS연구소(청해), 이신영·넥서스 TEPS연구소(문법), 오정우·넥서스 TEPS연구소(독해) 지음 | 청해: 16,000원, 문법: 15,000원, 독해: 19,000원

종합서

How to TEPS New Starter | 넥서스 TEPS연구소 지음 | 584쪽 | 25,900원
How to TEPS New Starter 모의테스트 | 넥서스 TEPS연구소 지음 | 296쪽 | 15,000원
How to TEPS Basic Listening | 고명희·넥서스 TEPS연구소 지음 | 320쪽 | 18,500원
How to TEPS Basic Reading | 박미영·넥서스 TEPS연구소 지음 | 368쪽 | 19,500원

유형별로 텝스 독해를 공략한다

How to TEPS

하우투 텝스

시크릿 독해편

Secret

정성수 지음

해설집

텝스 독해 최고 득점자가 밝히는 출제 비밀 파일

넥서스

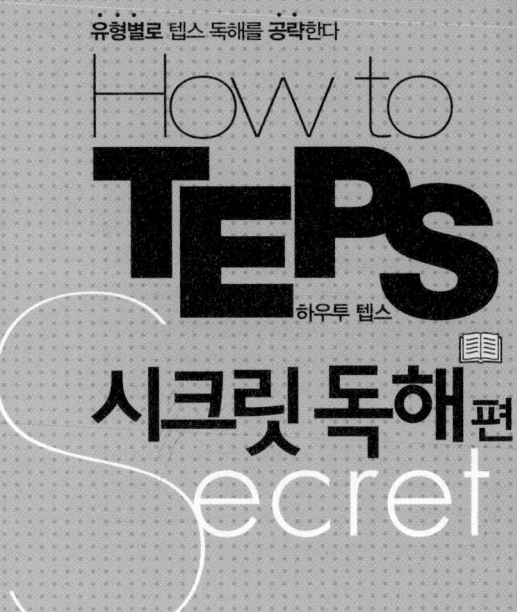

유형별로 텝스 독해를 공략한다

How to TEPS
하우투 텝스

시크릿 독해 편
Secret

정답 및 해설

Materials can often be improved by putting two of them together, so that each makes up for the deficiencies of the other. In this way several excellent, inexpensive materials have been created that make better products available at lower cost. Composites are usually made from pairs of materials that have opposite properties. One is often in the form of strands or fibers, which, though _____, are too floppy to stand up to being compressed. The other material can then be something that will simply stick the fibers together. Often this second material is quite weak or brittle.

(a) strong in tension
(b) sometimes breakable
(c) stable yet light
(d) chemically simple

번역 물질은 종종 둘을 하나로 혼합해 서로의 결함을 메워 줌으로써 개선될 수 있다. 이 방법으로 그 동안 몇몇 우수하면서도 값싼 물질이 만들어져 보다 나은 품질의 물건들을 저가로 이용할 수 있게 된 것이다. 합성물은 보통 서로 반대 성질을 가진 두 가지 물질에서 만들어진다. 그 중 한 가지는 흔히 섬유질의 형태를 취하는 물질로, 장력은 강하지만 너무 유연해서 압력에는 견디지 못한다. 이 경우, 함께 혼합할 다른 물질은 간단히 섬유질을 결합시켜 줄 수 있는 것이면 된다. 보통 이 물질은 아주 약하거나 쉽게 부서지는 성질을 가졌을 것이다.

(a) 장력은 강하지만
(b) 간혹 부서지는
(c) 가볍지만 안정된
(d) 화학적으로 단순한

해법 합성물은 보통 서로 반대 성질을 가진 두 가지 물질에서 만들어진다는 내용과 다른 물질은 섬유질을 결합시켜 주는 어떤 물질일 수 있다는 내용을 연계해 보면 다른 물질의 결합시켜 주는 성질에 반대되는 성질인 장력에 대한 내용이 와야 함을 알 수 있어 (a)가 정답이다. (c)는 빈칸이 있는 문장 다음에 stable에 반대되는 내용이 없다.

make up for ~을 메워 주다 **deficiency** 결핍, 결함 **composite** 합성, 혼성의, 합성물 **property** 재산, 소유물; 성질 **strand** (실·머리카락 등의) 가닥 **fiber** 섬유(조직) **floppy** 느슨한, 엉성한, 헐렁한 **compress** 압축하다, 요약하다 **brittle** 부서지기 쉬운, 덧없는, (태도가) 완고한

정답 (a)

Mr. Nevers,

Congratulations on your appointment to the new Summit Grain office in Halifax, Nova Scotia. Ms. Lou has told me that you are the perfect person to manage the office, and she looks forward to seeing good things from you there. I am writing to inform you that Ms. Lou will not be able to attend the kick-off meeting at the Halifax office on Tuesday. Summit Grain's board members have called a meeting in Marseille that same day, _____. I will be staying at the Highcrest Halifax on Morton Street while in Halifax. You are welcome to call me at the hotel to set up our meeting.

Cordially,
Jannette Choi

(a) but she cannot make it to the meeting
(b) and it looks like you should be there, too
(c) but she might be available later that day
(d) and apparently her presence is required

번역 노바스코샤 핼리팩스에 신설된 서밋 그레인 사무소 발령을 축하드립니다. 루 씨는 네버스 씨가 사무소를 경영할 적임자이며 그곳에서 훌륭하게 업무를 수행하실 것으로 기대한다고 말씀하셨습니다. 이 편지는 루 씨가 핼리팩스 사무소의 화요일 시무 행사에 참석하지 못한다는 것을 알려드리기 위해 띄우는 것입니다. 서밋 그레인의 이사회 위원들이 같은 날 마르세이유에서 회의를 소집했으며 루 씨는 그곳에 반드시 참석해야 합니다. 저는 핼리팩스에 머무는 동안 모턴 가에 있는 하이크레스트 핼리팩스에 머물 것입니다. 회의 일정을 잡으시려면 언제든지 호텔로 전화 주셔도 좋습니다.

(a) 루 씨는 참석할 수 없습니다
(b) 귀하도 참석해야 할 것 같습니다
(c) 루 씨는 이날 늦게나 시간이 날지도 모릅니다
(d) 루 씨는 그곳에 반드시 참석해야 합니다

해법 서밋 그레인 이사회 위원들이 핼리팩스 사무소 개점 행사에 회의 소집을 해서 루 씨가 개점 행사에 참석하지 못한다고 했으므로 이사회 위원들이 소집한 회의에 참석해야 한다는 흐름이 자연스러워 (d)가 정답이다. (a), (b), (c)는 지문에서 근거를 찾을 수 없다.

appointment 지정, 임명 **manage** 경영하다 **kick-off** 시작, 개시 **board** 이사회 **call a meeting** 회의를 소집하다

 정답 (d)

In recent research on college students' dating habits, studies found that _____ when it comes to choosing a partner for a casual date. What is intriguing is the explanation given by an evolutionary psychologist: For eons, it's been in the man's interest to spread his seed as widely and indiscriminately as possible, thus preserving the species. On the other hand, it's unwise for a woman to monkey around with just any suitor; her genetically inferior offspring could be at a disadvantage in attracting a mate and doing their part for civilization.

(a) how they look does not matter as much as it did
(b) men are less discriminating than women
(c) their parental influence is not important
(d) women are more picky than men

번역 대학생들의 데이트 습관에 관한 최근 연구 결과에서 가볍게 데이트할 상대를 고를 때 남자들이 여자들보다 덜 차별한다는 사실이 발견됐다. 흥미로운 것은 한 진화론 심리학자가 설명으로 제시한 내용이다. 인류 역사의 기나긴 세월을 살아오는 동안 남성의 관심사는 종족을 보존하기 위해 상대를 안 가리고 될 수 있는 한 광범위하게 자손을 퍼트리는 데 있어 왔다는 것이다. 한편 여성은 2세가 열성 유전자를 타고나 짝을 유혹하거나 문명을 이끌어가는 일에 맡은 바 역할을 제대로 해내지 못할 것에 대한 우려 때문에 주변의 아무 구혼자와 허튼 짓을 일삼는 것을 현명하지 못한 일로 여겨왔다는 것이다.

(a) 그들의 외모가 예전만큼은 중요치 않다
(b) 남자들이 여자들보다 덜 차별한다
(c) 그들 부모의 영향이 중요치 않다
(d) 여자들이 남자보다 더 까다롭다

해법 무궁한 시간 동안 자손을 될 수 있는 한 광범위하게 널리, 그리고 퍼트리고 가리지 않고 퍼트려서 종들을 보존하는 것이 남자의 관심사였고, 유전학적으로 열등한 자식은 배우자의 마음을 끌거나 문명을 위한 그들의 역할을 할 때 불리한 것이기 때문에 여성이 아무 구혼자와 놀아나는 것은 현명치 못하다고 했으므로 데이트 상대를 고를 때 남자들이 여자들보다 덜 차별한다는 (b)가 정답이다.

intriguing 흥미를 끄는 **eon** 무한한 시간(aeon) **seed** 자손
indiscriminately 가리지 않고 **monkey around with** ~와 장난하다, 놀아나다 **suitor** 구혼자(여자에게 구혼하는 남자) **genetically inferior** 유전적으로 열등한 **offspring** 자손; 결과

정답 (b)

Children quickly realize what roles society expects them to play. Researcher Douglas Hofstadter tells this story: ten boys and ten girls visited a hospital on a school trip. At the end of the visit, hospital staff gave each child a hat: doctors' hats for the boys, nurses' hats for the girls. The parents complained, saying it was an example of stereotyping. The hospital director supported them and promised this would change. The next year, at the end of a similar trip, the parents again found out that all the boys had doctors' hats and all the girls had nurses' hats! They went to the hospital director. This time he said, "_____."

(a) It was totally unexpected to see that happen
(b) We didn't have anything but hats for the children
(c) The children chose which hats they wanted
(d) I promise you we will teach them the principle of equality

번역 아이들은 사회가 그들에게서 바라는 역할이 무엇인지를 금세 깨닫는다. 더글라스 호프스테터 연구원의 이야기는 이렇다. 남자 아이 10명과 여자 아이 10명이 현장 학습으로 한 병원을 방문했다. 방문이 끝날 무렵 병원 직원이 아이들 각자에게 모자를 줬는데, 남자 아이들에게는 의사 모자를, 여자 아이들에게는 간호사 모자를 줬다. 부모들은 그것이 정형화의 예라고 말하면서 항의했다. 병원장은 부모들의 말에 일리가 있다고 하며 이를 시정하겠다고 약속했다. 그 다음 해에 비슷한 방문이 끝날 무렵에 부모들은 남자 아이들은 전부 의사 모자를, 여자 아이들은 모두 간호사 모자를 가지고 있는 모습을 또 발견했다. 부모들은 병원장을 찾아갔다. 그러자 그는 "이번에는 아이들이 그들이 원하는 모자를 선택했습니다"라고 말하는 것이 아닌가.

(a) 그런 일이 벌어지리라고는 전혀 예상할 수 없었습니다
(b) 아이들에게 줄 것이 모자밖에는 없었습니다
(c) 아이들이 그들이 원하는 모자들을 선택했습니다
(d) 아이들에게 평등 원칙을 가르칠 것을 약속합니다

해법 이 문제는 아이들이 그들의 사회적 역할을 빨리 배운다는 지문 첫 문장을 놓치지 않아야 한다. 지문을 읽다 보면 전개되는 내용 때문에 앞 내용을 깜박하는 경우를 조심하자. (a), (b), (d)는 빈칸이 있는 문장만 놓고 보면 그럴듯하지만 지문 첫 문장을 중심으로 지문 전체 흐름에 어울리지 않는다. 따라서 (c)가 정답이다.

stereotyping 정형화, 고정관념, 진부함 **principle** 원리, 원칙 **equality** 평등

정답 (c)

Shunning the somber hues and heavy shadows of earlier styles, the impressionists sought to paint on canvas what the eye sees in an instant. _____, they portrayed unposed subjects from unexpected angles. These artists also believed that the secret to visual impression is light. To emphasize the flickers of light reflected in the ever-changing scenes, impressionist painters daubed brilliant patches of color on the canvas with quick brush strokes.

(a) Being least attentive
(b) Trying to be prolific
(c) Breaking with tradition
(d) Creating natural looks

번역 인상파 화가들은 어두운 색조와 짙은 그림자가 특징인 초기의 스타일을 버리고 순간적으로 눈에 포착된 것을 캔버스 위에 그리고자 했다. 그들은 전통을 깨뜨리고 인위적으로 연출되지 않은 새로운 각도에서 대상들을 그렸다. 이 예술가들은 또한 시각적인 감명의 비밀은 빛이라고 믿었다. 끊임없이 변하는 장면들에 비치는 빛의 명멸을 강조하기 위해 인상파 화가들은 빠른 붓놀림으로 밝은 색상의 미세한 면들을 캔버스 위에 두툼하게 칠했다.

(a) 주의를 거의 기울이지 않고
(b) 많은 작품들을 만들어내고자 하면서
(c) 전통을 깨뜨리고
(d) 자연스러운 모습들을 만들면서

해법 지문 첫 문장에서 '초기 스타일의 음울한 색조와 짙은 그림자를 피하면서'라고 했으므로 전통을 깨뜨린다는 (c)가 지문 흐름에 어울린다. (a), (b)는 지문에서 근거를 찾을 수 없고, (d)는 빈칸 뒤 문장과 결국 같은 내용이므로 불필요한 의미 중복이다.

shun ~을 피하다　**somber** 어두컴컴한, 흐린　**hue** 색(조)　**unposed subject** 포즈를 취하지 않은 자연스러운 대상　**flicker** (불빛 따위) 명멸, 흔들림　**daub** (덕지덕지) 바르다, 칠하다　**prolific** (작가가) 다작의

정답 (c)

Clayton's educational fund budget is projected to be smaller than last year even though the district is continuing to grow. _____, and the district will have to hire more teachers. District officials point out, however, that over the past year many teachers have retired and, in most cases, have been replaced by younger, less experienced teachers. That keeps costs down because salaries are figured by seniority. Also, $680,000 was saved from the supply fund, which buys everything from rubber bands to construction paper. And a second look at the fund that pays for utility fees found that energy-saving efforts in schools will allow $250,000 to be spent elsewhere.

(a) Clayton has been growing for the last couple of years
(b) About 32,879 students are expected to enroll in the fall
(c) Education is regarded most highly in Clayton
(d) Efforts are being made to provide an inexpensive education

번역 클레이턴 지역은 계속 성장하고 있지만 교육 자금 예산은 작년보다 더 적을 전망이다. 32,879명의 학생들이 가을에 입학하기로 되어 있기에 관할기관은 교사들을 더 뽑아야 할 것이다. 그러나 지역 공무원들은 지난 한 해 동안 기존의 교사들 상당수가 퇴직했으며, 대부분의 경우 그들을 대신해서 더 젊고 경험이 적은 교사들이 배치되어 왔다는 사실을 지적한다. 급여는 근무 연수에 따라 책정되기 때문에 그로 인한 비용 절감이 이루어지고 있다는 것이다. 또한 교구 비용 68만 달러가 비축되어 있는데, 이 돈으로 고무 밴드에서 색상지에 이르는 다양한 교구를 구입할 수 있다. 그리고 시설 유지에 따른 공공요금의 예산을 다시 살펴보니 각 학교가 에너지 절약을 위해 노력한 결과 25만 달러를 다른 곳에 사용할 수 있다는 것을 알아냈다.

(a) 클레이턴 지역은 지난 2년 동안 성장해 오고 있다
(b) 32,879명 정도의 학생들이 이번 가을에 입학하기로 되어 있다
(c) 교육이 클레이턴 지역에서 가장 중요하게 여겨진다
(d) 저렴한 비용으로 교육을 제공하기 위한 노력이 진행되고 있다

해법 교사들을 더 뽑아야만 하는 내용에 대해 빈칸 앞에 올 만한 내용이 무엇인지 생각해보면 많은 수의 학생들이 입학할 예정이라는 (b)가 가장 적절하다. (a)는 지문 첫 문장 내용과 겹치고, 상대적으로 월급을 적게 받는 젊고 경험이 적은 교사들, 줄어든 비품 비용 25만 달러는 작년보다 더 적어질 교육 자금 예산에 대한 대비책들이므로 (d)도 오답이다.

fund budget 자금 예산　**be projected to** ~할 예정인, 전망인　**utility** 수도,전기 등 공익설비　**seniority** 연상, 근무 연수　**construction paper** 색상지　**enroll** 등록, 입학하다

정답 (b)

One day my brother Vincent had a minor pain in his hip. In an attempt to save both time and money, he tracked down his doctor on the phone. Seeking free advice, he described the pain. His doctor carefully said that he couldn't provide a diagnosis without a proper examination but obligingly suggested Vincent eat a good meal, take some paracetamol, and apply moist heat to his hip. "Hey, Doc," Vincent urged, "could it be arthritis?" "Hey, Vincent," the doctor asked, "_____?" Vincent got the point.

(a) do you need a prescription
(b) what do you think of the tie I'm wearing
(c) did I sound too serious
(d) why don't you come see me in person

📖 **번역** 어느 날 나의 형 빈센트는 골반에 경미한 통증을 느꼈다. 시간과 돈을 좀 절약해 보겠다는 생각으로 의사에게 전화를 걸었다. 공짜로 조언을 구하기 위해 그는 자신의 통증을 설명했다. 의사 선생님은 제대로 진찰하지 않고 진단을 내릴 수 없다고 조심스럽게 말하며 자상하게 빈센트에게 식사도 잘하고 해열 진통제를 먹고 골반에 온찜질을 하라고 제안했다. "선생님, 이게 혹시 관절염일까요?"라고 빈센트가 다급하게 묻자, "빈센트 씨, 지금 제가 매고 있는 넥타이가 어떤가요?"라고 의사가 대답했다. 빈센트는 의사 선생님이 하는 말이 무슨 뜻인지 알아차렸다.

(a) 처방전이 필요하신가요
(b) 제가 지금 매고 있는 넥타이가 어떤가요
(c) 제 말이 너무 심각하게 들렸나요
(d) 저를 보러 직접 오지 그래요

☀ **해법** 의사가 제대로 진찰을 해야만 진단을 내릴 수 있다고 했고 빈센트가 무슨 말인지 알아들었다는 지문 마지막 문장을 보면 빈칸은 어떤 의미를 내포하고 있음을 알 수 있어 직접 와서 진찰을 받아보라는 (b)가 정답이다. (a)와 (d)는 Vincent got the point라는 문장이 올 만큼 의미를 내포하고 있지 않다.

track down 찾다 **diagnosis** 진단 **examination** 진찰 **obligingly** 자상하게, 친절하게 **paracetamol** 해열 진통제 **arthritis** 관절염

✔ **정답** (b)

Architects _____ to design modern buildings. Usually after first spending time with the clients who want to build the structure, they draw some pen-and-paper sketches of buildings that might accommodate their clients' needs. Next, they usually use wooden blocks, much like the ones children play with, to build rough but easily altered models. They make it easy to determine the client's size requirements. In the next step, they build a series of scale models; the final one is a perfect miniature version of the full-size structure. Finally, they use the model to enter all of the building's measurements into a computer program that figures out the total costs for all of the necessary materials.

(a) work with computer graphic designers
(b) use a combination of high-tech and low-tech procedures
(c) spend a large amount of time with their clients
(d) go through six steps involving different skills

📖 **번역** 건축가들은 현대식 건물을 디자인하기 위해서 최첨단 기술과 재래식 방식을 혼합해서 적용한다. 일반적으로 처음에는 구조물을 짓고자 하는 의뢰인과 시간을 보낸 후 의뢰인의 요구 사항이 담겨 있는 건물을 스케치로 그려낸다. 다음 단계에서 그들은 이들이 가지고 노는 것과 비슷한 나무 블록을 사용해 변형이 쉬운 대략의 모형을 만든다. 이 과정은 의뢰인이 요구하는 구조의 규모와 관련된 요소를 쉽게 결정할 수 있도록 해준다. 다음은 여러 단계에 거쳐서 축소 모형을 만드는데, 그 중 맨 마지막 모형은 실물의 완벽한 축소판이다. 마지막으로 그들은 이 모형을 이용해서 필요한 자재의 총비용을 계산해 주는 컴퓨터 프로그램에 건축물의 모든 치수를 입력한다.

(a) 컴퓨터 그래픽 디자이너들과 작업한다
(b) 최첨단 기술과 재래식 방식을 혼합해서 적용한다
(c) 의뢰인들과 꽤 많은 시간을 보낸다
(d) 서로 다른 기술들을 수반하는 6단계를 거친다

☀ **해법** 지문 두 번째 문장의 펜과 종이, 세 번째 문장의 나무 블록 그리고 지문 마지막 문장의 컴퓨터 프로그램이 각기 다른 수준의 기술을 의미하므로 (b)가 정답이다. (a), (c)는 지문 마지막 문장과 두 번째 문장만을 이용했고, (d)는 의뢰인과 시간을 보내는 일부터 컴퓨터 프로그램 사용까지 5단계이므로 선택지의 six와 맞지 않다.

architect 건축가 **accommodate** 충족하다 **rough** 대충, 대강 **alter** 변경하다, 수정하다 **scale model** 비례 모형 (실제 모습을 축소해 놓은 모형) **procedure** 절차

✔ **정답** (b)

Your life is often ruled by rituals or beliefs that have no basis in fact. While this behavior is anxiety driven, the cause of the actual anxiety is your fundamental feeling of not being in control of your life. If you were in control of your life, you would see examples of your actions producing specific results. Without this control, you lose the ability to distinguish between things that happen to you and those that you make happen. This _____ rituals. You need to have some sense of control, so you draw your own correlation between an event and a behavior. After all, your actions give you the illusion of control.

(a) leads you to know about
(b) makes you a virtual slave to
(c) is the basic meaning of
(d) cannot be solved only by

A new labor union representing child care employees is starting to be organized to try to improve wages and welfare for one of the nation's lowest-paying professions. According to the U.S. Bureau of Labor Statistics, child care workers make an average of $7.86 an hour, less than animal caretakers, and _____. With low wages and little welfare, the turnover rate in child care jobs is 30 to 50 percent a year. "It's necessary to make a national union of child care workers to improve the quality of these jobs," said Denise Dowell, taking charge of organizing the United Child Care Union.

(a) their employees aren't making money
(b) it doesn't reflect the difficulty of the job
(c) this amount is expected to decrease soon
(d) many work without health care insurance

📖 **번역** 당신의 삶은 종종 사실에 근거를 전혀 두지 않은 의식이나 믿음에 의해 지배된다. 이런 행동은 불안에 의해 유발되지만 그 불안의 진짜 원인은 근본적으로 당신 스스로 자신의 삶을 통제할 능력을 가지고 있지 못하다는 마음에 있다. 만약 당신이 자신의 삶을 통제하고 있다면 자신의 행동이 구체적인 결과를 낳는 사례를 보게 될 것이다. 이런 통제력이 없으면 당신은 자신에게 일어나는 일과 자신이 일어나게 하는 일을 구분할 능력을 잃게 된다. 이와 같은 상황이 당신을 사실상 각종 의식의 노예로 만드는 것이다. 당신은 당신에게 일어나는 어떤 사건과 당신의 행동 사이의 상관 관계를 스스로 끌어낼 적절한 수준의 통제력을 가질 필요가 있다. 결국 당신의 행동이 스스로를 통제하고 있다는 환상을 심어주는 것이다.

(a) ~에 대해 알게 한다
(b) ~에 대해 사실상의 노예로 만든다
(c) ~의 기본적인 의미이다
(d) ~으로만으로 해결할 수 없다

☀ **해법** 당신의 삶이 실제로 근거 없는 의식이나 믿음에 의해 자주 지배되고 이런 행동의 원인인 불안, 근심은 삶에 대한 통제력의 부재에서 온다고 했으므로 이런 통제력이 없을 때를 말하고 있는 빈칸 앞 문장과 통제력을 가질 필요가 있다는 빈칸 뒤 문장을 보면 (b)가 지문 흐름에 알맞다. 즉, 근거는 없더라도 의식이나 믿음을 통해 통제력을 확보한다는 것이 지문 주요 내용이다.

ritual 의식(의) **anxiety driven** 불안에 의해 유발된 **fundamental** 근본적인 **distinguish** 구분하다 **draw** (결론 따위를) 끌어내다 **correlation** 상관 관계 **illusion** 환상

✓ **정답** (b)

📖 **번역** 국가에서 가장 낮은 임금을 받는 직업 중 하나인 보육사의 임금 인상과 복지 증진을 위해 노력하고자 이들을 대표하는 새로운 노동 조합이 결성되고 있다. 미국 노동 통계국에 따르면 보육사들의 평균 시급은 7달러 86센트로, 동물사육사들보다 낮은데다 그들 중 상당수는 건강 보험도 없이 일하는 것으로 드러났다. 낮은 임금과 거의 전무한 수준의 복지 혜택으로, 이직률은 연간 30~50퍼센트에 이른다. "직업의 질을 높이기 위해 보육사들로 구성된 전국적인 조합을 만들 필요가 있습니다"라고 공동 보육 조합을 조직하는 책임을 맡고 있는 드니스 도웰이 말했다.

(a) 그들의 고용주들은 수익을 얻지 못하고 있다
(b) 업무 난이도를 반영하지 못한다
(c) 이 액수는 곧 줄어들 것으로 예상된다
(d) 상당수는 건강 보험도 없이 일한다

☀ **해법** 보육사의 임금과 복지 향상에 대한 지문인데 이를 뒷받침하는 각각의 세부 내용으로 임금에 대한 언급은 있고 복지에 대한 내용이 없어 (d)가 정답이다. 빈칸에 지문 흐름상 임금과 복지에 대한 세부 내용이 필요한데 (a), (b), (c)는 모두 복지에 대한 내용이 아니므로 오답이다.

labor union 노동조합 **represent** 대표하다 **wage** 임금 **welfare** 복지 **profession** 직업 **Bureau of Labor Statistics** 노동 통계국 **turnover** 이직 **take charge of** ~을 맡다

✓ **정답** (d)

Dear Editor,

I noted with disappointment that, in an otherwise outstanding issue on the artists of the 20th century, your magazine failed to mention, arguably, the most distinguished figure of the century. The emergence of George Harris in 1982 was significant in that _____. Although his career eventually collapsed, it reflected a watershed in popular culture's debate on what an artist should pursue.

(a) it effectively changed the preconceived ideas of the public about art
(b) that was when styles of painting kept appearing and disappearing
(c) no other artists could produce the proper works of modern art
(d) he contributed to the development of new theories of art

번역 20세기의 예술가들을 다룬 귀 잡지의 지난 호가 다른 면에서는 모두 탁월했으나, 분명 20세기 최고의 예술인이라고 할 수 있는 인물을 언급하지 않았다는 사실에 실망했습니다. 1982년 조지 해리스의 등단은 사실상 예술에 대한 대중의 선입견을 변화시켰다는 점에서 중대한 의미를 갖습니다. 끝내 몰락의 길을 걷기는 했으나 그의 경력이 예술가가 추구해야 하는 바가 무엇인지에 대한 대중문화의 논쟁에 분수령이 되었던 것은 틀림없습니다.

(a) 사실상 예술에 대한 대중의 선입견을 변화시켰다는
(b) 그때가 많은 화풍이 계속 생기고 사라졌던 때였다는
(c) 다른 어떤 예술가들도 현대 예술의 적절한 작품들을 만들 수 없었다는
(d) 그가 새로운 예술 이론들을 만드는 데 공헌했다는

해법 1982년 조지 해리스의 등단이 중대한 의미를 갖는다는 내용과 그의 경력이 예술가가 추구해야 하는 바에 대한 대중문화의 논쟁에 분수령이 되었다는 내용을 연계해 보면 예술에 대한 대중의 선입견을 효과적으로 변화시켰다는 (a)가 지문 흐름에 어울린다. (b), (c), (d)는 지문에서 근거를 찾을 수 없다.

outstanding 현저한, 눈에 띄는 **arguably** 이론의 여지는 있지만, 거의 틀림없이 **distinguished** 저명한, 훌륭한 **figure** 인물 **emergence** 출현, 발생 **significant** 중요한 **watershed** 분수령, 전환점 **pursue** 추구하다, 쫓다 **preconceived idea** 선입견

정답 (a)

In this age of prospering commerce, one can be tempted to use the national wealth as a yardstick to decide how civilized a nation is. But could we call a nation which has all the gold of Peru but a vast majority of its people starving on the street a civilized nation? For me, being civilized is to develop the good sides of our human nature. That is to say, we should have compassion, pity, and understanding for people who are not like us. Thus, such terrible conditions for the poor _____.

(a) are not present in most civilized nations
(b) need nothing but our good will to improve
(c) can be found even in wealthy nations
(d) is a true mark of an uncivilized nation

번역 상업이 번성하는 이 시대에 사람들은 한 나라가 얼마나 문명화되었나를 결정하는 척도로 국부를 이용하고자 하는 유혹에 빠지기 쉽다. 그러나 페루 산 모든 금 덩어리를 갖고 있더라도 국민 대다수가 거리에서 굶고 있는 나라가 있다면 그 나라를 문명국이라고 할 수 있는가? 내 생각에 문명화된다는 것은 인간 본성의 좋은 면을 발전시키는 것이다. 즉, 우리는 우리와 상황이 다른 사람들에게 온정과 동정을 품고, 이해해야 한다. 그러므로 가난한 사람들에게 참혹한 조건은 비문명 국가임을 나타내는 진정한 지표이다.

(a) 대부분의 문명국에는 존재하지 않는다
(b) 필요한 것은 오로지 우리의 개선하고자 하는 선한 의지이다
(c) 부유한 나라들에서조차도 볼 수 있다
(d) 비문명 국가임을 나타내는 진정한 지표이다

해법 지문 마지막 문장 첫 부분의 Thus를 통해 국부가 나라의 문명화에 대한 척도가 아니라는, 즉 나라가 부유해도 빈곤 상태가 존재하면 문명화가 아닌 비문명화에 대한 척도라는 지문 주제가 반복됨을 알 수 있어 (d)가 정답이다. (a), (b), (c)는 지문 주제를 담고 있지 못하다.

prosper 번성, 번영하다 **commerce** 상업 **tempt** 유혹하다 **national wealth** 국부 **yardstick** 척도 **starve** 굶주리다 **compassion** 동정 **pity** 동정, 애석한 일

정답 (d)

We can't really afford to ignore the results from a recent survey. This survey was based on interviews conducted with senior managers in 300 corporations to find out what type of managers reach senior management positions. About 35% of the group of managers _____ reached senior management positions. On the other hand, 65% of the more individualistic managers who are decisive, dynamic, and able to make decisions on their own achieved senior management status. So, I think the conclusion is self-evident. If you want to reach the top of private-sector corporations, you have a much better chance if you adopt a fairly autocratic, top-down approach to management.

(a) who tend to depend on other people for important decisions.
(b) with abundant field experience rather than high education
(c) who do what they have to do without gaining attention
(d) classified as participative in their management style

It all began with a mysterious and seemingly innocent postcard, which changed the life of Bantock, a solitary artist living in Ireland. His logical world got turned upside down by Shiella, a strangely exotic woman living on an island in the South Pacific. This stunning original novel unfolds in a series of postcards and letters, all fascinatingly illustrated with whimsical designs, bizarre creatures, and darkly imagined landscapes. Inside the book, Bantock and Shiella's letters are to be found nestling in their envelopes, permitting the reader to _____.

(a) learn about some good examples of love letters for a lasting relationship
(b) keep so interested in the story that he/ she feels that it is a good book
(c) examine the intimate correspondence of these inexplicably linked strangers
(d) understand the different ways of thinking and living between the two characters

🔲 **번역** 우리는 최근 조사에서 얻은 결과를 무시하면 안 될 것 같다. 이 조사는 어떤 유형의 관리자가 고위 관리직까지 오르는지를 알아내기 위해 300개의 회사에 근무하는 고위 관리자들을 대상으로 인터뷰를 한 자료에 근거한 것이다. 고위 관리직에 오른 관리자의 35퍼센트 정도가 관리 방식이 참여적이라고 분류된 것으로 나타났다. 반면에 결단력 있고 활발하며 스스로 의사 결정을 잘하는 개인적 성향의 관리자인 65퍼센트가 고위 관리직을 차지한 것을 알 수 있었다. 여기에서 얻어지는 결론은 자명하다. 만약 당신이 사기업에서 고위직에 오르기 원한다면 비교적 독단적인 하향식 관리 방법을 채택하는 것이 당신의 바람을 이룰 확률을 높이는 길이다.

(a) 중요한 결정에 대해 다른 사람들에게 의존하려는 경향이 있는
(b) 고학력보다는 풍부한 현장 경험이 있는
(c) 주의를 끌지 않고 해야 할 일을 하는
(d) 관리 방법이 참여적이라고 분류된

☀️ **해법** 결단력 있고 활발하며 스스로 의사 결정을 할 수 있는 보다 개인적인 성향의 관리자들의 65퍼센트가 고위 관리직에 올랐다는 내용과, 사기업의 최고 자리까지 오르기 원한다면 관리에 있어 상당히 독단적이고 하향식 접근법을 채택하는 것이 확률이 높다는 내용을 연계해 보면 개인적이지 않고 참여적인 성향의 관리자 집단이 35퍼센트에 해당하므로 (d)가 정답이다.

cannot afford to ~할 수 없다 **self-evident** 자명한 **autocratic** 독재적인 **top-down** 하향식 (cf. bottom-up 상향식)

✅ **정답** (d)

🔲 **번역** 이 이야기는 아일랜드에 사는 고독한 예술가 반톡의 인생을 바꾸어 놓은 신비하면서도 겉으로 보기엔 평범해 보이는 엽서 한 장으로 시작되었다. 합리적이었던 그의 삶은 남태평양의 어느 섬에 살고 있는 실라라는 이름의 신기하도록 이국적인 여자 때문에 완전히 뒤집혀 버리고 만다. 이 멋지고 독창적인 소설은 일련의 엽서와 편지로 펼쳐지는데, 여기에는 모두 묘한 디자인과 특이한 생물체들과 어둡게 그려진 풍경 등을 담은 삽화가 그려져 있다. 책 속에는 반톡과 실라의 편지가 봉투 안에 그대로 들어 있어서 묘하게 연결된 남남이었던 이 두 사람의 내밀한 서신 왕래를 독자가 들여다볼 수 있도록 되어 있다.

(a) 오래 지속되는 관계를 위한 연애편지의 좋은 예를 몇 가지 알아볼 수 있도록
(b) 이야기에 너무나도 흥미를 갖게 되어 독자가 좋은 책이라고 느끼도록
(c) 묘하게 연결된 남남이었던 이 두 사람의 내밀한 서신 왕래를 독자가 들여다볼 수 있도록
(d) 두 등장인물들의 서로 다른 사고 및 생활 방식을 이해하도록

☀️ **해법** 별 뜻이 없어 보이는 엽서 때문에 반톡과 실라가 인연을 맺은 것이므로 '묘하게 연결된 이 두 사람'이라는 (c)가 정답이다. (a), (b), (d)는 지문에서 근거를 찾을 수 없다.

seemingly innocent 보기엔 별 뜻 없는 **solitary** 고독한 **turn upside down** 뒤집히다 **exotic** 이국적인 **whimsical** 변덕스러운, 별난, 묘한 **bizarre** 별난, 이상한, 색다른 **nestle** 차례로 포개어 넣다 **inexplicably** 이해할 수 없게

✅ **정답** (c)

The commercial for the Honda Accord wagon begins with one cog rolling down and touching another. And then, many other parts—tires, ball bearings, springs, windows, and cams—are sequentially triggered into action. One hundred and twenty seconds later, the wagon rolls down, spreading a banner with the Accord logo. Then, a low voice speaks: "Isn't it nice when things just work?" But two minutes is too long for a TV ad, and a lot of machine-indifferent women will tune out the last 1:45. _____, the ad seems to require that unnecessary complexity to accomplish the simple task of just showing their logo, so it might be more or less opposite to Honda's brand promise of dependable machines.

(a) Furthermore
(b) Resultantly
(c) In fact
(d) Thus

The modern supermarket is a scientifically designed human mousetrap. And you, the customer, are the mouse. If you don't believe that, consider this fact: average supermarket shoppers, even armed with a full shopping list, will buy an extra forty cents of goods for every one dollar they had originally intended to spend. If you asked them why they picked up the extra products, they would say something like, "Oh, I just happened to see something that caught my fancy." Do you think they came across them by chance? Certainly not. The truth is they didn't just "happen" to see that extra item—the supermarket carefully planned it that way. _____, the human mice fell into the trap.

(a) Namely
(b) Similarly
(c) Surprisingly
(d) Moreover

📖 번역   혼다 어코드 왜건 광고는 톱니바퀴 하나가 굴러 내려가서 다른 톱니바퀴를 건드리는 장면으로 시작한다. 그 뒤로는 또 다른 여러 가지 부품들, 즉 타이어, 볼베어링, 스프링, 창문, 캠이 계속해서 움직이도록 이어진다. 120초 후에 왜건이 굴러 내려오면서 어코드 로고가 쓰인 깃발이 펼쳐진다. 이어서 낮은 톤의 목소리가 말한다. "그저 잘 작동하니 다행스럽지 않습니까?" 그러나 TV 광고로 2분은 너무 길 뿐더러 기계에 무관심한 많은 여성들의 경우 나머지 1분 45초 동안 딴전을 부릴 것이다. 게다가 이 광고는 자신들의 로고를 보여주는 그 간단한 작업을 수행하기 위해 불필요하게 복잡함을 빚어낸 것처럼 보여서 '믿을 수 있는 자동차'라는 문구로 혼다 브랜드가 내건 다짐과는 다소 정반대 이미지로 다가올 수도 있는 것 같다.

(a) 게다가
(b) 결과적으로
(c) 사실은
(d) 그러므로

☀ 해법   빈칸 앞의 TV 광고로 2분은 너무 길다는 내용과 기계에 관심이 없는 여성들은 긴 광고에 신경 쓰지 않을 것이라는 내용에 대해 빈칸 뒤의 불필요한 복잡함이 추가되는 흐름이므로 (a)가 정답이다.

commercial 상업의, 영리적인, 광고   **cog** 톱니바퀴의 이   **sequentially** 연속적으로   **tune out** 무시하다, 딴전부리다   **complexity** 복잡함   **more or less** 다소

 정답 (a)

📖 번역   현대의 슈퍼마켓은 과학적으로 고안된 인간용 쥐덫이다. 그리고 고객인 여러분은 바로 쥐다. 이 말을 믿지 못하겠다면 다음 사실을 고려해 보라. 슈퍼마켓에서 물건을 구입하는 보통 사람들은 아무리 꼼꼼하게 작성한 쇼핑 목록으로 무장한다 하더라도 원래 물품 구입으로 지출하려던 금액 1달러당 평균 40센트 어치 물건을 더 구입한다고 한다. 사람들에게 왜 그 물건을 집었는지 물어 보면 그들은 "아, 우연히 사고 싶은 물건이 눈에 들어왔어요"라는 대답을 할 것이다. 진정 그들이 그 물건을 우연히 발견했다고 생각하는가? 절대로 아니다. 사실은 그들이 그 물건을 그저 '우연히' 발견한 게 아니라 슈퍼마켓 업자들이 그렇게 되도록 치밀하게 계획해 두었던 것이다. 즉, 인간 쥐가 덫에 걸려든 것이다.

(a) 즉
(b) 마찬가지로
(c) 놀랍게도
(d) 게다가

☀ 해법   빈칸 앞뒤 문장 내용이 결국 소비자들이 사지 않으려는 물건을 사게 되었다는 근본적으로 동일한 내용이므로 (a)가 정답이다. (c)가 답이 되려면 치밀한 계획에 알게 모르게 걸려든 내용이 와야 한다. 지문 문맥상 빈칸 뒤의 내용이 슈퍼마켓 업자들이 충분히 기대한 일이므로 맞지 않다.

mousetrap 쥐덫   **armed with** ~로 무장한, ~을 갖고 있는   **fancy** 충동, 애호   **come across** (우연히) 만나다, 발견하다

 정답 (a)

When nature hospitalizes an individual, whether he goes to bed in a hospital or in his own home, she takes him out of action so that she may use all of his energies for self-restoration purposes. Also, she gives the individual a much needed rest to discover the power of his own mind, as well as energy in meditation and thought regarding the cause of his pain. _____, he may discover that the cause came from a variety of sins which he might have avoided if he had listened to the voice of pain.

(a) For instance
(b) Ironically
(c) Thus
(d) Yet

 번역 자연이 나서서 사람을 병원이나 집안의 침상에 누워 있도록 할 경우에는 그 사람의 모든 에너지를 자연 치유라는 목적으로 사용하기 위해 그 사람이 움직이지 못하도록 한다. 또한 그가 지닌 마음의 힘을 비롯해서 통증의 원인에 관한 명상과 생각할 수 있는 에너지를 발견할 수 있도록 충분한 휴식을 취하게 해준다. 이렇게 하여 그가 아프게 된 것은 그가 고통의 목소리에 귀 기울였다면 피할 수 있었던 다양한 죄에서 온 것임을 알 수 있게 해준다.

(a) 예를 들면
(b) 아이러니하게도
(c) 이렇게 하여
(d) 그러나

해법 이 문제는 문맥을 정확히 읽어야 한다. 빈칸 앞 문장을 보면 통증의 원인에 관한 명상과 생각할 수 있는 에너지 발견이라고 했고 빈칸 뒤 문장에서 통증의 원인에 대해 알게 된다고 했다. 이때 빈칸 뒤 문장의 문맥은 (명상과 생각을 통해) 통증의 원인에 대해 알게 된다는 것이므로 (c)가 정답이다.

hospitalize 입원시키다 **self-restoration** 자연치유, 자기회복
meditation 명상 **sin** 죄

정답 (c)

There are at large among us today a considerable number of people who make it their business to correct the speech and writings of others. When Winston Churchill says, "It's me," in a radio address, they murmur "It's I," and sit down to write bitter letters to some leading newspaper about "What is Happening to the English Language." Reading "I only had five dollars," they circle only and move it to the right of had with a profound sense of morality. If these people were all retired school teachers of English, their weight in the community would be negligible; but unfortunately they are not. They are authors, businessmen, librarians; _____, they are to be found wherever educated people read and write English.

(a) nevertheless
(b) indeed
(c) even so
(d) thus

번역 오늘날 다른 사람의 연설이나 글을 수정하는 것을 일삼아 하는 사람들이 우리 사이에 상당수 있다. 윈스턴 처칠이 라디오 연설에서 It's me라고 말하면 그들은 It's I라고 중얼거리며 몇 군데 주요 신문사에 오늘날 영어에 무슨 일이 일어나고 있는지에 대해 신랄한 내용의 편지를 써보내기 위해 자리에 앉는다. I only had five dollars를 읽으면서 그들은 심오한 도덕적 관념으로 only에 동그라미를 치고는 그것을 had 오른쪽으로 옮긴다. 만약 이런 사람들 모두가 영어 교사로 일하다가 은퇴한 사람들이라면 우리 사회에서 그들이 차지하는 비중은 거의 무시해도 좋을 것이겠으나, 불행히도 그들은 은퇴한 영어 교사들만이 아니다. 그들은 작가, 사업가, 사서 등 그야말로 교양 있는 사람들이 영어를 읽고 쓰는 곳이라면 어디든 찾아볼 수 있다.

(a) 그럼에도 불구하고
(b) 그야말로
(c) 그렇다 할지라도
(d) 따라서

해법 빈칸 앞의 작가, 사업가, 사서들에 대한 내용과 빈칸 뒤의 이들에 대한 추가적이면서도 교양 있는 사람들이 영어를 읽고 쓰는 곳이라면 어디든 찾아볼 수 있다는 강조의 의미를 볼 때 (b)가 정답이다.

at large 자유로이, 자세히, 일반적으로 **considerable** 꽤 많은, 상당한
bitter 쓴, 신랄한 **profound** 심오한 **morality** 도덕(성) **weight** 무게, 비중

정답 (b)

TEPS Reading Practice | **1** (b)   **2** (a)   **3** (d)   **4** (d)   **5** (a)   **6** (c)   **7** (d)   **8** (b)   **9** (c)   **10** (b)   P25

해설 및 정답 **Unit 02**

Strong and resilient, polyurethane foam is now the most widely used filling for lift-out seat and back cushions. Because it is quite firm, it's most comfortable when wrapped with another material, such as down or polyester batting. To test the quality of a polyurethane-foam cushion, pick one up. If it is very light, it may be made of poor-quality material. _____, an 8-inch cushion that measures 2x3 feet shouldn't weigh less than 3 pounds.

(a) However
(b) In general
(c) Alternatively
(d) Most of all

First of all, if we used Chinese characters officially, traditional culture would be better understood, as most ancient Korean documents are written in Chinese characters. _____, wider use of Chinese characters would help expedite exchanges with Japan, China, and other Asian countries using Chinese characters. So, I think the Ministry has good reason to promote the use of Chinese characters in government papers and on street signs.

(a) In addition
(b) For example
(c) Undoubtedly
(d) For this reason

번역 질기면서도 원형 복구력이 강한 폴리우레탄은 접이식 의자나 의자의 등받이 방석을 채우는 재료로 요즘 가장 널리 사용되고 있다. 꽤 단단하기 때문에 오리털이나 폴리에스테르 솜과 같은 재료로 겉을 쌌을 때 가장 편안하다. 폴리우레탄 방석의 품질을 감정해 보려면 손으로 들어올려 보면 된다. 너무 가벼우면 질 나쁜 재료로 만들어진 것이다. 일반적으로 가로 세로의 길이가 2x3피트, 두께가 8인치인 방석이 3파운드 보다 가벼우면 안 된다.

(a) 그러나
(b) 일반적으로
(c) 대신
(d) 무엇보다

해법 폴리우레탄 방석의 질을 감정해 보려면 들어 봐서 너무 가벼우면 질 나쁜 재료로 만들어진 것이라고 했고, 지문 마지막 문장은 가벼운 제품에 대한 일반적인 기준에 대한 내용이므로 (b)가 정답이다.

resilient 원형 복구력이 있는, 탄성력이 있는 **lift-out seat** 접이식 의자, 이동이 가능한 의자 **batting** 이불 등에 넣는 탄 솜

✓ 정답 (b)

번역 대부분의 한국 고문서는 한자로 씌어 있기 때문에 한자를 공식적으로 쓰게 되면 무엇보다 먼저 전통문화에 대한 이해가 훨씬 쉬워질 것입니다. 게다가 한자 사용이 폭넓어지면 한자를 사용하는 일본, 중국, 기타 아시아 국가들과 교류를 촉진하는 데 도움이 될 것입니다. 그러므로 당국은 정부 문서와 도로표지판에서 한자 사용을 추진할 이유가 충분하다고 생각합니다.

(a) 게다가
(b) 예를 들어
(c) 분명히
(d) 이와 같은 이유로

해법 한자를 공식적으로 쓰게 되면 전통문화에 대한 이해가 쉬워진다는 긍정적인 내용에 일본, 중국, 기타 아시아 국가들과 교류를 촉진하는데 도움이 될 것이라는 내용이 추가된 것이므로 (a)가 정답이다. (c)는 앞 문장과 연결되지 않는다. (b)는 지문 앞에 있을 법한 공식적인 한자사용을 찬성한다는 전제 다음, 즉 지문 앞 부분의 First of all 대신에 올 수 있다.

character 문자 **expedite** 촉진하다, 신속히 처리하다, 급송하다
exchange 교역하다 **promote** 촉진하다

✓ 정답 (a)

When both parents have professional careers that are on the fast-track, their children can often be very anxious and competitive, and feel a lot of pressure to be as successful as their parents. They also show a lot of the problems that children of divorced parents show. _____, just like children who come from broken homes, they don't get enough parental supervision, nor attention.

(a) Obviously
(b) Hence
(c) Similarly
(d) Or

번역 부모가 모두 승승장구하는 전문 직업을 갖고 있을 경우 아이들은 종종 불안 심리와 경쟁 심리를 드러낼 수 있으며, 엄마, 아빠처럼 성공해야 한다는 압박감을 심하게 느끼기도 한다. 또한 이들은 이혼한 부모의 아이들이 보이는 문제점들을 많이 보이기도 한다. 즉, 결손 가정의 아이들처럼 이들은 부모로부터 충분한 감독과 관심을 받지 못한다는 것이다.

(a) 분명히
(b) 따라서
(c) 마찬가지로
(d) 즉

해법 빈칸 앞뒤 내용이 결국 같은 내용이므로 (d)가 정답인데 or가 '또는'이란 의미 외에 '즉'이란 의미도 있다는 것을 알아야 한다. (c)는 빈칸 앞 문장의 They와 빈칸 뒤 문장의 they가 결국 같은 대상이므로 오답이다. 즉, Similarly는 내용은 비슷하나 대상이 다를 때 사용한다.

fast-track 승진이 빠른 **competitive** 경쟁심이 강한 **broken home** 결손 가정 **supervision** 감독

정답 (d)

In this century, livestock is undergoing a dramatic change. You are still able to buy a steak at your local meat counter, but it comes from animals produced by new high-tech methods of farming. For example, the steers here are cloned: identical copies produced from the genes of one genetically superior animal. Bred to grow faster, with less fat, and needing less feed. But meat has an inherent problem—cholesterol. _____, numerous meat substitutes are being developed.

(a) Instead
(b) In conclusion
(c) For all that
(d) Consequently

번역 현 세기에 가축은 극적인 변화를 겪고 있다. 여전히 가까운 정육점에서 고기를 살 수는 있지만 이 고기는 새로운 첨단 목축 기술에 의해 생산된 것이다. 예를 들어 여기에서 판매하는 수송아지는 복제된 것으로, 유전적으로 우수한 송아지의 유전자로부터 복제해서 생산된 것이다. 이들은 더 빨리 자라고 지방은 적으며 사료도 덜 먹도록 키워진다. 그러나 고기는 콜레스테롤이라는 내재적 문제를 여전히 안고 있다. 따라서 다양한 육류 대체품들이 개발 중에 있다.

(a) 대신에
(b) 결론적으로
(c) 그럼에도 불구하고
(d) 따라서

해법 콜레스테롤이라는 내재적 문제를 해결하기 위해 육류 대체품들이 개발 중이라는 흐름이므로 (d)가 정답이다. (a) 다음에는 육류 대체품들의 좋은 점이 와야 한다.

livestock 가축 **undergo** 겪다 **steer** (식용의) 거세한 수소 **clone** 복제하다 **identical** 동일한 **gene** 유전자 **genetically** 유전적으로 **inherent** 내재적인, 타고난

정답 (d)

When we settled in the Upper East Side, it was filled with galleries. Its variety of cultural attractions reminded us of Mexico City, where we had grown up. But we were beginning to get tired of the neighborhood's party atmosphere. _____, when we were expecting our first baby, suddenly our apartment on the third floor of a brownstone didn't seem like the best place to live. It didn't have a second bedroom, and it posed the problem of stairs, which are intimidating with a baby in one arm and a stroller in the other.

(a) Furthermore
(b) Apart from that
(c) Worst of all
(d) Strangely

The investigating commission announced on Saturday that preliminary findings showed that the Kursk was involved in a collision with an object near the surface weighing 8,000 tons or more. The Russian government said it was possible that such an object could have been a ship or an old mine. _____, some unknown chain of events could have set off an explosion aboard the submarine. Whatever the case, Russian officials say most of the crew died in the first two minutes after the explosion, including all the officers on the bridge.

(a) Besides
(b) If so
(c) Alternatively
(d) By contrast

번역 우리가 어퍼 이스트 사이드에 정착했을 당시 그곳은 화랑들로 가득 차 있었다. 그곳 사람들의 다양한 삶의 형태는 우리가 자란 멕시코 시티를 연상시켰다. 그러나 서서히 이웃의 시끌벅적거리는 잔치 분위기가 지겨워지기 시작했다. 더구나 첫째 아이의 출산을 앞두자 갈색 건물 3층에 위치한 우리 아파트가 우리가 살기에 최상의 장소가 아닌 것으로 갑자기 느껴졌다. 침실도 하나밖에 없는 것만 문제가 되었던 게 아니라 아이를 한 팔에 안고 다른 손에는 유모차를 들고 오르내리기엔 겁이 나는 계단도 문제로 드러났다.

(a) 게다가
(b) 그것 말고는
(c) 최악인 것은
(d) 이상하게도

해법 시끌벅적한 이웃이라는 부정적인 내용에 아파트가 살기에 최상의 장소로 보이지 않았다는 또 다른 부정적인 내용이 첨가된 것이므로 (a)가 정답이다. (c)는 빈칸 뒤 내용이 최악의 상황으로 볼 만한 근거가 지문에 없고, (d)는 빈칸 앞 문장과 연결되지 않는다.

settle in ~에 정착하다 **brownstone** 적갈색의 사암(砂岩) **intimidate** 위협하다, 협박하다 **stroller** 유모차

정답 (a)

번역 토요일 조사 위원회는 예비 조사 결과 쿠르스크 호가 8,000톤 이상의 물체와 수면 가까이에서 충돌한 것으로 드러났다고 발표했다. 러시아 정부는 그런 물체는 선박이거나 낡은 수뢰일 가능성도 있다고 밝혔다. 그것이 아니라면 아직 밝혀지지 않은 일련의 사건들로 인해 잠수함에서의 내부 폭발이 촉발되었을 가능성도 있다. 어떤 경우이든 폭발 후 2분 안에 조종실의 장교들을 포함하여 대부분의 선원들이 사망했다고 러시아 관리들은 말한다.

(a) 게다가
(b) 그렇다면
(c) 그것이 아니라면
(d) 대조적으로

해법 지문 마지막 문장의 Whatever the case에서 정답 (c)에 대한 힌트를 얻을 수 있다.

investigating commission 조사 위원회 **preliminary findings** 예비 조사 결과 **mine** 지뢰, 수뢰 **set off** 폭발시키다 **submarine** 잠수함

정답 (c)

Computers are too clever to ignore but too stupid to be trusted entirely. For over 35 years researchers have been struggling to build a computer in man's image. They are not even close to doing so. Although scientists have succeeded in giving machines all sorts of human skills, the goal of creating a machine as clever as a person seems to recede all the time. _____, this failure may eventually change the way in which people work and live more comprehensively than if scientists had succeeded in getting a computer to sit up and say, "Mother!"

(a) Indeed
(b) Resultantly
(c) Additionally
(d) Ironically

Financial experts admit they are puzzled by the market's strange behavior during the previous day's trading. Although all the economic signs indicated that the market would rise, the market nosedived instead and lost over 5% of its value in the first three hours of trading. Experts stated there was no logical reason for this. Some economists insisted that investors were merely involved in profit taking. Experts stated that the market was due for a slight negative correction. _____, a large majority of brokers are high on the market and don't expect today's losses to reoccur any time in the near future.

(a) Unbelievably
(b) Nevertheless
(c) Eventually
(d) Meanwhile

 번역 컴퓨터는 무시하기엔 너무 똑똑하지만 전적으로 신뢰하기엔 너무 멍청하다. 35년이 넘도록 과학자들은 인간 형상의 컴퓨터를 만들어 내려고 안간힘을 써왔다. 그러나 그들은 아직 그 목표에 근접도 못하고 있다. 비록 과학자들이 인간의 온갖 기술을 컴퓨터에 부여하는 데 성공했지만 인간 못지않게 영리한 컴퓨터를 만들겠다는 목표는 줄곧 후퇴하는 것으로 보인다. 모순되는 것은 이 실패가 결국은 과학자들이 컴퓨터에게 일어나 앉아서 "엄마!"라고 말하게 하는 데 성공을 거두었을 경우보다 사람들이 일하고 생활하는 방식을 완전히 변화시킬지도 모른다는 것이다.

(a) 실로
(b) 결과적으로
(c) 게다가
(d) 모순되는 것은

해법 인간과 같이 영리한 컴퓨터를 만들겠다는 목표는 줄곧 후퇴하는 것으로 보인다는 내용과 이 실패가 결국 사람들이 일하고 생활하는 방식을 포괄적으로 변화시킬지 모른다는 내용은 반대되므로 (d)가 정답이다.

clever 똑똑한 **struggle** 애쓰다 **recede** 물러나다
comprehensively 완전히 **sit up** 일어나 앉다

✓ **정답** (d)

 번역 재정 전문가들은 전날 거래 동안 주식 시장이 이상하게 움직여 당황했음을 인정한다. 모든 경제 신호가 시장이 상승할 것으로 신호를 보냈음에도 올라가는 대신 곤두박질쳐서 거래 시작 초반 3시간 동안 시가가 5퍼센트 이상 손실되었다. 전문가들은 이러한 결과를 설명할 논리적 근거가 없다고 말했다. 어떤 경제학자들은 투자가들이 단지 이익을 챙기는 데 관여했던 것이라고 주장했다. 전문가들은 시장이 소폭 자율 반락을 하게 되어 있었다고 말했다. 그럼에도 불구하고 대다수의 주식 중개인들은 주식 시장을 낙관하면서 오늘의 손실이 조만간에는 다시 일어나지 않을 것이라고 보고 있다.

(a) 믿을 수 없게도
(b) 그럼에도 불구하고
(c) 결국
(d) 그 동안

해법 전문가들이 시장이 다소 소극적인 수정을 하게 되어 있었다고 말했다는 내용과 주식 중개인들이 주식 시장을 낙관하면서 오늘의 손실은 다시 일어나지 않을 것이라고 기대한다는 내용은 반대되므로 (b)가 정답이다. (a)는 빈칸 앞 문장과 연결되지 않는다.

puzzle 당황하게 하다 **nosedive** 급강하다, 폭락하다 **merely** 단지
broker 주식 중개인

✓ **정답** (b)

For their existence and comfort, men depend on certain products of the earth. These cannot be used in common, however, without certain disputes arising, nor do natural products suffice unless they are improved by human labor. Yet no one works unless he will receive some benefits to himself. Therefore, certain rules arise implying a mutual recognition of rights and the institution of private property. _____, such is a general utilitarian account of the origin of the ideal of justice and of its relation to human interests.

(a) Even so
(b) Yet
(c) Briefly
(d) Accordingly

번역 생존과 안락을 위해 인간은 지구의 산물에 의존한다. 그러나 이들 재화는 반드시 어떤 분쟁이 야기되지 않고는 공동으로 사용할 수 없으며, 또한 인간의 노동에 의해 개선되지 않은 자연 상태의 재화는 사용할 만큼 충분해지지 않는다. 그러나 자신에게 돌아오는 혜택이 없다면 아무도 일하지 않으려 한다. 따라서 권리에 대한 상호 인식과 사유 재산 제도를 암시하는 몇 가지 규칙이 발생하게 된다. 간단히 말해, 이런 것이 바로 일반적인 공리주의에서 말하는 이상적인 정의의 기원과 그 정의와 인간의 이익과의 관계에 대한 설명이다.

(a) 그렇다 할지라도
(b) 그러나
(c) 간단히 말해
(d) 따라서

해법 빈칸 앞에 나오는 권리에 대한 상호 인식과 사유 재산 제도를 암시하는 몇 가지 규칙의 발생이 빈칸 뒤에 나오는 이상적인 정의의 기원과 정의와 인간의 이익과의 관계는 결국 같은 의미이므로 (c)가 정답이다.

suffice 충분하다 **mutual recognition** 상호 인식 **the institution of private property** 사유 재산 제도 **utilitarian** 공리주의적인 **account** 설명

정답 (c)

Hamlet is possibly Shakespeare's—and the English language's—most famous play. Though it was written as a play, numerous film versions have also been produced since the early 1900s. Most notable of these are probably the 1948, 1990, and 1996 versions. Sir Laurence Olivier both directed and starred in the title role of the 1948 version. Olivier worked hard to change the play visually from a production intended for the stage to one for the movie screen. Interestingly, Olivier was 41 when he made his film. Hamlet is supposed to be 30. _____, the actress who played Hamlet's mother was in her late 20s when the movie was filmed! Nevertheless, Olivier's efforts won him Best Film and Best Actor Oscars.

(a) Likewise
(b) Furthermore
(c) Unfortunately
(d) On the other hand

번역 〈햄릿〉은 아마도 셰익스피어뿐만 아니라 영문학 중에서 가장 유명한 희곡일 것이다. 원래 희곡으로 쓰였지만 1900년대 초반 이후에는 영화로도 많이 만들어졌다. 이 중 가장 두드러지는 작품은 아마도 1948년, 1990년, 1996년 판일 것이다. 로렌스 올리비에 경은 1948년 판에서 감독과 주연을 맡았다. 그는 무대용으로 만들어진 작품을 영화에 맞게 시각적으로 변화시키려고 열심히 노력했다. 흥미로운 것은 올리비에가 그 영화를 만들었을 때 나이가 41세였다는 점이다. 햄릿의 나이는 원래 30세여야 하는데 말이다. 게다가 햄릿의 어머니 역할을 맡은 여배우가 그 영화를 찍을 때의 나이는 20대 후반이었다. 그럼에도 불구하고 올리비에는 노력의 대가로 최고 작품상과 최고 남우주연상을 받았다.

(a) 그와 마찬가지로
(b) 게다가
(c) 불행히도
(d) 다른 한 편으로는

해법 빈칸 앞에 영화 속 햄릿은 30세인데 햄릿 역을 맡은 로렌스 올리비에는 41세였고, 여기에 더불어 햄릿의 어머니 역을 맡은 여배우는 20대 후반이었음에도 불구하고 좋은 결과가 있었다는 흐름이므로 (b)가 정답이다.

possibly 아마 **play** 연극 **notable** 두드러진 **sir** 경 **star** 주연하다 **film** 촬영하다

정답 (b)

The Etruscans lived in a part of Italy that is called Tuscany today. They were good sailors, and after about 700 B.C. they were known in the Mediterranean area both as merchants and as pirates. An Etruscan empire began to spread throughout Italy and the surrounding lands. About 616 B.C., Rome, which was a very small village, was conquered without difficulty by the Etruscans. Under the Etruscans a great construction period turned Rome into a large, powerful city for the first time. Then, in 510 B.C., the Etruscan king was driven into exile, and Rome became an independent republic.

Q: What is the passage mainly about?
(a) The rise and fall of the Etruscan empire
(b) The Etruscans' construction technology
(c) The emergence of the Roman Empire
(d) The Etruscan influence on Rome

Many ferns grow in the rich soils of forests, but some seem to be growing out of rocks. These ferns can't grow in a place with rich soil. They only grow in rocky areas. They live in just a little bit of soil that is found in the cracks in rocks. That soil is different from soil that is on the ground. It takes many years for the soil to form there. Some of it is washed down into the rocks, and some is blown in by the wind. Part is made by plants that die on the rock, and part is made by frost, which causes tiny pieces of the rock to split off. The soil has the right combination of ingredients to support the life of a fern.

Q: What is the passage mainly about?
(a) Two kinds of soil for ferns
(b) Ferns growing in rocky areas
(c) Formation of soil in rocks that supports some ferns
(d) Factors that make rocks crack for ferns to live in

번역 에트루리아인들은 오늘날 토스카나라 불리는 이탈리아의 한 지역에서 살았다. 그들은 훌륭한 선원들이었는데 기원전 약 700년경 이후 지중해 지역에서는 상인과 해적으로 알려졌다. 에트루리아 제국은 이탈리아 전역과 주변 지역으로 세력을 확장하기 시작했다. 기원전 약 616년 당시 아주 작은 마을이었던 로마는 에트루리아인들에게 쉽게 정복당했다. 에트루리아인들의 통치 하에 이루어진 대대적인 건설은 로마를 처음으로 강력한 대규모 도시로 변모시켰다. 그 이후 기원전 510년에 에트루리아 왕이 추방당했고 로마는 독립 공화국이 되었다.

(a) 에트루리아 제국의 흥망
(b) 에투루리아의 건축 기술
(c) 로마 제국의 등장
(d) 로마에 끼친 에투루리아의 영향

해법 에트루리아인들에 대한 언급을 시작으로 지문 세 번째 문장에서 에트루리아 제국의 확장과 더불어 로마로부터 에트루리아 왕의 추방이 지문의 주요 내용이므로 (a)가 정답이다. (b)와 (d)는 지문의 Under the Etruscans a great construction period turned Rome into a large, powerful city for the first time을, (c)는 지문 마지막 문장을 이용한 것이다.

sailor 선원 **the Mediterranean** 지중해 **merchant** 상인 **pirate** 해적 **conquer** 정복하다 **exile** 추방(하다), 망명 **republic** 공화국

 정답 (a)

번역 많은 양치류는 토질이 풍부한 숲에서 자라지만 어떤 것들은 바위에서 자란다. 이런 양치류는 토질이 기름진 곳에서 자라지 못한다. 오직 바위 지역에서 자란다. 이들은 바위틈에 있는 극소량의 토양에서 산다. 이 흙은 땅의 흙과는 다르다. 이렇게 바위틈에 흙이 쌓이기까지는 여러 해 세월이 걸린다. 때로는 물에 씻겨 바위로 들어가는 경우도 있고 바람에 날려 들어가기도 한다. 또한 일부는 바위 위에서 죽은 식물로 인해서 생기는 경우도 있고 서리로 인한 경우도 있는데, 서리는 바위의 작은 조각들이 떨어져서 갈라지게 만든다. 그렇게 형성된 흙에는 양치류가 살기에 적합한 영양소가 조합되어 있다.

(a) 양치류를 위한 두 종류의 흙
(b) 바위 지역에서 자라는 양치류
(c) 일부 양치류를 위한 바위 안의 흙 생성
(d) 양치류가 살 수 있도록 바위를 갈라지게 하는 요인들

해법 지문의 They live in just a little bit of soil that is found in the cracks in rocks 이후 내용을 종합해 보면 양치류가 살기 적절한 흙 생성이 지문 핵심 내용이므로 (c)가 정답이다. (a)는 지문에 구체적으로 언급되지 않은 내용이고, (b)는 지문의 초점이 ferns가 아니라 바위 속에 생기는 흙이고, (d)는 지문에서 바위가 갈라지게 하는 원인으로 frost 한 가지만 나왔다.

fern 양치류 **rich** 풍부한, 기름진 **soil** 흙, 토양 **crack** 갈라진 틈; 갈라지다 **frost** 서리(로 덮다) **split off** 갈라지다 **combination** 조합 **ingredient** 성분

 정답 (c)

Ambrose Burnside would have preferred to be known as a war hero. Instead, his name makes us think of whiskers. Burnside was an army general. He fought for the Union Army in the Civil War. Unlike many men of the time, Burnside had no beard. But he did grow short whiskers down the sides of his face. The whiskers covered part of his cheeks. Other men began to imitate Burnside's unique whiskers. At first they called them "burnside," after the general. After a time, though, the name was changed to sideburns, possibly because they are grown on the sides of the face. If it doesn't seem to make much sense, think about this—it's better than naming them after the general by calling them Ambroses.

Q: What is the main topic of the passage?
(a) How whiskers had another name
(b) How "burnside" changed to "sideburns"
(c) Why whiskers are not called Ambroses
(d) Who first grew whiskers in history

The kudzu plant is considered an uncontrollable nuisance in the southern United States. Kudzu, introduced to the U.S. from Japan in 1876, is a spreading vine that moved into 18 American states stretching from Alabama to Massachusetts. In the south, kudzu plants can grow as much as a foot per day with root systems stretching 12 feet. The irony is that while kudzu is seen as an unwanted nuisance in the U.S., it is in demand in Japan where it is used to make starch and certain food products. Because of this, officials from Alabama cities traveled to Tokyo to discuss selling their surplus of kudzu to Japanese companies. They were interested and agreed to finance a kudzu farm in Alabama.

Q: What is the best title of the passage?
(a) The Past and Future of Kudzu
(b) Kudzu, America's New Business
(c) What's Good and Bad about Kudzu
(d) Popularity of Kudzu in Japan

번역 앰브로스 번사이드는 사람들이 자신을 전쟁 영웅으로 알아주기를 더 원했을 것이다. 그러나 그의 이름은 구레나룻을 생각나게 한다. 번사이드는 육군 장군이었다. 그는 미국 남북 전쟁에서 북부군으로 싸웠다. 번사이드는 당시의 많은 다른 남자들과는 달리 턱수염을 기르지 않았다. 그 대신 얼굴 양쪽을 타고 내려오는 짧은 구레나룻을 길렀다. 구레나룻은 그의 볼 일부를 덮었다. 다른 남자들이 번사이드의 독특한 구레나룻을 따라하기 시작했다. 처음에는 장군의 이름을 따서 구레나룻을 '번사이드'라고 불렀다. 시간이 흐른 후에 아마도 얼굴 양쪽에 기르는 것 때문이었는지 사이드번스로 이름이 바뀌었다. 이 이야기가 별로 말이 되지 않는 것 같이 느껴진다면 이렇게 생각해 보자. 장군의 이름을 따서 앰브로시스라고 부르는 것보다는 이 편이 낫다.

(a) 구레나룻이 어떻게 다른 이름을 갖게 되었나
(b) burnside가 어떻게 sideburns로 바뀌게 되었나
(c) 구레나룻이 왜 앰브로시스라고 불리지 않게 되었나
(d) 역사상 누가 최초로 구레나룻을 길렀나

해법 지문의 his name makes us think of whiskers와 Other men began to imitate Burnside's unique whiskers 이하의 내용들을 종합해 보면 (a)가 정답이다. (b)는 선택지의 burnside가 whiskers로 돼야 하고, (c)는 지문 마지막 문장을 이용했으며, (d)는 앰브로스 번사이드 장군이 역사상 가장 먼저 구레나룻을 기른 것은 아니다.

whiskers 구레나룻 general 장군 the Union Army 북부군
the Civil War 미국의 남북 전쟁 beard 턱수염 cheek 볼, 뺨

 정답 (a)

번역 칡은 미국의 남부지방에서 해결 방법이 없는 골칫거리로 여겨진다. 1876년에 일본에서 미국으로 도입된 칡은 앨라배마에서 매사추세츠에 이르기까지 18개 주에 퍼진 덩굴 식물이다. 남부지방에서는 근계가 12피트나 뻗어 나가며 칡은 하루에 최고 1피트까지 자랄 수 있다. 공교로운 사실은 미국에서는 원치 않는 골칫거리로 여겨지는 반면, 일본에서는 전분과 특정 음식을 만드는 데 사용되기 때문에 수요가 많다는 것이다. 이 때문에 앨라배마 주 각 시의 공무원들은 남아도는 칡을 일본 회사들에 판매하는 방안을 의논하기 위해서 도쿄를 방문했다. 일본회사들은 이 제안에 관심을 가졌고 앨라배마의 칡 농장에 재정적 지원을 하는 데 동의했다.

(a) 칡의 과거와 미래
(b) 칡, 미국의 새로운 사업
(c) 칡의 장단점
(d) 일본에서 칡의 인기

해법 이 지문 다섯 번째 문장을 보면 골칫거리였던 칡이 미국의 새로운 사업 아이템이 된 것이 지문 핵심 내용이므로 (b)가 정답이다. (a)는 지문에서 칡의 현재에 대한 내용도 있어 오답이고, (c)는 지문에서 구체적으로 나와 있지 않고, (d)는 지문의 it is in demand in Japan where it is used to make starch and certain food products 라는 지엽적인 내용을 이용했다.

kudzu 칡 nuisance 귀찮은 것, 골칫거리 vine 덩굴 식물 stretch 퍼지다, 뻗어나다 starch 녹말, 전분 surplus 과잉, 잉여 finance 자금을 조달하다

 정답 (b)

Infants are not self-conscious about cameras. They do not know what the camera is for, and this innocence allows us to capture their native actions. But the child learns very quickly, and by the age of five or six he may not be able to stand in front of a camera without frowning and feeling ill at ease. In most cases, this feeling is gradually brought under the control of an adjusting response which is a pose. Studying how poses change with time, in different social classes, in different cultures, and through the growth and maturation of the individual, is a first-class research problem.

Q: What is the passage mainly about?
(a) Infants becoming conscious of their surroundings
(b) The importance of studying what makes poses change
(c) Poses made by babies from different backgrounds
(d) Studying poses to take better pictures of infants

번역 아기들은 카메라를 의식하지 않는다. 카메라가 무엇인지도 모르는 순진함 때문에 자연스런 모습과 동작을 찍을 수 있다. 그러나 어린아이는 학습속도가 빨라 5~6세 정도에 이르러 카메라 앞에만 서면 얼굴을 찡그리고 불안해 한다. 대부분의 경우, 이런 감정은 점점 조정되어 결국 적응했다는 반응으로써 포즈를 취하는 동작을 보인다. 갓난아기가 시간의 흐름에 따라 다른 사회 계층에서, 다른 문화에서, 그리고 개인의 성장과 성숙을 통해 포즈가 어떻게 변하는지 연구하는 것이 최우선 과제다.

(a) 주변 환경을 의식하게 되는 아기들
(b) 포즈를 변하게 하는 것에 대한 연구의 중요성
(c) 다른 배경 출신의 아기들이 취하는 포즈
(d) 아기 사진을 더 잘 찍기 위한 포즈 연구

해법 글쓴이가 정작 말하고 싶은 내용은 시간이 지나고 기타 여러 요소들로 인해 포즈에 변화가 생기는 것을 연구하는 것이 최우선 과제라는 것이므로 (b)가 정답이다. (a)는 지문 앞부분만을 이용했고, (c)는 지문이 아기들의 다양한 포즈들에 대한 내용이 아니며, (d)는 지문에 없는 내용이다.

infant 아기, 유아   **conscious** 의식하는   **innocence** 순진, 천진
frown 얼굴을 찡그리다   **feel ill at ease** 불안한   **gradually** 점차적으로
maturation 성숙

 정답 (b)

Mathematics is a highly effective thinking system made even more effective by our invention of the computer. Thanks to mathematics we can perform such unthinkable operations as landing men on the moon, letting them drive round on the surface, hearing and watching them do it, and then bringing them safely back to earth. But getting to the moon is easier than solving social poverty, juvenile offense, or a simple strike. On the earth, most situations are interrelated, subjective, and vague, changing in value and dependent on human impulse. If we could translate every situation into definite relationships and symbols, we should never need to look beyond mathematics for our thinking.

Q: What is the passage mainly about?
(a) The necessity of creating a new mathematical thinking system
(b) Mathematical applications in astronomy and social science
(c) Computers as one of the greatest mathematical inventions to solve problems
(d) The usefulness and limitations of mathematics as a thinking system

번역 수학은 매우 효율적인 사고 체계로 컴퓨터의 발명으로 그 효율성이 강화되었다. 수학 덕분에 이전에는 상상도 못했던 일인 인간을 달에 착륙시켜서 달 표면을 운전하고 돌아다니게 하고, 또 이런 그들의 모습을 보고 목소리를 들을 수 있으며, 이들을 다시 지구로 안전하게 귀환시키는 일을 행할 수 있게 되었다. 그런데 달에 가는 것이 사회적 빈곤, 청소년 범죄 혹은 작은 파업 사태를 해결하는 것보다도 쉽다. 지구상 대부분의 문제는 서로 얽혀 있으며 주관적이고 애매해서 가치도 변하고 인간의 충동에 의해 좌지우지된다. 우리 주변의 모든 문제들을 딱 부러지는 관계와 기호로 해석해서 도식화만 할 수 있다면 우리의 사고는 수학 이상의 것을 볼 필요가 없을 것이다.

(a) 새로운 수학적 사고 체계를 만들 필요성
(b) 천문학과 사회학에서의 수학적 응용
(c) 문제 해결을 위한 가장 훌륭한 수학적 발명 중 하나로써의 컴퓨터
(d) 사고 체계로써 수학의 유용성과 한계

해법 지문 첫 문장과 지문의 But getting … a simple strike 이하의 내용을 종합해 보면 수학의 유용성과 한계가 지문 핵심 내용이므로 (d)가 정답이다. (a)는 지문 마지막 문장을 이용했고, (b)는 social science(사회학)에서 수학이 응용된 구체적인 내용이 지문에 없고, (c)는 지문 첫 문장을 이용했다.

highly 매우   **effective** 효율적인   **juvenile** 청소년   **interrelated** 서로 관련이 있는   **vague** 막연한, 애매한   **impulse** 충동

 정답 (d)

Dear Sirs,

Upon examination of the received order, we found that 12 SO 305 lenses had been sent by mistake in place of the ordered SO 307's. In view of the fact that this is not the first time such a mistake has been made and that we have to satisfy our customers immediately, we would appreciate it if you would send us the SO 307's by the quickest possible means at your expense. To simplify the handling of the SO 305's, we would be happy to take them off your hands at a 20% discount in order to save you the expense of having to pay for the return postage.

We look forward to your dealing with this matter without delay.

Very truly yours,
Bob Tracer

Q: What did Bob Tracer write the letter mainly for?

(a) To report a wrong delivery of SO 305 lenses
(b) To have a problem solved right after it's being recognized
(c) To order SO 307 lenses again at a discounted price
(d) To complain about a repeated mistake

The stripes stay striped in striped toothpaste because they get striped at the last minute. The red stripe color is stored in the cone-shaped part at the top of the tube. It surrounds an inner, slotted tube that extends part of the way into the main tube. The white paste fills the rest of the main tube. When it is squeezed up, the white paste presses on the red color. That forces the red color out through the slots in the small tube. And because the white paste has to pass through that same small tube, the two pastes meet. Therefore, just before they leave the main tube, the red color and the white paste join up to make big, bold stripes.

Q: What is the main topic of the passage?

(a) How to mix different kinds of toothpaste
(b) How striped toothpaste comes out striped
(c) What makes striped toothpaste popular
(d) What is in striped toothpaste

번역 수령한 주문 상품을 살펴보니 주문한 SO 307 렌즈 대신에 SO 305 렌즈 12개를 보내셨음을 알게 됐습니다. 이런 실수가 이번이 처음이 아니고 저희는 당장 고객들을 만족시켜야 한다는 점을 놓고 볼 때, 배송비는 귀사의 부담으로 가능한 최대의 빠른 방법으로 SO 307 렌즈를 보내주시면 감사하겠습니다. SO 305 렌즈의 처리 문제를 간소화하는 방법으로 귀사가 반송용 우편 요금을 지불하는 대신 20% 할인된 가격에 구입할 의사가 있음을 밝힙니다.
이 문제를 지체 없이 처리해 주시길 기대합니다.

(a) S 305 렌즈의 배달 착오를 알리기 위해
(b) 발견 즉시 문제 해결을 위해
(c) 할인된 가격으로 SO 307 렌즈를 재주문하기 위해
(d) 반복된 같은 실수에 대해 불만을 토로하기 위해

해법 지문 마지막에서 다시 한 번 이 문제를 지체하지 않고 처리해 달라고 했으므로 (b)가 정답이다. (c)는 SO 307 렌즈를 이미 주문했으므로 선택지의 again이 맞지 않고, (d)는 이런 실수가 이번이 처음이 아니라는 내용 때문에 착각할 수 있지만 편지를 쓴 사람이 정말 하고픈 이야기는 아니다.

in place of ~대신에(instead of) **in view of** ~을 고려하여 **means** 수단, 방법 **return postage** 반송용 우편 요금

정답 (b)

번역 줄무늬 치약의 줄무늬가 끝까지 남을 수 있는 것은 마지막 순간에 줄무늬가 되기 때문이다. 줄무늬를 내는 빨간색은 튜브 위 고깔 모양의 부분에 담겨져 있다. 이 고깔 모양 부분은 주 튜브 안으로 어느 정도 뻗어 있는 가늘고 긴 구멍이 난 튜브를 둘러싸고 있다. 하얀 치약은 주 튜브의 나머지를 채운다. 튜브를 짤 때 하얀 치약이 빨간색 치약에 압박을 가하게 된다. 이로 인해 작은 튜브 안에 있던 빨간색이 구멍을 통해 나온다. 그 순간 하얀 치약도 같은 작은 튜브를 통과해서 나와야 하기 때문에 두 치약이 만나게 된다. 그러므로 주 튜브를 떠나기 직전에 빨간색과 하얀 치약이 합쳐지게 되어 있어 크고 뚜렷한 줄무늬가 만들어질 수 있는 것이다.

(a) 다른 종류의 치약을 섞는 방법
(b) 줄무늬 치약이 줄무늬로 나오는 방법
(c) 줄무늬 치약이 인기 있는 이유
(d) 줄무늬 치약 안에 무엇이 있나

해법 지문 마지막 문장 Therefore, just before they leave the main tube, the red color and the white paste join up to make big, bold stripes를 중심으로 보면 지문 전반적으로 어떻게 줄무늬 치약이 섞이지 않고 줄무늬로 나오는지 설명하고 있으므로 (b)가 정답이다. (a), (c)는 지문에 없는 내용이고, (d)는 줄무늬 치약 자체에 무엇이 들어 있는지 지문에 없다.

stripe 줄무늬 **toothpaste** 치약 **cone-shaped** 고깔 모양의 **surround** 둘러싸다, 에워싸다 **slot** 구멍을 뚫다; 가늘고 긴 구멍 **extend** 뻗다, 연장하다 **squeeze up** 짜올리다 **bold** 굵은

정답 (b)

The game birds' play with the wind consists of practiced movements which are simply enjoyed for their own sake. These are not instinctive actions, but are carefully learned. Their accomplishments— use of the wind, amazing judgment of distances, and understanding of wind conditions—are all acquired skills. They play with the wind like cats play with mice. They let the wind throw them into the air. Then with a wave of wings, they turn themselves over and dive downward. Another snap of the wings returns them to their normal position. They playfully shoot away to the west to annoy the invisible monster that tries to drive them eastward.

Q: What is the main focus of the passage?
(a) Game birds flying against the wind
(b) Game birds teaching their young to fly
(c) Game birds using the wind for no reason
(d) Game birds practicing with the wind to have fun

 번역 엽조가 바람으로 장난치는 행위는 순전히 재미 삼아서 연마된 동작이다. 이것은 본능적인 행동이 아니라 주의 깊게 학습된 것이다. 바람을 이용하는 기술과 놀라운 거리감, 바람 상태 감지능력 등의 재주는 모두 연습을 통해 습득된 기술이다. 엽조는 고양이가 쥐를 가지고 놀듯이 바람을 가지고 논다. 바람이 가는 대로 몸을 맡긴다. 그러다가 한 번의 날갯짓으로 자세를 뒤집어 급하강한다. 또 다시 한 번의 날갯짓으로 원래 위치로 되돌아온다. 엽조는 자신을 동쪽으로 몰고 가려는 보이지 않는 괴물을 괴롭히려고 장난스럽게 서쪽으로 쏜살같이 날아가 버리기도 한다.

(a) 바람에 맞서 나는 엽조
(b) 새끼에게 나는 법을 가르치는 엽조
(c) 이유 없이 바람을 이용하는 엽조
(d) 재미 삼아 바람으로 연습하는 엽조

해법 지문 첫 문장을 중심으로 생각해보면 엽조가 재미를 위해 바람을 이용하는 것이 지문 핵심 내용으로 (d)가 정답이다. (a)는 지문 마지막 문장을 이용했고, (b)는 지문의 These are not instinctive actions, but are carefully learned 때문에 착각할 수 있지만 지엽적인 내용이다. (c)는 no reason이 지문 첫 문장의 simply enjoyed for their own sake와 맞지 않다.

consist of ~로 구성하다 **for one's own sake** ~만을 위해
instinctive 본능적인 **accomplishment** 이뤄놓은 일, 업적 **acquire** 습득하다, 익히다 **the invisible monster** 보이지 않는 괴물 (지문 문맥으로는 '바람'을 의미)

✓ 정답 (d)

When Cortez and his Spanish soldiers first met the Aztecs in 1520, they were greeted with a drink normally reserved for the god-king only—hot chocolate. However, it was quite a different drink from the cheery cocoa enjoyed today. It was really hot. The Aztecs served hot chocolate laced with ground chili peppers instead of sugar. Needless to say, the Spaniards weren't very impressed with the drink. The cocoa plant was very important to the Aztecs, however. They used the tree's flowers to cure apathy and timidity, its bark for stomach trouble, and its butter for burns. They even used the beans as currency.

Q: What is the best title of the passage?
(a) History of Chocolate
(b) The Aztec's Use of the Cocoa Plant
(c) How the Aztecs Treated Spanish Visitors
(d) How Chocolate was Used in the 1500s

번역 코테즈와 그의 스페인 군인들이 1520년에 아즈텍 사람들을 처음 만났을 때 보통 신과 왕만을 위해 마련된 핫 초콜릿을 대접받았다. 그러나 그것은 오늘날 기분 좋게 즐기는 코코아와는 꽤 달랐다. 그것은 아주 매웠다. 아즈텍 사람들은 설탕 대신 간 고추가 가미된 매운 초콜릿을 대접했던 것이다. 두말할 필요도 없이 스페인 사람들은 이 초콜릿 음료를 별로 달갑게 받아들이지 않았다. 그러나 아즈텍 사람들에게는 코코아 나무가 매우 중요했다. 그들은 냉담함과 소심함을 치유하기 위해 코코아 나무 꽃을, 배탈에는 나무껍질을, 그리고 화상에는 코코아 버터를 사용했다. 심지어 코코아 열매를 화폐로 사용하기도 했다.

(a) 초콜릿의 역사
(b) 아즈텍인들의 코코아 사용
(c) 아즈텍인들이 스페인 방문객들을 대접한 방식
(d) 1500년대에 초콜릿이 사용된 방식

해법 아즈텍 사람들은 일반적으로 신과 왕만을 위해 코코아로 만든 초콜릿 음료를 만들었다는 지문 앞부분과 지문 마지막 부분에서 코코아의 다양한 사용을 종합해 보면 (b)가 정답이다. (a)는 지문이 초콜릿의 역사로 보기에는 협소하고, (c)는 지문 중간 중간에 있는 Spanish soldiers, Spaniards를 이용했고, (d)는 지문 첫 문장을 이용했다.

reserve 준비해두다 **cheery** 기분 좋은 **laced with** ~가 가미된
ground 갈아 놓은 **apathy** 냉담함 **timidity** 소심함 **bark** 나무껍질
bean 열매 **currency** 돈, 화폐

✓ 정답 (b)

Forging strong partnerships with strategic local partners and investors in new markets is crucial to rapid, successful expansion. As one of the largest real estate companies in Asia, Captaland has garnered strong core competencies in real estate development and management of residential, retail, and commercial properties as well as serviced residences and real estate financial services. Through our strategic alliances, we have gained footholds in new markets and broken frontiers in existing ones, giving rise to our ever-growing presence in Asia Pacific, Europe, and the Middle East, with more than 100 cities in over 20 countries.

Q: What is the purpose of the passage?
(a) To encourage readers to be interested in Captaland
(b) To introduce what Captaland can do internationally
(c) To attract potential employees to Captaland to expand its business
(d) To discuss the importance of partnerships in new real estate markets

Suspension bridges are magnificent pieces of architecture. They can be found in many major cities that have bays and rivers that are crossed regularly by commuters. Most suspension bridges have tolls. Sometimes these tolls are extraordinarily high. Considering it takes less than 3 minutes to cross over most, a fee of $5.00 seems exorbitant. Suspension bridges generally only allow motor vehicles but some actually take foot traffic. The famous Golden Gate Bridge in San Francisco is one such bridge. You can see runners, walkers, and bicyclists going right along with drivers and enjoying the beautiful California weather way up high.

Q: What is the best title of the passage?
(a) Expensive Suspension Bridges to Cross
(b) People Crossing Urban Architectural Wonders
(c) Where Suspension Bridges are Found
(d) How Golden Gate Bridge is Different

번역 새로운 시장에서 전략적 지역 파트너와 투자자들과 굳건한 협력관계를 구축하는 것은 빠르고 성공적인 성장에 필수적입니다. 아시아에서 가장 큰 부동산 회사 중에 하나로 캡털랜드는 주택지와 부동산 금융 서비스를 해왔을 뿐만 아니라 부동산 개발과 거주, 소매, 상업적 소유물에 대한 강력하고도 핵심적인 힘을 키워왔습니다. 저희의 전략적 동맹을 통해 새로운 시장에 진출할 발판을 마련했으며, 현 시장의 한계를 뛰어넘어 20개국 이상의 100개가 넘는 도시와 더불어 아시아 태평양, 유럽, 그리고 중동에서 항상 성장하는 모습을 보이게 됐습니다.

(a) 독자로 하여금 캡털랜드에 관심을 갖도록 하기 위해
(b) 캡털랜드가 국제적으로 할 수 있는 일을 소개하기 위해
(c) 캡털랜드의 사업을 확장하기 위해 잠재적 직원들을 모으기 위해
(d) 새로운 부동산 시장에서의 협력의 중요성을 이야기하기 위해

해법 Captaland를 광고하는 지문이므로 (a)가 정답이다. (b)는 선택지의 what Captaland can do internationally에 대한 내용이 지문에 구체적으로 나와 있지 않고, (c)는 지문 마지막 문장을 보면 사업을 확장해 왔다는 것이지 앞으로 확장한다는 것은 아니며, (d)는 지문 내용만으로 discuss the importance of partnerships in new real estate markets라고 판단하기에는 부족하다.

forge 계획 등을 세우다 **crucial** 결정적인, 중대한 **rapid** 빠른, 신속한 **expansion** 확장 **real estate** 부동산 **garner** 축척하다 **core** 핵심, 중심 **residential** 주거의 **retail** 소매의 **commerial** 상업상의 **alliance** 결연, 동맹, 연합 **foothold** 발판 **give rise to** ~이 생기게 하다, ~의 근원이 되다

정답 (a)

번역 현수교는 참 아름다운 건축물이다. 현수교는 주로 통근자들이 항상 건너다니는 만과 강이 있는 많은 대도시에서 볼 수 있다. 대부분의 현수교를 통과하려면 통행료를 지불해야 한다. 때때로 이들 통행료는 터무니없이 비싸다. 건너는 데 3분도 안 걸리는 것을 감안하면 5달러의 요금은 터무니없는 것처럼 느껴진다. 현수교는 자동차의 통행만을 위한 것이지만 도보를 갖추고 있는 경우도 있다. 샌프란시스코에 있는 유명한 금문교가 바로 그러한 다리 중 하나다. 자동차 운전자들과 함께 나란히 저 높은 곳에서 캘리포니아의 아름다운 날씨를 즐기며 다리 위를 달리거나 걷거나 자전거를 타는 사람들을 볼 수 있다.

(a) 비싼 통행료를 내고 건너는 현수교
(b) 도시의 훌륭한 건축물을 건너는 사람들
(c) 현수교를 볼 수 있는 곳들
(d) 금문교는 어떻게 다른가

해법 지문 첫 문장과 두 번째 문장을 보면 훌륭한 건축물로써 현수교가 지문 핵심이므로 (b)가 정답이고, 지문의 in many major cities와 첫 문장이 선택지에서는 각각 Urban, Architectural Wonders로 paraphrasing되어 있다. 나머지 선택지들은 지문에 있긴 하지만 글쓴이가 주되게 말하고 싶은 내용은 아니다.

suspension bridge 현수교 **magnificent** 훌륭한, 근사한 **toll** 통행료 **extraordinarily** 엄청나게, 터무니없이 **exorbitant** 과도한, 지나친 **foot traffic** 도보

정답 (b)

Dear Mr. Chow,

We were pleased to receive your letter, and also remember fondly the few days you spent with us, as well as the interesting conversations we had. We are just now beginning to enjoy the fruits of your suggestions concerning improvements to our packing and labeling. We are happy to let you have copies of our annual reports for the current year and the previous two years. However, the full reports are published in Chinese and Thai only, although we do issue much-abridged versions of the reports in English. I am enclosing a copy of each publication, and would be glad to hear which version you would like to receive in the future.

Sincerely,
Ben McCameron

Q: Why did Ben McCameron write this letter?
(a) To thank Mr. Chow for his suggestions
(b) To reply to a request from a business partner
(c) To know what language Mr. Chow speaks
(d) To offer suggestions regarding packing and labeling

For people who can and will provide advanced care for their pets, a whole new scientific era has been born. It has been a technological explosion. Take a surgical robot. It can cut into and maneuver inside bones far more accurately than any human being ever could. The problem? The robot costs around 400,000 dollars. Pet owner Steve Ryan, however, says that he wouldn't mind the unavoidably high cost of the extremely advanced surgery using this robot as long as his dog can get back the quality of life he'd like him to have.

Q: What is the passage mainly about?
(a) The next scientific advancement for sick pets
(b) Pet owners' unreasonable concern for their pets
(c) The development of technology for pet lovers
(d) What is good and bad about surgical robots

The search for a logical explanation for the decline and fall of the Roman Empire has been more diligent than that in any other field of history. This is the only known instance of the decay of a more or less universal civilization, which might serve as something of an object lesson to our own; accordingly it has been very thoroughly studied, and the attempt to explain it has engaged some of the ablest historians who ever wrote about it. Almost any orator or politician can tell you why Rome fell, but the men who know most about it are not so ready with glib explanation. Even they must admit at critical moments the decisive interposition of chance.

Q: What is the main idea of the passage?

(a) The late history of the Roman Empire cannot be explained completely logically.

(b) The decline of the Roman Empire needs to be studied further.

(c) The collapse of the Roman Empire is a popular historical study subject.

(d) The fall of the Roman Empire came about unexpectedly.

번역　로마 제국의 쇠퇴와 몰락에 대한 논리적인 해석을 찾기 위한 연구는 역사학의 그 어느 분야보다도 가장 활발하게 진행되어 온 부분이다. 이는 한편으로는 역사상 전 인류의 문명이라고 할 수 있는 제국이 쇠퇴한 유일한 경우로서 현재 우리가 살고 있는 문명에도 객관적인 교훈이 될 수도 있기에 로마 제국의 쇠퇴와 몰락은 매우 철저하게 연구되어 왔고, 지금까지 존재한 역사학자들 중에서도 가장 뛰어난 몇몇 전문가들이 이를 설명하려고 시도했다. 연설가나 정치가라면 누구라도 로마가 멸망한 이유에 대해 말해줄 수 있지만 정작 그 내용을 가장 속속들이 많이 알고 있는 사람들은 미처 그리 유창하게 설명할 준비가 되어 있지는 못하다. 이 사람들조차도 결정적인 순간에는 우연의 개입이 있을 수 있다는 점을 인정할 수밖에 없는 것이다.

(a) 로마 제국의 후기 역사는 완전히 논리적으로 설명될 수는 없다.

(b) 로마 제국의 쇠퇴는 더 연구할 필요가 있다.

(c) 로마 제국의 붕괴는 인기 있는 역사 연구 주제이다.

(d) 로마 제국의 몰락은 예기치 않게 일어났다.

해법　지문 첫 문장과 마지막 문장을 중심으로 보면 로마 제국의 쇠퇴와 몰락에 대해 많은 논리적인 설명이 있었지만, 로마 제국이 쇠퇴하고 몰락하는 데는 우연적인 부분도 있기에 (a)가 정답이다. (b), (d)는 지문 마지막 문장을 이용했고, (c)는 지문에 없는 내용이다.

more or less 다소　**engage** ~를 끌어들이다　**orator** 연설자, 웅변가　**glib** 유창한, 입심 좋은　**interposition** 개입, 간섭

정답　(a)

The knowledge that you are punctual gives a feeling of calm security. But if you are always racing to catch up with your schedule, you are in a constant state of excitement; you are incapable of getting any enjoyment out of the present moment. The only moment you have to live is this one. Being urgent is not a virtue. It is merely a sign of bad management. A well-planned daily schedule has a few empty spaces, moments in which you can relax and think at ease about the problems at hand. Every day should have some pleasure, whether small or great. To rob yourself of that enjoyment because you are too busy is to miss the whole point of living.

Q: What is the main idea of the passage?

(a) Leading a busy life is not as beneficial as being urgent.

(b) Setting up a daily schedule helps understand life.

(c) Staying balanced between work and play is important in life.

(d) Planning an everyday schedule should be pleasant.

번역　시간을 잘 지켰다는 사실은 자신에게 편안한 안정감을 갖게 한다. 그러나 자신의 일정을 소화하기 위해 항상 바쁘게 움직이고 있다면 당신은 지속적인 긴장 상태에 있는 것으로 바로 지금 이 순간에 어떤 즐거움도 누리지 못하게 될 수 있다. 살아야 할 유일한 순간은 바로 지금이다. 쫓기는 것은 미덕이 아니다. 그저 잘못된 관리의 징표일 뿐이다. 제대로 계획된 일정에는 이곳저곳에 잠깐의 여유가 있기 마련이어서 긴장을 푼 상태에서 당장 처리해야 할 문제들에 대해 편하게 생각할 수 있게 해준다. 크건 작건 간에 매일매일 즐거움이 있어야 한다. 너무 바쁘다는 이유로 스스로 그 즐거움을 빼앗는 것은 삶 자체의 의미를 놓치는 것이다.

(a) 바쁜 삶을 영위하는 것은 쫓기는 것만큼이나 이롭지 않다.

(b) 매일의 계획을 세우는 것은 삶을 이해하는 데 도움을 준다.

(c) 일과 놀이 사이에서 균형을 유지하는 것이 삶에 있어서 중요하다.

(d) 매일의 계획을 짜는 것은 즐거워야 한다.

해법　지문의 A well-planned daily schedule has ... at hand 이하 내용을 종합해 보면 적당한 일과 휴식이 중요하다는 것이 지문 핵심 내용이므로 (c)가 정답이다. (a)는 지문 두 번째, 네 번째 문장을 이용했고 (b), (d)는 지문에 없는 내용이다.

punctual 시간[기한]을 엄수하는　**security** 안심　**catch up with** ~을 따라잡다　**state** 상태　**urgent** 다급한　**virtue** 미덕　**at hand** 가까이에　**rob A of B** A에게서 B를 빼앗다

정답　(c)

Project Mercury placed the first Americans into space. The pioneering project was organized to orbit a manned spacecraft, investigate man's reaction to and abilities in space flight, and recover both man and spacecraft. Project Mercury experiments demonstrated that the high-gravity forces of launch and atmospheric entry as well as weightlessness in orbit for as much as 34 hours do not impair man's ability to control a spacecraft. It proved that man can not only augment the reliability of spacecraft controls, but also can conduct scientific observations and experiments that expand and clarify information from instruments.

Q: Which of the following best summarizes the passage?
(a) America was the first nation to put a manned spacecraft into orbit.
(b) Project Mercury experiments produced unexpected results.
(c) Project Mercury was the first project to send people to space.
(d) Project Mercury helped gain knowledge about space flight.

📖 **번역** 머큐리 프로젝트는 최초의 미국인들을 우주로 보냈다. 이 선구적인 프로젝트는 유인 우주선을 궤도에 진입시키고, 우주 비행에 대한 인간의 반응과 능력을 조사하고 탑승 우주인과 우주선 둘 다 복구시키는 것을 목표로 계획되었다. 머큐리 프로젝트 실험을 통해 최장 34시간 동안 궤도에서 무중력 상태는 물론 우주선 발사와 대기권 진입 시 고중력이 탑승 우주인의 우주선 조종 능력을 손상시키지 않음이 증명되었다. 머큐리 프로젝트는 탑승 우주인이 우주선을 더 잘 조종할 뿐 아니라 실험 도구들로부터 얻은 정보를 부연하고 명확하게 하는 과학적 관찰과 실험을 행할 수 있음을 증명했다.

(a) 미국은 유인 우주선을 궤도에 진입시킨 최초의 나라였다.
(b) 머큐리 프로젝트 실험은 예상치 못했던 결과들을 낳았다.
(c) 머큐리 프로젝트는 사람을 우주로 보낸 최초의 프로젝트였다.
(d) 머큐리 프로젝트는 우주 비행에 대한 지식을 얻는 데 도움이 됐다.

☀ **해법** 지문 두 번째 문장과 다음 내용을 종합해 보면 우주 비행 시 인간이 겪는 그리고 할 수 있는 일들이 증명되었으므로 (d)가 정답이다. (a)는 미국이 최초로 유인 우주선을 궤도에 올렸다는 내용이 지문에 없고, (b)는 선택지의 the expected에 대한 내용이 지문에 없으며, (c)는 결국 (a)와 같은 말이다.

pioneering 선구적인 **orbit** 궤도 **manned** 유인(有人)
investigate 조사하다 **demonstrate** 증명, 설명하다 **gravity** 중력
launch 발사(하다) **atmospheric entry** 대기권 진입
weightlessness 무중력 **impair** 손상시키다 **augment** 증가시키다
reliability 신뢰성, 확실성 **conduct** 행하다 **observation** 관찰

✓ **정답** (d)

It is often said that one of man's most distinct needs is for security, but too much security can be boring. No one likes to be treated like a child. A man in bed in a hospital is pretty secure, but when he ceases to be sick, he soon becomes bored. The fact is that most people do not want to have security provided so much as to be in a position to create their own security. Man has a need to run his own life, to make his own decisions, which we may call the need for self-determination. Thus, just as we can have too much food or too much love, we can have too much security.

Q: Which of the following best summarizes the passage?
(a) Man should avoid having too much security in life.
(b) Man can have just as much security as he wants.
(c) Security, food, and love are man's most distinct needs.
(d) Those with too much security want to be adventurous.

📖 **번역** 인간에게 가장 확실하게 필요한 것 중 하나가 안정이라고들 하지만 지나친 안정은 지루할 수도 있다. 어린아이 취급받길 원하는 사람은 아무도 없다. 가령 병실에 있는 환자는 꽤 안정적이긴 하지만 건강을 되찾으면 곧 지루함을 느낀다. 사실 대부분의 사람들은 지나치게 안정을 제공받지 못해 안정으로부터 안정한 상태를 스스로 만들어야 하는 위치까지는 가고 싶지 않아 한다. 인간은 소위 자발적 결정이라고 표현할 수 있는 자신의 삶을 스스로 관리하고 결정할 필요성을 느끼는 것이다. 그러므로 음식도 너무 많이 먹을 수 있고, 사랑도 너무 과할 수 있듯이 안정을 너무 많이 누릴 수도 있는 것이다.

(a) 인간은 삶에서 지나친 안정을 멀리해야 한다.
(b) 인간은 원하는 만큼 안정을 취할 권리가 있다.
(c) 안정, 음식 그리고 사랑은 인간의 가장 뚜렷한 필요 사항이다.
(d) 지나친 안정을 취하고 있는 사람들은 모험적으로 되길 원한다.

☀ **해법** 지문 마지막 문장에서 너무 많은 안정을 취할 수 있다고 했고 지나친 안정은 지루할 수 있다는 것과 인간은 자신의 삶을 관리하고 결정을 내릴 필요가 있다고 했으므로 (a)가 정답이다. (b)는 인간이 원하는 만큼 안정을 취하는 것은 아니고, (c)는 지문에서 Security, food, and love가 인간의 가장 두드러진 필요라고 말하고 있지 않으며, (d)는 지문에 없는 내용이다.

distinct 명백한, 뚜렷한 **security** 안정 **cease** 멈추다
self-determination 자발적 결정 **adventurous** 모험적인

✓ **정답** (a)

TEPS Reading Practice | **1** (a) **2** (d) **3** (c) **4** (c) **5** (c) **6** (a) **7** (b) **8** (d) **9** (c) **10** (d) P45 ➔

해설 및 정답 Unit 04

Although many countries around the world have banned whaling, these gentle sea mammals are still at risk. Whales are still being hunted, and more than 10,000 have been killed since 1986. Some are hunted for scientific purposes; others are killed by "pirates." Endangered species include blue whales, sperm whales, and northern right whales. Because whales have very low rates of reproduction, marine biologists believe that some of these species may never recover from the damage that whale hunting has caused.

Q: What is the main idea of the passage?
(a) Whaling continues to the point where it is dangerous.
(b) Whales are being hunted for a variety of reasons.
(c) Ways to make whales more reproductive are needed.
(d) Whale hunting should be banned more strictly.

When a child fails, simply drawing her or his attention to the failure is unlikely to improve that performance. No doubt the child already knows she cannot read, or spell, or multiply. Her performance is more likely to benefit if she is shown that, just as she can control her breathing by panting, breathing deeply, or holding her breath, so too can she control her thinking. The child needs to understand that there are specific strategies for specific tasks and that the generation and use of these strategies is something she can do for herself.

Q: What is the main idea of the passage?
(a) Children are born to think and learn without any assistance.
(b) Pointing out failures that children make does not benefit them.
(c) Teaching how to control thinking matters when educating children.
(d) We should let children know that they are in charge of their thinking.

📖 **번역** 전세계 많은 나라가 고래잡이를 금지했음에도 불구하고 온순한 바다 포유동물인 고래는 여전히 위험에 처해 있다. 고래는 여전히 포획되고 있고 1986년 이후로 10,000마리 이상이 희생되었다. 과학적인 목적으로 포획되는 경우도 있고 해적들이 포획하는 경우도 있다. 멸종 위기에 빠진 고래로는 흰긴수염고래, 향유고래, 그리고 북쪽 지방의 참고래가 있다. 매우 낮은 고래의 번식률 때문에 해양 생물학자들은 이들 일부 종은 고래잡이로 인한 피해로부터 헤어나오기 매우 어려울 수 있다고 본다.

(a) 고래잡이가 위험한 수준까지 계속되고 있다.
(b) 다양한 이유로 인해 고래가 사냥되고 있다.
(c) 고래의 번식률을 높이는 방법들이 필요하다.
(d) 고래잡이가 더 엄격하게 금지되어야 한다.

💡 **해법** 많은 나라에서 고래잡이를 금지했음에도 불구하고 지속적인 사냥으로 고래가 여전히 위험에 처해 있고 고래는 새끼를 많이 낳지 않기 때문에 상황이 더 악화될 수 있다는 것이 주요 내용으로 (a)가 정답이다. (b)는 지문 세 번째 문장을 이용한 것이고, (c)와 (d)는 질문과 맞지 않다.

ban 금지하다 **whaling** 고래잡이 **at risk** 위험한 상태에 있는 **endangered** 위험에 처한, 멸종될 위기에 이른 **blue whale** 흰긴수염고래 **sperm whale** 향유고래 **right whale** 참고래 **reproduction** 번식

✅ **정답** (a)

📖 **번역** 어린아이가 실패를 했을 때 아이의 관심을 실패에만 집중시키면 성취 능력을 향상시키기 힘들다. 틀림없이 아이는 벌써 자신이 글을 읽거나 쓰거나 곱셈을 할 줄 모른다는 사실을 잘 알고 있을 것이다. 그보다는 오히려 헐떡거리거나 깊은 심호흡을 하거나 숨을 참아서 호흡을 조절할 수 있듯이 자신의 생각도 마음대로 조절할 수 있다는 사실을 알게 해주는 편이 훨씬 교육에 도움이 될 것이다. 아이는 특정한 일에는 특정한 전략들이 있으며 이런 전략을 만들어내고 사용하는 일은 자기 스스로도 할 수 있음을 깨달을 필요가 있다.

(a) 어린아이는 도움이 전혀 없이도 생각하고 배울 수 있도록 태어났다.
(b) 어린아이가 저지르는 실패를 지적하는 것은 아이에게 도움되지 않는다.
(c) 생각을 통제하는 법을 가르치는 것이 어린아이를 교육할 때 중요하다.
(d) 우리는 어린아이에게 그들의 생각을 조정할 능력이 있다는 것을 알려줘야 한다.

💡 **해법** 아이들이 자기주도적 사고 능력을 갖고 있음을 알게 해줘야 한다는 것이 지문의 주요 내용이므로 (d)가 정답이다. (a)는 without any assistance가 맞지 않고, (b)는 지문 앞부분 내용을 이용한 것으로 글쓴이가 가장 하고픈 말은 아니며, (c)는 지문 내용이 아이가 생각을 조절할 수 있는 능력을 갖고 있음을 알게 해주는 것으로 선택지의 Teaching how to control thinking이 맞지 않다.

draw (사람의 주의를) 끌다 **pant** 헐떡거리다 **strategy** 전략 **specific** 독특한, 특수한 **assistance** 조력, 원조 **educate** 교육하다

✅ **정답** (d)

The right to vote is a key benefit of a democratic system. Citizens in the U.S. have many opportunities to participate in the political life of their communities and the nation. They can participate by voting, by expressing their views to elected officials, and by voicing their opinions in newspapers and on radio and television. Unfortunately, many citizens don't take advantage of their rights. Fewer than fifty percent of all eligible voters have participated in recent national elections. Many citizens' groups, such as the League of Women Voters, work hard to encourage voters to participate, so that more and more citizens will exercise this important privilege.

Q: What is the main idea of the passage?
(a) More than 50% of the U.S. population should vote.
(b) Americans are less interested in politics than before.
(c) The right to vote is not exercised as much as it should be.
(d) Democracy is mainly characterized by people's voting power.

It is widely believed that the "hot dog" began on a cold day in New York's Polo Grounds in 1901, when a salesman began selling sausages in long buns. Sports cartoonist T. A. Dorgan captured the event in a drawing, depicting the sausages as dachshunds and calling them "hot dogs" because he couldn't spell "dachshunds." Nice story, but it's just nonsense. Jokes about dachshunds looking like sausages have been around for hundreds of years. The term "hot dog" was current at Yale in the fall of 1894, when sausages in a bun were sold at the dormitories. By the time T. A. Dorgan was "inventing" the term, "hot dog" was already replacing the other names for a sausage on a bun.

Q: What is the main idea of the passage?
(a) Nobody knows exactly who first created "hot dog."
(b) People disagree on when "hot dog" first came into use.
(c) The 20th century's explanation for the origin of "hot dog" is wrong.
(d) "Hot dog" is an example of replacing old words with new ones.

번역 투표권은 민주주의 제도의 중요한 장점이다. 미국 시민은 지역 사회나 국가의 정치적 삶에 참여할 수 있는 많은 기회가 있다. 투표를 하거나 선출된 관료에게 자신의 의견을 말하고 신문, 라디오, TV 등에 의사를 표명함으로써 정치에 참여할 수 있다. 불행하게도 많은 시민들이 자신의 권리의 이점을 이용하지 않고 있다. 최근 전국적인 선거에 참여한 사람은 전체 유권자의 50퍼센트에도 미치지 못했다. 여성 투표자 연맹 등을 비롯한 많은 시민 단체는 보다 많은 시민들이 이 중대한 특권을 행사하도록 하기 위해 유권자들에게 투표에 참여하도록 권장하는 일에 열심히 노력하고 있다.

(a) 미국 국민의 50% 이상은 투표를 해야 한다.
(b) 미국인들은 전보다 정치에 대해 관심이 적다.
(c) 투표권은 기대만큼 행사되어지지 않고 있다.
(d) 민주주의는 사람들의 투표 권력에 의해 특징지어진다.

해법 민주주의 제도의 중요한 장점으로써 투표권이 충분히 행사되고 있지 않다는 것이 지문의 주요 내용으로 (c)가 정답이다. (a)는 recent national elections에 국한된 내용이고, (b)는 지문 내용만으로 단정할 수 없는 비약이며, (d)는 지문 첫 문장만을 이용한 것으로 지문 전체를 아우르지 못한다.

democratic system 민주 제도   **voice** (생각 따위를) 말로 표현하다
exercise (권리를) 행사하다

 정답 (c)

번역 핫도그는 1901년의 어느 추운 날 뉴욕의 폴로 그라운즈에서 판매원이 길고 둥그런 빵 속에 소시지를 넣어 팔게 된 것이 그 시초라고 널리 알려져 있다. 스포츠 만평가인 T. A. 도건은 이 장면을 그림으로 포착하여 소시지를 닥스훈트로 묘사한 다음 닥스훈트의 철자를 몰라서 'hot dog'라고 불렀다는 것이다. 그럴싸하게 들리지만 이것은 말도 안 되는 이야기이다. 소시지처럼 생긴 닥스훈트에 대한 농담은 수백 년 동안 존재했다. 핫도그라는 용어는 빵 속에 든 소시지를 기숙사에서 팔던 때인 1894년 가을에 예일대학교에서 이미 사용하고 있었다. T. A. 도건이 그 이름을 발명하고 있을 때쯤에는 이미 핫도그가 길고 둥그런 빵 속에 든 소시지를 지칭하는 다른 말을 대신해 가고 있었다.

(a) 아무도 핫도그란 말을 누가 최초로 만들었는지 정확히 알지 못한다.
(b) 사람들은 언제 핫도그란 말이 최초로 사용되었는지에 대해 의견을 달리한다.
(c) 핫도그란 말의 기원에 대한 20세기 때 설명은 잘못됐다.
(d) 핫도그는 오래된 말을 새로운 말로 바꾸는 하나의 예다.

해법 지문 첫 문장과 지문의 Nice story, but it's just nonsense 이하 내용을 종합해 보면 (c)가 지문 핵심 내용으로 정답이다. (a)는 지문에서 말하고자 하는 내용이 아니고, (b)는 글쓴이 이외에 disagree하는 사람들의 이야기가 없고, (d)는 replacing old words with new ones에 대한 추가적이고 구체적인 내용이 없다.

long bun 핫도그용 긴 빵   **depict** 묘사하다   **dachshund** 닥스훈트 (짧은 다리에 몸이 긴 독일산 개)   **term** 말, 용어   **dormitory** 기숙사

 정답 (c)

It's true that we love technology, but the time will never come when we lose real person-to-person interaction. What with cell phones, computer games, and robots, the situation might seem troubling, but not all of us young people are socially withdrawn. I do not need super high-tech devices to kill time. Machines won't replace my friends. People of my generation don't have that much craving for technology, since we've grown up with it. We never needed to dream of having high-tech gadgets, because they have always been within reach.

Q: What is the main idea of the passage?
(a) Technology will not necessarily breed a total dependency.
(b) Different generations have different tastes for technology.
(c) Technology does not affect our social life as much as it appears to.
(d) Friends will not be replaced by machines for young people of this age.

According to the FBI, bombing incidents have almost tripled in the United States in the last 10 years. Last year alone, 2,577 explosives killed 193 people and caused over $105 million in property damage. Motives range from political terrorism to personal grudges to sheer thrill-seeking. In addition to real bombs, there are many false alarms and hoaxes. Each has to be treated seriously by expert technicians and professionals on bomb squads. A package from a jilted lover, a plain box found in an underground courthouse parking lot, a briefcase left under a table in a McDonald's—all are possible threats.

Q: Which of the following best summarizes the passage?
(a) Various potential causes of bombings account for increased bombing incidents.
(b) The increasing frequency of bombings has alerted the world to all bomb threats.
(c) False alarms and hoaxes remain serious until they are investigated by authorities.
(d) Three main reasons have been identified over the last decade for bomb threats.

번역 우리가 기술을 좋아하는 것은 사실이지만 사람과 사람이 직접 만나서 교류하는 일이 없어지는 날은 결코 오지 않을 것이다. 휴대폰과 컴퓨터 게임, 로봇 때문에 상황은 어려운 것처럼 보이지만 우리 젊은이들 모두가 사람과 만나는 일을 꺼리는 것은 아니다. 나는 시간을 때우기 위해 첨단 기술 장치를 필요로 하지 않는다. 기계가 내 친구를 대신할 일은 절대로 없을 것이다. 우리 세대의 사람들은 기술과 함께 자랐기 때문에 그것에 대해 그리 큰 갈망이 없다. 첨단 기술 기구들이 항상 우리가 손만 뻗으면 닿는 곳에 있었기 때문에 그것을 갖는 꿈을 꿀 필요가 없었다.

(a) 기술이 반드시 전적인 의존을 낳지는 않을 것이다.
(b) 서로 다른 세대들은 기술에 대해 서로 다른 생각과 취향을 갖고 있다.
(c) 기술은 생각만큼 우리 사회 생활에 영향을 미치지는 않는다.
(d) 이 시대의 젊은이들에게 있어 기계들이 친구들을 대신하지는 않을 것이다.

해법 보여지는 만큼 기술이 인간을 서로로부터 소외시키지는 않을 것이라는 것이 지문의 주요 내용이므로 (c)가 정답이다. (a)는 사람과 사람이 직접 만나서 교류하는 일이 없어지는 날은 결코 오지 않을 것이라고 했고, (d)는 지문의 우리 젊은이들 모두가 사람과 만나는 일을 꺼린다는 내용은 일부는 꺼린다는 것이므로 선택지와 같이 단정할 수 없다.

socially withdrawn 사람을 만나지 않는 **kill time** 시간을 때우다 **craving** 갈망, 열망 **gadget** 장치, 도구 **within reach** 손을 뻗으면 닿는 곳에 있는

 정답 (c)

번역 FBI에 따르면 지난 10년간 미국에서의 폭발 사고가 거의 3배 증가했다. 지난해 한 해 동안 2,577건의 폭발 사고로 193명의 사망자가 발생했고, 1억 500만 달러의 재산 피해가 났다. 동기는 정치적 테러에서부터 사사로운 원한과 순전히 스릴을 즐기는 데 이르기까지 다양하다. 진짜 폭탄뿐 아니라 가짜 경고와 장난도 많다. 이러한 경우 모두 일일이 폭탄 제거반 소속의 기술자와 전문가들에 의해 신중하게 처리되어야 한다. 실연당한 연인으로부터 온 꾸러미부터 법원 청사 지하 주차장에서 발견된 단순한 상자, 맥도날드 햄버거 가게 탁자 밑에 남겨진 서류 가방에 이르기까지, 이 모두가 위험 요소가 될 수 있다.

(a) 폭탄 사고의 증가는 폭탄 사용의 다양한 잠재적 원인에 있다.
(b) 폭탄 사용의 빈도가 증가함에 따라 세계 모든 폭파 위협 요소를 경계하게 되었다.
(c) 가짜 경고와 장난들은 관계 당국의 조사가 끝날 때까지는 심각한 사안으로 존재한다.
(d) 폭탄 사용 위협을 일으키는 3가지의 중대한 이유가 지난 10년간에 걸쳐 밝혀졌다.

해법 폭탄 사고가 증가했고 동기가 다양하다는 것이 지문의 주요 내용이므로 (a)가 정답이다. 지문의 all은 A package ... in a McDonald's를 받으며, 선택지의 all bomb threats와는 의미가 다르다. (c), (d)는 각각 지문 전체를 아우르지 못한다.

triple 3배가 되다 **explosive** 폭발하기 쉬운, 폭발물 **grudge** 원한 **sheer** 순전한 **bomb squad** 폭탄 제거반 **jilt** (애인을) 버리다

 정답 (a)

Let's assume that we can learn to speak someone else's language—not just a few polite phrases, but really learn to speak it fluently. We know that speaking a language fluently will certainly improve our communication with other speakers of that language, but something else happens as well. I think that learning another language can fundamentally change us as individuals—can change our worldview and even our personalities. For example, if we speak French fluently, we can form grammatically correct sentences, of course, but we can also begin to see the world in a way that is typically French.

Q: Which of the following best summarizes the passage?

(a) Studying grammar rules is part of learning a foreign language.

(b) Language skills mean more than simply the mastery of a foreign language.

(c) Learning another language improves communication and ways of thinking.

(d) Understanding a foreign culture helps one master a foreign language.

When you consider the enormous range of fitted units and elaborate accessories available today, it's difficult to believe that the kitchen has only recently been considered a suitable area for decoration. Although this room has always been extremely important, until the start of the First World War no sensible household would spend unnecessary time and effort on it since it was essentially the domain of servants, and even ordinary families had at least one maid whose responsibilities included the preparation of meals. Besides, cooking involved greasy work and thick smoke with soot made so that unnecessary units and acceccories meant nothing but extra nuisances.

Q: Which of the following best summarizes the passage?

(a) World War I changed the postwar image of the kitchen.

(b) The kitchen was not decorated with units and accessories until lately.

(c) Not all the households were interested in the kitchen.

(d) People's view on the kitchen is a far cry from that of the past.

🔄 **번역** 단순히 예의 바른 말 몇 마디 배우는 데 그치는 것이 아니라 유창하게 말을 할 수 있을 만큼 우리가 다른 나라의 언어를 배울 수 있다고 생각해 보자. 어떤 언어를 유창하게 구사할 수 있으면 그 언어를 사용하는 다른 사람들과 의사소통이 향상된다는 사실을 우리는 확실히 알고 있지만 이와는 별개로 또 다른 일이 생겨난다. 다른 나라의 언어를 배우는 것은 개인의 세계관과 인성을 포함해서 한 사람을 근본적으로 변화시킬 수 있다고 생각한다. 예를 들어 프랑스어를 유창하게 구사할 수 있게 된다면 문법적으로 옳은 문장을 만들어내는 것은 물론이고 전형적인 프랑스인의 시각으로 세상을 보게 될 수도 있을 것이다.

(a) 문법 규칙들을 공부하는 것이 외국어를 배우는 것의 일부분이다.

(b) 언어의 기술은 단순히 외국어를 습득하는 것 이상을 의미한다.

(c) 외국어 학습은 의사소통과 사고방식을 향상시킨다.

(d) 외국 문화를 이해하는 것은 외국어를 습득하는 데 도움된다.

✳️ **해법** 외국어를 유창하게 구사하는 것이 그 언어를 사용하는 사람들과의 의사소통 향상은 물론 우리의 세계관뿐 아니라 인성까지도 변화시킬 수 있다는 것이 지문의 주요 내용이므로 (b)가 정답이다. (c)는 사고방식을 개선한다는 내용이 지문에 없어 오답이다.

assume 생각하다 **fluently** 유창하게 **fundamentally** 근본적으로
worldview 세계관 **grammatically** 문법적으로 **mastery** 숙달

 정답 (b)

🔄 **번역** 오늘날 너무나도 폭넓은 종류의 짜임새 있는 가구와 그에 따른 수많은 장식과 부속물이 존재하는 것을 생각하면 주방이 최근에 와서야 비로소 장식하기 좋은 장소로 간주되었다는 사실이 좀처럼 믿기가 어렵다. 늘 지극히 중요한 공간으로 인식되었던 부엌은 1차 세계 대전이 발발할 때까지만 해도 양식 있는 가정에서는 주방을 꾸미는 데 불필요한 시간과 노력을 들이지 않았다. 부엌은 본래 하인들의 주거 공간이었기 때문이다. 당시에는 심지어 평범한 가정에서도 식사 준비를 담당하는 하녀가 최소한 한 명은 있었다. 더구나 요리는 기름기가 묻고 연기가 자욱하게 일며 검댕이 생기는 작업이었기 때문에 이와 상관없는 장식물은 단지 여분의 일거리만 생기게 할 뿐이었다.

(a) 1차 세계 대전이 부엌의 이미지를 바꿨다.

(b) 최근에 와서야 부엌이 부속물들로 장식됐다.

(c) 모든 가정이 부엌에 관심을 가진 것은 아니다.

(d) 부엌에 대한 사람들의 생각은 과거와 비교할 수 없을 만큼 다르다.

✳️ **해법** 현재와 과거의 주방 모습이 매우 달랐음이 지문의 주요 내용이므로 (d)가 정답이고, 선택지의 far cry는 '상당한 차이'라는 의미이다. (a), (b), (c)는 지문 전체를 아우르지 못한다.

enormous 엄청난, 대단한 **elaborate** 정성들여 만들다, 공들인
suitable 적당한, 적절한 **sensible** 분별 있는 **essentially** 본질적으로
domain 영역 **soot** 검댕(으로 더럽히다) **nuisance** 귀찮은 것

정답 (d)

If you were standing in a river, you would think the left bank would be the one to your left. But what if you were facing the other way? It seems as though the left and right banks of a river depend on where you are standing. However, there's a way to determine which is the left or right bank of a river no matter where you're standing. First, find the way the river flows. Now, face downstream. This means you're facing the same way the water is flowing. The left bank is now on your left. When people talk about the left and right banks of a river, they mean the left and right of the direction of flow.

Q: Which of the following best summarizes the passage?
(a) The direction of river flow has been confusing.
(b) How you face a river lets you know where it flows.
(c) Where a river flows decides its left and right orientation.
(d) One can tell left from right in a river by only one way.

When change is slow, the new is gradually assimilated, and only after a number of generations is it noticeable that the world is really different. In our century enormous changes in the circumstances of our lives and in our knowledge have occurred rapidly. It is not at all surprising that our intellectual, our social, and our political processes have failed to keep abreast of contemporary problems. It is not surprising that we become confused in the choice of our goals and the paths which we must take to reach them.

Q: Which of the following best summarizes the passage?
(a) Since the beginning of the century, things have been uncontrollable.
(b) These days, people find it more difficult to realize their goals.
(c) New things have become too difficult for our generation to catch up with.
(d) Recent changes have occurred at such a pace that they cannot be followed.

번역 여러분이 강에 서 있다면 왼쪽이 강의 왼쪽 제방일 것이라고 생각할 것입니다. 그러나 만약 여러분이 반대편을 바라보고 있다면 어떨까요? 강의 왼쪽 제방과 오른쪽 제방이 마치 여러분이 어디에 서 있느냐에 달려 있는 것으로 느껴집니다. 그러나 여러분이 어디에 어느 방향으로 서 있든지 상관없이 강의 왼쪽과 오른쪽 기슭을 결정하는 방법이 있습니다. 우선 강이 흐르는 방향을 알아내십시오. 이제 하류 쪽을 향하십시오. 즉, 강물이 흘러내려가는 방향과 동일한 방향을 향하라는 말입니다. 이제 왼쪽 강기슭이 여러분의 왼쪽에 있게 됩니다. 사람들이 강의 왼쪽과 오른쪽 제방을 언급할 때는 강물이 흐르는 방향을 기준으로 왼쪽과 오른쪽을 의미하는 것입니다.

(a) 강 흐름의 방향은 혼동을 유발해 왔다.
(b) 강을 바라보는 방식이 강이 어디로 흐르는지 알게 해준다.
(c) 강이 어디로 흐르는지가 강의 왼쪽, 오른쪽 방향을 결정한다.
(d) 강에서 왼쪽, 오른쪽을 한 가지 방법만으로 구분할 수 있다.

해법 지문의 However, there's a way to determine which is the left or right bank of a river no matter where you're standing과 강의 왼쪽과 오른쪽을 설명하고 있는 지문 마지막 문장을 보면 강이 흐르는 방향에 따라 강의 왼쪽과 오른쪽을 결정하는 것이므로 (c)가 정답이다.

bank 강기슭, 강둑 **downstream** 하류, 강 아래 **tell** 구별, 구분하다

 정답 (c)

번역 서서히 일어나는 변화의 경우 새로운 것이 점차적으로 흡수되어 수 세대가 지나서야 비로소 세상이 변했음을 감지할 수 있다. 현세기에는 우리 삶의 환경과 지식에 있어 엄청난 변화들이 빠르게 일어났다. 그러므로 우리의 지적, 사회적, 정치적 과정들이 현재의 문제들을 따라가지 못해온 것이 전혀 놀랄 만한 일이 아니다. 우리가 목표를 설정하고 이에 도달하기 위해 가야 할 길을 택하는 일에 혼돈을 느끼는 것 역시 놀랄 만한 일이 아니다.

(a) 금세기가 시작된 이래로 일들이 통제할 수 없게 되었다.
(b) 오늘날 사람들은 그들의 목표를 이루는 것을 더욱 어렵게 느낀다.
(c) 새롭게 변화된 것들은 우리 세대가 따라잡기에 너무 어려워졌다.
(d) 최근의 변화는 따라갈 수 없을 정도의 속도로 일어났다.

해법 지문의 In our century enormous changes in the circumstances of our lives and in our knowledge have occurred rapidly와 다음 내용을 종합해 보면 (d)가 성답이다. (c)는 변화가 빨리 일어나서 따라가기 어렵다는 것이지 일어난 새로운 변화 자체가 따라잡기 어려운 것은 아니다.

assimilate 받아들이다, 흡수하다 **noticeable** 눈에 띄는, 두드러진 **keep abreast of** ~에 뒤지지 않고 따라가다 **contemporary** 동시대의, 현대의 **circumstance** 상황, 환경

정답 (d)

The Philippine Islands have some of the richest coral reefs in the world. However, scientists are concerned that fishermen are destroying the reefs. One common practice used to catch a large number of fish is to throw explosives into the water. This kills many fish and destroys the reef where they live. Another practice is used to catch certain fish for use in aquariums overseas. Fishermen throw poison into the water around the reef. The poison stuns the fish, which float to the surface and are easily caught. The poison destroys the reef and kills the fish by poisoning them slowly. A result of these practices is the eventual loss of one of nature's most lovely works of art.

Q: Which of the following is correct according to the passage?
(a) The Philippine Islands boast the most beautiful coral reefs.
(b) Coral reefs make it hard for fishermen to increase their catch.
(c) Some of the world's coral reefs are being destroyed for fishing.
(d) Philippine fishermen are not interested in environmental issues.

번역 필리핀 제도에는 세계에서 가장 풍부한 산호초가 있다. 그러나 과학자들은 어부들이 산호초를 파괴하고 있다고 염려한다. 많은 양의 물고기를 잡기 위해 흔히 사용하는 방법 하나로 물 속에 폭발물을 던지는 것이 있다. 이 방법은 많은 물고기들을 죽이고 물고기들이 살고 있는 산호초를 파괴한다. 또 다른 방법은 해외에 있는 수족관에서 사용할 특정 물고기들을 잡는 용도로 사용된다. 어부들은 산호초 주변의 물에 독약을 푼다. 독약이 물고기를 기절시켜 수면 위로 떠오르게 해 쉽게 잡을 수 있게 해주는 것이다. 그 독약은 산호초를 파괴하고 물고기들을 서서히 오염시켜 죽인다. 이러한 행위의 결과는 자연이 창조한 가장 아름다운 예술품 중 하나를 서서히 잃는 것이다.

(a) 필리핀 제도는 가장 아름다운 산호초를 뽐낸다.
(b) 산호초 때문에 어부들이 어획량을 늘리기 어렵다.
(c) 전 세계 산호초 일부가 어업 때문에 파괴되고 있다.
(d) 필리핀 어부들은 환경 문제에 관심이 없다.

해법 필리핀 제도에는 세계에서 가장 풍부한 산호초가 있다고 했고, 물고기 잡이의 결과로 산호초들이 파괴된다고 했으므로 결국 물고기 잡는 일 때문에 전 세계 산호초 일부가 파괴되고 있다는 (c)가 정답이다. (a)는 필리핀 제도의 산호초가 가장 아름다운 것은 아니고 (d)는 지문 내용만으로는 진위를 판단할 수 없다.

coral reef 산호초 **practice** 방법 **explosive** 폭발물 **aquarium** 수족관 **poison** 독 **stun** 기절시키다 **float** 떠오르다

 정답 (c)

Our Concept Auto, which will be on the market within five years, is different from any car ever made. Most of the features in the car are voice activated, so you won't have to take your hands off the wheel or your eyes off the road. Instead of reaching down to turn on the radio, the driver only has to say "radio on." Furthermore, the Concept Auto will be extremely lightweight, yet strong enough to stand up in accidents with the same performance as the cars we know today. Because of the weight, the car will use less energy. Any way you look at it, this car is an exciting prospect for the future.

Q: How will the car advertised interest potential buyers?
(a) Most of its features will be automatic.
(b) It will be able to use a special kind of fuel.
(c) It will be lighter and stronger than its competitors.
(d) It will be able to carry out its driver's oral instructions.

번역 5년 안에 시중에 나올 저희 컨셉트 오토는 지금까지 생산된 여느 차와는 다릅니다. 차에 있는 거의 모든 기능이 음성으로 작동되므로 운전대에서 손을 떼거나 도로에서 눈을 뗄 필요가 없습니다. 라디오를 켜기 위해 아래로 손을 뻗치는 대신 운전자는 "라디오 켜기"라고만 말하면 됩니다. 게다가 컨셉트 오토는 그 무게가 매우 가벼운 것에 비해 견고함도 갖추고 있어 사고 시 현재 우리가 알고 있는 일반 차량들과 대등한 수준으로 견딜 것입니다. 가벼운 차 무게 덕분에 에너지 소비는 줄어들 것입니다. 어떠한 관점에서 보더라도 이 차는 우리 미래의 흥미로운 기대주입니다.

(a) 대부분의 기능은 자동일 것이다.
(b) 특별한 종류의 연료를 사용할 수 있을 것이다.
(c) 경쟁 제품들보다 가볍고 견고할 것이다.
(d) 운전자의 음성으로 전해지는 명령을 수행할 수 있을 것이다.

해법 지문의 voice activated가 (d)에서 carry out its driver's oral instructions로 paraphrasing되어 있다. (a)는 지문의 voice activated와 선택지의 automatic은 각각 '음성으로 작동되는', '자동의'라는 다른 의미이고, (c)는 현재 우리가 알고 있는 차들과 같은 성능으로 사고에도 견딜 만큼 충분히 강하다고 했으므로 선택지의 stronger가 맞지 않다.

activate 작동시키다 **lightweight** 가벼운 **stand up** 견디다
prospect 기대 **fuel** 연료 **oral** 구두의

 정답 (d)

Turner was a quiet but determined woman. She, a retired government officer, enjoyed going to antique auctions. She also loved gardens, especially Brookside Garden. She made up her mind to do something for the Garden. In 1986, she asked to see Els Benjamin, then the director of the Garden. The public garden, with its museum and lakeside jogging course, is a 50-acre oasis. Turner found solace there and wanted to leave something for others to remember her. She asked Benjamin for a list of items Brookside might want. The list included some paintings and a piece of sculpture for the garden. Benjamin thought Turner would leave as much as $10,000, but her donation reached $800,000 when she died in 1990.

Q: Which of the following is correct about Turner?

(a) She saved money for Brookside Garden for about 4 years.

(b) She once didn't know what to do for Brookside Garden.

(c) She felt that something about Brookside Garden was worth sharing.

(d) She wanted Brookside Garden to have some artworks.

📖 **번역** 터너는 조용하지만 결단력 있는 여성이었다. 은퇴한 공무원인 그녀는 골동품 경매에 가는 것을 즐겼다. 그녀는 또한 정원을 좋아했는데 특히 브룩사이드 정원을 좋아했다. 그녀는 그 정원을 위해 뭔가를 해야겠다고 결심했다. 1986년, 그녀는 당시 그 정원의 관리자였던 엘스 벤저민에게 만날 것을 요청했다. 박물관과 호수 주변으로 조깅 코스가 있는 그 공공 정원은 50에이커 면적의 오아시스이다. 터너는 그곳에서 위안을 얻었으며 다른 사람들이 그녀를 기억할 수 있도록 무언가를 남기고 싶어 했다. 그녀는 벤저민에게 브룩사이드 정원에 필요할 것으로 생각되는 물품의 목록을 요청했다. 그 목록엔 정원을 위한 그림 몇 점과 조각상 한 개가 포함되어 있었다. 벤저민은 터너가 많아야 1만 달러 정도를 남기리라고 생각했으나 1990년에 세상을 뜬 그녀가 남기고 간 금액은 80만 달러에 이르렀다.

(a) 약 4년 동안 브룩사이드 정원을 위해 돈을 모았다.

(b) 브룩사이드 정원을 위해 뭘 해야 할지 몰랐던 때가 있었다.

(c) 브룩사이드 정원에 대해 뭔가 나눌 가치가 있다고 느꼈다.

(d) 브룩사이드 정원에 예술품들이 있었으면 했다.

💡 **해법** 터너는 벤저민을 만나기 전까지는 브룩사이드 정원을 위해 무엇을 할 수 있을지 몰랐으므로 (b)가 정답이다. (a)는 지문 내용만으로는 알 수 없고, (c)는 선택지의 worth sharing에 대한 근거가 지문에 없다. (d)는 그림들과 조각상을 터너가 아닌 벤저민이 생각한 것이다.

determined 결단력 있는　**retire** 은퇴하다　**antique auction** 골동품 경매　**solace** 위안　**sculpture** 조각품　**donation** 기부금

 정답 (b)

Dear Mr. Cousen,

We are writing to notify you that the Everycard credit card you hold with our company has been showing usage, including online and in-store locations, that is not characteristic of past purchasing patterns. We are writing to make sure that you are in possession of your card ending in the digits 3248 and that you are in fact making the purchases being charged to your card. Please contact us by phone or e-mail as soon as possible to confirm that your card or identity has not been stolen and is not being abused. We hope that you will understand that this is a necessary step to protect your credit, your money, and your identity.

Chris Wilkens
Everycard
Customer Service

Q: Which of the following is supported by the letter?

(a) Mr. Cousen's Everycard credit card has more than 4 digits.

(b) Mr. Cousen will call Chris Wilkens right after reading the mail.

(c) Mr. Cousen's Everycard credit card is being used by another person.

(d) There are two ways for Chris Wilkens to contact Mr. Cousen.

📖 **번역** 이 편지는 귀하가 소유하고 계신 저희 회사의 에브리 카드가 온·오프라인 상에서 사용되고 있으며, 이는 지금까지의 구매 형태와는 다른 점이 포착되어서 알려 드리고자 보내는 것입니다. 귀하께서 현재 귀하의 명의로 발급된 끝자리가 3248인 신용 카드를 가지고 계시며 귀하의 카드에 청구되는 구매를 실제로 하고 계신지 확인하고자 편지를 띄웁니다. 귀하의 카드나 개인 정보가 도난당해 부정한 방법으로 잘못 사용되지 않은 사실을 최대한 빨리 전화나 이메일로 저희에게 연락주시기 바랍니다. 이것은 귀하의 신용, 돈, 그리고 개인 정보를 보호하기 위해 필요한 조치임을 이해해 주시기 바랍니다.

(a) 코젠 씨의 에브리 카드는 4자리 수 이상이다.

(b) 코젠 씨는 편지를 읽은 후 바로 크리스 윌킨스에게 전화할 것이다.

(c) 코젠 씨의 에브리 카드는 다른 사람에 의해 사용되고 있다.

(d) 크리스 윌킨스가 코젠 씨에게 연락할 방법은 두 가지이다.

💡 **해법** 코젠이 끝자리가 3248로 끝나는 카드 소유자라고 했으므로 그의 신용 카드 일련번호는 4자리 이상임을 알 수 있어 (a)가 정답이다. (b)는 코젠 씨가 전화를 할 것인지 이메일을 쓸 것인지는 아직 알 수 없고, (c)는 카드나 개인 정보가 도난당해 잘못 사용되고 있는지 아직 확인되지 않았으며, (d)는 선택지의 크리스 윌킨스와 코젠이 바뀌어야 한다.

✓ **정답** (a)

Most of the world's largest cities have existed for centuries, over the course of which they have grown and evolved to meet the ever-changing needs of their populaces. This process must continue today, particularly through the removal of old, run-down buildings that currently take up space in many metropolitan areas. While many individuals favor a system of urban revitalization that attempts to renovate and modernize old buildings, that process is simply not efficient and does not do enough to solve problems faced by expanding and modernizing cities.

Q: Which of the following is correct according to the passage?
(a) The number of needs of city residents has multiplied.
(b) The growth of the world's largest cities must continue.
(c) Much land in large cities is occupied by centuries-old buildings.
(d) Some old buildings in the world's largest cities have collapsed.

번역 세계의 대도시들 대부분은 수백 년의 역사를 지니고 있으며 끊임없이 변화하는 주민들의 요구들을 충족시키기 위해 그동안 계속 성장과 변천의 과정을 겪어왔다. 이러한 과정은 오늘날에도 지속되어야 하는데, 특히 여러 대도시 지역 내에 자리를 차지하고 있는 오래되고 황폐한 건물들을 철거하는 사업을 통해 이루어져야 한다. 낡은 건물을 개조하고 현대화하는 방식의 도심 재개발 방식을 선호하는 사람들도 많지만, 이러한 방법은 한마디로 효율적이지도 못하며 날로 커지고 현대화되어가는 도시가 직면한 문제점들을 해결하기에는 충분치 못하다.

(a) 도시 주민들의 요구가 증가해왔다.
(b) 세계 대도시들의 성장은 지속되어야 한다.
(c) 대도시 땅의 많은 부분을 수백 년 된 건물들이 차지하고 있다.
(d) 세계 대도시들의 몇몇 오래된 건물들이 무너졌다.

해법 세계의 대도시 대부분은 수백 년 동안 성장하면서 끊임없이 변화하는 주민들의 요구를 충족시켜 왔고 이런 과정이 오늘날에도 여전히 지속되어야 한다고 했으므로 (b)가 정답이다. (a)는 지문 내용이 주민들의 요구가 끊임없이 변화했다는 것이지 증가한 것은 아니고, (c)는 Much가 맞지 않고, (d)는 지문에 없는 내용이다.

meet 충족시키다 **populace** 주민 **take up** 차지하다 **revitalization** 새로운 활력, 힘 따위를 줌 **renovate** 개조하다 **efficient** 효율적인

✓ 정답 (b)

iBridge is the standard software for connecting digital cameras and printers of different manufacturers and printing out pictures directly. By connecting the camera to an iBridge-compatible printer with the USB cable, you can print out recorded pictures directly. With the camera connected to the printer, select the pictures you want to print and the number of prints on the camera's monitor. It is also possible to print out pictures using the print reservation data. All printers that support iBridge have standard print settings. If [STANDARD] is selected on the settings screens, images are printed according to these settings. Refer to the instruction manual for its standard settings or contact the manufacturer.

Q: Which of the following is correct according to the passage?
(a) iBridge-compatible printers can print out pictures in different settings.
(b) iBridge is a software that can be installed using a USB cable.
(c) Both printers and cameras should have iBridge installed to print out pictures.
(d) The print settings can change the number of pictures to print out.

번역 아이브리지는 각기 다른 제조사의 디지털 카메라와 프린터를 연결해서 사진을 직접 출력해주는 표준 소프트웨어입니다. USB 케이블로 카메라를 아이브리지 호환 프린터와 연결하면, 저장된 사진들을 직접 출력할 수 있습니다. 카메라를 프린터에 연결한 채, 카메라 모니터 상에서 출력하고자 하는 사진들과 장수를 선택합니다. 프린트 저장 데이터를 이용해서 사진을 출력할 수도 있습니다. 아이브리지를 지원하는 모든 프린터들은 표준 프린트 세팅이 있습니다. 세팅 화면에서 [표준]이 선택되면 이 세팅에 맞춰 사진들이 출력됩니다. 프린터 표준 세팅에 관해서는 사용 설명서를 참조하거나 제조사에 연락해보세요.

(a) 아이브리지 호환 프린터들은 다른 세팅으로 사진을 출력할 수 있다.
(b) 아이브리지는 USB 케이블을 이용해 설치 가능한 소프트웨어이다.
(c) 사진 출력을 위해 프린터와 카메라 각각 아이브리지가 설치돼야 한다.
(d) 프린트 세팅으로 출력할 사진 매수를 바꿀 수 있다.

해법 지문의 If [STANDARD] is selected on the settings screens, images are printed according to these settings를 보면 (a)가 정답이다. (b), (c)는 지문에 install(설치)에 대한 내용이 없고, (d)는 출력하고자 하는 사진 장수는 카메라 모니터에서 정하는 것이지 프린트 세팅과는 상관없다.

 정답 (a)

Top designer Clay Depp, 38, is pleased to announce that he will show his latest line of evening clothes starting this Saturday. The exhibition of the new collection will be held at So Chic Gallery in Manhattan, located at 2745 W. 74th Ave. The world famous designer, who grew up on a farm in Kansas, first became prominent in 1992 in Paris, at the Le Chateau Noir, the stylishly modern street shop, where he sold his first line of women's clothing and startled the world with wild colors, ragged hemlines, and flaring sleeves. "My newest line mixes raw urban emotion with romantic sophistication," said Depp, speaking by phone from his New York City penthouse apartment, near the new exhibition.

Q: Which of the following is correct about Clay Depp?
(a) He was once involved in farming.
(b) He became internationally renowned in 1992.
(c) He made a phone call at his house to be interviewed.
(d) He lived in Paris before coming to Kansas.

Pirates would take the combs of all the people on board the ships they robbed. Earlier combs, from around nine hundred years ago, were made of bone. They had animal shapes carved on them. Unlike plastic combs used today, these combs could last longer. Later, combs made of gold were used in church. It was a custom of the Greek Church to comb the priest's hair. The combing was a part of the service. Today, the Japanese place more value on combs than do people in the West. Japanese women always combed thier hair neatly, and some Japanese people feel that to throw away a comb brings bad luck. But, to get one as a parting gift is good luck. The comb is supposed to make all future paths straight. That is because the comb makes the hair straight.

Q: Which of the following is correct about combs?
(a) They are sometimes used for religious purposes.
(b) They are believed to mean shortcuts to future goals.
(c) They were first made about 900 years ago.
(d) They were sometimes not paid for when taken.

번역 38세의 일류 디자이너 클레이 뎁이 이번 토요일부터 그의 최신 이브닝 의상 모음을 선보인다는 소식을 기쁜 마음으로 알립니다. 그의 새로운 컬렉션을 소개하는 이번 전시회는 맨해튼 소재 2745 W. 74번가에 위치한 소 시크 갤러리에서 열립니다. 세계적으로 유명한 디자이너인 클레이 뎁은 캔자스 주의 한 농장에서 자랐으며, 1992년 파리의 세련된 현대식 길거리 가게인 르 샤토 누아르에서 전 세계를 놀라게 한 강렬한 색상에 들쑥날쑥한 옷단과 나팔 소매가 특징인 그의 첫 여성복 라인을 판매하면서 세계적으로 알려지게 되었다. "저의 최신 작품은 있는 그대로의 도시 감각과 낭만적인 세련됨을 결합시켰습니다"라고 뎁은 새롭게 시작되는 전시장 근처에 위치한 그의 뉴욕 시내 아파트 펜트하우스에서 전화로 말했다.

(a) 한때 농사를 지은 적이 있다.
(b) 1992년에 세계적으로 유명해졌다.
(c) 인터뷰를 위해 자택에서 그가 전화를 걸었다.
(d) 캔자스에 오기 전에 파리에 살았다.

해법 1992년 파리의 르 샤토 누아르에서 최초로 유명해졌는데 이곳에서 그의 첫 번째 여성복을 판매했고 강렬한 색상, 들쑥날쑥한 옷단, 그리고 나팔 소매로 전 세계를 놀라게 했다고 했으므로 (b)가 정답이다. (a)는 농장에서 자란 것이지 농업 종사 여부까지는 알 수 없고, (c)는 누가 전화했는지 지문에서 확인할 수 없으며, (d)는 캔자스에서 태어났고 그 이후에 파리에 간 것이다.

prominent 유명한 **startle** 놀라게 하다 **ragged hemlines** 들쑥날쑥한 옷단 **flaring sleeves** (아래로 갈수록 넓어지는) 나팔 소매 **raw** 있는 그대로의 **urban** 도시의 **sophistication** 세련

정답 (b)

번역 해적들은 약탈한 배에 탄 모든 사람들의 빗을 가져갔다. 더 오래 전인 약 900년 전의 빗은 뼈로 만들어졌다. 이 빗에는 동물 모양이 새겨져 있었다. 오늘날의 플라스틱 빗과는 달리 이 빗은 더 오래 쓸 수 있다. 나중에는 금으로 만들어진 빗이 교회에서 사용되었다. 성직자의 머리를 빗는 것이 그리스 정교회의 관습이었다. 이러한 빗질은 예배의 한 부분이었다. 오늘날에는 일본인들이 서양인들보다 빗에 더 많은 가치를 둔다. 일본 여성들은 항상 빗으로 머리를 가지런하게 했고 어떤 일본인들은 빗을 버리면 불운이 닥쳐온다고 여긴다. 그러나 이별의 선물로 빗을 받는 것은 행운을 가져온다고 여긴다. 빗은 미래를 향해 펼쳐진 모든 길을 반듯하게 만든다고 한다. 왜냐하면 빗이 머리를 반듯하게 해주기 때문이다.

(a) 종교적인 목적으로 사용되기도 한다.
(b) 때로는 미래 목표를 향한 지름길을 의미한다고 믿어진다.
(c) 약 900년 전에 최초로 만들어졌다.
(d) 대가를 지불하지 않고 가져가는 경우가 있었다.

해법 해적들이 약탈할 때는 돈을 내고 물건을 가져가지 않으므로 (d)가 정답이다. (a)는 선택지의 현재시제와 같이 현재도 그런지 지문에 없고, (b)는 빗이 모든 미래의 진로를 반듯하게 한다는 것과 빗이 미래 목표의 지름길을 의미한다는 것은 다르며, (c)는 최초의 빗에 대한 내용이 지문에 없다.

pirate 해적 **carve** 새기다 **custom** 관습 **priest** 성직자 **service** 예배 **part** 헤어지다 **shortcut** 지름길

정답 (d)

The finch is found throughout most grassland areas of the world. It is believed that finches were caught in Australia and taken to England in the early 1800s, where they soon became popular due to their quiet song and wonderful coloration. The wild finch is grey, but captive breeding programs have produced more than 100 variations such as blue, silver, white, black, etc. Finches are social birds and should not be kept in small cages as a solitary bird. As they are not usually aggressive to other birds, they may be kept with some other species. Finches are quite cheap to purchase and easy to breed. So they are ideal for novices.

Q: Which of the following is correct according to the passage?
(a) The world has more than 100 kinds of finch.
(b) Although finches sing, they often stay quiet.
(c) Finches are aggressive to each other.
(d) Australians took finches to England.

Aircraft, of course, impact not only the environment but the passengers who fly them and the companies that operate them. So the challenge is to design jets so that everyone wins—creating models that are fuel-efficient, emissions-friendly, comfortable, and cost-effective. With its groundbreaking new aircraft, the A380, Airworld shows that these goals can be achieved. The Airworld A380—the most technically advanced civil aircraft in operation—sets new standards for environmental performance. By building roughly 25% of the A380 out of lightweight carbon fiber composite materials, Airworld was able to decrease the weight of the aircraft. Lower weight means less fuel is required, which means fewer emissions.

Q: What is Airworld?
(a) It is a newly developed plane.
(b) It is an award given to the best aircraft.
(c) It is a company that makes products.
(d) It is a group that improves air traffic.

 번역 핀치는 전 세계 대부분의 초원에서 발견된다. 핀치는 1800년대 초반에 호주에서 잡힌 뒤 영국으로 옮겨졌고 거기서 조용한 지저귐과 화려한 색깔 때문에 곧 사랑받았다. 야생 핀치는 회색이지만 포획 사육 프로그램으로 파란색, 은색, 흰색, 검정색 등 100종 이상의 변종이 만들어졌다. 핀치는 사회성이 있는 새라서 작은 새장에 혼자 키우면 안 된다. 대개 다른 새들에게 공격적이지 않기 때문에 다른 종들과 함께 키워도 된다. 핀치는 가격이 꽤 저렴하고 키우기 쉬워서 초보자들에게 적격이다.

(a) 전 세계적으로 100종 이상의 핀치가 있다.
(b) 핀치는 지저귈지라도 종종 침묵을 지킨다.
(c) 핀치는 서로에게 공격적이다.
(d) 호주 사람들이 핀치를 영국으로 가져갔다.

해법 사육 프로그램에 의해 100종 이상의 변종 핀치가 생겨났다고 했으므로 (a)가 정답이다. (b)는 지문에서 지저귐 소리가 조용하다고 했지 지저귈지라도 종종 지저귀지 않는다는 것은 아니고, (d)는 19세기 초반에 핀치가 호주에서 잡혀 영국으로 옮겨졌으나 누가 옮겼는지는 지문에 없다.

finch 핀치(되새류 새) **grassland** 초원 **captive** 포로의 **breeding** 사육 **variation** 변종 **solitary** 혼자의 **aggressive** 공격적인

정답 (a)

 번역 당연히 비행기는 환경뿐만 아니라 비행기를 타는 승객들과 비행기를 운용하는 회사들에도 영향을 줍니다. 따라서 연료 효율도 좋고, 배기가스도 적게 나오며 편하고 비용 효율이 높은 비행기를 만들어서 관련된 대상 모두를 만족시키는 것이 관건입니다. 획기적인 에어월드의 새로운 항공기 A380은 이런 목표가 이뤄질 수 있다는 것을 보여줍니다. 운용 중인 항공기 중에서 기술적으로 가장 앞선 항공기인 에어월드 A380은 환경적인 면에서 새로운 표준을 정합니다. 기체의 25퍼센트 정도를 가벼운 탄소 섬유 합성 물질로 만듦으로써 에어월드는 A380의 무게를 줄일 수 있었습니다. 가벼워진 무게로 필요한 연료의 양도 줄고 배기가스도 따라서 줄게 됨을 의미합니다.

(a) 새로 개발된 비행기이다.
(b) 가장 좋은 비행기에 주어지는 상이다.
(c) 제품을 생산하는 회사이다.
(d) 항공 교통을 개선하는 단체이다.

해법 A380의 25퍼센트 정도를 가벼운 탄소 섬유 합성 물질로 만듦으로써 에어월드는 비행기 무게를 줄일 수 있었다고 했으므로 에어월드는 비행기 제조사임을 알 수 있어 (c)가 정답이다. (a)는 A380에 대해 묻는 질문에 해당하는 답이고, (b), (d)는 지문에 없는 내용이다.

impact 영향을 주다 **operate** 운영하다 **challenge** 도전 **fuel-efficient** 연료 효율이 좋은 **cost-effective** 비용 효율이 높은 **groundbreaking** 획기적인 **roughly** 대략 **carbon fiber** 탄소 섬유

정답 (c)

The Tunguska Event occurred in 1908 over a remote region of Russia. Locals observed a bright light moving across the sky, followed by an enormous explosion and earthquake. Thanks to modern-day research and study, we can conclusively say that the explosion of a comet fragment caused the Tunguska Event. The results of this massive explosion can still be viewed, as trees were felled and burned in an area of roughly 50 square kilometers. The lack of an impact crater suggests that the object completely vaporized in midair. This supports the conclusion that the event was caused by a piece of comet, which became superheated upon atmospheric entry and exploded 5-10 kilometers above the earth's surface.

Q: Which of the following is stated about the passage?
(a) The Tunguska Forest has not been fully restored.
(b) The cause of the event was not studied until recently.
(c) The comet did not complete its course to impact the earth.
(d) The comet was not large enough to resist heat upon atmospheric entry.

In the event of Lessee being transferred other than temporarily by his present employer to a location for work so distant from the country, as to render it impractical for Lessee to maintain residence in the country while performing such work, Lessee may terminate this lease by providing Lessor with a statement in writing from both Lessee and Lessee's employer setting forth the fact of the transfer, the place to which Lessee is to be transferred, and in general the nature of the work Lessee will perform when transferred. Upon receipt of both such statements, the Lease will terminate as of the first day of the first full calendar month which is more than thirty (30) days after the date of receipt by Lessor of the two required statements.

Q: Which of the following claims is made about the passage?
(a) An employer should prove his or her relocation by providing written statements.
(b) Lessee should submit the written reason for stopping paying the rent in time.
(c) Lessee must provide the documents by the first day of a month.
(d) A transferring employee should inform the employer of the new location.

번역 통구스카 강 유역 폭발 사건은 1908년 러시아의 한 외딴 지역에서 일어났다. 인근 주민들은 하늘을 가로질러 움직이는 밝은 빛을 목격하는 것에 이어 엄청난 폭발과 지진을 경험했다. 현대의 조사와 연구 덕택에 우리는 혜성 파편이 통구스카 대폭발을 일으켰다고 확실한 결론을 내릴 수 있다. 반경 약 50킬로미터 지역에 걸쳐 나무들이 잘려나가고 불타버렸기 때문에 이 대폭발 사건이 남긴 흔적은 오늘날까지도 눈으로 확인할 수 있다. 분화구가 없다는 사실로 미루어 물체가 대기 중에서 완전히 소멸했음을 시사한다. 이는 이 사건이 혜성 파편에 의한 것이었으며 혜성 파편이 대기권에 진입함과 동시에 과열되어 지표면으로부터 5~10킬로미터 떨어진 상공에서 폭발했다는 결론을 뒷받침해 준다.

(a) 통구스카 숲은 아직 완전히 복구되지 않았다.
(b) 통구스카 사건의 원인은 최근에 와서야 연구되었다.
(c) 혜성 진로 과정 중 지구와 충돌하지 않았다.
(d) 혜성이 대기권 진입 시 열을 견딜 만큼 크지 않았다.

해법 혜성 파편이 대기권에 진입하면서 과열되어 지표면으로부터 5~10킬로미터 상공에서 폭발했다는 것은 지구 표면에 도달하지 못한 것이므로 (c)가 정답이다. (a)는 일단 통구스카 복구가 시작됐다는 내용이 지문에 없어 오답이다. (b)는 통구스카 사건의 원인이 최근에 와서야 연구되었다는 내용이 지문에 없고, (d)는 혜성의 크기에 대한 언급은 없다.

remote 외딴 **local** 주민 **observe** 목격하다 **conclusively** 결정적으로, 확실히 **comet fragment** 혜성 파편 **fell** (잘라서) 넘어뜨리다 **vaporize** 증발하다 **midair** 공중 **atmospheric** 대기의

 **정답** (c)

번역 임차인이 임시적인 상황이 아닌 그의 현재 고용주로부터 새로운 업무 수행을 위해 본국에서 계속 거주하는 것이 비효율적이라는 판단이 내려질 정도의 먼 거리에 위치한 국가로 전근 발령을 받게 될 경우 임차인은 임차인 본인과 임차인의 고용주가 작성한 전근 사실, 전근 장소, 그리고 전근지에서 담당할 업무의 성격을 담은 서면 신고서를 임대인에게 제출함으로써 임대 계약을 종료할 수 있다. 임대인이 이에 해당하는 서면 신고서 2매를 수령하는 날로부터 최소 30일 이상 존재하는 달로 1개월 이상 경과한 이후의 첫째 달, 첫날부터 임대 계약이 효력을 잃게 된다.

(a) 고용인은 서면 신고서를 제출함으로써 본인의 전근 사실을 증명해야 한다.
(b) 임차인은 기일 내 임대료 지불 정지 사유를 서면으로 제출해야 한다.
(c) 임차인은 한 달의 첫날까지 서류를 제출해야 한다.
(d) 전근 가는 고용인은 고용주에게 새로운 거주지를 알려야 한다.

해법 서면 신고서를 임대인에게 제출하고 임대인이 신고서를 받은 날로부터 30일 이상 떨어져 있는 달의 첫날부터 임대 계약이 효력을 잃을 것이라고 했으므로 (b)가 정답이다. (a)는 employer가 아니라 employee가 돼야 하고, (c)는 선택지의 by the first day of a month가 맞지 않다. (d)는 지문에 없는 내용이다.

lessee 임차인 **render** ~로 만들다, ~이 되게 하다 **impractical** 불가능한 **residence** 거주 **terminate** 종료하다 **lease** 임대 계약 **set forth** 설명하다, 명시하다 **nature** 성격 **as of** ~로부터 (시간적 개념)

정답 (b)

Low literacy rates are common in the United States: a decade ago, 40 million adult Americans scored on the lowest of five levels (level 1) of the National Adult Literacy Survey (NALS). This low literacy level corresponds to having trouble finding pieces of information or numbers in a lengthy text, integrating multiple pieces of information in a document, or finding two or more numbers in a chart and performing a calculation. Consequently, it may damage functioning in the health care environment, affect patient-physician communication relation, and unintentionally lead to poor quality of medical care. It is related to the fact that people poorly understand medical advice in a written or spoken form so that their health is adversely affected.

Q: Which of the following is supported by the passage?
(a) U.S. medical care is negatively influenced by low illiteracy rate.
(b) Some patients cannot understand properly doctors' advice to get well.
(c) NALS surveys the literacy rate in the U.S. every 10 years.
(d) About 40 million of the U.S. population turned out to be illiterate.

The pawnshop industry has been in decline in most parts of the world. In the United States, however, the pawnshop business actually grew during the same time period, from under 2,000 to more than 7,000 today. One of the reasons for the growth of pawnshops is that many states have relaxed their restrictions on the maximum interest rates that can be charged. Pawnshops in these states can now legally charge the high rates needed to stay in business. Further, the percentage of U.S. citizens classified as low-income has risen in recent decades. These individuals cannot get loans from mainstream financial institutions, such as banks and savings and loan associations, and so must turn to alternatives, one of which is the pawnshop.

Q: Why did the pawnshop business grow in the United States?
(a) There have been changes to restrictions on pawnshops.
(b) The U.S. economy has been impacted by the world economy.
(c) The most recent decades have seen the increased patronage of pawnshops.
(d) The pawnshops have become more competitive than mainstream financial institutions.

번역 높은 문맹률은 미국에서 흔한 일이다. 10년 전, 전국 성인 식자율 조사(National Adult Literacy Survey (NALS)) 결과 4천만 명의 미국 성인이 총 5개 등급 중 최하인 1급을 받았다. 이런 높은 문맹률은 긴 지문에서 정보나 숫자를 찾거나 한 문서에서 여러 개의 정보를 취합하는 것, 또는 도표에서 2개 이상의 숫자를 찾아 계산을 하는 데 있어 문제를 겪는 상황에 비할 수 있다. 결과적으로 문맹은 의료 환경의 기능을 손상시키거나 환자와 의사 간의 의사 소통에 영향을 끼치며, 본의 아니게 의료 수준을 떨어뜨리는 결과를 빚을 수도 있다. 이는 사람들이 글이나 말로 전달되는 의학적 충고를 제대로 이해하지 못함으로 인해 그들의 건강에 부정적인 영향을 받게 되는 것과 관련 있다.

(a) 미국 의료 서비스가 높은 문맹률의 부정적인 영향을 받고 있다.
(b) 어떤 환자들은 본인의 회복을 위해 전달하는 의사들의 충고를 제대로 이해하지 못한다.
(c) NALS는 매 10년마다 미국의 식자율을 조사한다.
(d) 약 4천만 명의 미국 인구가 문맹이라고 드러났다.

해법 문맹은 의료 환경의 기능을 손상시킬 수 있고 환자와 의사 간의 의사 소통 활동에 영향을 끼친다고 했으므로 (b)가 정답이다. (a)는 지문 내용이 미국의 low illiteracy rate가 아닌 low literacy rate에 대한 것이고, (c)는 National Adult Literacy Survey (NALS)이 조사기관이 아닌 일종의 설문지이다. (d)는 지문 내용이 미국 국민이 아니라 미국 성인 중에서 4천만 명의 문맹률이 높다는 것이다.

literacy rate 식자율   **correspond to** ~에 해당하다   **integrate** 통합하다   **calculation** 계산   **consequently** 결과적으로   **unintentionally** 본의 아니게   **adversely** 반대로, 부정적으로   **illiterate** 문맹의

번역 전당포 산업은 세계 대부분의 지역에서 감소 추세를 보여왔다. 하지만 동일한 기간 동안 미국의 전당포 사업은 그 수가 과거 2,000개 미만에서 현재 7,000개 이상으로 실질적으로 늘어났다. 전당포가 증가한 이유 중 하나는 여러 주에서 청구 가능한 최대 이자율에 대한 규제를 완화했기 때문이다. 이제 이들 주 내에서는 전당포가 살아남는 데 필요한 높은 이자율을 합법적으로 매길 수 있게 된 것이다. 게다가 저소득층으로 분류되는 미국 시민의 비율이 최근 몇십 년 사이에 늘어났다. 이런 사람들은 은행이나 신용 금고 등과 같은 제1금융권에서 대출을 받을 수가 없으며, 따라서 다른 대안에 의존해야 하는데 그 중 하나가 전당포이다.

(a) 전당포에 대한 규제가 바뀌었다.
(b) 미국 경제가 세계 경제에 영향을 받았다.
(c) 지난 몇십 년 동안 전당포 사용자가 늘었다.
(d) 전당포가 제1금융권보다 더 경쟁력 있게 됐다.

해법 최근 몇십 년 사이에 제1금융권에서 대출받을 수 없는 저소득층 비율이 증가했고 이들이 대안으로 전당포를 이용하게 됐다는 내용을 보면 (c)가 정답이다. (a)는 전당포에 취해진 규제를 완화한 것으로 최대이자율을 낮춘 것 하나만 지문에서 나왔으므로 복수형 changes가 맞지 않고, (d)는 지문 내용이 제1금융권에서 대출받을 수 없어 전당포를 찾는 저소득층이 증가했다는 것이지 전당포가 제1금융권보다 더 경쟁력 있게 됐다는 것은 아니다.

pawnshop 전당포   **restriction** 규제   **interest rate** 이자율
mainstream financial institutions 제1금융권

 정답 (b)

정답 (c)

Model Test | 1 (d) 2 (a) 3 (c) 4 (c) P63

Traditional Korean painting can be divided into two distinct categories. The first is the Confucian style which was first introduced by China in the 14th century. These paintings originally imitated the style of the Chinese scholar-gentry artists, but soon developed many characteristics which were distinctly Korean. Most of these paintings are of pastoral settings— landscapes, birds, and flowers. The other tradition of Korean painting is the folk painting, which is not bound by Confucian restrictions, but instead reflects Korea's shamanistic and spiritual heritage. These delightful pictures depict tigers, mountain spirits, and household gods. Most Buddhist temples are gaily decorated with pictures of this type.

Q: Which of the following is correct about traditional Korean painting?
(a) It began around the 14th century.
(b) It was greatly influenced by Chinese artists.
(c) It did not have its own restrictions.
(d) Its Confucian style is not seen at temples.

번역 한국 전통 회화는 두 개의 뚜렷한 범주로 나눌 수 있다. 하나는 14세기에 중국에서 최초로 유입된 유교식 회화이다. 이 그림들은 처음에는 중국 문인 화가들의 화풍을 모방했지만 오래지 않아 한국만의 고유한 특징을 많이 개발했다. 대부분의 이 그림들은 풍경, 새, 그리고 꽃과 같이 목가적인 배경이다. 한국 회화의 다른 전통으로는 유교에 얽매이는 대신에 한국의 샤머니즘과 정신적인 유산을 반영하는 민속화가 있다. 화려한 민속화는 호랑이, 산신령, 그리고 집안의 신들을 그린다. 대부분의 절은 이런 종류의 그림들로 익살스럽게 장식되어 있다.

(a) 14세기경에 시작됐다.
(b) 중국 예술가들의 영향을 많이 받았다.
(c) 고유의 방식이 없었다.
(d) 유교식 스타일은 절에서 볼 수 없다.

해법 한국 전통 회화가 유교식 회화와 유교 방식에 제한되지 않은 종류로 나뉜다는 내용과 후자가 대부분의 절을 장식하고 있다는 내용을 연계해 보면 (d)가 정답이다. (a)는 유교식 그림이 14세기에 중국으로부터 한국에 도입됐다는 것이지 한국 전통 회화 자체가 14세기에 시작됐다는 것은 아니고, 지문의 in the 14th century와 선택지의 around the 14th century는 다르다.

distinct 뚜렷한 **Confucian** 유교의 **scholar-gentry** 선비, 문인 **pastoral** 목가적인 **folk painting** 민화 **be bound by** ~에 의해 제한되다 **depict** 그리다 **gaily** 유쾌하게

 정답 (d)

For centuries the Nez Perce Indians lived among the grassy hills and plateaus of the area that is now part of Washington, Idaho, and Oregon. In 1877 the people, under the leadership of Chief Joseph, were told that they would have to leave the area within 30 days. Several battles followed in which the Indians were victorious under the leadership of their great war chief. Finally, the Nez Perce were defeated. Joseph chose to retreat rather than surrender. This was one of the most skillfully planned and performed retreats in American military history. The Indians traveled over 2,500 kilometers and were stopped just before reaching the Canadian border, where they would have been safe from U.S. soldiers.

Q: Which of the following is correct according to the passage?
(a) The Nez Perce Indians lost only one battle against U.S. soldiers.
(b) U.S. soldiers and the Nez Perce Indians fought each other for a month.
(c) Chief Joseph provided military training to his people.
(d) The Nez Perce Indians wanted to cross the Canadian border.

번역 수세기 동안 네즈퍼스 인디언들은 지금의 워싱턴, 아이다호, 그리고 오리건 주 일부 지역의 풀이 우거진 언덕과 고원에서 살았다. 1877년에 조셉 추장의 지휘 하에 이 인디언들은 30일 이내에 그 지역을 떠나야 할 것이라는 말을 들었다. 이후 훌륭한 전쟁 추장의 통솔로 인디언들이 승리했던 몇몇 전투가 이어졌다. 그러나 결국 네즈퍼스 인디언들은 패배했다. 조셉 추장은 항복보다는 후퇴를 선택했는데, 이것은 미군 역사상 가장 치밀하게 계획되고 수행된 후퇴 중 하나였다. 네즈퍼스 인디언들은 2,500킬로미터가 넘는 거리를 이동했으나, 도착했더라면 미국 군인들로부터 안전했을 캐나다 국경에 다다르기 직전 저지당했다.

(a) 네즈퍼스 인디언들은 미군들과의 전투에서 한 번만 졌다.
(b) 미군들과 네즈퍼스 인디언들은 한 달 동안 싸웠다.
(c) 조셉 추장은 그의 동족들에게 군사 훈련을 시켰다.
(d) 네즈퍼스 인디언들은 캐나다 국경을 넘고 싶었다.

해법 조셉 추장이 이끈 네즈퍼스 인디언들이 계속해서 전투에서 승리를 했다는 내용과 결국 패배했다는 내용을 연계해 보면 이는 단 한 번 패배했다는 말과 같으므로 (a)가 정답이다. (b), (c)는 지문에 구체적으로 나와 있지 않다.

plateau 고원, 대지 **retreat** 후퇴하다 **surrender** 항복하다

 정답 (a)

Homelessness has arisen from at least three social forces. One is the increased shortage of inexpensive housing for poor families and poor unattached persons because of diminishing government subsidization of such housing. Another social force is the decreasing demand for unskilled labor that has occurred since the 1980s, which has resulted in extremely high unemployment among young men in general and African Americans in particular. A third social force is the erosion of the public welfare benefits that has occurred over the last two decades. These three social forces enlarged the ranks of the extremely poor, thereby increasing the chances of these people becoming homeless.

Q: Which of the following is supported by the passage?
(a) The government will increase public housing subsidization in the future.
(b) African Americans have been affected most by the three social forces.
(c) Homelessness and unemployment among young men have become more serious.
(d) There has been little demand for unskilled labor since the 1980s.

번역 노숙은 적어도 세 가지 사회적 요인에 의해 생겨났다. 하나는 가난한 사람들과 가난한 독신자들을 위한 저렴한 주택의 부족 현상이 심화되었기 때문인데, 이는 이러한 주거 환경에 대한 정부의 보조가 줄어들었기 때문이다. 또 다른 사회적 요인은 1980년대 이래로 일어나고 있는 비숙련 노동에 대한 수요 감소 현상으로, 이는 젊은층 전반에 걸쳐 높은 실업률을 가져왔는데, 특히 흑인들 사이에서 더욱 두드러졌다. 세 번째 사회적 요인은 지난 20년에 걸쳐 일어난 공공복지 혜택 붕괴이다. 이들 세 가지 사회적 요인들은 극도로 가난한 사람들을 더 많이 양산했고, 따라서 이들이 노숙자가 될 가능성도 커졌다.

(a) 정부는 앞으로 공공주택 보조금을 늘릴 것이다.
(b) 흑인들은 이 세 가지 사회적 요인들에 영향을 가장 많이 받아왔다.
(c) 젊은이들의 노숙과 실직이 더 심각해졌다.
(d) 1980년대 이래로 비숙련 노동에 대한 수요가 거의 없었다.

해법 노숙을 생기게 한 세 가지 요인들에 대한 내용과 이런 요인들로 가난한 사람들이 더 많이 생겼고 이들이 노숙자가 될 가능성도 커졌다는 내용을 연계해 보면 젊은이들의 노숙과 실업이 더 심각해졌다는 (c)가 정답이다. (a)는 지문 내용만으로 선택지와 같이 단정할 수 없고, (d)는 선택지의 little이 declining이 돼야 한다.

unattached 독신의 **subsidization** 보조금 **housing** 주거
unemployment 실업 **erosion** 붕괴 **enlarge** 확대하다 **thereby** 그 때문에 **chance** 가능성

  정답 (c)

A Whitesville police officer, responding to an incident call in his private car near Port Ericsson, crashed into another vehicle around 2:40 p.m. Sunday, killing its driver, according to Whitesville State Highway Patrol reports. Patrick T. Houston, 32, an assistant inspector of the Port Ericsson Police Department, remains hospitalized in moderate condition at the Cooper County Regional Medical Center, according to the hospital authority, while Debora Hammersmith, 58, the assistant principal of Port Ericsson Industrial High School, was confirmed dead at the center. A witness said Houston was driving a 2005 Toyokuni 3000 convertible westbound when he entered the intersection and struck Hammersmith's 1999 ABM SUV traveling from downtown.

Q: Which of the following is NOT correct?
(a) Patrick is not on duty temporarily.
(b) Debora's car was manufactured before Patrick's.
(c) The incident in Port Ericsson was not taken care of.
(d) Patrick and Debora were driving toward different directions.

번역 일요일 오후 2시 40분쯤에 화이츠빌 소속인 한 경찰관이 에릭슨 항구 근처에서 사고 소식을 듣고 자신의 차로 출동하다가 다른 차량과 충돌해서 상대 차량 운전자가 사망했다고 화이츠빌 주 고속도로 순찰대가 전했다. 병원 당국에 따르면 32세의 에릭슨 항구 경찰서 소속 패트릭 T. 휴스턴 경사는 쿠퍼군 지역 병원에 양호한 상태로 입원 중인데, 58세의 에릭슨 항구 공업 고등학교 데보라 해머스미스 교감은 병원에서 사망한 것으로 확인되었다. 목격자에 따르면 휴스턴은 교차로에 진입했을 때 2005년 토요쿠니 3000 컨버터블을 몰고 서쪽으로 가고 있었고 시내에서 오는 해머스미스 씨의 1999년 ABM SUV와 충돌했다고 한다.

(a) 패트릭은 당분간 근무하지 않는다.
(b) 데보라의 차는 패트릭의 차보다 먼저 제조되었다.
(c) 에릭슨 항구의 사고는 처리되지 않았다.
(d) 패트릭과 데보라는 서로 다른 방향을 향해 운전하고 있었다.

해법 에릭슨 항구에서 어떤 사건이 발생했는지가 지문에 없어 발생 여부가 불분명한 사건에 대해 처리 여부를 말할 수 없으므로 (c)가 정답이다. (b)는 지문의 2005 Toyokuni 3000 convertible과 Hammersmith's 1999 ABM SUV를 연계해 보면 알 수 있으며 (d)는 지문의 the intersection(교차로)을 보면 서로 다른 방향에서 오다가 충돌했음을 알 수 있다.

hospitalize 입원시키다 **moderate** 온건한 **authority** 당국
westbound 서쪽으로 가는 **intersection** 교차로 **on duty** 근무 중인
temporarily 일시적으로

  정답 (c)

해설 및 정답 **Unit 06**

One had to light this alarm clock to make it work. The Chinese called it the dragon clock. It belonged to a second-century ruler. It was a figure of a dragon with pegs evenly spaced along its body. The pegs made it look like a dragon-shaped coat rack. A wooden bar was laid across the pegs every night. When lighted, the bar burned from one peg to the next in about an hour. The alarm for this clock was a cord with weights on the ends. It was hung on the peg of the hour that the king wanted to wake up. When the burning bar got to the cord, it burned through it. The weights would fall into a copper basin on the floor. The sound of the weights landing was this clock's alarm.

Q: What should be done first to set the alarm clock?
(a) It has to be lit.
(b) It should be placed in a bedroom.
(c) A wooden bar needs to be put across the pegs.
(d) Weights should be put back on the ends of the cord.

This certificate entitles you to purchase one $149 round-trip Coach Class companion ticket with the purchase of one qualifying published round-trip Coach Class adult fare ticket with a minimum stay requirement. This certificate applies for travel solely on Great Lakes Airlines within the forty-eight contiguous United States. Exception: travel to or from Minnesota or Michigan is not permitted. A Saturday night stay is required. Tickets must be issued by March 31 for travel between April 5 and September 15. Passenger Facility Charges of $1 to $3 per airport may apply, up to a maximum of $12 round-trip, depending on your itinerary. Void if sold, bartered or exchanged for compensation.

Q: Which of the following is correct according to the passage?
(a) Those with certificates can travel right after they get their tickets issued.
(b) Valid certificates must be exchanged for tickets before March 31 for travel.
(c) It is impossible to sell, barter, or exchange certificates for compensation.
(d) Certificate holders must stay at their travel destination for at least one night.

번역 이 자명종을 작동시키기 위해서는 불을 붙여야 했다. 중국인들은 이것을 용 시계라고 불렀다. 이것은 2세기 한 지배자가 소유했던 물건이다. 용의 형상을 한 이 시계는 몸통을 따라 고른 간격으로 못이 박혀 있었다. 그 못들 때문에 시계는 용 모양의 코트 걸이처럼 보였다. 매일 밤 그 못들을 가로질러 나무 막대기가 놓였던 것이다. 불을 붙이면 막대기는 한 못에서 다른 못까지 타는 데 약 한 시간 걸렸다. 이 시계의 자명종은 끝에 추가 달린 끈이었다. 이 끈을 왕이 일어나고자 하는 시간에 해당하는 못에 걸었다. 막대기의 타는 부분이 끈에 닿으면 끈을 태운 뒤 바닥에 있는 구리 대야로 추가 떨어지게 되는 것이다. 추가 떨어지는 소리가 이 시계의 자명종이었다.

(a) 불을 붙여야 한다.
(b) 침실에 놓여야 한다.
(c) 못을 가로질러 나무 막대기가 놓여야 한다.
(d) 끈 끝에 추가 다시 달려야 한다.

해법 질문을 자세히 읽지 않으면 지문 첫 문장 때문에 (a)를 선택하기 쉽다. What should be done to make the alarm clock work?와 같은 질문이 나왔다면 (a)가 정답이 될 수 있다. 그러나 '자명종을 맞춰놓기 위해 가장 먼저 할 일은 무엇인가?'라는 질문을 되짚어 보면서 지문 첫 문장과 그 다음에 이어지는 자명종을 준비하는 과정을 연계해 보면 (c)가 정답이다.

light 불을 붙이다 **belong to** ~의 것이다 **figure** 형상 **peg** 못 **coat rack** 코트 걸이 **weight** 추 **copper** 구리 **basin** 대야

✓ 정답 (c)

번역 이 할인권은 최소한의 숙박 요건을 포함한 정규 일반석 성인 왕복 항공권 1매 구입을 전제로 일반석 동승 왕복권 한 장을 149달러에 구입하실 수 있습니다. 이 할인권은 그레이트 레이크 항공을 이용하여 미국 내 인접 48개 주를 여행할 경우에만 적용됩니다. 단, 미네소타 주 혹은 미시건 주에서의 출발 및 도착은 해당되지 않습니다. 토요일 밤 하루는 반드시 포함되어야 합니다. 4월 5일에서 9월 15일 사이에 여행을 하기 위해서는 3월 31일까지 항공권을 발급받아야 합니다. 공항에 따라 1달러에서 3달러 사이의 공항 이용료가 발생할 수 있으며, 여행 일정에 따라 왕복 최대 12달러까지 부과될 수 있습니다. 상기 조건은 증서의 판매, 물물 교환, 또는 보상금으로 교환 즉시 그 효력을 상실합니다.

(a) 할인권 소유자는 항공권을 발급받자마자 여행할 수 있다.
(b) 여행을 하려면 유효한 할인권을 3월 31일 전에 항공권으로 교환해야 한다.
(c) 할인권을 판매, 물물 교환, 또는 대가를 받고 교환하는 것은 불가능하다.
(d) 할인권 소유자는 여행 목적지에서 최소한 하룻밤을 머물러야 한다.

해법 여행지에서 최소한의 숙박 기간을 요구한다는 내용과 토요일 하룻밤을 머물러야 한다는 내용을 보면 (d)가 정답이다. (a)는 3월 31일까지 항공권을 발급받아야 탑승할 수 있다고 했으므로 옳지 않고, (c)는 무효가 된다는 것이지 그런 행위 자체를 할 수 없다는 것은 아니다.

certificate 증명서 **contiguous** 인접하는 **itinerary** 여행 일정표

✓ 정답 (d)

Attackers had to pass the drawbridge of a medieval castle. If the drawbridge had been pulled up, the attackers had to find some way of crossing the moat. While they were finding a way across, the defenders could shoot arrows at them from the safety of the castle battlements. If the attackers did succeed in crossing the moat, they had to get past a heavy iron gate called the "portcullis." From slits above them, the defenders could pour down boiling water, hot lead, or burning oil. Once inside the castle itself, the attackers had to fight their way through the different buildings and storerooms. Sometimes a wall divided the castle into two parts: the outer and inner yards.

Q: Which of the following is correct according to the passage?
(a) More ways were developed to easily attack castles.
(b) The wall of a castle was divided into two parts.
(c) There were not many ways to get to the portcullis.
(d) Buildings and storerooms made up a complete castle.

 번역 중세의 성을 공격하려면 도개교를 지나가야 했다. 만약 도개교가 걷혀져 있다면 공격자들은 해자(垓子)를 건널 방법을 찾아야만 했다. 공격자들이 건널 방법을 찾고 있는 동안에 성을 지키는 호위대는 안전한 성벽에서 공격자들을 향해 화살을 쏠 수 있었다. 공격자들이 해자를 건너는 데 성공했다 하더라도 '내리닫이 쇠창살문'이라고 불리는 육중한 철재 성문을 통과해야만 했다. 그 철문 위의 틈새로 호위대는 끓는 물이나 뜨거운 납, 혹은 타고 있는 기름을 부을 수 있었다. 일단 성 안에 들어가면 공격자들은 여러 건물과 창고를 뚫어 싸워 나가야만 했다. 때로는 벽 하나로 성을 바깥뜰과 안뜰의 두 부분으로 나누어 놓은 경우도 있었다.

(a) 성을 쉽게 공격할 수 있는 더 많은 방법들이 개발되었다.
(b) 성벽은 두 부분으로 나뉘어 있었다.
(c) 내리닫이 쇠창살문에 도달할 수 있는 방법은 많지 않았다.
(d) 건물과 창고가 모여 성 전체를 구성했다.

※ 해법 도개교를 통과해야만 했다는 내용과 도개교가 올라가 있으면 해자(垓子)를 건널 방법을 찾아야만 했다는 내용을 연계해 보면 도개교를 이용하거나 해자를 건너 내리닫이 쇠창살문에 도달할 수 있었으므로 (c)가 정답이다. (d)는 성문도 성의 일부분이므로 선택지와 같이 건물들과 저장실들로만 성이 이뤄져 있었다고 할 수 없다.

medieval 중세의 **drawbridge** 도개교 **moat** 해자(垓子) **defender** 방어자 **battlements** 총안이 있는 흉벽 **portcullis** 내리닫이 쇠창살문 **slit** 틈

✓ 정답 (c)

Probably the most famous example of primate language use is Koko, a female lowland gorilla studied by scientists at Stanford University. Born and raised in captivity, Koko has been scrutinized intensely ever since her training in a slightly modified American Sign Language began at the age of one. Since then, Koko has gained proficiency in over 1,000 signs and developed an understanding of roughly 2,000 words of spoken English. Her mastery of these language aspects is not based on a vague idea that the symbols will earn her treats, however. Instead, Koko has been shown to use language in a novel, independent, and critical thinking-based manner.

Q: Which of the following is correct according to the passage?
(a) Koko could translate signs into English words.
(b) Koko sometimes used sign language simply to be fed.
(c) Stanford scientists saw Koko's creative use of signs.
(d) It is not clear why animals use symbols to communicate.

번역 영장류의 가장 유명한 언어 사용 사례는 아마도 스탠퍼드 대학교 과학자들이 연구한 암컷 저지대 고릴라 코코일 것이다. 포획 상태로 태어나 길러진 코코는 한 살 때부터 약간 변형된 미국 수화 교육을 받기 시작하며 면밀히 조사되었다. 그 이후로 코코는 1천 개가 넘는 수화를 능숙하게 구사할 수 있게 되었고 약 2천 개에 이르는 영어 구술 표현을 이해할 수 있게 되었다. 그러나 코코의 이런 언어 능력은 손짓을 잘 구분하면 먹을 것이 생긴다는 막연한 생각에 근거한 것이 아니다. 대신에 코코는 새롭고 독립적이며 비판적인 사고가 반영된 방식으로 언어를 사용한다는 것이 입증되었다.

(a) 코코는 수화를 영어 단어로 번역할 수 있었다.
(b) 코코는 종종 단지 음식을 얻어먹기 위해 수화를 사용했다.
(c) 스탠퍼드 과학자들은 코코의 창의적인 수화 사용을 목격했다.
(d) 동물들이 의사 소통을 위해 왜 기호들을 이용하는지 불분명하다.

※ 해법 스탠퍼드 대학교 과학자들이 고릴라 코코를 연구했다는 내용과 코코가 참신하고 독립적이며 비판적인 사고가 반영된 방식으로 언어를 사용한다는 것이 입증됐다는 내용을 연계해 보면 (c)가 정답이다. (a), (b)는 지문에 없는 내용이고, (d)는 선택지 animals의 범위가 너무 넓다.

primate 영장류 **captivity** 포획 **scrutinize** 면밀히 조사하다 **modified** 변형된 **sign language** 수화 **proficiency** 능숙 **mastery** 숙달 **vague** 막연한 **symbol** 기호 **novel** 새로운

✓ 정답 (c)

The United States' forest management policy for much of the mid-20th century advocated preventing and extinguishing fires. This practice led to a buildup of dead timber, brush, and other combustible material on the forest floor. After years of drought, that debris dried into volatile tinder that fed inordinately large and hot fires beginning in the late '90s and recurring every summer. Because of the unnatural amount of fuel in forests that had not been allowed to burn for decades, fires that should have been moderate became massive raging infernos that engulfed everything in their paths.

Q: Which of the following is correct according to the passage?
(a) Forest fire extinguishing operations have often failed for some years.
(b) The U.S. forest management policy seemed to work for about 50 years.
(c) Droughts are severest in summer with many forests being burned out.
(d) The buildup of dead timber was not cleared until the late 1990s.

The most practical method of employing hydrogen as a widespread source of power is through the use of fuel cells. In such devices, hydrogen is combined with oxygen in the presence of an electrolyte, creating energy. Just as importantly, the process releases only water vapor and heat as waste products, neither of which is truly harmful. Hydrogen fuel cells come in a variety of sizes, and can be joined together in circuits to yield higher voltage and stronger current. Thus, they can provide power for a wide variety of industrial and personal applications without harming the environment.

Q: Which of the following is correct according to the passage?
(a) Hydrogen is being used for different industrial and personal applications.
(b) Hydrogen fuel cells are replacing some popular types of energy.
(c) Hydrogen must be mixed with oxygen to produce energy.
(d) Hydrogen fuel cells cause no environmental problems.

 번역 대부분의 20세기 중반 동안 미국의 삼림 관리 정책은 산불 예방 및 진압을 옹호했다. 이런 정책 시행으로 인해 죽은 목재와 덤불, 기타 타기 쉬운 땔감들이 숲 바닥에 계속 쌓여가는 결과를 초래했다. 지속되는 가뭄으로 그와 같은 나무 부스러기들이 건조되어 휘발성 불쏘시개로 바뀌어 갔고, 그로 인해 90년대 후반부터 맹렬한 초대형 산불들이 일어나기 시작하여 매년 여름철마다 되풀이되고 있다. 수십 년간 태우는 것이 금지된 숲 속에 비정상적으로 많은 양의 땔감 때문에, 그리 크지 않았을 산불은 지나가는 길목마다 모든 것을 집어삼켜 버리며 맹렬한 속도로 번지는 대화재로 바뀌었다.

(a) 산불 진압 활동이 몇 년 동안 종종 실패했다.
(b) 미국의 삼림 관리 정책이 약 50년 동안은 효과적인 것으로 보였다.
(c) 많은 숲이 다 타버리는 여름에 가뭄이 가장 심하다.
(d) 쌓여 있는 죽은 목재는 1990년대 후반에 이르기까지 치워지지 않았다.

해법 20세기 중반 대부분 동안 미국의 삼림 관리 정책이 산불 예방 및 진압을 밀어붙였다는 내용과 90년대 후반부터 맹렬한 초대형 산불들이 일어나기 시작했다는 내용을 연계해 보면 (b)가 정답이다. (a)는 선택지의 have often failed에 대한 객관적인 근거가 지문에 없고, (c)는 선택지의 out이 빠져야 하며, (d)는 선택지의 was not cleared에 대한 객관적인 근거가 지문에 없다.

advocate 옹호하다 extinguish 끄다 practice 실행 brush 덤불, 잡목림 combustible 타기 쉬운 volatile 휘발성의 inordinate 과도한 recur 반복되다 raging 맹렬한 inferno 지옥, 불 engulf 삼키다

정답 (b)

번역 수소를 광범위한 에너지원으로 활용할 수 있는 가장 현실적인 방법은 연료 전지를 사용하는 것이다. 이러한 장치로 수소가 전해질이 있는 데에서 산소와 결합하면서 에너지를 창출한다. 마찬가지로 중요한 것은 이 화학 과정을 통해 폐기물로 배출되는 것은 별로 해롭지 않은 수증기와 열뿐이라는 점이다. 수소 연료 전지는 다양한 크기가 있으며 회로를 연결해서 더 높은 전압과 강한 전류를 얻을 수 있다. 따라서 환경에 무해하면서 각종 다양한 산업용 및 가정용 에너지원을 제공할 수 있다.

(a) 수소가 다른 산업용 및 가정용 에너지원으로 사용되고 있다.
(b) 수소 연료 전지가 널리 보급된 몇몇 에너지원을 대체하고 있다.
(c) 수소는 에너지를 생산하기 위해 산소와 결합해야 한다.
(d) 수소 연료 전지는 환경 문제를 발생시키지 않는다.

해법 수소를 광범위한 에너지원으로 활용할 수 있는 가장 현실적인 방법으로 수소 연료 전지에 대한 내용과 폐기물로 배출되는 것이 결코 해롭지 않은 수증기와 열뿐이라는 내용, 혹은 환경에 무해하다는 내용을 연계해 보면 (d)가 정답이다. (a), (b)는 시제가 맞지 않고, 특히 (b)는 선택지의 some popular types of energy는 지문에 없다. (c)는 수소가 아니라 수소 연료 전지에만 해당한다.

employ 사용하다 hydrogen 수소 in the presence of ~가 있는 데에서 electrolyte 전해질 water vapor 수증기 waste product 폐기물 circuit 회로 yield 산출하다 voltage 전압 current 전류 application 이용

정답 (d)

Dear Mr. Henry,

We extend our gratitude for your special attention to our company the other day. With your detailed presentation, we learned a lot about propane and propane accessories. We have known propane as barbecue grill fuel but did not know it could be efficient and environmentally friendly as well. We were also impressed by the propane-powered refrigerator. We came to realize that propane is ideal for our business operation. We are planning to make an infrastructural building project next month, and are happy to tell you that we will revise our business practices to use this natural resource soon. Before we launch this project, we would like you to visit us once again and help us implement propane accessories safely. We are looking forward to hearing from you at your earliest convenience.

Sincerely,
Lola William

Q: Which of the following is correct about Lola William?
(a) She gave a presentation about propane and its accessories.
(b) She thought that she knew everything about propane.
(c) She wants Mr. Henry to help her with a building project.
(d) She has ordered propane from Mr. Henry before.

The "1421 hypothesis," based on ideas proposed in the book *1421: The Year China Discovered the World*, by Gavin Menzies, suggests that Chinese sailors actually reached the Americas by sailing across the Indian Ocean, around the southern tip of Africa, and across the Atlantic Ocean roughly 70 years before Columbus made his famous journey. The evidence for the "1421 hypothesis" is fairly scattered, as it has to be pulled from what remains today, almost six centuries later. Three categories can be used to organize the supporting evidence: maps, Chinese records, and assorted historical oddities. Menzies uses maps to bolster his revolutionary contentions, which seem to show that the Chinese had an outstanding understating of world geography prior to Columbus.

Q: Which of the following claims is made about the passage?
(a) Evidence shows that the Chinese knew how to get to the Americas.
(b) Chinese sailors discovered the Americas in the early 14th century.
(c) The Chinese made maps to the Americas that were first found by Menzies.
(d) Menzies does not believe that Columbus discovered the Americas.

번역 일전에 저희 회사에 보여주신 귀하의 특별한 관심에 감사드립니다. 귀하의 꼼꼼한 프레젠테이션 덕분에 프로판과 프로판 가스 기기들에 대해 많은 것을 배웠습니다. 저희는 프로판을 바비큐 그릴 연료로는 알고 있었으나 효율이 좋고 환경친화적일 수 있다는 것은 몰랐습니다. 프로판으로 작동되는 냉장고도 정말 놀라웠습니다. 저희는 프로판이 저희 사업 운영에 이상적이라는 것을 알게 되었습니다. 다음 달에 추진할 기반 시설 건설 프로젝트에 조만간 이 천연 자원을 사용하는 방향으로 수정해서 진행할 계획이라는 점을 기쁜 마음으로 알려드립니다. 프로젝트를 시작하기에 앞서 다시 한번 저희를 방문해 주셔서 안전하게 프로판 가스 기기들을 사용할 수 있도록 도와주시면 좋겠습니다. 가급적 빠른 시일 안에 소식 주시기를 기대합니다.

(a) 프로판과 프로판 가스 기기들에 대해 프레젠테이션을 했다.
(b) 프로판에 대해 모든 것을 알고 있다고 생각했다.
(c) 헨리 씨가 건설 프로젝트에 도움을 주길 원한다.
(d) 전에도 헨리 씨로부터 프로판을 주문한 적이 있다.

해법 로라 씨가 건설 프로젝트에 프로판 가스를 사용하려 하고, 헨리 씨로부터 프로판 가스 기기 작동법을 알고 싶어 한다는 점을 연계해 보면 (c)가 정답이다. (a)는 헨리 씨가 프레젠테이션을 했고, (b)는 선택지의 everything이 맞지 않다. (d)는 지문에서 알 수 없다.

 정답 (c)

번역 개빈 멘지스가 쓴 〈1421년: 중국, 세계를 발견한 해〉라는 책에서 제시된 이론을 바탕으로 한 '1421년 가설'의 주장에 따르면 중국 선원들이 콜럼버스가 그 유명한 항해를 하기 70년 전에 이미 실제로 인도양을 건너 아프리카 남단을 돌고 대서양을 횡단하여 아메리카 대륙에 도착했다고 한다. '1421년 가설'을 뒷받침하는 증거들은 거의 6백 년의 세월이 흐른 오늘날까지 남아 있는 자료들에서 끌어내야 하므로 꽤 산재되어 있는 편이다. 가설을 뒷받침하는 증거 구성을 위해 지도, 중국 역사 기록, 역사적으로 이례적인 사건들이라는 세 가지 부류의 자료가 활용될 수 있다. 멘지스는 자신의 혁명적인 이론을 뒷받침하기 위해 지도를 활용하는데, 이 지도들은 중국인들이 콜럼버스에 앞서 이미 세계의 지형을 훌륭히 파악하고 있었음을 보여주는 듯하다.

(a) 중국인들이 아메리카 대륙에 가는 법을 알았다는 증거가 있다.
(b) 중국 선원들은 14세기 초에 아메리카 대륙을 발견했다.
(c) 중국 사람들이 아메리카 대륙으로 가는 지도를 만들었고 멘지스에 의해 이 지도들이 최초로 발견됐다.
(d) 멘지스는 콜럼버스가 아메리카 대륙을 발견했다고 믿지 않는다.

해법 가설을 뒷받침하는 증거 구성을 위해 지도 등이 활용될 수 있다는 내용과 멘지스가 자신의 혁명적인 이론을 뒷받침하기 위해 활용한 지도들을 통해서 볼 때 중국인들이 콜럼버스에 앞서 세계의 지형을 파악하고 있었던 듯하다는 내용을 연계해 보면 (a)가 정답이다. (c)는 선택지의 first found by Menzies에 대한 근거가 지문에 없으며, (d)는 지문에서 확인할 수 없다.

hypothesis 가설 **oddity** 이상함 **bolster** 뒷받침하다, 강화하다

정답 (a)

Paleontology is the branch of science focused on the study of prehistoric life, which is accomplished through careful examination of the fossilized remains those creatures have left behind. It is closely related to two other specialties: archaeology, which studies past human cultures, and paleoanthropology, which studies prehistoric human ancestors. Paleontology, however, is confined to the study of prehistoric animals. Even though the organisms studied by paleontologists have been extinct for thousands or millions of years, they still provide substantial scientific evidence for close research and discovery. Fossils provide an intriguing glimpse into the wildlife that roamed the earth long before humans became the dominant life form on the planet.

Q: Which of the following is stated about the passage?
(a) Paleontology is also studied by archaeologists and paleoanthropologists.
(b) Scientists study carefully the animals that died millions of years ago.
(c) The creatures that roamed the earth have been found by paleontologists.
(d) Paleontologists examine the fossils of the animals that took over the world.

In the 19th century, people began to recognize that clearing breeding grounds for mosquitoes was supremely effective at curbing malaria's spread and effects. Scientists started to understand that just as rats propagated the bubonic plague, mosquitoes carry and transmit malaria. This critical fact ultimately proved paramount in purging malaria from the U.S. As settlers moved into the Upper Mississippi Valley during the 18th and 19th centuries, outbreaks of malaria were triggered by land use habits. Because the Anopheles mosquitoes dislike shade, coolness, and dryness, the settlers' efforts to clear land and irrigate created perfect mosquito breeding grounds. Thus, through their efforts to make land more productive for their use, early settlers also inadvertently improved mosquito habitat.

Q: Which of the following is supported by the passage?
(a) Most Mississippi settlers died of malaria carried by mosquitoes.
(b) The Upper Mississippi Valley was developed by settlers.
(c) Scientists found out that malaria is actually spread by humans.
(d) Settlers did not know that their efforts could damage the land.

번역 고생물학은 선사 시대의 생명체를 중심으로 하는 과학 분야로, 화석화된 유해를 면밀히 분석하여 완성해가는 학문이다. 이 분야와 밀접한 관계가 있는 전문 분야 두 가지는 고대 인류의 문화를 연구하는 고고학과 선사 시대에 살았던 인류의 조상들을 연구하는 고인류학이다. 그러나 고생물학은 선사 시대 동물들에 대한 연구로 국한되어 있다. 고생물학자들이 연구하는 생물들은 비록 수천 또는 수백만 년 전에 멸종해 버렸지만 여전히 정밀한 연구와 발견을 위한 상당한 과학적 증거를 제공한다. 화석은 인류가 지구의 지배자가 되기 훨씬 오래 전에 지구에 돌아다녔던 야생 생물의 모습을 엿볼 수 있는 흥미로운 기회를 제공한다.

(a) 고생물학은 고고학자들과 고인류학자들에 의해 연구되기도 한다.
(b) 과학자들은 수백만 년 전에 죽은 동물들을 자세히 연구한다.
(c) 지구에 돌아다녔던 동물들은 고생물학자들에 의해 발견되어 왔다.
(d) 고생물학자들이 세상을 지배했던 동물들의 화석을 연구한다.

해법 고생물학이 선사 시대 동물들에 대한 연구에 국한되어 있다는 내용과 화석들이 인류가 지구의 지배자가 되기 훨씬 오래 전에 지구에 살았던 야생 생물의 모습을 엿볼 수 있는 기회를 제공한다는 내용을 연계해 보면 (d)가 정답이다. (b)는 선택지의 Scientists가 Paleontologists로, the animals가 the fossils of the animals가 돼야 한다.

paleontology 고생물학 **fossilize** 화석화되다 **specialty** 전문 **archaeology** 고고학 **paleoanthropology** 고인류학 **substantial** 상당한 **intriguing** 아주 흥미로운 **glimpse** 흘끗 봄 **roam** 돌아다니다

정답 (d)

번역 19세기에 사람들은 모기들의 번식지를 없애는 것이 말라리아의 유행과 영향을 억제하는 데 매우 효과적이라는 사실을 깨닫기 시작했다. 과학자들은 쥐들이 림프절 페스트를 퍼뜨렸던 것처럼 모기들이 말라리아 병균을 지니고 전염시킨다는 사실을 인지하기 시작했다. 이 결정적인 사실이야말로 미국의 말라리아 근절에 있어 궁극적으로 가장 큰 역할을 했다. 18세기와 19세기 동안에 정착민들이 미시시피 상류 계곡으로 이주해 가면서 토지 이용 행태로 인해 말라리아가 창궐하게 되었다. 학질 모기는 그늘, 시원함, 건조함을 싫어하므로 정착민들이 토지를 개간하고 물을 대자 모기들이 서식할 수 있는 최적의 환경이 조성되었다. 따라서 용도에 맞게 토지의 생산성을 더욱 높이려고 애쓰는 과정에서 초기 정착민들은 무심코 모기들의 서식지를 더욱 좋게 만들어주는 결과 또한 초래하고 말았다.

(a) 대부분의 미시시피 정착민들은 모기가 전파하는 말라리아로 죽었다.
(b) 미시시피 상류 계곡은 정착민들에 의해 개발됐다.
(c) 과학자들은 말라리아가 실제로 인간들에 의해 퍼진다는 것을 알아냈다.
(d) 정착민들은 그들의 노력이 땅에 피해를 입힐 수 있다는 것을 몰랐다.

해법 정착민들이 미시시피 상류 계곡으로 이주했다는 내용과 이들이 토지를 개간하고 물을 댔다는 내용을 연계해 보면 (b)가 정답이다. (c)는 actually spread by humans 역시 spread from mosquito habitat improved by humans가 돼야 한다. (d)는 could damage the land가 맞지 않다.

propagate 번식시키다 **trigger** 유발하다 **irrigate** 물을 대다

정답 (b)

As part of our commitment to serving your investment needs, we are striving to ensure that you receive timely information from the fund company in which you are investing. The enclosed information is from New Century Funds and the Paulson Investment Group. If you prefer not to receive this sort of information material from fund companies, please return the enclosed card. We will remove your name from future correspondence. Of course, there are legally required fund materials, such as prospectuses and reports, which we will continue to send you. We thank you for investing through Shahill & Sons and hope you will continue to take advantage of our low-cost, wide selection of investing services.

Q: What can be inferred from the passage?
(a) Shahill & Sons works with investment companies.
(b) Shahill & Sons sent the requested information.
(c) Shahill & Sons provides special information.
(d) Shahill & Sons has a list of financial aid seekers.

It has become usual to refer to the revolution that occurred in the seventeenth century—the revolution in ways of knowing that led to the establishment of science as the ultimate authority about material reality—as the Copernican Revolution. But this, I think, is unjust. Copernicus, if in fact he desired to bring about a major change in thinking about the world, was afraid to produce it in his lifetime. He may never have had any such idea. Furthermore, his proposal that the earth revolves around the sun was not a revolutionary idea at all. Six ancient Greeks said the same thing before he did.

Q: Which of the following would the writer of the passage most likely agree with?
(a) Copernicus was given astronomical teachings in Greece.
(b) A revolutionist should stand up against a popular belief.
(c) The 17th century is marked most by the Copernican Revolution.
(d) Ancient Greek astrology did not develop much until the 17th century.

번역 귀하가 투자에 필요한 요소를 제공하는 일이 저희 의무 중 하나이기에 귀하가 투자한 투자 회사의 시의적절한 정보를 받아볼 수 있도록 최선을 다하고 있습니다. 동봉된 정보는 뉴 센트리 펀드와 폴슨 투자 그룹에서 제공한 것입니다. 투자 회사로부터 이런 종류의 정보 자료를 받고 싶지 않으시다면 동봉된 카드를 반송해 주십시오. 앞으로의 발송 명단에서 귀하의 이름을 삭제하겠습니다. 물론 귀하께 지속적으로 발송될 투자 설명서 및 보고서와 같이 법으로 정해진 투자 자료가 있습니다. 저희 샤힐 & 선스를 통해 투자한 귀하께 감사드리며 앞으로도 저렴한 수수료로 제공해 드리는 폭넓은 투자 서비스 혜택을 계속 누리시기를 바랍니다.

(a) 샤힐 & 선스는 투자 회사들과 일한다.
(b) 샤힐 & 선스는 요청받은 정보를 보냈다.
(c) 샤힐 & 선스는 전문적인 정보를 제공한다.
(d) 샤힐 & 선스는 재정적인 도움이 필요한 대상의 목록을 갖고 있다.

해법 투자한 투자 회사의 시의적절한 정보를 받아볼 수 있도록 노력하고 있고 지속적으로 보낼 투자 설명서, 기록들과 같이 법으로 정해진 투자 자료가 있다고 했으므로 샤힐 & 선스는 일종의 정보를 제공하는 기관임을 알 수 있어 (c)가 정답이다. (b)는 requested가 맞지 않고, (d)는 지문의 investment와 선택지의 financial aid는 각각 '투자,' '재정 지원'으로, 다른 의미이다.

commitment 의무   **timely** 적시의, 때에 알맞은   **enclose** 동봉하다
correspondence 서신, 서한   **prospectus** 매출 안내서

 정답 (c)

번역 17세기에 일어났던 혁명, 즉 사물의 실재에 대한 궁극적 권위로 과학의 정립을 앞세운 지식의 혁명을 코페르니쿠스적 혁명이라고 부르는 것이 일반화되었다. 그러나 내 생각에 이것은 부당하다. 코페르니쿠스는 사실 그가 세상에 대한 시각을 크게 변화시키고 싶어 했을지라도 그것을 자신이 살아 있는 동안에 발표하기를 두려워했다. 그는 발표할 생각조차도 없었을 것이다. 게다가 지구가 태양 주위를 공전한다는 그의 주장은 전혀 혁신적인 생각이 아니었다. 고대 그리스인 6명이 그에 앞서 똑같은 이야기를 이미 했었다.

(a) 코페르니쿠스는 그리스에서 천문학을 배웠다.
(b) 혁명가라면 대중의 믿음에 맞설 수 있어야 한다.
(c) 17세기에 일어난 가장 특징적인 일은 코페르니쿠스적 혁명이다.
(d) 고대 그리스 천문학은 17세기 전까지는 크게 발전하지 않았다.

해법 코페르니쿠스가 세상에 대한 시각을 크게 변화시키고 싶어 했을지라도 자신이 살아 있는 동안에 발표하기를 두려워했으므로 혁명가는 많은 사람이 믿고 있는 것에 맞설 수 있어야 한다고 추론할 수 있어 (b)가 정답이다. (a), (d)는 지문에 없는 내용이고, (c)는 선택지의 most에 대한 내용이 지문에 없다.

refer 부르다   **reality** 실재   **lifetime** 생애   **revolve** 공전하다
astronomical 천문학의   **mark** 특징짓다

 정답 (b)

Actually, the practical result of all material progress ought to be increase of leisure, but too often new activities are born of the old, not all of which are beneficial, so leisure is decreased rather than increased. Life was so strenuous for a primitive man that his whole time, or very nearly his whole time, was taken up in providing for the necessities of life. To work for his very existence, to eat, and to sleep were all he could do in the twenty-four hours of each day. Now we have, or ought to have, ample leisure for all sorts of other activities, and indeed the insistence on the eight-hour working day as the standard ensures that we do have this leisure.

Q: What can be inferred from the passage?
(a) The meaning of leisure changes with time.
(b) The amount of leisure time changes with time.
(c) More leisure is not always beneficial.
(d) Some primitive leisure activities do not live on.

번역 실제로 모든 물질적 진보의 실제적 결과는 여가의 증가여야 하나, 새로운 활동이 예전 활동에서 생겨나는 것이 매우 빈번하고 이 활동이 모두 유익하진 않아 여가가 늘기보다는 줄게 된다. 원시인의 삶은 매우 고된 것이어서 평생 혹은 평생에 가까운 시간 동안 생필품을 구하면서 보냈다. 살기 위해 애쓰고 먹고 자는 것이 매일 24시간 동안 원시인이 할 수 있는 전부였다. 현재 우리는 온갖 종류의 다른 활동을 위한 충분한 여가가 있거나 있어야 하고, 실로 평일 8시간 근무하는 것을 일반적인 원칙으로 지킬 것을 주장하는 일도 이런 여가를 보장해 준다.

(a) 여가의 의미는 시간이 흘러감에 따라 변한다.
(b) 여가의 양은 시간이 흘러감에 따라 변한다.
(c) 더 많은 여가가 항상 좋은 것은 아니다.
(d) 어떤 원시 여가 활동은 더 이상 남아 있지 않다.

해법 시간이 흘러감에 따라 여가의 양이 달라졌음을 알 수 있어 (b)가 정답이다. (c)는 지문의 new activities는 increase of leisure 가 아니라, the practical result of all material progress를 의미하므로 선택지의 More leisure는 new activities나 the practical result of all material progress에 해당하는 내용이 돼야 한다.

practical 실제적인 **beneficial** 유익한 **strenuous** 노력을 요하는 **primitive** 원시의 **necessity** 필수품 **ample** 충분한 **insistence** 주장 **live on** 존재하다

정답 (b)

Dear Mr. Brockman,

As you no doubt know, commodity prices have increased dramatically over the past several months. Not surprisingly, our costs have increased as well. In this difficult business climate, we have had to acknowledge the impossibility of maintaining our prices at their past levels while continuing to provide the superior quality and service that you have come to expect from us. As a result, we have revised our price list. The enclosed list shows the prices that apply to all purchases effective the first of the month.
On behalf of Faremont Foods, I would personally like to thank you for your past purchases and continuing support.

Sincerely,
Brian Weiss
Account Representative

Q: What will Mr. Brockman do after reading the letter?
(a) Decrease the current order volume
(b) Check the prices
(c) Look for another food company
(d) Contact Brian for a new product catalog

번역 잘 알고 계시겠지만 지난 몇 달 동안 물가가 급격히 상승했습니다. 당연히 이에 따라 저희 비용도 상승했습니다. 이런 어려운 사업 환경에서는 기대하시는 만큼의 품질과 서비스를 계속 제공하면서 과거 수준의 가격을 유지하는 것은 불가능하다는 사실을 받아들여야만 했습니다. 이에 따라 저희 정가표를 수정했습니다. 동봉된 가격 일람표에 익월 1일부터 모든 구매에 적용되는 가격이 표시되어 있습니다.
페어먼트 식품을 대표하여 지금까지의 귀사의 거래에 감사드리며 앞으로도 계속될 지속적인 지원에 대해서도 감사를 드립니다.

고객 담당 브라이언 와이스 드림

(a) 현재 주문량을 줄인다
(b) 가격을 확인한다
(c) 다른 식품 회사를 찾는다
(d) 새로운 제품 카탈로그를 얻기 위해 브라이언에게 연락한다

해법 동봉된 가격 일람표에 다음 달 1일부터 모든 구매에 적용되는 가격들이 표시되어 있다고 했으므로 브락맨 씨는 편지를 읽고 가격을 확인할 것임을 알 수 있어 (b)가 정답이다. 나머지는 우선 가격을 확인해 보고 결정할 내용이므로 단정할 수 없다.

commodity 일용품 **dramatically** 극적으로 **climate** 환경 **acknowledge** 인정하다 **on behalf of** ~을 대표하여

정답 (b)

The film preview for *Atlantic News* readers will be a special screening of *Happy Days*, Francis Kitano's film of Arthur Nelson's long-running musical. It is nominated for seven Oscars including best film. The screening will take place at 11:00 a.m. on Saturday, February 10th, at the Atlantic Club. The film runs for two and a half hours. To obtain a free ticket, present this coupon from 9:00 a.m. next Monday at the Atlantic News office in the Central building. Tickets will be given to the first 100 applicants. Only one coupon per person will be accepted. This film will resonate better with those who have speculated on the meaning of happiness.

Q: What can be inferred from the passage?
(a) The movie is even for those who have not pondered happiness.
(b) The ticket holders will have to skip their lunch to see the whole film.
(c) February 5 is the first day to use the coupons for the tickets.
(d) 100 coupons have been issued for *Atlantic News* readers.

Some people say that it is bad to read old-fashioned fairy tales to little children because they make them afraid. But, like very primitive people, they already live in a world that they cannot begin to understand. Fairy tales could do for small children, and indeed did for many years, what myth, ritual, and religion did for primitive people—give their fears a name and an identity, a handle to take hold of and perhaps to cast them out by. A child who can channel his fear of the unknown into a fear of ghosts, witches, giants, and the like, may be able to rid himself of much of that fear when he finds that such things do not exist.

Q: What can be inferred about fairy tales?
(a) They help children understand what scares them.
(b) They are as old as primitive people.
(c) They secretly reveal how primitive people lived.
(d) They teach children how to solve problems.

번역 아서 넬슨의 장기 공연 뮤지컬을 프랜시스 키타노가 영화화한 〈행복한 날들〉을 〈애틀랜틱 뉴스〉 독자들을 위한 영화 시사회로 특별 상영합니다. 이 작품은 최고 작품상을 포함해 오스카상 7개 부문에 후보로 올랐습니다. 시사회는 애틀랜틱 클럽에서 2월 10일 토요일 오전 11시에 있습니다. 이 영화의 상영 시간은 2시간 30분입니다. 무료 티켓을 받으려면 다음 주 월요일 오전 9시부터 센트럴 빌딩의 애틀랜틱 뉴스 사무실로 본 쿠폰을 가져오세요. 선착순으로 100명의 신청자에게 티켓이 제공될 것입니다. 1인당 쿠폰 1매로 한정 지급됩니다. 이 영화는 행복의 의미에 대해 숙고해 본 적이 있는 사람들에게 더 큰 감동을 줄 것입니다.

(a) 이 영화는 행복에 대해 숙고해 본 적이 없는 사람들도 볼 수 있다.
(b) 티켓 소지자들은 영화를 끝까지 보려면 점심을 걸러야 할 것이다.
(c) 2월 5일이 영화 쿠폰을 사용할 수 있는 첫 날이다.
(d) 〈애틀랜틱 뉴스〉 독자들을 위해 쿠폰 100매가 발행됐다.

해법 행복의 의미에 대해 숙고해 본 적이 있는 사람들에게 더 큰 감동을 줄 것이라는 것은 그렇지 않은 사람들도 감동을 느낄 수 있다는 것으로 (a)가 정답이다. (b)는 영화 후에도 점심 식사를 할 수 있으므로 단정할 수 없고, (c)는 다음 월요일이 2월 5일이라고 단정할 수 없다. (d)는 선착순 100명에게 티켓이 제공된다는 것과 쿠폰 100매가 발행됐다는 것은 다르다.

film preview 영화 시사회   **run** 계속되다   **nominate** 지명하다
resonate 공명하다   **speculate** 사색하다   **ponder** 숙고하다

 정답 (a)

번역 어떤 사람들은 옛날 동화가 아이들을 무섭게 하기 때문에 읽어주는 것은 좋지 않다고 말한다. 그러나 원시인들과 마찬가지로 이미 아이들은 이해하기 힘든 세상에 살고 있다. 신화와 각종 의식, 종교가 원시인에게 그랬듯이 동화는 아이들의 두려운 대상의 정체를 알게 하고 그 두려움을 내던져 버릴 수 있도록 해주는 역할을 수년 동안 아이들을 위해 해왔고 앞으로도 할 수 있을 것이다. 미지의 것에 대한 두려움을 유령, 마녀, 거인과 같은 대상으로 돌릴 수 있는 아이는 그런 것들이 실제로는 존재하지 않는다는 것을 깨닫게 될 때 그런 두려움에서 상당 부분 벗어날 수 있을 것이기 때문이다.

(a) 아이들 자신이 두려움의 대상을 이해할 수 있도록 돕는다.
(b) 원시인만큼이나 오래됐다.
(c) 원시인이 어떻게 살았는지 내밀히 보여준다.
(d) 아이들에게 문제를 해결하는 법을 가르쳐 준다.

해법 동화가 아이들이 두려워하는 것들에 이름을 붙이고 규명해 준다고 했으므로 (a)가 정답이다. (b)는 지문 내용이 원시인들에게 전설, 의식, 종교가 있었는지 동화도 있었다는 것은 아니고, (c)는 동화가 원시인의 생활을 보여준다는 근거가 지문에 없다. (d)는 지문 내용이 동화가 두려움을 없애 준다는 것이지 여러 문제를 해결하는 데 도움이 된다는 것은 아니다.

fairy tale 동화   **primitive** 원시의   **myth** 신화   **ritual** 의식   **channel** 돌리다   **take hold of** 잡다   **witch** 마녀   **and the like** 기타 등등
rid A of B A에게 B를 없애다

정답 (a)

This year, as every year, the Annual Ventriloquist Convention will be held the last weekend in June at Fort Mitchell, Kentucky. For four days and nights, men, women, and dummies will converse, debate, argue, and generally enjoy themselves. Ventriloquism is the art of speaking in such a way that the voice seems to come from some source other than the speaker. When watching ventriloquists perform, it is clear that they have a very close relationship with their dummies. Some people speculate that this is because often ventriloquists were lonely as children and invented an alter ego, a separate personality, that followed them around and kept them company.

Q: What can be inferred from the passage?
(a) Ventriloquists do not have as many friends as others do.
(b) The convention is more than two years old.
(c) The convention is open to members only.
(d) Part of ventriloquism is imitating other people.

Fast readers cannot understand completely the whole meaning of a book. It's because they just skim and guess the meaning of it. But there seems to be one person who can read about 20,000 words a minute with near-perfect comprehension. His name is Kim Peek and he has the ability to read two pages simultaneously, one with each eye, with 98% comprehension. It's not clear how it works for him, but he didn't have a corpus callosum upon his birth. However, others born without it couldn't show such reading or comprehension abilities. He was partly the model for the idiot savant in the movie *Rain Man*.

Q: What can be inferred from the passage?
(a) Kim Peek wanted to teach others how they should read.
(b) Some people born without a corpus callosum were studied.
(c) *Rain Man* is partly about how Kim Peek influenced educators.
(d) Other fast readers do not know as many words as Kim Peek does.

번역 예년처럼 올해도 연례 복화술사 대회가 켄터키 주 포트 미첼에서 6월 마지막 주말에 열릴 것입니다. 나흘간 밤낮으로 남녀 그리고 인형들이 대화와 토론, 논의를 하고 전반적으로 즐거운 시간을 보낼 것입니다. 복화술은 목소리가 화자 외의 다른 데에서 들리는 것처럼 말하는 기술입니다. 복화술사가 복화술하는 모습을 보고 있으면 그들이 자신의 인형과 매우 친밀한 관계를 맺고 있다는 사실이 분명합니다. 어떤 사람들은 이것이 종종 복화술사들이 외로운 어린 시절을 보냈기에 제2의 나, 즉 그들을 따라다니며 친구 역할을 해주는 또 하나의 자아를 만들었기 때문이라고 추측하기도 합니다.

(a) 복화술사들은 다른 사람들만큼 친구들이 많지 않다.
(b) 이 대회는 2년 이상 됐다.
(c) 이 대회는 회원들만 참석할 수 있다.
(d) 다른 사람들을 흉내내는 것도 복화술의 일부이다.

해법 '예년처럼 올해도'라는 말은 2년을 넘은 것으로 딱 2년이 됐다면 This year, as last year와 같이 써야 하므로 (b)가 정답이다. (a)는 지문 내용이 복화술사들이 어렸을 때 외로웠다는 것이지 지금도 친구들이 적다고 단정할 수 없고, (c), (d)는 지문에 없는 내용이다.

ventriloquist 복화술사 **dummy** 인형 **converse** 이야기하다 **art** 기술 **speculate** 추측하다 **alter ego** 제2의 나, 분신 **personality** 자아 **keep company** 친구가 되어 주다 **imitate** 흉내내다

 정답 (b)

번역 속독하는 사람들은 책 전체의 의미를 완전히 이해하지는 못한다. 내용을 그냥 훑어 읽고 그 의미를 추측하기 때문이다. 그러나 1분에 약 2만 개의 단어를 읽으면서도 그 내용을 거의 완벽하게 이해할 수 있는 사람이 한 명 있는 것 같다. 그의 이름은 킴 피크로 양쪽 눈으로 각각 한 페이지씩 두 페이지를 동시에 읽으면서도 이해도는 98퍼센트이다. 어떻게 이것이 가능한지는 불분명하지만 그는 뇌량 없이 태어났다. 그러나 뇌량이 없는 다른 사람들은 그와 같은 독서와 이해 능력을 보이지는 않았다. 영화 〈레인 맨〉의 백치 천재가 그를 부분적으로 모델로 삼은 캐릭터이기도 했다.

(a) 킴 피크는 다른 사람들에게 읽는 법을 가르치길 원했다.
(b) 뇌량이 없이 태어난 사람들 일부가 연구되었다.
(c) 〈레인 맨〉의 일부 내용은 킴 피크가 교육자들에게 어떤 영향을 끼쳤는지에 대한 것이다.
(d) 속독하는 다른 사람들은 킴 피크만큼 단어를 많이 알지 못한다.

해법 뇌량이 없는 다른 사람들의 독해 또는 이해 능력이 뇌량이 없는 킴 피크의 능력과 다르다고 했으므로 결국 뇌량이 없는 킴 피크의 능력을 연구하기 위해 뇌량이 없는 사람들을 연구한 것이므로 (b)가 정답이다. 나머지는 객관적인 근거를 지문에서 확인할 수 없다.

skim 훑어 읽다 **simultaneously** 동시에 **corpus callosum** 뇌량 (腦梁) **idiot savant** 백치 천재

정답 (b)

The number of people taking cruises continues to rise, and so does the number of complaints about cruise lines. A prime concern that has arisen with the proliferation of cruise-line mergers—as it did with airline consolidation—is the apparent decline in staff courtesy, service, and cuisine. One reader reported "less than coffee-shop quality." Another writes that food "was never hot." Travel arrangements like fly/cruise programs, late port arrival, and confusing disembarkation procedures were also criticized. When asked about these irregularities, industry spokespeople say they are trying to improve their service and ask that the public report dissatisfaction to the appropriate management.

Q: What can be inferred from the passage?
(a) Cruise lines have not made their service better.
(b) Coffees provided by cruise lines were cheap.
(c) Cruise lines are trying to cancel mergers.
(d) Complaints about the service were not heard.

번역 크루즈 여행을 하는 사람들이 계속 늘고 있어 선박 회사들에 대한 불만도 늘어나고 있다. 항공사들이 그랬던 것처럼 선박 회사들의 합병 확산과 함께 생긴 가장 큰 문제는 직원들의 예의, 서비스 그리고 음식의 질이 눈에 띄게 떨어졌다는 것이다. 한 독자는 "커피숍 수준만도 못하다"라고 했고, 다른 사람은 음식이 "따뜻한 적이 없었다"라고 글을 썼다. 항공—선박 프로그램들과 같은 여행 준비, 도착 지연, 그리고 복잡한 입국 절차들도 불만 사항으로 드러났다. 이런 불미스러운 문제들에 대해 질문을 받은 업계 관계자들은 서비스 개선을 위해 노력 중이라고 하면서 사람들에게 해당 부서에 불만을 제기할 것을 부탁했다.

(a) 선박 회사들은 서비스를 개선하지 않았다.
(b) 선박 회사들이 제공하는 커피는 값이 싼 것이었다.
(c) 선박 회사들은 합병을 취소하려고 한다.
(d) 서비스에 대한 불만 사항들을 듣지 않았다.

해법 서비스 개선을 위해 노력 중이라고 했으므로 (a)가 정답이다. (b)는 지문에 없는 내용이고, 지문의 less than coffee-shop quality의 주체는 앞 문장의 staff courtesy, service, and cuisine이다. (c)는 지문 내용이 합병을 취소하는 것은 아니고, (d)는 지문에서 서비스 개선을 위해 노력하고 있다는 것은 불만 사항들을 들었다는 것이므로 선택지의 not heard가 맞지 않다.

cruise 크루즈 여행 **prime** 가장 중요한, 근본적인 **proliferation** 확산 **merger** 합병 **consolidation** 합병 **staff courtesy** 직원 예의 **cuisine** 요리 **travel arrangements** 여행 준비 **disembarkation** 입국 **irregularity** 불규칙(성) **spokespeople** 대변인, 대변하는 사람들

정답 (a)

Many people say that the statue called *The Thinker* shows a man in deep thought over a serious topic. That makes sense because this statue was designed to be placed over a set of great doors which would show the things that happened to people in hell. Both *The Thinker* and the doors were designed by Auguste Rodin, an artist who lived and worked in France around the same time as the painter Claude Monet. Like Monet, Rodin was much criticized for his non-traditional style. In the 1800s there was a strict standard for realistic sculpture. Some people thought a smooth finish was one of the essential marks of fine sculpture. However, the surface of *The Thinker* is wrinkled and rippled.

Q: What can be inferred from the passage?
(a) *The Thinker* was liked by many people for a long time.
(b) Auguste Rodin was inspired by Claude Monet.
(c) Auguste Rodin and Claude Monet taught each other.
(d) Most sculptures in the 19th century shared something similar.

번역 많은 사람들은 〈생각하는 사람〉이라 불리는 조각상이 심각한 주제에 대해 깊은 생각에 빠진 남자의 모습이라고 말한다. 이러한 평을 받아 마땅한 것은, 이 조각상이 지옥에서 사람들에게 일어나는 일들을 보여 주는 여러 개의 커다란 문 위에 놓여지도록 만들어졌기 때문이다. 〈생각하는 사람〉과 문은 모두 클로드 모네와 비슷한 시기에 프랑스에 살며 작업했던 화가 오귀스트 로댕이 만들었다. 모네처럼 로댕도 전통을 벗어난 그의 스타일 때문에 많은 비판을 받았다. 1800년대에는 현실주의 조각에 대한 엄격한 기준이 있었다. 매끄럽고 부드러운 마무리가 훌륭한 조각품의 중요한 특징 중 하나라고 생각하는 사람들이 있었다. 그러나 〈생각하는 사람〉의 표면은 주름지고 굴곡이 있다.

(a) 〈생각하는 사람〉은 많은 사람들로부터 오랫동안 사랑을 받았다.
(b) 오귀스트 로댕은 클로드 모네에게 영감을 받았다.
(c) 오귀스트 로댕과 클로드 모네는 서로 가르쳤다.
(d) 19세기 대부분의 조각은 공통점이 있었다.

해법 1800년대에는 현실주의 조각에 대한 엄격한 기준이 있었다고 했으므로 (d)가 정답이다. (a)는 지문 내용이 모네처럼 로댕도 그의 비전통적인 스타일 때문에 많은 비판을 받았다고 했으므로 오답이고, (b), (c)는 지문에 없는 내용이다.

statue 조각(상) **make sense** 말이 되다 **criticize** 비판하다 **strict** 엄격한 **standard** 기준 **realistic** 현실적(인) **sculpture** 조각(작품) **surface** 표면 **wrinkled** 주름진 **rippled** 굴곡이 있는

정답 (d)

Among the Crowell Museum's collections is the world-famous glass flower exhibit, featuring over one hundred delicate hand-blown replicas of actual floral species. The glass flower display was donated by a benefactor who was the force behind the museum in its early years, the nephew of the enigmatic Elberth Crowell, founder of the museum. The collection is part of the museum's permanent display of collections. It is a curious fact that although Elberth Crowell founded the museum when only forty-three, he never visited it or inquired as to the collections it housed. The collection is housed in the West Gallery and may be visited weekdays from 9:00 AM to 5:00 PM.

Q: What can be inferred from the passage?
(a) Elberth Crowell founded the museum for his nephew.
(b) The display was donated when Elberth Crowell was forty-three.
(c) Elberth Crowell did not create the glass flowers.
(d) West Gallery is owned by Elberth Crowell's nephew.

🔲 **번역** 크로웰 박물관의 소장품 중에는 세계적으로 유명한 생화 모양을 그대로 일일이 유리로 불어서 만든 100여 종이 넘는 섬세한 유리 꽃 전시물이 있다. 이 유리 꽃 전시물은 박물관 설립 초기의 후원자인 정체를 알 수 없는 박물관 설립자 엘버스 크로웰의 조카가 기부했다. 이 소장품은 크로웰 박물관의 상시 전시물 일부분이다. 엘버스 크로웰이 43세 때 박물관을 설립했지만 박물관을 방문하거나 전시물에 대해 물어본 적이 전혀 없었다는 사실은 호기심을 끈다. 이 소장품은 웨스트 갤러리에 전시되어 있으며, 평일 오전 9시부터 오후 5시 사이에 방문할 수 있다.

(a) 엘버스 크로웰은 그의 조카를 위해 박물관을 설립했다.
(b) 전시품은 엘버스 크로웰이 43세 때 기증됐다.
(c) 엘버스 크로웰은 유리 꽃을 만들지 않았다.
(d) 웨스트 갤러리는 엘버스 크로웰의 조카 소유이다.

❋ **해법** 유리 꽃 전시물은 엘버스 크로웰의 조카가 기증했다고 했으므로 (c)가 정답이다. (a)는 지문에 없는 내용이고, (b)는 지문 내용이 엘버스 크로웰이 박물관을 설립했을 때 43세였다는 것이지 43세 때 기증한 것은 아니다. (d)는 지문에 West Gallery가 누구 소유인지 나와 있지 않다.

delicate 섬세한, 우아한 **hand-blown** 손으로 잡고 불은 **replica** 복제품. 모사품 **species** 종류. 종(種) **benefactor** 후원자, 기증자 **force** 힘, 영향력 **nephew** 조카 **enigmatic** 알 수 없는 **founder** 설립자 **curious** 호기심 가는 **permanent** 영원한, 불변의 **house** 들여놓다

 정답 (c)

Dear Mr. Washburn,

Thank you for your payment of $543.78. We are removing the penalty based on your explanation of why you paid your tax late. We charge interest on any unpaid tax, however, regardless of whether you had a reasonable cause. If you have already paid the penalty and you have no other outstanding balances, you will receive a refund of the penalty amount you paid within six to eight weeks from the date of this letter.
If your tax return is selected for examination later, the examiner may review this decision about the penalty and ask for your explanation or additional information about it. If you have any questions, please call our Taxpayer Customer Service area telephone number.

Sincerely yours,
Rodney Foxfield
Accounts Representative

Q: What can be inferred from the letter?
(a) Washburn has paid interest for paying tax late.
(b) Washburn did not tell Rodney whether he paid the penalty.
(c) Washburn's tax return will be selected for examination.
(d) Washburn will call Taxpayer Customer Service.

🔲 **번역** 534달러 78센트를 지불해 주셔서 감사합니다. 귀하가 제시한 세금이 지연된 사유를 근거로 벌금을 면제해 드리겠습니다. 그러나 사유의 타당성 여부와는 무관하게 미납된 세금에 대한 이자가 부과됨을 알려드립니다. 이미 벌금을 지불했고 여타 미납금이 없다면 이 편지에 명시된 날짜를 기준으로 6주 내지 8주 사이에 귀하가 지급한 만큼의 벌금을 환불받을 것입니다.
만약 귀하의 소득 신고가 나중에 감사 대상으로 선정되면 조사관이 본 벌금에 대한 결정을 검토하고 이에 대한 설명이나 더 자세한 사항을 요구할 수도 있습니다. 궁금한 사항은 납세자 고객 센터 지역 전화번호로 전화하십시오.

(a) 워시번은 세금을 늦게 내서 이자를 냈다.
(b) 워시번은 로드니에게 벌금 수납 여부에 대해 알려 주지 않았다.
(c) 워시번의 소득 신고가 감사 대상으로 선정될 것이다.
(d) 워시번은 납세자 고객 센터에 전화할 것이다.

❋ **해법** 지문의 If you have already paid the penalty를 보면 (b)가 정답이다. (a)는 미납분 세금에 대한 이자가 부과된다는 사실이 지문 내용에 추가된 것으로 선택지는 Washburn will have to pay interest…정도가 돼야 하고, (c), (d)는 지문 내용만으로는 단정할 수 없다.

penalty 벌금 **charge** 부과하다 **cause** 명분 **outstanding balance** 미납금. 체불액

 정답 (b)

The early colonists in the United States did not build in stone. In the southern and Dutch colonies, the important buildings were mostly of brick, but for other buildings, wood was most commonly used. Wood frequently determined the form and style, but there was not much architectural elegance until the influence of Sir Christopher Wren's work had some effect on the middle and southern colonies in the eighteenth century. Williamsburg Town Hall in Williamsburg, Virginia, and St. Michael's Church in Charleston, South Carolina, were attributed to Wren, but they had no special architectural elegance, although they were of simple and pleasing design.

Q: What can be inferred from the passage?
(a) Wood is most frequently used as a building material in the U.S.
(b) Brick buildings in the southern colonies were not architecturally elegant.
(c) St. Michael's Church in Charleston, South Carolina, was built during the 1900s.
(d) Sir Christopher Wren supposedly designed only two buildings in the 18th century.

Refreshment stands can be found everywhere. These concession stands give the "small guy" a chance to make really good money and be his own boss at the same time. There are a variety of stands. Some are permanent. Others are actually moving vehicles that can be parked anywhere. Concession owners usually have to pay license fees to be able to set up in particular places. Their wares range from Coke made from syrup and seltzer water to homemade baked goods to organic health food smoothies. A concession stand is a welcome sight in extreme weather conditions: an ice cream stand in the sweltering heat or a place to get a cup of hot chocolate by an ice rink!

Q: What can be inferred from the passage?
(a) Concession owners pay license fees instead of taxes.
(b) Seltzer water is one of the wares that concession owners sell.
(c) Weather decides where refreshment stands are set up.
(d) There are two main kinds of refreshment stands.

🗨 **번역** 미국 초기 식민지 개척자들은 돌로 건물을 짓지 않았다. 남부와 네덜란드 식민지의 중요한 건물들은 대부분 벽돌로 지어졌지만 그 밖의 건물들에는 목재가 가장 흔히 사용됐다. 목재가 흔히 형태와 양식을 결정했지만 18세기에 크리스토퍼 렌 경의 작품이 중부 및 남부 식민지에 영향을 미칠 때까지는 건축학적으로 우아한 맛은 별로 없었다. 버지니아 윌리엄스버그에 있는 윌리엄스버그 시청과 남부 캐롤라이나의 찰스턴에 있는 성 마이클 교회가 렌의 작품으로 여겨졌으나 그 건물들은 단순하고 유쾌한 디자인이긴 해도 특별한 건축학적인 우아함은 없었다.

(a) 미국의 건축 자재로 목재가 가장 흔히 사용된다.
(b) 남부 식민지의 벽돌 건물들은 건축학적으로 우아하지 않았다.
(c) 사우스 캐롤라이나 주의 찰스턴에 있는 성 마이클 교회는 1900년대에 지어졌다.
(d) 크리스토퍼 렌 경은 18세기에 두 개의 건물만을 디자인했을 것이다.

🔆 **해법** 목재가 형태와 양식을 결정해 줬다고 했으므로 벽돌은 그렇지 않았음을 알 수 있어 (b)가 정답이다. (a)는 현재도 그런지 알 수 없어 선택지의 is가 맞지 않고, (c)는 지문에 없는 내용이며, (d)는 크리스토퍼 렌 경이 18세기에 지은 건축물의 개수가 지문에 없다.

colonist 식민지 개척자 **Dutch colony** 네덜란드 식민지 **attribute A to B** A를 B의 것으로 추정하다 **supposedly** 생각컨대, 추측건대

 정답 (b)

🗨 **번역** 간식 판매대는 어디에서나 볼 수 있다. 이런 판매대는 '별 볼 일 없는 사람'이 사장이 되는 동시에 많은 돈을 벌 수 있는 기회를 제공한다. 판매대의 종류는 다양하다. 정해진 장소가 있는 경우와 이동식 차량형으로 어디든 세울 수 있는 경우가 있다. 판매대 주인들은 대개 지정된 장소에 판매대 설치에 따른 허가증을 구입해야 한다. 여기에서 판매하는 상품은 시럽과 탄산수로 만든 콜라, 집에서 직접 구워 만든 식품, 그리고 유기농 건강식품 스무디에 이르기까지 다양하다. 판매대는 날씨가 극도로 덥거나 추운 상황일 때 특히 반가운 장소로 환영받는다. 푹푹 찌는 더위에 아이스크림 판매대 혹은 아이스 스케이트장 옆에서 파는 따뜻한 코코아 한잔처럼 말이다.

(a) 간식 판매대 주인들은 세금 대신 허가증 구입 비용을 낸다.
(b) 탄산수는 간식 판매대 주인들이 파는 물건 중 하나이다.
(c) 간식 판매대가 세워지는 장소는 날씨가 결정짓는다.
(d) 크게 두 종류의 간식 판매대가 있다.

🔆 **해법** 간식 판매대의 종류는 다양하다고 했지만 지문에 언급된 종류는 영구적인 것과 이동식 두 가지만 있으므로 (d)가 정답이다. (a)는 지문에 instead of taxes에 대한 내용이 없고, (b)는 지문 내용이 시럽과 탄산수로 만든 콜라를 판매한다는 것이지 탄산수를 판매한다는 것은 아니다. (c)는 Weather decides what refreshments are sold 정도가 돼야 한다.

refreshments 간식 **concession** 매점 **permanent** 영구적인 **seltzer** 탄산수 **sweltering** 푹푹 찌는

정답 (d)

UNIT 08

Model Test | **1** (a)   **2** (a)   **3** (b)   **4** (a)   P83

1

To refresh yourself and get rid of the boredom of everyday life, fly from America to Southeast Asia with the extras you'll need for a free 2-night luxury holiday. We invite you to relax at the first-class hotel. We also give you a chance to play a free round of golf on the championship course. You can also choose from four other free options: Car hire for two days. A half-day city tour in a private, chauffeur-driven car. A Jungle Safari with dinner. Or a voucher worth $120 to spend at the Duty Free shop. To accept our offer, fly First or Business Class with Asianlines between America and Southeast Asia before June 17.

Q: What can be inferred from the passage?
(a) Qualified Asianlines passengers can visit a jungle in Southeast Asia.
(b) Car rental provided by Asianlines in a travel destination is $60 per day.
(c) Asianlines passengers are eligible for a free hotel stay before June 17.
(d) A free golf lesson is provided to First or Business Class passengers.

🗨 **번역**　에너지를 충전하고 일상 생활의 지루함에서 벗어나기 위해 이틀간의 무료 고급 휴가를 위한 짐을 챙겨 미국 동남아시아 항공편을 이용해 보세요. 저희는 귀하를 1등급 호텔에 모십니다. 또한 챔피언십 코스에서 무료 골프를 할 수 있는 기회도 제공합니다. 이외에도 4가지 다른 무료 옵션 중에서 하나를 고를 수도 있습니다. 이틀간의 차량 임대, 운전기사가 딸린 승용차로 즐기는 반나절의 시내 관광, 저녁 식사가 포함된 밀림 속 사파리 관광, 혹은 면세점에서 사용할 수 있는 120달러 상당의 상품권이 그것입니다. 6월 17일 전에 미국–동남아시아 아시안 항공의 퍼스트 혹은 비즈니스 클래스를 이용하시면 이와 같은 혜택을 누릴 수 있습니다.

(a) 자격을 갖춘 아시안 항공 승객들은 동남아시아 정글을 방문할 수 있다.
(b) 여행 목적지에서 아시안 항공 제공 차량 대여는 하루당 60달러이다.
(c) 아시안 항공 승객들은 6월 17일 전에 무료로 호텔에 숙박할 수 있다.
(d) 무료 골프 레슨이 퍼스트 혹은 비즈니스 클래스 승객들에게 제공된다.

✳ **해법**　fly from America to Southeast Asia와 A Jungle Safari with dinner, 그리고 자격 요건이 나온 마지막 문장을 연계해 보면 (a)가 정답이다. (b)는 자격을 갖춘 승객들에게 행사 기간에만 적용되는 지문 내용과 달리 특별한 조건이 없는 일반적인 내용이므로 오답이다. (c)는 지문 마지막 문장을 보면 모든 아시안 항공 승객들에게 해당되지 않는다.

refresh 원기를 회복시키다　**chauffeur** 운전기사　**voucher** 상품권

 **정답** (a)

2

Many changes in cultural attitudes and social values are responsible for the increased later marriages. There is the growing acceptance of cohabitation in which adults live together in a sexual relationship without being married. Cohabitation has increased rapidly since the 1970s. This change in marriage patterns has various implications. One of them is smaller family size because couples marry later and have a shorter time when they can have children. Another is the increasing number of older parents; people getting married and having a child in their 30s means they will be in their 50s as the child graduates from high school. No matter how late people marry, marriage, in one form or another, is functional in so many ways that it keeps existing in every society.

Q: What can be inferred from the passage?
(a) Birth rates have been on the decline since the 1970s.
(b) People getting married in their 20s will retire in their 50s.
(c) The meaning of marriage is different in every society.
(d) Certain social attitudes are responsible for illegal activities.

🗨 **번역**　문화적 인식과 사회적 가치의 많은 변화가 늦은 결혼이 증가한 원인이다. 점점 더 성인 남녀의 혼전 동거를 인정하는 인식이 확대되고 있다. 1970년대 이래로 동거가 빠른 속도로 증가해 왔다. 결혼 패턴의 이러한 변화는 많은 부분에 영향을 미친다. 그 중 하나는 가족 규모의 축소인데, 이는 늦은 결혼으로 인해 부부가 아기를 낳을 수 있는 기간이 더 짧아지기 때문이다. 또 다른 영향은 고령 부모의 증가로, 30대에 결혼해서 낳은 아이가 고등학교를 졸업할 때가 되면 부모의 나이가 50대가 된다는 것을 의미한다. 사람들이 아무리 늦게 결혼하더라도 어떤 형태로든지 결혼은 아주 많은 방식들로 기능을 하기 때문에 모든 사회에 계속 존재한다.

(a) 1970년대 이래로 출생률이 감소해 왔다.
(b) 20대에 결혼하는 사람들은 50대에 은퇴할 것이다.
(c) 사회마다 결혼의 의미는 다르다.
(d) 일부 사회적 태도들은 불법 활동의 원인이 된다.

✳ **해법**　1970년대 이래로 가족 규모가 축소되었고 아기를 낳을 수 있는 기간이 짧아진다는 내용을 연계해 보면 (a)가 정답이다. (b), (d)는 지문에 없는 내용이고, 결혼의 기능이 다양하다고 했으므로 (c)는 오답이다.

cohabitation 동거　**implication** 영향　**functional** 작용하는　**on the decline** 내리막에　**retire** 은퇴하다

 **정답** (a)

It may bear the scars of past abandonment, but the Dohany Street Synagogue, here on the edge of what was once Budapest's Jewish ghetto, has finally triumphed over the successive onslaughts of the Holocaust and Communism. During World War II, as much of its congregation perished at the hands of the Nazis, this imposing Moorish-style temple, which is one of Europe's largest with a seating capacity of almost 3,000, was completely neglected. For nearly half a century its twin turrets and elaborate mosaic floors deteriorated. Then in the early 1990s the newly democratic Hungarian government, working in concert with private donors from abroad, began restoring this magnificent 137-year-old synagogue.

Q: What can be inferred from the passage?
(a) Hungary had to be democratic to be aided in repairing the synagogue.
(b) The synagogue had been used for about 87 years following its construction.
(c) Hungarian and foreign architects will work together to restore the synagogue.
(d) People who stayed in the synagogue survived World War II.

🔲 번역 지난날 방치된 상처가 아직 남아 있을지도 모르지만 한때 부다페스트의 유대인 거주지였던 지역의 끝자락에 위치한 도하니 스트리트 유대 교회는 대학살과 공산주의의 계속적인 공세에도 굴하지 않고 결국 승리를 거두었다. 유럽에서 가장 큰 사원 중 하나로 3천 명 가까이 수용할 수 있는 이 인상적인 무어 양식의 사원은 제2차 세계 대전 동안 많은 신도들이 나치의 손에 의해 희생되면서 완전히 방치되었다. 거의 반세기 동안 이곳의 쌍둥이 탑과 모자이크로 정교하게 장식된 바닥은 황폐화되었다. 그러던 중 1990년대 초반, 헝가리에 새롭게 들어선 민주 정부는 해외의 개인 기부자들과 협력해 137년의 역사를 지닌 이 아름다운 유대 교회를 복구하기 시작했다.

(a) 유대 교회를 수리하는 도움을 받기 위해 헝가리는 민주주의가 돼야만 했다.
(b) 유대 교회는 건립 이래로 약 87년간 사용됐다.
(c) 유대 교회를 복구하기 위해 헝가리와 외국 건축가들이 합작할 것이다.
(d) 유대 교회에 머문 사람들은 제2차 세계 대전에서 살아남았다.

※ 해법 유대 교회가 137년의 역사를 지니고 있으며 거의 반세기 동안 황폐화되었다는 내용을 연계해 보면 약 87년 동안은 사용됐음을 알 수 있어 (b)가 정답이다. (c)는 지문에 foreign architects에 대한 내용이 없고 이미 복구 작업을 시작한 것으로 선택지의 will work together to restore the synagogue가 맞지 않는다.

synagogue 유대 교회 ghetto 유대인 거주 지역 successive 계속적인 onslaught 맹공격 holocaust 유대인 대학살 turret 작은 탑 deteriorate 악화되다 in concert with ~와 협력하여

✓ 정답 (b)

Inspired by the popularity of ferns during the Victorian period, cast iron fern-leaf furniture was first introduced in Great Britain in the 1870s. Now, more than a century later, it thrives again, thanks to Marbletown Craftsmen, Ltd., which in cooperation with the Appleton Institution has issued heavy cast aluminum versions of licensed adaptations of the historic leafy-design furniture. Although Garden White is the most popular color, the replica furniture is also available in Appleton Green, Baltimore Blue, and Federal City Yellow.

Q: What can be inferred from the passage?
(a) Leafy-design furniture was not popular in the middle of the 20th century.
(b) Original leafy-design furniture of the 1870s was made in Garden White.
(c) Fern-leaf furniture is made by two independent manufacturers.
(d) Adapting the old furniture is regulated by law in Great Britain.

🔲 번역 빅토리아 시대 양치류의 인기에 영향을 받아 주철로 된 양치류 잎 무늬 가구가 1870년대 영국에 최초로 소개되었다. 이 가구는 마블타운 크래프츠맨 덕분에 1세기 이상의 시간이 흐른 지금 또 다시 인기를 끌고 있고 마블타운 크래프츠맨 주식회사는 애플턴 협회와 협력해서 묵직한 알루미늄 주조 형태로 변형 제작된 전통적인 나뭇잎 무늬가 들어간 가구의 생산 허가를 받았다. 가장 인기 있는 색상은 가든 화이트이지만 원형을 복원해 생산되고 있는 이 가구는 애플턴 그린, 볼티모어 블루, 그리고 페더럴 시티 옐로 색상으로도 나온다.

(a) 나뭇잎 디자인의 가구는 20세기 중반에는 인기가 없었다.
(b) 1870년대에 제작된 나뭇잎 디자인 가구 원형은 가든 화이트 색상으로 만들어졌다.
(c) 양치류 잎 무늬 가구는 서로 다른 두 제조사가 만든다.
(d) 영국에서는 오래된 가구를 변형해서 복제하는 것을 법으로 제재한다.

※ 해법 주철로 된 양치류 잎 무늬 가구가 1870년대 영국에 최초로 소개됐다는 내용과 1세기 이상 시간이 흐른 현재 다시 인기를 끌고 있다는 내용을 연계해 보면 다시 인기를 끈 시점이 1970년대 이후이다. 따라서 20세기 중반, 즉 1950년대에는 인기가 없었음을 추론할 수 있어 (a)가 정답이다. (d)는 지문 내용만으로 오래된 가구를 수정하는 것이 영국에서 법적 제재를 받는지 알 수 없다.

inspire 영감을 주다 fern 양치류 cast iron 주철 thrive 번영, 성공하다 in cooperation with ~와 협력해서 adaptation 개조, 변형 replica 복제

✓ 정답 (a)

TEPS Reading Practice | **1** (c) **2** (a) **3** (c) **4** (a) **5** (d) **6** (d) **7** (d) **8** (c) **9** (a) **10** (b) P85

해설 및 정답 Unit 08

American artist Georgia O'Keefe attracted much attention when the first of her many floral scenes was exhibited. Everything about these paintings—their color, size, point of view, and style—overwhelmed the viewer's senses, just as their creator had intended. In one of her familiar poppies, O'Keefe directed the viewer's eye down into the poppy's center, much as the flower naturally attracts an insect for reproduction purposes. By contrasting the light tints of the outer ring of petals with the darkness of the poppy's center, the viewer's eye is pulled beelike into the heart of the flower. The overwhelming size and detailed interiors of O'Keefe's flowers give an effect similar to the photographer's close-up camera angle.

Q: What can be inferred from the passage?
(a) The viewers appreciated Georgia O'Keefe's works as photographers would.
(b) Georgia O'Keefe's first exhibition of poppies was a success.
(c) The subject of the exhibit was what Georgia O'Keefe often worked on.
(d) Georgia O'Keefe was also interested in photography.

The Department of Linguistics at Stanford University invites applications for the tenure-track position of assistant professor of phonetics to begin in fall next year. Responsibilities will include teaching courses in phonetics; directing the master's and doctorate programs; engaging in an active program of research and publication; and rendering service at the departmental, college, and university levels. Candidates must have a Ph.D. in phonetics, or other appropriate discipline. Please send a letter of application, a CV, and three letters of recommendation. Salary commensurate with qualifications and experience. Minority and women candidates are encouraged to apply.

Q: What can be inferred from the passage?
(a) Phonetics classes can be taught by an inexperienced professor.
(b) Foreign applicants are not to apply for the position.
(c) One of the phonetics professors left Stanford University.
(d) Applications must be submitted by next fall at the latest.

번역 스탠퍼드 대학교 언어학과에서는 내년 가을부터 근무할 음성학 종신직 조교수를 채용하고자 신청서를 접수합니다. 업무는 음성학 강의를 비롯하여 석사 및 박사 프로그램 관리 업무, 활발한 연구 및 출판 활동, 그리고 학과, 단과 대학, 또는 전체 대학에서의 행정 업무가 포함됩니다. 신청자는 음성학 또는 관련 분야의 박사 학위 소지자여야 합니다. 지원서와 이력서 및 3장의 추천서를 보내주십시오. 급여는 자격 및 경력에 따라 결정됩니다. 소수 민족 및 여성 지원자도 적극 신청하시길 바랍니다.

(a) 음성학 수업은 경험이 없는 교수가 지도할 수도 있다.
(b) 외국인 지원자들은 지원할 수 없다.
(c) 스탠퍼드 대학교의 음성학 교수들 중 한 명이 학교를 떠났다.
(d) 지원서가 늦어도 내년 가을까지 제출되어야 한다.

해법 채용되는 지원자가 음성학 강의를 하게 될 것이고, 급여는 자격 및 경력에 따라 결정된다는 내용을 연계해 보면 가르친 경험이 없는 지원자가 채용되어 강의를 할 수도 있어 (a)가 정답이다. (c)는 근거가 지문에 없다.

linguistics 언어학 **tenure-track** 종신 재직이 인정되는 **phonetics** 음성학 **rendering service** 행정 업무 **discipline** 훈련, 학문 분야 **CV** 이력서(Curriculum Vitae) **commensurate with** ∼와 비례한

 정답 (a)

번역 미국의 화가인 조지아 오키프는 자신의 첫 꽃그림 전시회에서 많은 주목을 받았다. 이들 그림의 색상, 크기, 관점, 스타일 등 모든 면에서 화가가 의도한 대로 관람객의 감각을 압도했다. 익숙한 그의 양귀비 그림 중 하나에서 오키프는 마치 번식을 목적으로 벌레를 유인하는 꽃처럼 관람객의 시선을 양귀비 중앙으로 돌렸다. 양귀비 중심부의 짙은 색조와 꽃잎 바깥쪽의 밝은 색조를 대비시킴으로써 관람객의 시선은 벌처럼 꽃의 심장으로 빨려 들어간다. 오키프가 보여주는 꽃의 압도적인 크기와 내부 구조의 상세한 묘사는 사진작가의 근접 촬영과 비슷한 효과를 낸다.

(a) 관람객들은 조지아 오키프의 작품들을 사진작가들처럼 감상했다.
(b) 조지아 오키프의 첫 양귀비 전시회는 성공적이었다.
(c) 전시회는 조지아 오키프가 자주 작업했던 내용을 주제로 삼았다.
(d) 조지아 오키프는 사진에도 관심이 있었다.

해법 미국의 화가인 조지아 오키프의 첫 꽃그림 전시회가 많은 주목을 받았다는 내용과 그녀에게 익숙한 양귀비 그림에서 관객의 시선을 양귀비 중앙으로 이끌었다는 내용을 연계해 보면 (c)가 정답이다. (b)는 선택지의 poppies가 flowers나 floral scenes가 돼야 한다.

overwhelm 압도하다 **reproduction** 번식 **contrast** 대비하다

 정답 (c)

Most people have no idea how much effort is devoted to influencing their eating habits by large-scale food corporations and lobbyist groups. From creating food to putting products on shelves and advertising, almost every aspect of most food is overseen by some large companies. Such firms want people to eat more of the foods and products bearing their name regardless of health consequences, and will go to great lengths to enhance and protect those products' images. Considering this, rather than wasting time combating such staggering lobbying and advertising powerhouses, health crusaders would be wise to focus their efforts on giving healthy foods similar exposure and treatment.

Q: What can be inferred from the passage?
(a) Some popular foods have been proved unhealthy by health-concerned groups.
(b) Minor food companies produce more healthy foods than major ones do.
(c) Healthy foods should gain as much public attention as those of large companies.
(d) People's eating habits will change with healthy foods being consumed more.

A small island in central Caribbean Bay was once called Treasure Island because of the riches pearl cultivation brought to its residents. In 1992, a deadly red tide of poisonous plankton struck the bay. The mortality rate of oysters increased from about 40 percent to more than 55 percent. In 1996, a more threatening scourge hit the oysters. The mystery disease rapidly spread to other pearl-cultivating sites. In the case of red tide, oysters can be moved to a safe place. At some point in the season, growers usually clean the oysters to remove any attachments from the shells. But the new disease makes the shells so fragile that cleaning is impossible.

Q: What can be inferred from the passage?
(a) Economic difficulties began to emerge on the island in 1992.
(b) Between 1993 and 1996, no cases of red tide were reported.
(c) Red tide made the mystery disease spread on the island.
(d) The mortality rate of oysters jumped by about 15% in 1996.

번역 대부분의 사람들은 로비 단체와 거대 식품 회사들이 대중의 식습관을 좌지우지하기 위해 얼마나 노력을 쏟는지 전혀 모른다. 일부 대기업은 식품을 개발하는 것에서 판매대에 제품을 올리고 선전하는 것까지 모든 면을 철저하게 관리한다. 이런 회사들은 자사의 제품이 대중의 건강에 미치는 영향과는 관계없이 사람들이 자사 상표가 붙은 식품과 제품을 더 많이 먹기만을 원해 제품의 이미지를 높이고 보호하는 데 많은 애를 쓴다. 이런 점으로 미루어 볼 때, 건강 지킴이들은 엄청난 로비 공세와 광고 공세에 맞서 싸우느라 시간을 낭비하기보다는 건강 식품이 이와 비슷한 수준과 방법으로 사람들에게 노출될 수 있도록 하는 일에 집중하는 편이 오히려 현명할 것이다.

(a) 일부 대중 식품들은 건강 관련 단체들에 의해 건강에 해롭다고 증명됐다.
(b) 소규모 식품 회사들이 거대 식품 회사들보다 건강에 좋은 식품들을 더 많이 생산한다.
(c) 건강에 좋은 식품들이 거대 식품 회사들의 제품들만큼이나 대중에게 노출되어야 한다.
(d) 건강에 좋은 식품들이 더 많이 소비됨으로써 사람들의 식습관이 변할 것이다.

해법 일부 대기업은 식품을 개발하는 것에서 판매대에 제품을 올리고 선전하는 것까지 모든 면을 철저하게 관리한다는 내용과 건강한 식품이 비슷한 관심과 대우를 받을 수 있도록 노력해야 한다는 내용을 연계해 보면 (c)가 정답이다. (d)는 지문 내용만으로는 알 수 없다.

devote 쏟다 **oversee** 감독하다 **regardless of** ~에 상관없이 **go to great lengths** 많은 애를 쓰다 **staggering** 엄청난

정답 (c)

번역 카리브 만의 중앙에 위치한 작은 섬은 진주조개 양식으로 주민들이 거두어들인 부 때문에 한때는 보물섬으로 불리기도 했다. 1992년에 치명적인 독성 플랑크톤의 적조가 이곳을 덮쳤다. 약 40%였던 진주조개의 치사율이 55% 이상까지 증가했다. 1996년에 더 위협적인 재앙이 진주조개를 강타했다. 알 수 없는 병이 빠른 속도로 다른 진주 양식 지역으로까지 퍼져나갔다. 적조의 경우엔 진주조개를 안전한 곳으로 옮겨 놓을 수 있다. 조개 양식업자들은 대개 한 철 중 적당한 시기에 껍질에 달라붙은 이물질을 제거하기 위해 조개를 청소한다. 그러나 이 새로운 질병은 조개 껍질을 너무 연약하게 만들어 껍질 청소를 불가능하게 한다.

(a) 1992년부터 이 섬에 경제적 어려움이 나타나기 시작했다.
(b) 1993년과 1996년 사이에는 적조 현상이 보고되지 않았다.
(c) 적조로 인해 그 섬에 알 수 없는 병이 퍼졌다.
(d) 1996년에 진주조개 치사율이 약 15%정도 뛰었다.

해법 진주조개 양식을 통해 주민들이 거두어들인 부 때문에 보물섬으로 불리기도 했고, 1992년에 치명적인 독성 플랑크톤의 적조가 이곳을 덮쳐 진주조개 치사율이 증가했다는 내용을 연계해 보면 (a)가 정답이다. (d)는 1992년에 진주조개 치사율이 15% 증가했다.

cultivation 양식 **deadly** 치명적인 **red tide** 적조 **mortality rate** 사망률 **oyster** 진주조개 **scourge** 재앙 **attachment** 부착물 **fragile** 연약한

정답 (a)

The Opium War, though often considered a conflict centered simply on the smuggling of contraband opium into China by British merchants, effectively made China's resources a massive source of British commerce. It was less a war about drugs, and more one about British imperialist designs. When declaring war, British officials acknowledged that its citizens had been breaking Chinese law by importing opium into China. However, England's Prime Minister argued that the Chinese government had mistreated those issues because the laws applied only to foreigners. In short, the British felt wronged at being subject to laws that the Chinese themselves did not obey. So, England enacted a naval blockade of Chinese ports in 1840, beginning the Opium War.

Q: What can be inferred from the passage?
(a) England's Prime Minister thought that importing opium was not against international law.
(b) After the Opium War, the Chinese government illegalized domestic opium sale.
(c) The Chinese government did not try to apply its laws to its citizens.
(d) Before 1840, England did not have access to China's resources.

📖 번역   아편 전쟁은 비록 단순히 영국 상인들이 불법 마약을 중국으로 밀수하다가 빚어진 충돌을 중심으로 발생한 전쟁이었다고 흔히 알려져 있지만 중국의 자원이 영국의 막대한 교역원이 되는 계기를 만들어 주었다. 이는 마약을 둘러싼 전쟁이라기보다는 영국의 제국주의적 책략의 일환이었다. 전쟁을 선포했을 때 영국 관리들은 영국인들이 중국으로 아편을 밀반입함으로써 중국 법을 어긴 사실은 인정했다. 그러나 영국 수상은 중국 법이 외국인들에게만 적용된다는 점을 들어 그 사안에 대한 중국 정부의 처리 방법에 문제가 있다는 이의를 제기했다. 요컨대 영국인들은 중국인 스스로는 지키지 않는 법에 자신들이 제재를 당해야 하는 것이 부당하다고 생각했다. 그래서 영국은 1840년에 중국의 항구를 함대로 봉쇄하고 아편 전쟁을 선포했다.

(a) 영국 수상은 아편 수입이 국제법에 어긋나지 않는다고 생각했다.
(b) 아편 전쟁 후, 중국 정부는 국내 아편 판매를 불법화했다.
(c) 중국 정부는 자국민들에게 법을 적용하려고 하지 않았다.
(d) 1840년 이전에는 영국이 중국의 자원에 접근할 수 없었다.

💡 해법   아편 전쟁으로 중국의 자원이 영국의 막대한 교역원으로 전락했다는 내용과 1840년에 아편 전쟁이 발발했다는 내용을 연계해 보면 (d)가 정답이다. (c)는 선택지의 did not try에 대한 여부까지 지문에서 알 수 없어 오답이다.

opium 아편   smuggle 밀수하다   contraband 불법의   imperialist 제국주의(자)의   be subject to ~에 영향을 받다   blockade 봉쇄(하다)

✅ 정답   (d)

All middle class families would like a larger living space. Doesn't this then mean that the proliferation of the middle class and economic success will eventually lead to the mass production of children who, proudly armed with individuality, show no consideration whatsoever toward other people? Many studies indicate that personal space affects the formation of one's personality and values. The residential space of the poor is structured in such a way that they have to interact with one another, whereas the living space of the upper class is secluded enough to ensure privacy, completely blocking public access.

Q: What can be inferred from the passage?
(a) Changing living conditions is important for middle class families.
(b) Most of today's living spaces have little educational value for children.
(c) Middle class families became richer and want privacy more than the poor.
(d) The children of the rich should interact with family members in their house.

📖 번역   중산층 가족은 모두 더 넓은 주거 공간을 원한다. 그렇다면 중산층의 확산과 경제적 성공은 결국 당당한 개성으로 무장한, 타인을 전혀 배려할 줄 모르는 아이들을 양산하는 결과를 낳지 않을까? 주거 공간이 성격과 가치관 형성에 영향을 준다는 사실은 여러 연구를 통해 밝혀졌다. 빈곤층의 주거 공간은 서로 소통할 수밖에 없는 구조로 짜여 있는 반면, 상류층은 타인의 접근을 완전히 차단하여 사생활이 보장될 정도로 주거 공간이 격리되어 있다.

(a) 주거 환경을 바꾸는 것은 중산층 가족들에게 중요하다.
(b) 오늘날 대부분의 주거 공간들은 아이들에게 교육적 가치를 거의 갖고 있지 않다.
(c) 중산층 가족들이 더 부유해졌고 빈곤층보다 사생활이 보장되길 더 원한다.
(d) 상류층 아이들은 집에서 가족들과 서로 소통해야만 한다.

💡 해법   주거 공간이 성격과 가치관 형성에 영향을 준다는 내용과 상류층은 타인의 접근을 완전히 차단하여 사생활이 보장될 정도로 주거 공간이 격리되어 있다는 내용을 연계해보면 (d)가 정답이다. (a)는 living conditions에 해당하는 것으로 지문에 a larger living space 한 가지만 나왔고, (b)는 Most가 맞지 않고, (c)는 more than the poor라고 단정적으로 비교할 수 없다.

middle class 중산층   proliferation 확산   eventually 결국   be armed with ~으로 무장하다   individuality 개성   indicate 나타내다   residential 주거의   one another 서로   seclude 은둔하다. 격리시키다   privacy 사생활

✅ 정답   (d)

The Marxist theory of history as a series of class struggles has had powerful consequences for what many people believe about the world. Many of the political and social conflicts around the world involve people acting on or acting against this vision of human organization. In a less dramatic way, this theory has had a serious impact on the study of history, politics, economics, sociology, and even art and literature. The far-reaching effect of Marxism demonstrates forcibly that theories are not just empty abstractions, with little relation to reality.

Q: What can be inferred about the Marxist theory according to the passage?
(a) It changed every field of study profoundly.
(b) World views did not change until its introduction.
(c) It turned out to be more real than any other theory.
(d) It produced literary works that supported class struggle.

Columbus's personal life turned out to be an abject failure despite his astounding success as a greatly mistaken but even more greatly fortunate navigator. A magnificent seaman, he was an abysmal administrator. Ferdinand and Isabella soon saw this. They had made him promises, and they never ceased to be generous and affectionate toward this strange, mad, wonderful man who had made them almost as famous as he was. But they could not endure his autocratic claim that he was the king of the Western World, and they merely the Spanish viceroys.

Q: What can be inferred from the passage?
(a) Ferdinand and Isabella helped Columbus rule the Western World.
(b) Columbus stepped down after all those years as an administrator.
(c) Columbus's belief about himself was different from his actual status.
(d) Ferdinand and Isabella were not as good as their word with Columbus.

 번역 역사를 계급 투쟁의 연속으로 보는 마르크스주의 이론은 많은 사람들의 세계관에 지대한 영향을 끼쳤다. 세계 각지에서 벌어지는 많은 정치적, 사회적 분쟁에도 이러한 인간의 사회 구조를 지지하거나 반대하여 행동하는 사람들이 관련되어 있다. 이렇게까지 극단적인 경우가 아니더라도 그의 이론은 역사, 정치학, 경제학, 사회학과 심지어 예술과 문학에도 중대한 영향을 미쳐 왔다. 마르크스주의의 원대한 영향이야말로 이론이 현실과 거의 무관한 공허한 추상에 불과한 것이 아님을 확실하게 보여준다.

(a) 모든 학문 분야를 완전히 바꿨다.
(b) 이 이론이 알려지기 전까지는 세계관이 바뀌지 않았다.
(c) 다른 어떤 이론보다 더 현실적이라고 밝혀졌다.
(d) 계급 투쟁을 지지하는 문학 작품들이 만들어졌다.

해법 마르크스주의가 역사를 계급 투쟁의 연속으로 본다는 내용과 이 이론이 문학에도 중대한 영향을 미쳤다는 내용을 연계해 보면 (d)가 정답이다. (a)는 every라고 하기에는 무리가 있다.

struggle 투쟁 **consequence** 영향 **conflict** 분쟁 **act against** ~에 반(反)하다 **impact** 영향 **far-reaching** 원대한 **forcibly** 강력하게 **abstraction** 추상

정답 (d)

 번역 콜럼버스 개인의 삶은 비록 엄청난 오류를 범하긴 했으나 그보다 한층 더 엄청나게 운 좋은 항해자로서 놀라운 성공을 거두었음에도 불구하고 비참한 실패로 끝났다. 그는 탁월한 선원인 한편 지독히 못 된 통치자였다. 페르디난드 왕과 이사벨라 비는 이를 곧 알아차렸다. 그들은 콜럼버스에게 여러 약속을 했고, 두 사람을 자신만큼이나 유명하게 해 준 이 괴팍스러우면서도 멋진 남자를 끊임없이 후하고 다정하게 대했다. 그러나 그들은 자기 자신은 서방 세계의 왕이며 그네들은 스페인 총독에 불과하다고 여기는 콜럼버스가 가진 독재적인 생각을 참아 넘길 수 없었다.

(a) 페르디난드 왕과 이사벨라 비는 콜럼버스가 서방 세계를 다스리도록 도왔다.
(b) 콜럼버스는 장기간 통치자로 지낸 끝에 자리에서 물러났다.
(c) 콜럼버스 자신에 대한 생각과 그의 실제 지위는 달랐다.
(d) 페르디난드 왕과 이사벨라 비는 그들이 말한 만큼 콜럼버스에게 잘해 주지 않았다.

해법 콜럼버스 개인의 삶이 비참한 실패로 끝났다는 내용과 자신을 서방 세계의 왕으로 확신했다는 내용을 연계해 보면 (c)가 정답이다. (a)는 페르디난드 왕과 이사벨라 비가 콜럼버스에게 서방 세계를 다스리도록 도왔다는 근거가 지문에 없고, (b)는 선택지의 stepped down에 대한 근거가 지문에 없다.

abject 비참한, 비굴한 **astounding** 엄청난 **magnificent** 탁월한, 굉장한 **abysmal** 끝없이 깊은, 지독한 **cease** 멈추다 **endure** 견디다 **autocratic** 독재적인 **viceroy** 총독

정답 (c)

Well known throughout the world, black powder was invented by the Chinese. This invention opened the first era of human utilization of explosives—the black powder era. As early as 220 B.C., the Chinese laboring people already had primary knowledge of it. Around the 11th to 12th centuries, it began to spread to Arabian countries, and then to Europe. In about 1627, black powder was used for mining. Compared to the original method of breaking rock by fire, it proved to be more effective to blast rock by black powder. It remained in use as the world's only explosive until the mid-1870s.

Q: What can be inferred from the passage?
(a) Black powder was used exclusively in China for more than a millennium.
(b) People stopped using black power from the mid-1870s.
(c) China was the first to use black powder for mining.
(d) Nations around the world shared the knowledge of explosives.

번역 전 세계적으로 잘 알려진 흑색 화약은 중국인들에 의해 발명되었다. 이 발명품으로 인해 인류가 폭약을 최초로 사용한 시대인 흑색 화약 시대가 열렸다. 기원전 220년에 중국 노동자들은 이미 흑색 화약에 대한 기본적인 지식이 있었다. 흑색 화약은 11세기에서 12세기경 아랍 국가들에 이어 유럽으로 퍼지기 시작했다. 대략 1627년쯤에 흑색 화약은 채광 작업에 사용됐다. 불로 암석을 깨던 기존의 방법과 비교했을 때 흑색 화약으로 암석을 폭파하는 것이 더 효과적임이 드러났다. 흑색 화약은 1870년대 중반까지 유일한 폭약으로 꾸준히 사용되었다.

(a) 흑색 화약은 천 년 이상 중국에서만 사용됐다.
(b) 사람들은 1870년대 중반부터 흑색 화약의 사용을 중단했다.
(c) 중국이 최초로 채광 작업을 위해 흑색 화약을 사용했다.
(d) 전 세계 나라들이 폭약에 대한 지식을 공유했다.

해법 기원전 220년에 중국 노동자들이 이미 흑색 화약에 대한 기본적인 지식이 있었다는 내용과 흑색 화약이 11세기에서 12세기경 아랍 국가들과 유럽으로 퍼지기 시작했다는 내용을 연계해 보면 흑색 화약이 천 년 이상 중국에서만 사용됐으므로 (a)가 정답이다. (b)는 유일한 폭약으로 흑색 화약이 1870년대 중반까지 사용됐다는 지문 내용과 다르다.

black powder 흑색 화약 **utilization** 사용 **explosive** 폭약 **primary** 기본적인 **mining** 채광 **blast** 폭파하다 **exclusively** 오로지

 정답 (a)

After Alexander the Great died in 323 B.C., the rule of Egypt passed to one of his generals, the Macedonian Ptolemy. In 305 B.C., Ptolemy became king of Egypt, and moved his capital to Alexandria on the Mediterranean coast, and it became a great center of trade and scholarship. From 285 B.C., he ruled jointly with his son, Ptolemy II, who went on, after his father's death in 282 B.C., to further strengthen the country's commerce. Ptolemy III continued to consolidate the power of the dynasty, but his successors were weak. The Ptolemaic dynasty ended when a joint Egyptian and Roman fleet under Mark Antony was defeated by Octavian, Caesar's heir, at the Battle of Actium in 31 B.C.

Q: What can be inferred from the passage?
(a) Ptolemy gave financial help to poor students.
(b) The Ptolemaic dynasty lasted for about 270 years.
(c) Mark Antony was against the Ptolemaic dynasty.
(d) Caesar was involved in battles in Alexandria.

번역 기원전 323년 알렉산더 대왕이 사망한 후, 이집트 통치권은 대왕의 장군 중 한 명인 마케도니아 출신의 프톨레미에게로 넘어갔다. 프톨레미는 기원전 305년에 이집트 왕이 되고 나서 수도를 지중해 연안에 있는 알렉산드리아로 옮겼고, 이곳은 곧 무역과 학문의 중심지가 됐다. 그는 기원전 285년부터 아들인 프톨레미 2세와 공동으로 통치를 시작했고, 기원전 282년 부친의 사망 이후에도 프톨레미 2세가 계속해서 통치를 이어 나라의 무역을 더욱 강화시켜 나갔다. 프톨레미 3세도 왕조의 권력을 계속해서 강화해 갔으나 후계자들은 힘이 미약했다. 프톨레미 왕조는 시저의 후계자인 옥타비안에게 마크 앤토니가 이끈 이집트와 로마 연합군이 기원전 31년에 악티움 해전에서 패한 후 막을 내렸다.

(a) 프톨레미는 가난한 학생들에게 재정적 도움을 줬다.
(b) 프톨레미 왕조는 약 270년간 지속됐다.
(c) 마크 앤토니는 프톨레미 왕조에 대항했다.
(d) 시저는 알렉산드리아 전투에 관여했다.

해법 기원전 305년에 프톨레미가 이집트 왕이 됐고 프톨레미 왕조가 기원전 31년에 악티움 해전에서 패한 후 막을 내린 것을 연계해 보면 프톨레미 왕조는 약 270년간 지속됐음을 알 수 있어 (b)가 정답이다. (a), (d)는 지문에 없는 내용이므로 오답이고, (c)는 지문에서 마크 앤토니는 프톨레미 왕조 편이었으므로 오답이다.

rule 통치 **general** 장군 **the Mediterranean** 지중해 **scholarship** 학문 **jointly** 공동으로 **consolidate** 강화하다 **dynasty** 왕조 **successor** 후계자 **heir** 후계자

정답 (b)

그

Ray Novaco has been observing commuters since the late 1980s. (a) His research shows that a stressful car trip can cause astounding physical effects. (b) He found, for example, that the number of times a person commutes seemed to increase the individual's risk of getting the flu or a cold. (c) Novaco links his research finding to the "deleterious effects of stress on the immune system," adding that commuters who encountered a lot of traffic jams also took sick days more frequently than those with a relatively hassle-free route to work. (d) Novaco also found out that blood pressure goes up in proportion to how far commuting distance is.

번역 레이 노바코는 1980년대 후반부터 통근자들을 관찰해 오고 있다. (a) 그의 연구는 스트레스를 동반한 차량 이동이 신체적으로 엄청난 영향을 유발할 수 있다고 밝히고 있다. (b) 예를 들어, 그는 한 사람이 통근하는 횟수가 독감이나 감기에 걸릴 위험성을 증가시키는 것 같다고 밝혔다. (c) 그는 이런 연구 결과를 '스트레스가 면역체계에 주는 해로운 영향'과 연결시키며 교통 체증을 많이 겪은 통근자들이 비교적 편한 길로 통근한 사람들보다 더 병가를 자주 낸 것으로 드러났다고 덧붙였다. (d) 그는 또한 통근 거리와 비례해서 혈압도 올라간다는 사실을 발견했다.

해법 (b)에 for example이 있는 것으로 봐서 (a)에 대한 예가 나와야 하므로 (b)에는 차로 이동할 때 겪는 스트레스가 신체적으로 끼치는 영향의 예들이 나와야 하는데 통근 횟수의 영향이 나와 있으므로 (b)가 지문 흐름에 어긋난다.

observe 지키다, 관찰하다 **commuter** 통근자 **astounding** 놀라운, 엄청난 **deleterious** 해로운 **immune system** 면역체계 **encounter** 경험하다 **sick day** 병가(sick leave) **hassle-free** 편한 **in proportion to** ~와 비례해서

정답 (b)

른

The bed and breakfast, or B&B, is a form of holiday accommodation for which Britain is world-famous. (a) It gives you the opportunity to learn how British villagers used to live. (b) And you can have the chance to make friends and see some of the most attractive and less well-known parts of the country, ranging from John O'Groats to Land's End. (c) Generally, it will be run by the owner of the premises, and you will be treated like a royal guest. (d) The welcome will be friendly and warm, but you can have all your meals in a separate dining room for your privacy.

번역 숙박과 아침 식사, 혹은 B&B는 세계를 통틀어 영국의 가장 유명한 휴가용 숙박 시설의 한 형태이다. (a) 이것은 영국의 마을 사람들이 살아온 방식을 배우는 기회를 제공한다. (b) 그리고 친구도 사귀면서 존 오그로츠에서 랜즈 앤드까지 걸쳐 있는 영국의 가장 매력적이면서도 덜 알려진 몇몇 지역을 볼 수 있는 기회를 가질 수도 있다. (c) 이러한 숙박 시설은 일반적으로 해당 숙소에 기거하는 주인이 운영하며 손님을 왕족처럼 대접한다. (d) 친절하고 따뜻한 환대를 받긴 하겠지만 개인적인 시간을 갖고자 하는 투숙객들은 별도의 식당에서 모든 식사를 할 수 있다.

해법 영국의 유명한 숙박 시설인 B&B에 대한 지문으로, 영국 마을 사람들이 어떻게 살았는지에 대한 내용의 (a)는 숙박의 범위를 넘기 때문에 지문 흐름에 맞지 않다. (b)의 And는 지문의 주제를 담고 있는 첫 문장 내용을 망각하도록 유도하는 함정이다.

accommodation 숙박 시설 **world-famous** 세계적으로 유명한 **villager** 마을 사람 **premises** 토지, 부지 **royal** 왕족의

정답 (a)

Every role we play in life has an onstage and backstage area; in one we're on our best behavior, and in the other we can be more relaxed. (a) For example, in the dining room, a waiter is onstage. (b) No matter how rushed he is or how annoyed he feels, a waiter is expected to be polite and helpful to his customers. (c) Once he returns to the kitchen, however, he is backstage and can let his true feelings show. (d) In the kitchen, the waiter can take it easy for a minute and get ready for another round of serving.

번역 인생의 모든 역할에는 무대 위의 영역과 무대 뒤의 영역이 있다. 우리는 무대 위에서 가장 바른 태도를 보이고, 무대 뒤에서는 좀 더 편안한 상태로 있을 수 있다. (a) 예를 들어, 식당 홀에서 웨이터는 무대 위에 있다. (b) 아무리 바쁘고 화가 나더라도 웨이터는 손님들에게 예의 바르게 대하고 도움이 되어야만 한다. (c) 그러나 일단 그가 주방으로 돌아가면 그는 무대 뒤에 있고 자신의 진실된 감정을 보여줄 수 있다. (d) 주방에서 웨이터는 잠시 휴식을 취하고 나서 다시 서빙할 준비를 할 수 있다.

해법 모든 역할에는 무대 위의 영역과 진짜 감정을 드러내는 무대 뒤의 영역이 있다면서 그 예로 웨이터를 들었다. 웨이터는 그의 무대 뒤인 주방에서 진짜 감정을 드러낸다고 했고, (d)에는 이 진짜 감정에 해당하는 내용이 없어 지문 흐름에 어긋난다.

onstage 무대 위의 **rushed** 성급한 **annoyed** 화난 **polite** 예의 바른 **feeling** 감정

정답 (d)

The governments of several South American nations, including Brazil and Argentina, jointly announced a number of changes in their monetary exchange policies. (a) Long considered some of the most stringent in the world, the liberalization of their financial markets was applauded by economists throughout the region. (b) A number of recessions have plagued Brazil and Argentina, and implementing monetary reform has long been cited as one way to cure their economic ills. (c) The major change announced was that the transfer of capital from one country to another would become a quicker, more efficient process. (d) This should help encourage investment in the region and spur the economies of South America to future success.

번역 브라질과 아르헨티나를 포함한 몇몇 남미 국가 정부들은 환율 정책의 여러 가지 변화를 연대해서 발표했다. (a) 오랫동안 전 세계에서 가장 자금이 절박한 곳으로 여겨졌던 이들 국가들의 금융 시장 자유화는 그 지역 전역의 경제학자들에게 박수갈채를 받았다. (b) 브라질과 아르헨티나에 닥친 수 차례의 불경기는 이들 나라를 괴롭혔고, 화폐 개혁을 이행하는 것이 그들의 경제적인 병고를 치료하는 한 가지 방법으로 오랫동안 언급되어 왔었다. (c) 발표된 주요 변화는 한 국가에서 다른 국가로의 자금 이체 과정이 보다 효율적이고 빨라진다는 것이다. (d) 이것은 이 지역 투자를 촉진하고 남미 경제가 성공적인 미래로 나아가도록 박차를 가하는 데 도움이 될 것이다.

해법 브라질과 아르헨티나를 포함한 몇몇 남미 국가 정부들의 환율 정책 변화와 이런 변화로 인한 결과에 대한 지문으로 브라질과 아르헨티나에 대한 이야기만 나온 (b)가 지문 흐름에 어긋난다. 즉, 지문 첫 문장의 several South American nations, including Brazil and Argentina를 모두 받을 수 있는 these countries 정도로 바꿔야 한다.

stringent (자금이) 절박한 **plague** 괴롭히다 **recession** 불경기 **implement** 이행하다 **capital** 자본 **spur** ~에 박차를 가하다, 자극하다

정답 (b)

Much has been said about the need for industrialization as the quickest and most effective way to raise the income and the level of living of underdeveloped countries. (a) But they cannot industrialize successfully with a substantial improvement in their food and human efficiency. (b) This depends primarily on the improvement of their agriculture and utilization of food. (c) In these countries 60 to 80 percent of the people are engaged in farming, but their productivity is so low that it falls far short of feeding the population. (d) Unless they improve their food-producing efficiency, any efforts of turning their working force to industry will only make their food problem more hopeless.

번역 저개발 국가의 수입과 삶의 수준을 향상시키는 가장 빠르고 효율적인 방법으로 산업화에 대한 필요성이 많이 논의되어 왔다. (a) 그러나 식량과 인력의 상당한 개선 없이는 성공적으로 산업화될 수 없다. (b) 이것은 주로 농업과 식량 이용의 향상에 달려 있다. (c) 이들 나라는 국민의 60에서 80퍼센트가 농업에 종사하지만 생산성이 너무 떨어져 자국민이 먹기에도 턱없이 부족하다. (d) 이들 나라가 식량 생산의 효율성을 향상시키지 않으면 노동력을 산업 분야로 전환하려고 아무리 노력해도 오히려 자국의 식량 문제는 더 절망적인 수준이 될 것이다.

해법 저개발 국가의 수입과 삶의 수준을 향상시키기 위해 산업화가 필요하고, 인구 대부분이 농업에 종사하는 이들 나라의 농업이 향상되는 것이 선결 과제라는 것이 지문의 주된 내용이다. 따라서 식량과 인적 효율성의 근본적인 향상만으로는 산업화를 성공적으로 할 수 없다는 (a)가 지문 흐름에 어긋난다.

industrialization 산업화 **underdeveloped country** 저개발국 **substantial** 상당한 **improvement** 개선 **agriculture** 농업 **utilization** 이용 **fall short of** ~에 미치지 못하다

정답 (a)

In a dry climate like that of Egypt, papyrus is stable, but storage in humid conditions can result in destroying the material. (a) By 800 AD the use of vellum had replaced it in many areas, though it continued to be used in Egypt until it was replaced by cheaper paper introduced by the Arabs. (b) The reasons for this switch result from the fact that it was quite expensive to make paper using papyrus. (c) People gradually began not to use sheets of papyrus, and the latest certain date for the use of it is 1057. (d) Although it was used as late as the 12th century in the Byzantine Empire, there remain no known surviving examples.

번역 이집트처럼 건조한 기후에서 파피루스는 안정적이지만, 습한 환경에 보존하면 파손될 수 있다. (a) 서기 800년경에 이르자 타 지역에서는 송아지 피지가 파피루스를 대체했으나, 이집트에서는 아랍인들에 의해 소개된 보다 저렴한 종이로 대체될 때까지 파피루스를 계속 사용했다. (b) 이런 변화의 이유는 파피루스를 이용해서 종이를 만드는 것이 꽤 비싸서이다. (c) 사람들은 점차 파피루스 종이를 사용하지 않게 되어 1057년까지 사용하였다. (d) 비잔틴 제국에서 12세기까지 사용했지만, 현재까지 남아 있는 실례는 없다.

해법 파피루스는 습한 상태에서 보존하면 파손될 수 있어서 송아지 피지로 대체하였고, 그 이유는 송아지 피지가 습한 곳에서도 보존할 수 있기 때문이라는 정도의 흐름이 자연스럽다. 파피루스 종이를 뜻하는 지문의 papyrus가 (b)에서만 파피루스 종이가 아니라 종이를 만드는 파피루스 식물, 즉 재료의 의미로 쓰여 (b)가 지문 흐름에 어긋난다.

stable 안정적인 **humid** 습한 **vellum** 송아지 피지(皮紙) **gradually** 점차로 **as late as** 바로 ~만큼 최근에

정답 (b)

Tonight the whole park had become a small forest of blossoming cherry trees. (a) Under the calm cloudy sky the blossoms formed a mass of solid whiteness. (b) The paper lanterns that hung from wires between the trees had been put out; in their place electric light bulbs, red, yellow, and green, shone dully beneath the blossoms. (c) It was well past ten o'clock with most of the flower viewers having gone home and all the lights had been turned off. (d) As passers-by strolled through the park, they would kick aside empty bottles or crush waste paper beneath their feet.

번역 오늘 밤 공원은 온통 꽃을 피우고 있는 벚꽃 나무들로 하나의 작은 숲이 되었다. (a) 구름 낀 고요한 하늘 아래에 벚꽃이 커다란 하얀 덩어리를 형성했다. (b) 나무 사이사이에 철사로 매단 종이등은 꺼져 있었다. 그 자리에 빨강, 노랑, 그리고 녹색 전구들이 꽃 아래에서 희미한 빛을 발하고 있었다. (c) 밤 10시는 족히 지나 꽃구경 나온 대부분의 사람들이 귀가했으며 모든 조명은 꺼져 있었다. (d) 행인들이 공원을 거닐면서 빈 병을 발로 차거나 버려진 종이를 밟고 다니곤 했다.

해법 벚꽃이 만발한 공원의 밤 풍경을 다룬 지문으로 (b)에서 종이등은 꺼졌지만 빨강, 노랑, 그리고 녹색 전구들이 반짝거렸다고 했으므로 (c)에서 모든 조명이 꺼졌다는 부분이 지문 흐름에 어긋난다.

blossom 꽃 피다 cherry tree 벚나무 mass 큰 덩어리 paper lantern 종이등 put out 끄다 light bulb 전구 dully 희미하게 passer-by 행인 stroll 거닐다

정답 (c)

Truth as ultimate reality, if it is actually in existence, must be eternal, imperishable, unchanging. (a) But that infinite, eternal, and unchanging truth cannot be apprehended in the fullness of it by the finite mind of man. (b) It is natural that the mind of man can only grasp, at most, some small aspect of it, limited by time and space and by the state of development of that mind. (c) As the mind develops and enlarges the scope of it, new aspects of it come to light. (d) Not to mention, the fact that the core of truth may yet be the same doesn't need to be reconfirmed.

번역 궁극적 사실로서 진실은, 만약 실제로 존재한다면 영원하고 불멸하며 한결같아야만 한다. (a) 그러나 그런 무한하고 영원하며 변하지 않는 진실은 한정된 인간의 지성만으로는 완전히 이해될 수 없다. (b) 인간의 지성은 기껏해야 시간과 공간 그리고 지성의 발전 상태에 의해 제약을 받기에 진실의 작은 한 부분만을 이해할 수 있을 뿐인 것은 자연스러운 일이다. (c) 지성이 발전하고 범위를 넓혀 감에 따라 새로운 면모가 밝혀진다. (d) 물론 진실의 핵심은 변하지 않고 그대로일 것이라는 점은 다시 확인할 필요가 없다.

해법 궁극적 사실로서 진실이 존재한다면 영원하고 불멸하며 한결같아야 하고, 한정된 인간의 지성은 그런 진실을 충분히 이해할 수 없으므로 지성의 한계에 따라 진실을 부분적으로 이해한다는 것이 지문의 주요 내용이다. 따라서 지성이 발전하고 범위를 넓혀 감에 따라 지성의 새로운 측면들이 드러나게 된다는 (c)가 지문 흐름에 어긋난다. (c)의 it은 모두 the mind를 지칭한다.

eternal 영원한 imperishable 불멸의, 영속적인 infinite 무한한 apprehend 이해하다 grasp 이해하다 at most 기껏해야 enlarge 넓히다 not to mention ~은 말할 것도 없고, ~은 물론 core 핵심

정답 (c)

The quartet, consisting of the United States, the European Union, the United Nations, and Russia, has invented a plan for Israeli-Palestinian peace, a "Road Map." (a) However, this new peace plan contains more questions than answers. (b) It is so lacking in important details that even the most experienced navigators will have to find or create their own trail markers in order not to get lost on the way. (c) Therefore, the quartet doesn't welcome the peace plan. (d) But they agree that despite all its many flaws, it is the only game in town for the present.

번역 미국, 유럽 연합, UN, 러시아로 구성된 4자 단체가 '로드 맵'이라는 이스라엘–팔레스타인 평화를 위한 계획을 만들었다. (a) 그러나 이 새로운 평화안은 해답보다 문제가 더 많다. (b) 중요한 세부 사항들이 너무 부족해서 심지어 가장 경험 있는 항해자도 길을 잃지 않기 위해 안내 표시를 찾거나 직접 새로운 표시를 만들어야만 한다. (c) 그 결과 4자 단체는 평화안을 반기지 않는다. (d) 그러나 그들은 많은 결점에도 불구하고 현재로서는 그것이 유일한 대안이라는 것에 동의한다.

해법 미국, 유럽 연합, UN, 러시아로 구성된 단체가 '로드 맵'이라는 이스라엘–팔레스타인 평화안을 만들었는데 이 안은 문제점들이 더 많다고 했으므로 (c)의 the quartet이 many Israelis and Palestinians 정도로 바뀌어야 한다.

quartet 4인조 **consist of** ~로 구성되다 **navigator** 항해자

정답 (c)

Now is the time to subscribe to the *Dunhill Networker*. (a) To add your name to the *Dunhill Networker* mailing list, just detach, fill out, and mail the postpaid card below. (b) We will be sure each quarterly issue of the *Dunhill Networker* is addressed to you by name—no guesswork for your mailroom or administrative staff. (c) The *Dunhill Networker* is a quarterly publication prepared by Dunhill International particularly for managers dealing with the complexities of human resources. (d) If you would like to forward any comments, reactions, questions, or suggestions related to the Dunhill International, please write to the *Dunhill Networker*.

번역   지금 〈던힐 네트워커〉를 구독 신청하십시오. (a) 〈던힐 네트워커〉 우편 발송 목록에 여러분의 이름을 올리시려면 아래의 우편 요금 후불 엽서를 떼어내 내용을 기입하셔서 우송해 주시기만 하면 됩니다. (b) 저희는 〈던힐 네트워커〉의 계간호가 모두 여러분의 이름으로 발송되도록 만전을 기할 것입니다. 따라서 여러분의 배달원이나 행정 직원들이 추측해서 일하지 않을 것입니다. (c) 〈던힐 네트워커〉는 던힐 인터내셔널에서 특히 복잡한 인적 자원을 관리하는 관리자들을 위해 발행하는 계간지입니다. (d) 던힐 인터내셔널과 관련된 어떤 논평이나 반응, 질문 혹은 제안이 있으면 〈던힐 네트워커〉로 글을 보내 주세요.

해법 던힐 인터내셔널이 잡지사이고 〈던힐 네트워커〉가 잡지이므로 (d)의 던힐 인터내셔널과 던힐 네트워커가 바뀌어야 한다.

subscribe to ~을 구독하다 **detach** 떼어내다 **postpaid card** 우편 요금 후불 엽서 **quarterly** 계간지 **administrative** 행정상의 **human resources** 인적 자원

정답 (d)

Today's top story is on an extreme daring that has baffled senior detectives nationwide. (a) In this morning's early hours it appears that several robbers managed to enter the palace grounds, bypassing guard dogs, a sensor-activated alarm system, and electric fencing before making their way inside the building. (b) Once inside, they stole four original paintings by Goya, a diamond necklace, three Persian rugs, and a bronze statue. (c) They are believed to have then made their getaway in a hijacked taxi cab that was recovered later, in a wood in Essex. (d) The royal family are currently staying at their Greek holiday home while the palace security system is being fixed.

번역 오늘의 주요 뉴스는 전국의 고참 형사들을 황당하게 만든 매우 대담한 사건입니다. (a) 오늘 아침 이른 시간에 강도 몇 명이 궁정에 몰래 침입해서 경비견과 센서로 작동되는 경보 시스템, 그리고 전기 울타리를 우회하여 건물 안으로 침입한 것으로 보입니다. (b) 안에 들어간 다음에 고야의 원화 넉 점과 다이아몬드 목걸이 한 점, 페르시아 양탄자 석 장, 청동상을 훔쳤습니다. (c) 그들은 택시를 납치해 도주한 것으로 여겨지는데 그 택시는 나중에 에섹스의 숲에서 발견됐습니다. (d) 왕실 가족은 현재 궁전의 보안 시스템이 수리되는 동안 그리스의 별장에 머물고 있습니다.

해법 강도가 여러 방범 장치들을 우회해서 궁정에 침입하여, 절도 사건을 벌이고 납치한 택시로 도주했다는 내용이다. 그런데 궁정의 방범 시스템이 고장 났다는 내용이 지문에 없어 (d)가 맞지 않아 지문 흐름에 어긋난다.

daring 대담한 **baffle** 당황케 하다 **nationwide** 전국적인 **bypass** 우회하다 **make one's getaway** ~가 도주하다 **hijack** 납치하다 **holiday home** 별장

정답 (d)

Korean food begins to tickle the world's taste buds. (a) Many food manufacturers are continuously working on various kinds of Korean food to make them appeal to foreigners' tastes and their efforts bear fruit. (b) A bowl of rice topped with Kimchi has become very popular among many European gourmets or food-lovers. (c) In Russia, many people enjoy Korean soy sauce instead of salt, and they are also known to be big fans of Korean dumplings. (d) In addition, "Hot & Joy," a red pepper paste sauce, is also made from many different ingredients, including Korean pepper.

번역 한국 음식이 세계의 미각을 자극하기 시작하고 있다. (a) 많은 음식 제조업체들은 한국 음식을 외국인의 취향에 맞게 하려고 꾸준히 다양한 한국 음식을 만들고 있으며 그들의 노력이 결실을 맺고 있다. (b) 김치를 얹은 밥은 많은 유럽 미식가들과 음식 애호가에게 매우 인기를 얻었다. (c) 러시아에서는 많은 사람들이 소금 대신 한국 간장을 즐기며 한국 만두도 매우 좋아하는 것으로 알려져 있다. (d) 게다가 '핫 & 조이'라는 고추장이 한국 고추를 포함한 다양한 재료로 만들어졌다.

해법 한국 음식이 세계적으로 인기를 끌고 있다는 지문으로 (a), (b), (c)는 한국 음식의 세계적 인기를 이야기하고 있으나, (d)는 단지 한국 고추를 포함한 다양한 재료로 만든 '핫 & 조이'라는 고추장만을 이야기하고 있어 지문 흐름에 어긋난다.

tickle 간지럽히다, 자극하다 **taste bud** (혀의) 미뢰, 혀의 미각 기관 **bear fruit** 결실을 맺다 **topped with** ~를 얹은 **gourmet** 미식가 **soy sauce** 간장 **red pepper paste sauce** 고추장

정답 (d)

Dr. Carlo Bellieni, a pediatrician at the University of Siena in Italy, announced that TV can be helpful for numbing pain. (a) The study involved 50 children, ages 5 to 12, who were separated into three groups and told to rate their pain on a numerical scale when they were poked with a needle. (b) Those watching TV cartoons were soothed by a parent but reported the full pain. (c) However, when compared to children who just sat in a hospital with mothers who didn't try to soothe them, the TV watchers recorded one-third the pain. (d) Dr. Bellieni has found that TV can be a great aid for children going through painful medical procedures.

The funny word "couch-potato" was created because many people usually eat snacks like potato chips while watching TV on a couch. (a) And now a fresh new word, "mouse-potato," has been coined to refer to those who spend time surfing the Internet all day. (b) Researchers from the University of Glasgow in Scotland said that the number of these mouse-potatoes is increasing rapidly among teenagers. (c) For 6 to 16-year-olds in the U.K., the average time for exercising is only 25 minutes a day. (d) These habits cause severe child obesity, and 16% of them are now classed to be too fat.

번역 이탈리아 시에나 대학의 소아과 의사인 칼로 벨리에니는 TV가 고통을 완화시키는 데 도움이 될 수 있다고 발표했다. (a) 연구 대상으로는 5세에서 12세에 이르는 50명의 아이들이 선정되어 세 그룹으로 나뉘어져 진행되었으며 이들에게 주사 바늘에 찔렸을 때의 고통을 숫자로 표시하도록 했다. (b) TV 만화를 보는 아이들은 부모가 달랬지만 고통을 전부 나타냈다. (c) 그러나 아이들을 달래지 않은 엄마와 병원에서 그냥 앉아 있던 아이들과 비교해서 TV를 시청한 아이들은 고통의 3분의 1을 표시한 것으로 나타났다. (d) 벨리에니 박사는 TV가 고통스러운 치료 과정을 겪고 있는 아이들에게 큰 도움이 될 수 있다는 것을 발견했다.

해법 주사 바늘로 찔러서 TV가 고통을 완화시키는 데 도움이 되는지 실험했고 효과가 있다는 지문으로 (b)의 Those watching TV cartoons가 Those poked with a needle 정도가 되어야 한다.

pediatrician 소아과 의사 **numb** 완화시키다 **separate** 분류하다 **rate** 평가하다 **numerical** 숫자로 나타낸 **poke** 찌르다 **needle** (주사) 바늘 **soothe** 달래다, 가라앉히다

정답 (b)

번역 '카우치 포테이토(couch-potato)'라는 재미있는 말은 많은 사람들이 소파에 앉아 TV를 볼 때 감자칩 같은 간식을 주로 먹기 때문에 만들어졌다. (a) 이제는 그에 이어 '마우스 포테이토'라는 신조어가 하루 종일 인터넷을 하며 시간을 보내는 사람들을 지칭해서 만들어졌다. (b) 스코틀랜드 글래스고 대학 연구원들은 이런 마우스 포테이토 수는 십대들 사이에서 급속도로 증가하고 있다고 말했다. (c) 영국의 6세에서 16세 사이 아이들의 평균 운동 시간은 하루 25분에 불과하다. (d) 이런 습관은 심각한 어린이 비만을 일으켜 현재 그들 중 16%는 고도 비만으로 분류된다.

해법 인터넷을 하루 종일 하는 사람들을 의미하는 mouse-potato를 소개하는 지문으로 (b)의 teenagers와 (c)의 For 6 to 16-year-olds in the U.K.가 연결되지 않음을 알 수 있어 둘 중 하나가 흐름에 어긋남을 알 수 있다. 그런데 (d)의 child를 보면 (c)의 For 6 to 16-year-olds in the U.K.와 연결되므로 (b)가 지문 흐름에 어긋난다.

couch 소파 **coin** 신조어를 만들다 **obesity** 비만 **class** 분류하다, 분류되다

정답 (b)

Actual Test 01

1 (b)	**2** (c)	**3** (a)	**4** (d)	**5** (d)	**6** (b)	**7** (a)	**8** (c)	**9** (c)	**10** (a)	**11** (d)	**12** (b)	**13** (d)	**14** (b)	**15** (c)
16 (a)	**17** (d)	**18** (b)	**19** (d)	**20** (d)	**21** (b)	**22** (c)	**23** (b)	**24** (b)	**25** (c)	**26** (b)	**27** (a)	**28** (d)	**29** (b)	**30** (c)
31 (d)	**32** (b)	**33** (c)	**34** (a)	**35** (b)	**36** (a)	**37** (c)	**38** (d)	**39** (a)	**40** (c)					

P102

Each year malaria kills about one million people, most of whom are African children under the age of 5. The Gates Foundation donates more than 30% of the world's malaria-research funds, and _____. Artemisinin, the most effective medicine for the disease, is in very short supply. But the scientists funded by the foundation made an announcement last month that they succeeded with development of the technology to create artemisinin in the laboratory. They expect the cost of artemisinin to drop from $2.40 to 25 cents within the next 5 years.

(a) the number of patients is decreasing
(b) it appears to be paying off
(c) improved treatments will be available
(d) the percentage is expected to increase

번역 매년 말라리아로 백만 명의 사망자가 발생하고 이들 대부분은 5세 이하 아프리카 아동이다. 게이츠 재단은 현재 전 세계 말라리아 연구 자금의 30% 이상을 기부하고 있는데 그들의 노력이 성과를 거둔 것으로 보인다. 말라리아에 가장 효과적인 치료약인 아테미시닌은 매우 부족한 상황이다. 그러나 지난달 게이츠 재단의 자금을 지원받는 과학자들이 기술 발전으로 자체 실험실에서 아테미시닌을 만드는 데 성공했다고 발표했다. 그들은 5년 이내로 아테미시닌의 가격이 2달러 40센트에서 25센트로 떨어질 것으로 기대하고 있다.

(a) 환자 수가 줄고 있다
(b) 성과를 거둔 것으로 보인다
(c) 개선된 치료법이 나타날 것이다
(d) 그 비율이 늘어날 것으로 전망된다

해법 게이츠 재단의 자금을 지원받는 과학자들이 실험실에서 말라리아 치료제인 아테미시닌을 만들 수 있는 기술 개발에 성공했다고 했으므로 게이츠 재단은 현재 전 세계의 말라리아 연구 자금의 3분의 1 이상을 제공하고 있고 성과를 거두고 있는 것 같다는 흐름이 적절하므로 (b)가 정답이다. (c)는 the technology to create artemisinin in the laboratory 자체가 improved treatments는 아니다.

foundation 재단 **donate** 기부하다 **in short supply** 필요한 물품이 부족하여 **fund** 자금을 제공하다 **artemisinin** 아테미시닌 **laboratory** 실험실

✓ **정답** (b)

The first thing to remember about an angry customer is that, while his/ her behavior is directed at you, _____. The person is usually angry with you not as a person but as an employee of an organization that is perceived as cold, unfeeling, and unhelpful. Since it is difficult to yell at or abuse an entire organization, he/ she will direct the anger towards you. It is important to know that angry people want a chance to express their anger and want to have their voice heard. If you fail to acknowledge their anger and act too fast to try to work out the problem, you will probably make them angrier.

(a) you should first listen, not ask what the problem is
(b) he/ she is actually talking to a whole company
(c) the real source of his/ her anger is elsewhere
(d) your proper explanation should be made in no time

번역 화가 난 고객에 대해 가장 먼저 기억해야 할 것은 고객의 언행이 당신에게 향해 있는 반면에 고객이 화난 진짜 원인은 다른 곳에 있다. 그 사람은 대개 개인적으로 당신에게 화난 것이 아니라 차갑고 감정이 없으며 도움이 되지 못하는 것으로 인식되는 한 조직에 속한 직원인 당신에게 화를 내는 것이다. 조직 전체에게 소리를 치거나 욕하기는 어려우므로 고객은 당신에게 화풀이를 하는 것이다. 화가 난 사람들은 화를 표현할 기회를 원하고 그들의 의견을 들어주기 바란다는 것을 깨닫는 것이 중요하다. 만약 그들의 분노를 받아들이지 않고 문제를 해결하기 위해 너무 서두르는 것이 오히려 그들을 더욱 더 화나게 할지도 모른다.

(a) 무엇이 문제인지 묻지 말고 처음에는 들어야 한다
(b) 고객은 실제로 회사 전체에게 이야기하고 있는 것이다
(c) 고객이 화난 진짜 원인은 다른 곳에 있다
(d) 즉각 적절한 설명을 해줘야 한다

해법 빈칸이 있는 문장의 while이 '반면에'라는 의미가 있다는 것만 알아도 (b), (c)가 정답 후보임을 알 수 있다. 빈칸 다음 문장의 an organization의 종류에는 company만 있는 것은 아니므로 (b)가 아니라 (c)가 정답임을 알 수 있다.

direct at ~에게 돌리다, ~로 향하게 하다 **perceive** 감지, 인식하다 **yell at** ~에게 소리치다 **abuse** 욕하다 **acknowledge** 인정하다

✓ **정답** (c)

Of all the natural forces, gravity is the most implacable and controls our lives from birth to death. No wonder that, conscious of their earth-bound slavery, men have always _____. Mysterious as it may seem, most of the creatures on this planet are hardly aware that gravity exists. Dominant as it is over all the lives of large land animals to anything much smaller than a mouse, it is seldom more than a mild inconvenience. To the insects it is not even that; flies are so light and fragile that the air buoys them up, and gravity bothers them no more than it does a fish.

(a) pictured the sky as the abode of the gods
(b) looked for ways to free themselves from gravity
(c) went about looking for suitable places to settle
(d) wondered about invisible natural forces including gravity

---

Six senior citizens aged between 60 and 80 died in a car accident on the coast in Hawaii Saturday. At about 5 P.M., their vehicle _____ and crashed into a fish farm 1.5 meters below the main street, killing all passengers onboard, police said. According to the investigation authorities, they were on their way back home after having spent the afternoon at a nearby beach, which opened that day. Although the case is still under investigation, police authorities say the accident was most likely caused by the driver's inability to control the vehicle as the road forked to the right just prior to the scene of the accident.

(a) ran into a dead end sign
(b) skidded on the road
(c) broke the speed limit
(d) veered off the road

번역 자연의 모든 힘 가운데 중력이 피하기가 가장 어려우며 태어나서 죽을 때까지 우리의 생활을 지배한다. 지구에 매어 있는 노예 상태를 의식하는 인간이 항상 하늘을 신들이 사는 곳이라고 상상해 온 것은 당연하다. 이상하게 보일지는 모르지만 지구상의 생물 대부분은 중력이 존재한다는 것을 거의 의식하지 않고 있다. 비록 중력이 큰 육상 동물에서 쥐보다 훨씬 작은 모든 동물들에 이르기까지 지구상의 모든 동물의 생활을 지배하고 있지만 조금의 불편도 주지 않는다. 심지어 곤충에게도 중력은 조금의 불편이 되지 않는다. 파리들은 매우 가볍고 연약하기 때문에 공기 자체가 파리를 공중으로 띄워주는 역할을 하기에 중력이 물고기에게 별다른 불편을 주지 않듯이 파리에게도 특별한 불편을 주지 못한다.

(a) 하늘을 신들이 사는 곳이라고 상상해 온
(b) 그들 자신을 중력으로부터 자유롭게 할 방법들을 찾아 온
(c) 정착할 적절한 장소들을 찾아 여기저기 다닌
(d) 중력을 포함해서 눈에 보이지 않는 자연의 힘에 대해 궁금해 온

해법 일단 abode(거주지)라는 단어를 알아야 하고 지구에 매어 있는 노예 상태를 의식하는 인간에게 있어 당연한 것이 무엇일지 생각해 보면 인간이 하늘을 신들이 사는 곳이라고 항상 상상해 왔다는 내용이 자연스러워 (a)가 정답이다. (b), (c)는 뒷받침하는 내용이 이어지지 않고, (d)는 invisible natural forces에 해당하는 내용이 지문에 없다.

gravity 중력 **implacable** 달래기 어려운, 화해할 수 없는 **conscious of** ~을 의식하는 **earth-bound** 지구에 매어 있는 **dominant** 지배적인 **buoy** 뜨게 하다, 띄다 **A no more than B** A하지 않는 것이 B하지 않는 것과 같다

정답 (a)

번역 60세에서 80세에 이르는 노인 6명이 토요일에 하와이 해안에서 자동차 사고로 사망했다. 오후 5시경에 그들을 태운 자동차가 길을 벗어나 간선 도로에서 1.5미터 아래의 양어장에 추락하여 차에 타고 있던 승객 전원이 사망했다고 경찰이 밝혔다. 수사 기관에 따르면 그들은 그 날 개장한 근처 해변에서 오후를 보내고 귀가 중이었다고 한다. 아직 수사 중이지만 도로가 사고 현장 바로 앞 양갈래 길에서 오른쪽으로 굽어 있으므로 사고의 원인은 아마도 운전자의 운전 미숙일 가능성이 크다고 경찰이 밝혔다.

(a) 막다른 길 표지판으로 돌진했다
(b) 길에서 미끄러졌다
(c) 제한 속도를 어겼다
(d) 길을 벗어났다

해법 도로가 사고 현장 바로 앞에서 오른쪽으로 굽어 사고 원인은 분명 운전 미숙일 것이라고 했으므로 커브를 제대로 틀지 않아 사고가 발생한 것으로 (d)가 정답이다. (a), (b), (c)는 빈칸이 있는 문장만 놓고 보면 그럴듯하지만 사고 현장 바로 앞 양갈래 길에서 오른쪽으로 굽은 도로와 연결되지 않는다. 지문을 끝까지 읽는 것이 중요한 문제다.

senior 손위의 **vehicle** 탈 것, 차 **crash** 추락하다 **fish farm** 양어장 **investigation** 수사 **authority** 당국 **inability** 무능 **fork** 갈라지게 하다, 갈라지다 **scene** 현장

정답 (d)

If not cared for by some other human being, a child _____. This kind of helplessness is in distinct contrast with the ability of many newly born animals to get to their feet within minutes of birth and to run with the herd within a few hours. This long period of vulnerability would seem to be the price that mankind has to pay for the long learning process which fits man for survival as a species. It is during this very long period in which the human infant is totally dependent on others that it reveals the feature which it shares with all other human infants: a capacity to learn a language.

(a) cannot stay healthy enough
(b) will be slow to learn to speak
(c) may have a hard time walking
(d) is not likely to survive

번역 아기는 다른 사람의 보살핌 없이는 생존하기 어려울 것이다. 이런 무력함은 태어나자마자 몇 분 이내로 걷고 몇 시간 이내로 무리들과 뛰어다닐 수 있는 다른 새끼 동물의 능력과는 확실히 대조적이다. 오랜 기간의 이런 무력함은 인간이 이 세상에서 하나의 종으로 생존할 수 있게 해주는 아주 오랜 학습 기간에 대한 인간이 치러야 할 대가인 것 같다. 이렇게 다른 사람에게 완전히 의존해서 살아가는 긴 기간 동안에 아기는 다른 모든 아기들이 갖고 있는 공통된 특징이 나타나는데, 이는 다름 아닌 언어를 배우는 능력이다.

(a) 충분히 건강하게 지낼 수 없다
(b) 말하는 것을 늦게 배울 것이다
(c) 걷기를 시작하는 게 어려울 수도 있을 것이다
(d) 생존하기 어려울 것이다

해법 빈칸 다음 문장의 This kind of helplessness와 지문 세 번째 문장의 This long period of vulnerability를 중심으로 보면 (d)가 정답이다. 지문에서 어른들의 보살핌이 있을 때와 없을 때 언어를 배우는 속도 차이와 걷기를 배우는 속도 차이에 대하여는 언급되지 않으므로 (b)와 (c)는 맞지 않다.

in distinct contrast with ~와 상당히 대조적인 **herd** 짐승 떼, 무리 **vulnerability** 약함 **survival** 생존 **reveal** 드러내다, 보이다

 정답 (d)

Acne has been plaguing mankind for thousands of years. Although acne is often called "teenage acne," this is wrong because it is not evidence of maturation. While more than 80 percent of teenagers develop some kind of acne, almost 95 percent of the population will suffer from acne at some time in their adulthood. As a matter of fact, acne is a disease that some people never outgrow. Besides, some people become adults before they suffer from acne. The _____ doesn't make any difference in treating acne.

(a) prominent symptom
(b) age of onset
(c) long history of the disease
(d) best-known treatment

번역 여드름은 수천 년 동안 인류를 괴롭혀 오고 있다. 여드름은 성숙의 상징이 아니기 때문에 이것이 '십대 여드름'이라고 즐겨 불리는 것은 잘못이다. 청소년의 80퍼센트 이상이 어떤 형태로든 여드름이 나는 반면, 거의 95퍼센트에 육박하는 사람들이 성인 시절 한때 여드름으로 고통받게 된다. 사실 여드름은 일부 사람들에게는 어른이 되어도 없어지지 않는 질병이다. 게다가 어떤 사람들은 여드름이 나기 전에 어른이 된다. 여드름의 치료법은 그것의 발병 나이와는 상관이 없다.

(a) 두드러지는 증상들
(b) 발병 나이
(c) 여드름의 긴 역사
(d) 최선의 치료법

해법 여드름이 청소년 시절에만 겪는 것이 아니라 성인 시절에도 많이 겪고 어른이 되어도 없어지지 않거나 어른이 되어도 여드름이 나지 않는 사람들도 있다는 것으로 여드름 발생 시기는 나이와 상관없다고 추론할 수 있어 (b)가 정답이다. (c)는 지문 내용이 여드름의 긴 역사가 아닌 생기는 다양한 시점이므로 맞지 않다.

acne 여드름 **plague** 괴롭히다 **maturation** 성숙 **adulthood** 성인기 **outgrow** 성장해서 벗어나다 **symptom** 증상 **onset** 발병

정답 (b)

Dear Editor,

The author of the editorial piece "What about the Children?" that appeared in last Sunday's paper is uninformed and has his facts completely wrong. Additionally, he is not looking at the big picture of what is happening in the field of medicine. The Ministry of Health has enacted several new requirements for doctors who treat children. The Association of Health Care Professionals is currently involved in a legal battle with the Ministry on the grounds that, with the current workload, most doctors cannot meet the requirements. Infant vaccination and nutrition education are extremely important for the proper development of our youth, but the Ministry itself should be following through with its commitment _____. Your readers should understand the background of all the issues before blaming hard-working medical professionals.

(a) instead of putting the responsibility on overwhelmed physicians
(b) to develop new vaccines to help sick children in underdeveloped countries
(c) and realize once again what is going on in the field of medicine
(d) to publish journals that provide reliable medical information to readers

번역 지난 일요일 신문에 실린 사설 〈아이들을 어떻게 할 것인가?〉의 필자는 제대로 된 정보가 아닌 사실과는 완전히 다른 정보를 가지고 계십니다. 게다가 의학계에서 벌어지고 있는 전반적인 상황에 대한 큰 그림을 잘못 그리고 계십니다. 보건부는 소아과 의사들에게 몇몇 새로운 요구 사항들을 제정했습니다. 의료인 협회는 현재의 업무량으로는 대부분의 의사들이 그 요구 사항들을 충족할 수 없다는 이유로 보건부와 현재 법적 분쟁에 휘말린 상태입니다. 유아 예방 접종과 영양 교육이 우리 아이들이 올바르게 성장하는 데 매우 중요하지만 과중한 업무에 시달리고 있는 의사들에게 책임을 넘기는 대신 보건부부터 본연의 임무에 충실해야 할 것입니다. 귀하의 독자들은 업무에 충실한 의사들을 비난하기 전에 모든 문제들의 배경을 우선 이해해야 합니다.

(a) 과중한 업무에 시달리고 있는 의사들에게 책임을 넘기는 대신
(b) 개발 도상국의 아픈 아이들을 도울 새로운 백신 개발을 위한
(c) 그리고 의학 분야에 무슨 일이 벌어지고 있는지 다시 한번 깨달아야 한다
(d) 독자들에게 신뢰할 수 있는 의학 정보를 제공하는 간행물을 출판하기 위한

해법 과중한 업무에 시달리는 의사들에 관련된 건으로 의료인 협회와 보건부가 공방을 벌이고 있다고 했으므로 (a)가 정답이다. (c)는 선택지의 once again에 해당하는 한때에 보건부가 의료계에서 무슨 일이 벌어지고 있는지 깨닫지 못했다는 내용이 지문에 없다.

editorial 사설 **field** 분야 **overwhelm** 압도하다, 질리게 하다

정답 (a)

William Jesperson, 47, bit his neighbor's dog in a dispute about her garden fence yesterday. Mrs. Carol Ramsey complained to the police and her dog had to be stitched four times. The argument between the two started when Mrs. Ramsey took down the fence between their two backyards. She told her neighbor she was going to replace it with a newer one, but she has not yet done so because, she claims, she cannot afford to. When the fence was removed, Mrs. Ramsey's dog used Mr. Jesperson's yard to play in, on one occasion frightening his two-year-old son. Despite repeated complaints, Mrs. Ramsey did nothing, and when the dog chased Mr. Jesperson's pet rabbit, _____.

(a) Mr. Jesperson was arguing with Mrs. Ramsey
(b) the man decided to complain about the dog
(c) the angry father and pet-lover took action
(d) Mrs. Ramsey ran after them to stop the chase

번역 윌리엄 제스퍼슨 씨(47세)는 어제 이웃집 여자의 울타리 문제로 논쟁을 하던 중 그녀의 개를 물었다. 캐럴 램지 씨는 이 사실을 경찰에 신고했고 그녀의 개는 네 바늘을 꿰매야 했다. 둘 사이의 말다툼은 램지 씨가 두 집의 뒤뜰 사이에 있는 울타리를 헐어 버리면서 시작됐다. 그녀는 제스퍼슨 씨에게 그것을 새것으로 교체하겠다고 말했지만 시간이 지나도 여전히 설치하지 않았으며, 그 이유로 내세운 내용은 그럴 만한 여유 자금이 없기 때문이라는 것이었다. 울타리가 제거되자 램지 씨의 개는 제스퍼슨 씨의 뜰을 놀이 공간으로 사용했고, 한번은 그의 두 살짜리 아들을 놀라게 한 적도 있었다. 계속되는 항의에도 불구하고 램지 씨는 아무런 행동도 취하지 않았고 그 개가 제스퍼슨 씨의 애완용 토끼를 뒤쫓자, 성난 아버지이자 애완동물 애호가인 그가 조치를 취했다.

(a) 제스퍼슨 씨는 램지 씨와 언쟁을 벌이는 중이었다
(b) 제스퍼슨 씨가 그 개에 대해 항의를 하고자 결심했다
(c) 성난 아버지이자 애완동물 애호가인 그가 조치를 취했다
(d) 램지 씨는 추격을 멈추기 위해 그들을 뒤쫓아서 달려갔다

해법 지문 마지막 문장을 보면 램지 씨의 개가 제스퍼슨 씨의 토끼를 뒤쫓았을 때 제스퍼슨 씨는 뭔가 행동을 취했을 것이고 이 행동이 논쟁을 하다가 램지 씨의 개를 물었다는 지문 첫 문장과 연결되는 구조이므로 (c)가 정답이다. (d)는 지문에서 드러난 제스퍼슨 씨와 램지 씨의 행태로 보아 선택지의 Mrs. Ramsey가 Mr. Jesperson이 돼야 그나마 적절하다.

dispute 논쟁(하다) **fence** 울타리 **stitch** 바느질하다 **argument** 말다툼 **replace** 교체하다 **occasion** 경우, 때 **run after** ~를 뒤쫓다

정답 (c)

Music has always influenced fashion, especially among teenagers and young adults. In the late 1980s and early 1990s, Seattle, Washington, was home to a new sound—grunge—that came out of garages and small clubs. Rock music by bands like Nirvana, Pearl Jam, and Soundgarden became the rage. The Seattle sound was loud, and the look was down-to-earth, affordable, and not at all flashy. As the music became more popular, so did copying the style of the musicians. This translated to fashion that mixes work clothes like flannel shirts and long johns with vintage clothes. Fashion designers are often influenced by pop culture, so _____.

(a) the designers at that time were very knowledgeable about rock music
(b) music, a form of pop culture, can be said to be influenced by fashion
(c) it didn't take long for the grunge look to make it to the runaway
(d) the fashion industry began to reflect various cultural factors

 번역 음악은 늘 패션에 영향을 끼쳐왔는데 십대와 젊은이들 사이에서는 특히 더 그래왔다. 1980년대 말과 1990년대 초 워싱턴 주의 시애틀은 차고와 작은 클럽에서 나온 새로운 사운드인 그런지의 산실이었다. 너바나, 펄 잼, 사운드가든 같은 밴드의 록 음악은 대유행이 됐다. 시애틀의 사운드는 요란스러웠으나 그 모습은 수수하고 실용적인 것으로 입을 만하고, 전혀 요란하지 않았다. 음악이 점점 인기를 더 끌면서 사람들은 음악가들의 스타일 또한 더욱 더 모방하게 되었다. 이런 현상은 패션으로 옮겨가 융 재질의 셔츠나 긴 내의와 빈티지 의상 같은 작업복을 패션에 접목시키는 현상으로 나타났다. 패션 디자이너들은 종종 대중문화의 영향을 받으므로 그런지 패션이 유행하는 데는 오랜 시간이 걸리지 않았다.

(a) 그 당시 디자이너들은 록 음악에 대한 지식이 풍부했다
(b) 대중문화의 한 형태인 음악 역시 패션에 영향을 받는다고 할 수 있다
(c) 그런지 패션이 유행하는 데는 오랜 시간이 걸리지 않았다
(d) 패션 업계가 다양한 문화적 요소들을 반영하기 시작했다

해법 그런지 록 음악이 유행했고 이런 유행이 패션에 옮겨왔다는 것이 지문 주요 흐름이므로 (c)가 정답이다. (a)는 영향을 준 록 음악에 대해 디자이너들이 잘 알았다는 객관적인 근거가 지문에 없고, (b)는 음악이 패션에 영향을 준다는 지문 주요 내용에 반대된다. (d)는 선택지의 various cultural factors에 대한 내용이 지문에 없다.

rage 대유행 **down-to-earth** 실제적인 **flashy** 요란한 **long johns** (손목, 발목까지 덮는) 긴 내의 **make it to the runaway** 승승장구하다

정답 (c)

The Employment Opinion Survey is an excellent communication and feedback tool that can provide management with crucial organizational improvement information. It can be used to build trust, confidence, and mutual respect between the management and the workforce as it demonstrates management's interest in learning about employees' concerns, opinions, and suggestions. It is a great way to help establish the foundation and communication process necessary for _____. It is suitable for all organizational levels and requires only twenty-five to thirty minutes to administer. Easy scoring instructions show you how to calculate the percentage of employees positively responding to survey issues.

(a) total quality performance
(b) organization-wide management
(c) quick results to share and show
(d) better supervision of employees

 번역 직원 의견 조사는 경영진에게 중요한 조직 개선 정보를 제공해줄 수 있는 훌륭한 의사소통 및 의견 수렴 수단이다. 경영진이 직원들의 관심사, 의견 및 제안 사항을 알고자 한다는 것을 표출하기에 경영진과 근로자 사이에 믿음, 확신, 그리고 상호 존중을 구축하는 데 사용될 수 있다. 직원 의견 조사는 업무 전반에 걸쳐 우수한 성과를 올리는 데 필요한 기반 및 의사소통 절차를 확립하는 데 도움이 되는 방법이다. 직원 의견 조사는 모든 규모와 단계의 조직에 적용이 가능하며 조사에는 불과 25분에서 30분밖에 소요되지 않는다. 간단한 점수 측정 지침이 있기 때문에 조사 항목에 긍정적으로 응답하는 직원들의 비율을 쉽게 산출할 수 있다.

(a) 업무 전반에 걸쳐 우수한 성과를 올리는 데
(b) 조직 전체를 관리하는 데
(c) 공유하고 보여줄 빠른 결과를 내는 데
(d) 더 나은 직원 관리를 위해

해법 직원 의견 조사는 경영진에게 중요한 조직 개선 정보를 제공해줄 수 있는 훌륭한 의사소통 및 의견 수렴 수단이라고 했으므로 조직 개선과 관련된 업무 전반에 걸쳐 우수한 성과를 올리는 데 필요한 기반 및 의사소통 절차라는 내용이 지문 흐름에 어울린다. 따라서 (a)가 정답이다.

crucial 결정적인, 중요한 **mutual** 서로의, 상호의 **foundation** 설립 **administer** 실시하다, (약 따위를) 복용시키다

정답 (a)

Determinism, which means that every event has natural causes, has been hypothesized as a natural law _____. According to scientific laws, a certain set of conditions will undoubtedly bring about a predetermined outcome. However, studies in physics have shown that the speed and location of tiny particles such as electrons are the results of irregular behaviors rather than predictable results determined by previously existing conditions. These studies made Werner Heisenberg formulate the principle of indeterminacy in 1925. From a philosophical viewpoint, those who regard human beings as creatures with free will show the greatest opposition toward the principle.

(a) but it needs to be studied further in physics and philosophy
(b) to help people accept what they go through in their lives
(c) and it still applies to every cause and effect in nature
(d) yet is under criticism in other fields of study

📖 **번역**　모든 자연 사건에는 자연적인 원인이 있음을 의미하는 결정론은 자연 법칙으로 가정되었지만 여전히 다른 학문 분야로부터 공격을 받고 있다. 과학적 법칙에 따르면 일련의 정해진 조건들은 반드시 이미 정해진 결과를 가져온다고 한다. 그러나 물리학 분야의 여러 연구들로 전자와 같은 미세한 입자들의 위치와 속도가 이미 존재하는 조건들에 의해 정해진 예상 가능한 결과라기 보다는 임의적인 작용의 결과임이 증명됐다. 이런 연구들로 인해 1925년 웨너 하이젠버그가 불확실성 원리를 구체화했다. 철학적인면에서 보면 인간을 자유의지가 있는 창조물로 보는 사람들이 결정론에 대해 가장 반대한다.

(a) 그러나 물리학과 철학에서 더 깊이 연구될 필요가 있다
(b) 사람들이 인생에서 겪는 일들을 받아들이도록 돕기 위해
(c) 그래서 그것은 자연의 모든 원인과 결과에 아직도 적용된다
(d) 그러나 여전히 다른 학문 분야로부터 공격받고 있다

✳️ **해법**　물리학에서 전자와 같은 미세한 입자들의 위치와 속도가 이미 존재하는 조건들에 의해 정해진 예상 가능한 결과라기보다는 임의적인 작용의 결과임이 증명됐다고 했고 지문 마지막 문장을 보면 철학에서도 결정론을 반대하는 부분이 있으므로 (d)가 정답이다. (a)는 연구가 이미 되어 있어 맞지 않고 (b)는 결정론에 반대하는 지문 내용과 맞지 않는다. (c)는 지문 내용과 정반대다.

determinism 결정론 **hypothesize** 가설을 세우다 **predetermined** 이미 정해진 **outcome** 결과 **physics** 물리학 **particle** 입자 **electron** 전자 **behavior** (물체, 물질의) 성질, 반응 **formulate** 공식화하다. 명확하게 말하다 **principle** 원리, 원칙 **indeterminacy** 불확실성

✅ **정답**　(d)

The decade of prosperity that the stock market crash of 1929 ended had been dazzling. In 1919, the First World War was over and the nation had turned its attention to making money. It succeeded beyond its wildest dreams. With a friendly Republican government in Washington fully committed to business growth, United States industry mushroomed. Mechanization, electrification, and the spread of assembly-line techniques led to a manufacturing output increase of 64 percent between 1919 and 1929. Wages and real earnings rose, but _____.

(a) they did not affect the number of job seekers
(b) profits rose far higher
(c) demand dwindled
(d) the stock market did not rebound

📖 **번역**　1929년 주식 시장 붕괴로 막을 내린 10년간의 번영은 눈부셨다. 1919년에 1차 세계 대전이 끝나자 국가는 부의 축적에 눈을 돌려 상상도 못한 정도로 성공을 거두었다. 공화당 정부가 우호적으로 기업 성장에 전념했기 때문에 미국 기업들은 우후죽순 늘어났다. 기계화, 전력화, 조립 생산 라인 기법의 확산으로 1919년과 1929년 사이에 제조업 생산량이 64퍼센트나 증가했다. 임금과 실질 소득도 증가했지만 이윤은 훨씬 많이 증가했다.

(a) 구직자 수에 영향을 주지 않았다
(b) 이윤은 훨씬 많이 증가했다
(c) 수요가 감소했다
(d) 주식 시장이 반등하지 않았다

✳️ **해법**　1919년에 1차 세계 대전 이후 미국의 경제 성장에 대한 지문으로 (b)가 정답이다. (a), (c)는 빈칸 앞의 but 때문에 그럴듯한 의미를 형성하지만 지문에 없는 내용이고, (d)는 지문 첫 문장의 1929년 주식 시장 붕괴 전 10년간 번영했다는 내용을 보면 1919년에서 1929년에는 주식 시장이 붕괴되지 않았음을 알 수 있어 선택지와 같은 내용 자체가 나올 수 없다.

prosperity 번영 **dazzling** 눈부신 **mushroom** 우후죽순 생겨나다 **mechanization** 기계화 **electrification** 전력화

✅ **정답**　(b)

The signs of math anxiety vary: students sometimes get in a bad mood when it's time for math class, ignore low grades by saying they didn't try, or simply complain that they hate the subject. _____; scientific research has shown that these feelings can have negative effects on students' ability to do math. What happens is that anxious thoughts crowd the brain and occupy memory that would otherwise be dedicated to computation. Experts believe that teachers can help relieve the anxiety. The first step is to acknowledge that a student's anxiety is real but fixable. Then they go back over the curriculum to figure out where the student started getting lost.

(a) This kind of anxiety, in most cases, influences students for a long time
(b) The culprit of the trouble is not clearly understood by teachers
(c) These students are tired of working to reverse the situation
(d) The anxiousness at the root of such behavior isn't an emotional matter

You know that modern organizations must continuously improve to thrive. _____. There is no shortage of people offering to help deliver high performance. Yet recent research shows that there is room for improvement. 49% of business executives believe that consultants put forward solutions that cannot be sustained in the short to medium term, let alone the longer term. Ernst&Young's Performance Improvement services are different because we recognize that you are. So we focus on helping you achieve sustained improvement by developing an approach that draws on our considerable experience in performance improvement.

(a) Employees are also required to be more competitive than ever
(b) Success today should be matched tomorrow
(c) They, however, do not know how to make that possible
(d) Some of them have been more successful than others

  번역 수학에 대해 드러나는 불안한 마음은 다양하다. 학생들은 수학 시간이 되면 기분이 안 좋아지기도 하고, 충분한 노력을 기울이지 않았다고 하면서 낮은 점수가 나온 것을 무시하거나 그냥 수학이 싫다고 불평하기도 한다. 그런 행동의 근원에 있는 불안감은 정서적인 문제는 아니다. 과학적 연구를 통해 이런 감정들이 학생들의 수학 공부 능력에 부정적인 영향을 줄 수 있다고 밝혀졌다. 사실은 불안한 생각들이 머리 속을 채워 계산에 필요한 기억력을 잠식해 버리는 것이다. 전문가들은 교사들이 이런 불안을 완화하는 데 도움을 줄 수 있다고 믿고 있다. 우선은 학생의 불안한 마음이 실제로 존재하지만 해결 가능하다는 사실을 인정하는 것이다. 그리고 어디서부터 학생이 헤매게 됐는지 알기 위해 교과 과정을 되돌아가서 다시 살펴보는 것이다.

(a) 대부분의 경우에 있어 이런 종류의 불안은 학생들에게 장기간 영향을 준다
(b) 교사들은 문제의 원인을 명확히 이해하지 못하고 있다
(c) 이 학생들은 그런 상황을 뒤집기 위해 노력하는 데 지쳤다
(d) 그런 행동의 근원에 있는 불안감은 정서적인 문제는 아니다

해법 빈칸 다음 문장에서 수학에 대한 감정이 학생의 수학 학습 행위에 부정적 영향을 준다고 했으므로 수학에 대한 걱정이 단지 정서상의 문제에서 그치는 것이 아니라 수학 학습 행위에 실제적인 부정적 영향을 준다는 내용이 자연스러워 (d)가 정답이다. (a)는 선택지의 for a long time이 맞지 않고, (c)는 뒤 문장과 연결되지 않는다.

dedicate 전념하다 **computation** 계산 **acknowledge** 인정하다 **fixable** 고칠 수 있는, 해결할 수 있는 **curriculum** 교육[교과]과정

✓ 정답 (d)

 번역 현대의 조직은 성공하기 위해 발전을 거듭해야 함을 알고 계실 것입니다. 오늘의 성공은 내일로 이어져야 합니다. 높은 수행 능력을 제공하도록 도와주겠다는 사람들은 많습니다. 그러나 최근의 연구에 따르면 여전히 개선의 여지가 있는 것으로 나타납니다. 기업체 중역의 49%는 기업 컨설팅 담당자가 장기간은 물론 단·중 기간 동안에도 유지될 수 없는 해결책들만을 제안한다고 믿고 있습니다. 귀하는 다르다는 것을 알기에 어니스트&영스의 수행 능력 개선 서비스는 다릅니다. 그렇기에 저희는 수행 능력 개선의 상당한 경험에 바탕을 둔 접근법을 개발함으로써 귀하가 지속적인 개선을 할 수 있도록 돕는 데 집중합니다.

(a) 직원들도 그 어느 때보다 경쟁력을 더 갖출 것도 요구받습니다
(b) 오늘의 성공은 내일로 이어져야 합니다
(c) 그러나 그들은 어떻게 하면 그 일을 가능하게 할 수 있을지 모릅니다
(d) 그들 중 몇몇은 다른 조직들보다 더 성공적이었습니다

해법 현대 조직들은 성공을 위해 개선을 거듭해야 하고 어니스트&영스가 돕겠다는 지문으로 sustained improvement가 키워드이므로 (b)가 정답이다. (a)는 지문이 직원 경쟁력 향상에 대한 내용이 아니고, (c)는 높은 수행 능력을 제공하도록 도와주겠다는 사람들이 많다고 했으므로 성공을 위해 지속적인 개선을 위한 방법들 자체를 모른다는 것은 맞지 않는다. (d)는 지문에 없다.

thrive 번창, 성공하다 **room** 여지 **executive** 중역 **put forward** 제안하다 **sustain** 유지하다, 견디다 **term** 기간 **let alone** ~은 말할 것도 없고 **draw on** ~에 의존하다 **match** 조화시키다, 맞추다

✓ 정답 (b)

115

Culture evolves naturally, but we need "education and training" to make it become part of our chemistry. And to do so, we need to develop various programs for people to participate in cultural club activities as families and develop a system of funding to reward exemplary cases. _____, we should establish a social environment in which a person's experience in cultural activities can be counted into his/ her resume. Let us now say goodbye to our old, wasteful, uniform culture of the adults and develop cultures for workplaces, families, and couples instead.

(a) For example
(b) As a result
(c) Above all
(d) Hence

📖 **번역** 문화는 자연스럽게 형성되지만 그것이 몸에 베기까지 교육과 훈련이 필요하다. 그러려면 문화 동호회에 가족 단위로 함께 참여할 수 있는 다양한 프로그램을 개발하고 모범적인 문화 모임에 보조금 지원 시스템도 마련해야 한다. 그리고 무엇보다 문화 활동 체험을 그 사람의 경력으로 인정해 우대하는 사회 분위기를 만들어야 한다. 이제 낭비적이고 획일적인 성인 문화와 결별하고 다양한 직장, 가족, 부부 문화를 만들어 보자.

(a) 예를 들면
(b) 결과적으로
(c) 무엇보다
(d) 그러므로

☀️ **해법** 문화가 몸에 베기까지 교육과 훈련을 위해 가족 단위로 문화 동호회에 함께 참여할 수 있는 프로그램이 제시되고 있고 이런 프로그램을 지원하기 위한 보조금 지원 시스템도 마련해야 한다는 내용으로 보아 지문 빈칸 뒤에 제시된 사회 분위기는 지문 첫 문장의 교육과 훈련을 포함하는 개념이므로 (c)가 정답이다.

evolve 발전하다 **chemistry** 마음의 움직임 **reward** 보상하다
exemplary case 모범적인 사례 **count** 포함되다 **wasteful** 낭비적인
uniform 획일적인

✅ **정답** (c)

116

Will widespread disapproval or resentment of the English language have any significant impact on its use? It seems that many non-native speakers around the world have a love-hate relation with English. Whether it is reflected in wearing baseball caps or eating fast food, the habit of imitating American culture seems inescapable, especially among the young and even among those who disapprove of American politics. _____, using English is a desirable habit to be acquired and imitated around the world, even among those who dislike English for the role it plays in spreading Western values and for its effect on other languages.

(a) Similarly
(b) In fact
(c) Relatively
(d) Hence

📖 **번역** 영어를 반대하고 싫어하는 현상이 만연해짐은 영어 사용에 어떤 중대한 영향을 줄까? 전 세계의 많은 비 영어권 사람들이 영어와 애증 관계를 맺고 있는 것 같다. 이런 관계가 야구 모자를 쓰는 것에 나타나 있든지 패스트푸드를 먹는 것에 나타나 있든지 특히 젊은이들과 심지어 미국 정치를 반대하는 사람들조차 미국 문화를 모방하는 습관을 버릴 수 없는 것 같다. 마찬가지로 영어가 서양의 가치관을 퍼트리고 다른 언어들에 영향을 주는 역할 때문에 영어를 싫어하는 사람들에게조차 영어 사용은 전 세계적으로 습득해서 모방할 바람직한 습관으로 인식되고 있다.

(a) 마찬가지로
(b) 사실
(c) 상대적으로
(d) 그러므로

☀️ **해법** 빈칸 앞의 영어를 싫어하고 미국의 정치를 반대하는 사람들조차 미국 문화를 모방하고 있다는 내용과 빈칸 뒤의 영어가 서양의 가치관들을 퍼트리고 다른 언어들에 영향을 주는 역할 때문에 영어를 싫어하는 사람들에게조차 영어 사용은 전 세계적으로 바람직하다는 내용은 비슷한 논리이므로 (a)가 정답이다.

disapproval 반대 **resentment** 분개, 원한 **significant** 중대한
love-hate 좋아하면서도 싫어하는, 애증의 **reflect** 반영하다, 나타내다
imitate 모방하다 **inescapable** 피할 수 없는 **desirable** 바람직한
acquire 획득, 습득하다

✅ **정답** (a)

해설 및 정답 Actual Test 01

Because power over people is shown in forcing them do what they don't want to do, the person who acts upon the love of power is more likely to inflict pain than to allow pleasure. If you ask your boss for leave of absence from the workplace on some reasonable occasion, his/ her love of power will bring more satisfaction from a refusal than from approval. If you need a building permit, the narrow-minded official in charge will obviously feel more pleasure from saying "No" than from saying "Yes." It is this kind of thing which makes the love of power a very dangerous motive.

Q: What is the best title of the passage?
(a) Who Should Gain Power?
(b) Results Made by Power
(c) Ways Power Makes People Satisfied
(d) What Is a Power Lover Like?

The rise of circulating libraries helped literature expand. At a time when the prices of books were very high in relation to the purchasing power of the great number of the population, the libraries were a meaningful social invention. They furnished those who had acquired a taste for reading with access to books otherwise out of their reach. They helped reduce the gap between interest in reading and purchasing power. The first circulating library was opened to the public in London in 1740. Rivals quickly sprang up in London and in the provinces as well. By the end of the century, about 1,000 libraries dotted the country. Their quick success attested to the growing interest in reading.

Q: What is the main topic of the passage?
(a) The different kinds of circulating libraries
(b) The influence of circulating libraries
(c) The reason for the success of circulating libraries
(d) The beginning of circulating libraries

📖 번역　사람들 위에서 행사하는 권력은 사람들이 하고 싶지 않은 일을 하게 만드는 데에서 드러나기 때문에 권력을 사랑하는 사람은 즐거움보다는 고통을 유발할 가능성이 더 크다. 상사로부터 정당한 사유로 휴가를 요청하는 경우에도 상사가 권력을 사랑하는 사람이라면 허락보다는 거절을 함으로써 만족감을 느낄 것이다. 건축 허가가 필요하다면 편협한 담당 공무원은 "그렇게 하세요"라고 말하기 보다는 "안 됩니다"라고 말함으로써 분명히 더 큰 즐거움을 얻을 것이다. 권력에 대한 욕심을 동기로 갖는 것이 위험한 이유가 바로 여기에 있다.

(a) 누가 권력을 가져야 하나
(b) 권력이 만든 결과들
(c) 권력이 사람들을 만족시키는 방법들
(d) 권력을 사랑하는 사람의 특징

☀ 해법　지문 첫 문장을 중심으로 보면 지문은 힘에 대해 애착을 느끼는 사람의 특성에 관한 것임을 알 수 있어 (d)가 정답이다. (a)는 힘에 대한 애착을 위험한 동기로 만든다고 했으므로 Who Shouldn't Gain Power?가 돼야 하고, (b)는 지문에 Results Made by the Love of Power에 대한 내용은 있지만 Results Made by Power에 대한 내용은 없다. (c)는 선택지의 Ways가 맞지 않다.

inflict (타격·고통 따위를) 가하다　leave of absence (회사·학교 등에서의) 휴가　reasonable 합법적인, 정당한　occasion 경우, 이유　building permit 건축 허가　motive 동기

✓ 정답　(d)

📖 번역　순회 도서관의 번성은 문학의 확산을 도왔다. 인구 대부분의 구매력에 비해 책값이 매우 비싼 때에 순회 도서관은 사회의 의미 있는 고안품이었다. 독서의 맛을 깨달은 사람들이 다른 방법으로는 접할 수 없었을 책들을 접할 수 있도록 해줬다. 독서에 대한 관심과 구매력 사이의 간격을 좁히는 데도 도움이 됐다. 최초의 순회 도서관은 1740년 런던에서 대중들에게 선보였다. 런던 시내와 다른 여러 지역에도 유사한 도서관이 경쟁적으로 빠르게 생겨났다. 17세기 말에 이르자 약 1,000개의 순회 도서관이 전국에 흩어져서 생겼다. 순회 도서관의 빠른 성공은 독서에 대한 커져가는 관심을 증명해 준다.

(a) 다양한 종류의 순회 도서관
(b) 순회 도서관의 영향
(c) 순회 도서관의 성공 이유
(d) 순회 도서관의 시초

☀ 해법　순회 도서관의 영향이 지문 주요 내용이므로 (b)가 정답이다. (a), (c), (d)는 각각 경쟁 도서관, 1740년 런던에서 문을 연 최초의 순회 도서관 그리고 독서에 대한 커져가는 관심이 나오나 지문 전체를 아우르지 못하는 지엽적 내용이다.

circulating 순환, 순환하는　in relation to ~에 관해, ~에 비해　purchasing power 구매력　furnish 공급, 갖추다　spring up 생기다　province 지방, 지역　dot 흩어져 있다　attest to ~을 입증하다

✓ 정답　(b)

You may think that some books will be too difficult for you to understand because you don't have any previous knowledge of the subjects. But knowledge is not as necessary for understanding as you suppose. You will not become a better reader if you read books always within your ability. You must read books that are beyond you, books that will make you work to understand them, and unless you work, you will not learn. Each time you read books beyond you, you will discover something new. You should keep in mind that the mind has no limit to growth and development, unlike the body.

Q: What is the passage mainly about?
(a) Books beyond one's understanding
(b) The doubt about the benefit of previous knowledge
(c) How to gain new knowledge through reading
(d) The necessity of reading difficult materials

번역 사람들은 책에 담긴 내용에 관한 선행 지식이 없기 때문에 어떤 책은 이해하기 너무 어려울 것이라고 생각할지도 모른다. 그러나 생각하는 것만큼 지식이 이해에 꼭 필요한 것은 아니다. 만약 자신의 능력 내에 있는 책들만 읽는다면 더 나은 독자가 될 수 없을 것이다. 누구든 자신이 가진 능력의 범위를 넘는 책들을 읽어야 하는데, 그래야 그 내용을 이해하기 위해 노력을 하게 되고 노력을 해야만 배움이 있는 것이다. 자신의 수준을 넘는 책을 볼 때마다 뭔가 새로운 것을 발견할 것이다. 사람의 신체와는 달리 정신은 성장과 발달에 한계가 없다는 것을 명심해야 한다.

(a) 한 개인의 이해력을 뛰어넘는 책들
(b) 선행 지식의 혜택에 대한 의문
(c) 독서를 통해 새로운 지식을 얻는 법
(d) 어려운 내용들을 읽을 필요성

해법 지문 앞부분의 선행 지식이 책을 이해하는 데 꼭 필요한 것이 아니라는 내용이 독자의 능력 범위를 넘는 책들을 읽어야 하는 필요성이라는 지문의 주요 내용을 유도하는 구조로 (d)가 정답이다. (a), (b)는 지엽적인 내용이고, (c)는 지문에 구체적인 내용이 없다.

previous[background] knowledge 선행 지식 suppose 생각하다
beyond ~을 넘어서 discover 발견하다 keep in mind 명심하다

정답 (d)

For about 700 years, Japan was officially ruled by an emperor, while the real power was in the hands of the shogun. Under the shogun came the daimyo, provincial governors. Society was like a rigidly controlled pyramid, with the peasant at the bottom. The glue that held that structure together was the military caste that served the daimyo: the samurai. That system began to come apart in 1854, when the U.S. Navy forced Japan to join the modern world—at gunpoint. Japanese leaders decided that they needed a modern army equipped with the most up-to-date weapons and trained by the best officers of the day. Suddenly, 2 million samurai found themselves unqualified for careers that had once been theirs alone.

Q: Which of the following best summarizes the passage?
(a) The Japanese imperial army was aided in being reorganized.
(b) The samurai helped the shogun to rule Japan for 700 years.
(c) The U.S. intervened in Japan's internal affairs in 1854.
(d) The samurai suddenly became obsolete in the mid-nineteenth century.

번역 약 700년 동안 일본은 공식적으로는 황제에 의해 통치되었지만 실권은 쇼군이 쥐고 있었다. 쇼군 아래에 지방 영주인 다이묘가 있었다. 사회는 소작농을 맨 밑바닥에 둔 엄격히 통제된 피라미드 형태와 같았다. 이러한 구조가 유지될 수 있었던 것은 다이묘 밑에서 충성을 다해 일하는 군사 계급인 사무라이가 접착제 역할을 했기 때문이었다. 이 체제는 1854년 미 해군이 일본을 총으로 위협하며 강제로 근대화에 편승하라는 협박을 받았을 때 붕괴되기 시작했다. 일본의 지도자들은 최신 무기로 무장하고 그 당시 최고 교관에 의해 훈련받은 신식 군대가 필요하다는 결정을 내렸다. 갑자기 2백 만의 사무라이들은 한때 자신들의 전유물이었던 직업에 자기 스스로가 부적합한 존재가 되었음을 통감해야만 했다.

(a) 일본 황군은 재조직되는 데 도움을 받았다.
(b) 사무라이들은 쇼군이 700년 동안 일본을 통치하도록 도와줬다.
(c) 1854년에 미국은 일본의 내정에 간섭했다.
(d) 사무라이들은 19세기 중반에 이르러 갑자기 쓸모없는 존재로 전락했다.

해법 현대식 군대가 필요하게 됨에 따라 사무라이 계층이 쓸모없는 존재가 되어 (d)가 정답이다. (a)는 aided에 대한 내용이 지문에 없고, (b)는 지엽적이며, (c)는 미국이 일본에 간섭한 일이 지문에 한 가지만 나와 있어 맞지 않다.

rigidly 엄격하게 peasant 소작인, 농부 glue 접착제 caste 카스트 제도, 특권계급 at gunpoint 총으로 위협하여 imperial 황제의

정답 (d)

Fifty years ago there was a general, though vague, belief that it was the duty of grammarians to lay down rules for the correct use of the language, and the duty of everybody else to obey them. This belief has not entirely disappeared, but it is no longer respectable. Today's linguists generally believe that grammar is dependent on usage and that a grammarian cannot say how people should talk just like a chemist defines how molecules should act upon each other. The laws of grammar are similar to those of any other science, merely general statements about what happens, not directions about what should happen—and they can change as soon as any new evidence is suggested.

Q: What is the main idea of the passage?
(a) Grammar changes through linguistic studies.
(b) Grammar is based on usage rather than rules.
(c) Grammar describes how a language is used.
(d) Grammar is less important than it used to be.

Even though you see beautiful people in ads drinking together, alcohol itself doesn't make you beautiful or guarantee you'll meet a great guy. Alcohol slows down your central nervous system by blocking messages to your brain. So, even when you drink small amounts, your responses to everything are slower. Also, because your head is not clear, you can make bad judgments like drunk driving. If you drink too much, you may vomit because alcohol is toxic and vomiting is the body's way of getting rid of an unwanted poison. If you consume large amounts of alcohol in a very short time, you can get alcohol poisoning.

Q: What is the best title of the passage?
(a) What Drinking Does to Our Brain
(b) Untold Truths about Drinking
(c) How Our Body Reacts to Alcohol
(d) Effects of Alcohol Poisoning

🟰 **번역** 애매하긴 했어도 50년 전에는 바른 언어의 사용을 위한 규칙들을 정하는 것이 문법학자들의 의무였고 다른 모든 사람들은 이 규칙을 지키는 것이 의무라는 일반적인 믿음이 있었다. 이런 믿음이 완전히 사라진 것은 아니지만 더 이상 존중되지는 않는다. 오늘날 언어학자들은 일반적으로 문법은 사용에 토대를 둔다고 믿으며, 마치 화학자가 분자가 서로 어떻게 반응해야 한다고 말하지 못하듯이 문법학자들도 사람들에게 어떻게 말하는 것이 옳다고 말할 수는 없다. 문법 규칙은 다른 여느 과학 분야와 다를 바가 없어서, 이러이러한 작용이 일어나야만 한다고 하는 지시 사항이 아니라 이러한 작용이 일어난다고 하는 일반적인 현상을 설명하는 것에 불과하며 새로운 증거가 제시되는 즉시 바뀔 수 있다.

(a) 문법은 언어학 연구를 통해 변한다.
(b) 문법은 규칙들 보다는 용법에 토대를 둔다.
(c) 문법은 언어가 사용되는 방식을 기술한다.
(d) 문법은 예전보다 덜 중요하다.

❇ **해법** 문법은 규칙보다 용법에 토대를 둔다는 내용의 지문으로 (b)가 정답이다. (a)는 문법이 언어학 연구를 통해 바뀌는 것이 아니라 문법이 쓰여지는 실제 생활에서 발견되는 증거들로 인해 바뀐다는 것이 지문 내용이므로 맞지 않고, (c)는 지문이 문법의 변화에 대한 내용이지 문법의 정의에 대한 내용은 아니다. 지문 내용이 문법의 중요성에 대한 것이 아니므로 (d)는 옳지 않다.

vague 막연한, 애매한 **duty** 의무 **lay down** 정하다 **respectable** 의미 있는, 존중되는 **linguist** 언어학자 **molecule** 분자

✔ **정답** (b)

🟰 **번역** 광고에서 함께 술을 마시는 멋진 사람들을 본다 하더라도 술 자체가 당신을 아름답게 만들어 주거나 당신이 멋진 사람을 만나게 될 거라는 보장을 해주지는 않는다. 술은 뇌에 보내는 신호를 차단함으로써 중추신경계의 반응을 느리게 만든다. 그래서 적은 양을 마셔도 모든 반응이 더 느려진다. 또한 머리가 맑지 않기 때문에 음주운전과 같은 잘못된 판단을 내릴 수도 있다. 술을 너무 많이 마시면 구토를 할 것이다. 왜냐하면 알코올은 독성이 있고 구토란 원하지 않는 독성 물질을 몸에서 제거하는 방법이기 때문이다. 당신이 아주 짧은 시간에 다량의 알코올을 섭취한다면 알코올 중독에 걸릴 수 있다.

(a) 음주가 우리 뇌에 어떤 일을 하나
(b) 음주에 대해 알려지지 않은 진실
(c) 우리 몸이 알코올에 어떻게 반응하나
(d) 알코올 중독의 영향

❇ **해법** 지문 전반적으로 술에 대한 우리 몸의 반응에 대해 말하고 있으므로 (c)가 정답이다. (a)는 지문에 뇌뿐 아니라 술에 대한 우리 몸의 반응도 있으므로 제목으로 보기에는 협소하고, (b)는 선택지의 Untold에 대한 근거가 지문에 없고, (d)는 지문 마지막 문장을 이용한 것으로 지문에 없는 내용이다.

guarantee 보장하다 **central nervous system** 중추신경계 **vomit** 구토하다(throw up) **toxic** 독성의 **alcohol poisoning** 알코올 중독

✔ **정답** (c)

Based on a new survey on the cost of living in the world's major cities, Tokyo is the most expensive place for expatriate business people or diplomats to live. Prices in the Japanese capital are more than double those in New York. Western Europe is also relatively pricey—lunch in Zurich or Paris will cost over 20% more than in New York. Moscow is becoming an increasingly expensive place to live; last year the Russian capital was already 4% more expensive than New York; this year the difference is 10%. Moscow is now about as expensive as Hong Kong. The cost-conscious would do well to stay in Central Europe; life in Prague is half as expensive as in New York.

Q: Which of the following is correct according to the passage?
(a) Prices in Hong Kong stayed the same as last year.
(b) Prices in Prague are less than 25% of those in Tokyo.
(c) Prices in Paris are less than 20% of those in New York.
(d) Prices in Moscow have more than doubled since last year.

🔲 번역 세계 주요 도시의 물가에 관한 새로운 조사에 따르면 도쿄는 외국인 사업가나 외교관들이 살기에 제일 비싼 곳이다. 도쿄 물가는 뉴욕 물가의 두 배 이상이다. 서유럽도 상대적으로 물가가 비싸서 취리히나 파리의 점심값은 뉴욕보다 20퍼센트 이상 높다. 모스크바는 점차 살기에 비용이 많이 드는 곳이 되고 있다. 러시아의 수도는 작년에 이미 뉴욕보다 물가가 4퍼센트 더 비쌌으며 올해는 그 차이가 10퍼센트나 된다. 모스크바는 이제 거의 홍콩만큼이나 물가가 비싸다. 물가에 신경 쓰는 사람들이라면 중앙 유럽 지역에 머무르는 것이 좋을 것이다. 프라하에서의 생활비는 뉴욕의 반밖에 들지 않기 때문이다.

(a) 홍콩 물가는 작년과 같다.
(b) 프라하 물가는 도쿄 물가의 25% 이하이다.
(c) 파리 물가는 뉴욕 물가의 20% 이하이다.
(d) 모스크바 물가가 작년보다 두 배 이상 증가했다.

🔆 해법 도쿄 물가가 뉴욕 물가의 두 배 이상이라는 점과 프라하 물가가 뉴욕의 반밖에 되지 않는 점을 연계해 보면 프라하 물가가 도쿄 물가의 4분의 1 미만이므로 (b)가 정답이다.

expatriate 해외에 거주하는 (사람) **diplomat** 외교관 **capital** 수도 **cost-conscious** 가격 따위에 예민한

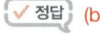 정답 (b)

A truck carrying electronics valued at over $200,000 was hijacked yesterday morning. The truck belonged to the Ruby Star Company, and the driver, Nicolas Estrella, was making deliveries to the customers in the Bedford section. This is the eleventh truck hijacking in the first five months of this year. Over the last four years there have been 38 hijackings in the metropolitan area. The hijackers target trucks carrying cargoes that can be sold fast for cash. Drivers have been warned to lock their doors and not to pick up hitchhikers. But some insurance investigators believe that as many as one-third of these cases are not hijackings at all. They believe that some drivers steal their own cargoes.

Q: Which of the following is correct according to the passage?
(a) Nicolas Estrella is believed to have stolen his cargo.
(b) This year's 11th truck hijacking happened yesterday.
(c) The electronics stolen yesterday were sold for cash.
(d) Up to 30% of all the hijackings have been investigated.

🔲 번역 어제 아침, 시가 20만 달러가 넘는 전자 제품들을 실은 트럭이 약탈당했다. 이 트럭은 루비 스타 회사 소유로 운전기사인 니콜라스 에스트렐라는 베드퍼드 구역의 거래처에 배달을 하는 중이었다. 이번이 올해 첫 5개월 동안에 11번째로 발생한 트럭 약탈이다. 지난 4년 동안 수도권 지역에서 38건의 약탈이 있었다. 약탈자들은 빨리 팔아서 현금을 만들 수 있는 화물을 실은 트럭을 목표로 삼는다. 이들 운전기사들은 차문을 잠그고 차량 편승 여행자들을 태우지 말라는 주의를 받아왔다. 그러나 몇몇 보험 조사관들은 적어도 약탈 사건의 3분의 1 정도는 약탈이 아닌 것으로 추정하고 있다. 일부 운전기사들의 경우 본인의 화물을 본인이 직접 훔치는 것이라고 믿고 있는 것이다.

(a) 니콜라스 에스트렐라가 자신의 화물을 훔친 것으로 추정된다.
(b) 올해의 11번째 트럭 약탈이 어제 발생했다.
(c) 어제 도난당한 전자 제품들이 현금으로 거래되어 팔렸다.
(d) 약탈 사건의 30%까지 조사가 끝났다.

🔆 해법 20만 달러가 넘는 전자 제품들을 실은 트럭 한 대가 어제 아침에 약탈당했다는 내용과 이번이 올해 1월부터 5월 안에 발생한 11번째 트럭 약탈이라는 내용을 연계해 보면 (b)가 정답이다. (a)는 Nicolas Estrella가 화물을 훔치는 운전수들에 속하는지 알 수 없고, (d)는 조사 여부가 지문에 없다.

hijack 강탈, 약탈, 납치하다 **belong to** ~에 속하다 **metropolitan** 수도권의, 대도시의 **hitchhiker** 히치 하이커

🔲 정답 (b)

Researchers at TechnoGear reported on Tuesday that they had succeeded in developing an affordable type of portable reading device that could revolutionize the way books are consumed. The team of researchers produced a bendable, portable, waterproof reading device that is 90 percent cheaper than similar devices produced using other technologies developed so far. The device is tentatively called E-BookPlus. The technology is also capable of displaying moving images and generating sounds. This raises the possibility that in the future this medium could be used for enjoying movies as well as music. Apart from this, TechnoGear officials said they are looking at other ways to differentiate their product in the marketplace.

Q: Which of the following is correct about E-BookPlus?
(a) It was developed using technology that already existed.
(b) It should be used in water.
(c) It might have its name changed.
(d) It is being purchased by cost-conscious buyers.

번역 테크노기어의 연구원들은 화요일 독서 방식에 혁신을 일으킬 저렴한 휴대용 전자책을 개발하는 데 성공했다고 발표했다. 연구팀은 지금까지 개발된 다른 기술들을 이용해서 만들어진 유사 제품들보다 90% 저렴한 가격으로 접을 수도 있고 휴대 가능하며 방수도 되는 전자책을 만드는 데 성공했다고 발표했다. 이 제품은 가칭 이북 플러스라고 불린다. 이 제품에는 동영상이나 음향도 재생할 수 있는 기술이 적용된다. 이와 같은 특징은 이 매체가 미래에 음악뿐 아니라 영화도 즐기는 데 사용될 가능성을 높여준다. 이런 점 외에도 테크노기어 측 관계자들은 이 제품을 시장에서 차별화할 다른 방법들도 살펴보고 있다고 전했다.

(a) 기존의 기술로 만들어졌다.
(b) 물속에서 사용해야 한다.
(c) 제품명이 바뀔지도 모른다.
(d) 가격에 민감한 소비자들에 의해 구매되고 있다.

해법 임시적으로 E-BookPlus라고 불린다는 것은 이름이 바뀔 수 있다는 것으로 (c)가 정답이다. (a)는 혁신을 일으킬 저렴한 휴대용 전자책이라고 했으므로 신기술로 만들어졌음을 알 수 있다. (b)는 지문의 waterproof는 물속에서 사용해야 한다는 의미가 아니다. (d)는 시장에서 차별화할 다른 방법들을 살펴보고 있다고 했으므로 아직 판매되고 있지 않음을 알 수 있어 오답이다.

portable 휴대용 **revolutionize** 혁명, 혁신을 일으키다 **bendable** 구부릴 수 있는 **waterproof** 방수 **tentatively** 임시적으로 **medium** 매체 **apart from** ~외에

 정답 (c)

The paramecium is larger than the amoeba. Like an amoeba, it also is only one cell in size and can move. It can be found in ponds. It is rounded at one end and pointed at the other. It is covered with microscopic hairs that make it move. These hairs are referred to as cilia. The paramecium can move in every direction with its cilia. It eats minuscule algae, plants, and so on. The cilia thrusts the food into a small opening in the middle of the paramecium. Then, the food is pushed down a gullet which looks like a little tube. The food is held in the food vacuole. There is an opening called an anal pore near the pointed end of the paramecium.

Q: Which of the following is correct about the paramecium?
(a) It does not have a symmetrical figure in any way.
(b) It uses its cilia to eat tiny algae or plants.
(c) It is one of the smallest creatures living in ponds.
(d) It has its mouth in the middle of its back.

번역 짚신벌레는 아메바보다 크다. 아메바와 마찬가지로 단세포이며 움직일 수 있고 연못에서 찾아볼 수 있다. 한쪽 끝은 둥글고 다른 쪽은 뾰족하다. 미세한 털로 뒤덮여 있는데, 이 털 때문에 움직일 수 있다. 이 털들은 섬모라고 불린다. 짚신벌레는 이 섬모를 이용해서 사방으로 움직일 수 있다. 먹이로 매우 작은 이끼나 식물 등을 먹는다. 섬모는 짚신벌레의 가운데 있는 작은 구멍으로 음식을 넣는다. 그리고 나면 이 음식은 작은 관처럼 생긴 식도를 통해 밀려서 내려간다. 이렇게 내려간 음식은 식포에 머문다. 짚신벌레의 뾰족한 모양의 끝부분 가까운 곳에 항문이라고 불리는 구멍이 있다.

(a) 몸의 모양이 어느 방향으로든지 대칭되지 않는다.
(b) 작은 이끼나 식물을 먹기 위해 섬모를 이용한다.
(c) 연못에 사는 생물 중 가장 작은 것에 속한다.
(d) 등 가운데에 입이 있다.

해법 섬모는 짚신벌레의 가운데 있는 작은 구멍으로 음식을 넣는다고 했으므로 (b)가 정답이다. (a)는 지문에 없는 내용이고, (c)는 일단 지문의 짚신벌레가 아메바보다 크다는 내용과 연못에 사는 가장 작은 생물체에 대한 내용이 지문에 없다. (d) 또한 지문에 its back(짚신벌레의 등)에 대한 구체적인 내용이 지문에 없다.

paramecium 짚신벌레 **amoeba** 아메바 **microscopic** 매우 작은 **cilia** 섬모 **minuscule** 매우 작은 **algae** 조류, 이끼 **thrust** 밀어 넣다 **gullet** 식도 **food vacuole** 식포 **anal pore** 항문

정답 (b)

Dear Mr. Johnson,

I am writing to inquire about the possibility of procuring parts for a 1995 Magenta 323 RX coupe. I was referred to your company by Mike Ward of Performance Auto here in Madison. He thought you might be able to help me locate the parts I need to rebuild the turbocharger. I acquired the car recently and the turbo gave out almost immediately. If you have any of the necessary parts, please contact me at (608) 661-3457. I am willing to pay shipping and handling on all parts if you can find them within the next two weeks. I have an interested buyer and must get the car in working order by the 29th of this month. If you can help me out in this regard, please let me know.

Sincerely,
Micky Smith

Q: Which of the following is NOT correct?
(a) Mr. Johnson has parts for a 1995 Magenta 323 RX coupe.
(b) Micky Smith wants to sell his car.
(c) Micky Smith is not worried about the shipping and handling costs.
(d) Mike Ward knows Micky Smith.

For all Bert Snelling fans, you're in for a real treat with his latest book, *Through the Sands of Time*, a historical novel set in ancient Egypt. As with his previous publications, this one will please history buffs as it is well-researched and true to the time period in every detail. Readers who like less history and more intrigue will also be satisfied with Snelling's fast-paced plot and fascinating characters. The story opens with the beautiful but headstrong heroine, Serafina, daughter of the ruling Pharaoh. She uncovers a secret plot to dethrone her father, devised by his most trusted advisor, Artemis. Her courageous and inventive plan to reveal the king's enemies is successful, but comes at a high price for her.

Q: Which of the following is correct about *Through the Sands of Time*?
(a) It is about the rise and fall of an Egyptian king.
(b) One of its characters, Serafina, gets killed eventually.
(c) It was written by a historian as an addition to a series.
(d) Its audience will be wider than that of the other books of its kind.

🔳 **번역** 1995년형 마젠타 323 RX 쿠페 차량 부품들을 구할 수 있는지 알아보고자 편지를 씁니다. 이곳 매디슨에 있는 퍼포먼스 오토를 운영하는 마이크 워드 씨로부터 귀사를 소개받았습니다. 그분은 터보 과급기를 다시 만드는 데 필요한 부품들을 찾는 데 귀하께서 도움이 될지도 모른다고 했습니다. 제가 이 차량을 최근에 구하자마자 터보 과급기가 망가졌습니다. 귀하께서 제가 필요한 부품 중 어느 하나라도 갖고 계시다면 (608) 661-3457로 연락주시길 바랍니다. 2주 안으로 부품을 구할 수 있다면 부품 모두에 대한 배달료와 수수료를 부담할 의사가 있습니다. 제 차를 사려고 하는 사람이 있어서 이번 달 29일까지 차가 잘 작동되도록 조치를 취해야 합니다. 이와 관련해서 저에게 도움을 주실 수 있다 면 연락을 부탁드립니다.

(a) 존슨 씨는 1995년형 마젠타 323 RX 쿠페 부품을 갖고 있다.
(b) 미키 스미스는 그의 차를 팔길 원한다.
(c) 미키 스미스는 배달료와 수수료에 대해 걱정하지 않는다.
(d) 마이크 워드는 미키 스미스를 안다.

☀ **해법** 편지를 쓴 미키 스미스가 필요한 부품을 갖고 있으면 연락해 달라고 했으므로 지문 내용만으로 존슨 씨가 부품을 갖고 있다고 단정할 수 없어 (a)가 정답이다. (d)는 미키 스미스가 마이크 워드로부터 존슨의 회사를 소개받았기 때문에 미키 스미스는 마이크 워드를 안다.

procure (어렵게) 구하다 **turbocharger** 터보 과급기 **give out** 배포하다. (소리, 빛 따위를) 발하다 **working order** 제대로 작동되는 상태

✓ 정답 (a)

🔳 **번역** 버트 스넬링의 팬들을 위한 희소식입니다. 그의 최신작 〈Through the Sands of Time〉은 고대 이집트를 배경으로 한 역사 소설입니다. 그의 기존 작품과 마찬가지로 이번 책도 꼼꼼한 조사를 통해 세세한 부분 모두에 걸쳐 당시의 상황이 제대로 담겨 있기에 역사 팬들을 즐겁게 해줄 것입니다. 역사보다는 흥미진진한 음모를 담은 내용을 좋아하는 독자들도 스넬링의 빠른 내용 전개와 매력적인 등장인물들에 만족할 것입니다. 이 책은 아름답지만 고집 센 여주인공인 당시 파라오의 딸 세라피나의 이야기로 시작합니다. 그녀는 아버지가 가장 신뢰하는 보좌관인 아르테미스가 아버지인 파라오를 자리에서 물러나게 하기 위해 비밀스럽게 꾸민 음모를 알게 됩니다. 아버지 파라오의 적들을 밝혀내기 위해 그녀가 짜낸 용감하고 기발한 계획은 성공으로 돌아가지만, 그로 인해 그녀가 치러야 하는 대가는 엄청납니다.

(a) 어느 이집트 왕의 흥망에 대한 것이다.
(b) 등장인물 중에 하나인 세라피나는 결국 죽음을 당한다.
(c) 시리즈에 추가된 것으로 역사가에 의해 쓰여졌다.
(d) 이런 종류의 다른 책들의 독자보다 독자층이 넓을 것이다.

☀ **해법** 역사를 좋아하는 사람들과 역사보다는 음모 같은 것을 더 좋아하는 사람들도 만족할 것이라고 했으므로 (d)가 정답이다. (b)는 지문의 a high price가 반드시 죽음을 의미한다고 단정할 수 없고, (c)는 Bert Snelling이 역사가라는 내용이 지문에 없고 〈Through the Sands of Time〉이 어떤 시리즈에 연결되는 책이라는 언급이 없다.

be in for ~를 경험하기로 되어 있다 **buff** 팬 **intrigue** 음모 **dethrone** 왕위에서 물러나게 하다 **devise** 고안하다 **inventive** 창의적인

✓ 정답 (d)

The National Bird Watchers' Association is now accepting nominations for the Person of the Year, or POY Award. This prize was founded in 2002 with the intention of raising interest, appreciation, and concern for the birds on our planet. The nomination form is two pages long and has to be sent with at least one letter specifying why the nominee deserves consideration for the award. The names of the five finalists will be released by October 31 with their nominations and summaries of their activities posted on our website. The winner will be announced at the NBWA's annual convention and receive 10,000 dollars with 5,000 dollars to be donated to his or her favorite charity.

Q: Which of the following is correct according to the passage?
(a) The POY Award has been given in October since 2002.
(b) The winner will take only part of the prize money.
(c) The NBWA was established by bird watchers from all over the world.
(d) The winner will be announced on the NBWA's website as well.

Americans used to eating hamburgers will soon be trying Asian fast food. Thailand's government is planning to open about 1,000 new Thai restaurants in the U.S. Many of them will be fast-food places called Elephant Jump. These restaurants, which probably would be jointly funded by private investors and the Thai government, would compete with other leading fast-food chains. In addition, Jollibee, a Filipino fast-food chain with restaurants across Asia, recently opened its first U.S. store. Japanese food is hitting the American fast-food market, too. Yoshinoya, a Japanese chain specializing in beef and rice dishes, already has over 75 restaurants in North America, and is planning an expansion. Yoshinoya reports that by 2014 it hopes to have over 2,000 restaurants outside Japan.

Q: Which of the following is correct according to the passage?
(a) Thailand has the greatest fast-food market share in North America.
(b) Yoshinoya will add more than 2,000 restaurants in the U.S.
(c) Competition in the fast-food market in America is getting stiffer.
(d) Americans used to have more hamburgers than Asian fast food.

번역 전국 조류 관찰자 협회는 올해의 인물에 수여되는 포이 대상 수상자 추천을 받고 있습니다. 이 상은 우리 지구 상의 조류에 대한 관심과 이해를 증진시키고자 하는 의도로 2002년에 제정되었습니다. 2페이지 분량의 추천 서류에 해당 후보 추천 이유를 상세히 기록한 최소 한 통 이상의 추천인의 추천서를 함께 동봉해야 합니다. 10월 31일 5명의 최종 수상 후보자 이름이 각자의 추천서와 요약된 활동 내용과 함께 저희 홈페이지에 게재되어 발표될 것입니다. 최종 수상자는 NBWA 연례 총회에서 발표되며 본인이 가장 선호하는 자선 단체에 기부할 5,000달러를 포함한 상금 1만 달러를 수상할 것입니다.

(a) POY Award는 2002년 이래로 10월에 시상했다.
(b) 수상자는 상금의 일부만을 가져갈 것이다.
(c) NBWA는 전 세계 조류 관찰자들에 의해 설립됐다.
(d) 수상자는 NBWA 홈페이지 상에도 발표될 것이다.

해법 총 상금 1만 달러 중 5천 달러는 수상자가 가장 좋아하는 자선 단체에 기부하게 되므로 (b)가 정답이다. (a)는 2002년 이래로 매년 10월에 시상을 해왔다는 내용이 지문에 없고, (c)는 지문 첫 문장의 National과 선택지의 from all over the world는 다르다. (d)는 NBWA 연례 총회 외에 수상자가 발표될 방법이 지문에 없다.

bird watcher 조류 관찰자 **nomination** 추천 **found** 설립하다
intention 의지, 의도 **nominee** 추천된 사람 **deserve** ~할 만하다
convention 집회, 정기총회 **charity** 자선 단체

 정답 (b)

번역 햄버거 먹는 일에 익숙한 미국인들은 곧 아시아의 패스트푸드를 맛보게 될 것이다. 태국 정부는 미국에 약 1,000개의 태국 음식점을 새로 열 계획이다. 그 중에서도 가장 많은 비율을 차지하는 곳은 엘리펀트 점프라고 불리는 패스트푸드 음식점이 될 것이다. 개인 투자자들과 태국 정부 공동 투자로 진행되는 사업일 것으로 사료되는 이 음식점은 다른 유수한 패스트푸드 체인점들과 경쟁할 것이다. 게다가 아시아 전역에 지점이 퍼져 있는 필리핀의 패스트푸드 체인점인 졸리비도 최근 들어 미국에 첫 매장을 열었다. 일본 음식도 미국 패스트푸드 시장에 진출하고 있다. 소고기와 쌀 요리를 전문으로 하는 일본 체인인 요시노야는 북미 지역에만 벌써 75개가 넘는 지점들을 가지고 있으며, 확장 계획을 세우고 있다. 요시노야는 2014년까지 일본 외 지역에 2,000개 이상의 지점을 갖는 것을 목표로 삼고 있다고 전했다.

(a) 태국이 북미에서 가장 높은 패스트푸드 시장 점유율을 갖고 있다.
(b) 요시노야는 미국에 2,000개 이상의 음식점을 추가할 것이다.
(c) 미국 내 패스트푸드 시장의 경쟁이 더 심해지고 있다.
(d) 미국인들은 아시아계 패스트푸드보다 햄버거를 더 먹었다.

해법 태국 정부가 미국에 약 1,000개의 태국 음식점을 새로 열 계획이고 필리핀과 일본의 패스트푸드 체인도 미국에 문을 엶으로써, 미국 내에서 경쟁이 더 치열해지고 있음을 알 수 있어 (c)가 정답이다.

jointly 공동으로 **dish** 요리 **specialize in** ~을 전문으로 하다

정답 (c)

The sounding line, the navigator's first instrument, was created because of dangerous hidden rocks and sandbanks. It had a lead weight at its end and had knots that marked distance along its length. People considered the sounding line such an important tool in early navigation that ships kept back in port for not paying taxes, or for other reasons, had their sounding lines taken away by the police. This practice continued even when ships carried more modern tools like compasses. Samuel Clemens chose Mark Twain as his pen name on the basis of the sailors' custom of employing the sounding line on board going down the Mississippi River in the 19th century.

Q: Which of the following is correct according to the passage?
(a) Samuel Clemens changed his name.
(b) Compasses were not used when they were first introduced.
(c) Sounding lines were made for safety and tax collection.
(d) Some sounding lines were taken away for an official reason.

Today, chamber music has evolved into small ensemble music in which each performer in the ensemble plays an individual part. The compositions written for this type of performance can easily be classified into three distinct periods. In the earliest period (1450-1650), the violin and other instrumental families developed considerably, and instrumental music took its first steps toward equal footing with vocal music. In the second period (1650-1750), trio sonatas dominated. These ensemble compositions were often written for two violins and a cello; the harpsichord was also featured in various compositions of this period. In the modern period (after 1750), the preponderance of chamber music was written for the string quartet, an ensemble composed of two violins, a viola, and a cello.

Q: Which of the following is supported by the passage?
(a) The harpsichord began to disappear in the middle of the 1700s.
(b) Chamber music is characterized by the periods of its development.
(c) Chamber music got its name because only a few people enjoyed it.
(d) The earliest period of chamber music is the longest.

🔁 **번역** 최초의 항해 도구인 측심줄은 위험한 암초와 모래톱 때문에 만들어졌다. 이 도구는 한 쪽 끝에 납 덩어리가 달려 있는 긴 줄의 형태로 줄을 따라 거리를 표시하는 매듭이 매어져 있었다. 경찰이 세금 체납이나 기타 사유로 항구에 정박 중인 배의 측심줄을 압수해갈 정도로 초기 항해 시기에는 사람들이 측심줄을 너무나도 중요한 도구로 여겼다. 이러한 관행은 나침반 등의 보다 현대화된 기구를 배에 싣고 다닐 때까지도 계속되었다. 사무엘 클레멘스는 19세기에 미시시피 강을 따라 운항하는 배에 뱃사람들이 측심줄을 싣고 다니는 관행을 두고 자신의 필명을 마크 트웨인으로 선택했던 것이다.

(a) 사무엘 클레멘스가 그의 이름을 바꿨다.
(b) 나침반이 처음으로 등장했을 때 사람들은 그것을 사용하지 않았다.
(c) 측심줄은 안전과 세금 징수를 위해 만들어졌다.
(d) 어떤 측심줄은 공적인 이유로 압수되었다.

☀ **해법** 측심줄은 초기 항해에 매우 중요한 도구로 여겨져서 세금 체납이나 다른 여러 가지 이유로 항구에 정박 중인 배들의 측심줄을 경찰이 가져가기도 했으므로 공무상의 이유로 측심줄을 압수한 적도 있다는 (d)가 정답이다. (a)는 필명을 갖게 된 것과 원래 이름 자체를 바꿨다는 것은 다르고, (c)는 선택지의 and tax collection이 맞지 않다.

sounding line 측심줄(sounding lead line) **navigator** 항해자
sandbank 모래톱, 사구 **lead** 납 **knot** 매듭 **compass** 나침반
pen name 필명, 아호

 정답 (d)

🔁 **번역** 오늘날 실내악은 연주자가 각자 맡은 부분을 연주하는 소규모 앙상블 음악으로 발달되었다. 이런 식의 연주를 위해 작곡된 작품들은 각각의 음악, 기악 편성 스타일과 함께 세 개의 뚜렷한 시기로 쉽게 구분될 수 있다. 초창기(1450년~1650년)에는 바이올린과 다른 종류의 악기들이 상당히 발달했으며, 처음으로 기악이 성악과 동등한 위치로까지 올라서게 된 시기이기도 하다. 두 번째 시기(1650년~1750년)에는 트리오 소나타가 인기를 독차지했다. 이런 앙상블 작품들은 종종 바이올린 두 대와 첼로 한 대로 연주하기 위한 음악으로 작곡되었으나 하프시코드 또한 이 시기에 다양한 작품에 등장했다. 근대(1750년 이후)에는 대부분의 실내악 작품이 바이올린 두 대, 비올라 한 대, 그리고 첼로 한 대로 구성된 앙상블인 현악 4중주용으로 작곡되었다.

(a) 하프시코드는 1700년대 중반에 사라지기 시작했다.
(b) 실내악은 발달 시대별로 특징지워진다.
(c) 실내악은 오직 소수의 사람들만 즐겼기 때문에 그 이름이 붙여졌다.
(d) 실내악의 역사는 초창기가 가장 길다.

☀ **해법** 실내악은 세 개의 뚜렷한 시기로 쉽게 구분될 수 있다고 했으므로 (b)가 정답이다. 실내악이 작은 공간(실내)에서 연주되기 때문에 실내악이란 이름이 붙은 것이며, 근대가 1750년부터 지금(2000년대)까지로 가장 길기 때문에 (c)와 (d)는 맞지 않다.

chamber music 실내악 **instrumental music** 기악 **footing** 기반, 관계 **vocal music** 성악 **harpsichord** 하프시코드(16~18세기에 쓰인 피아노의 전신) **preponderance** 우위, 다수

✓ **정답** (b)

해설 및 정답 Actual Test 01

Thomas Osborne was a millionaire who hailed from Auburn, New York. Twice he held the post of town mayor. Later he became a banker and newspaper owner. Then, in 1913, Thomas Osborne became Convict 3333X. Osborne went to prison even though he had not committed a crime. Why did a leading citizen like Osborne go to jail? He wanted to help the governor of New York. The governor had asked Osborne to suggest the best way to improve life in the state's prisons. Osborne decided that the best way to learn about prisons was to become a prisoner himself. He spent one week in Auburn Prison. He found many things that shocked and angered him. Prisoners and guards were afraid of each other.

Q: What can be inferred from the passage?
(a) The governor was asked to improve conditions in prisons.
(b) Thomas Osborne wanted to stay in Auburn Prison a week ago.
(c) Thomas Osborne's idea about what it is like in prisons changed.
(d) Thomas Osborne was not afraid of prisoners and guards.

번역 토마스 오스본은 뉴욕 주 오번 출신의 백만장자였다. 그는 시장직을 두 번 역임했다. 후에 그는 은행가와 신문사 사장이 됐다. 그런 뒤 토마스 오스본은 1913년에 3333X라는 수감번호를 단 죄수가 되었다. 오스본은 죄도 없이 감옥에 가게 되었다. 오스본 같은 모범 시민이 감옥에 간 이유가 무엇일까? 그는 뉴욕 주지사를 돕고 싶어 했다. 주지사는 그에게 주 교도소 내의 삶의 질을 향상시킬 최선의 방법을 제안해 달라는 부탁을 했던 것이다. 그는 감옥에 대해 알 수 있는 가장 좋은 방법은 본인이 직접 죄수가 되는 것이라는 결론을 내렸던 것이다. 그는 오번 감옥에서 일주일을 보냈다. 그곳에서 그는 자신을 놀라게 하고 화나게 하는 많은 것들을 발견했다. 죄수와 교도관이 서로를 두려워한다는 것도 알게 되었다.

(a) 주지사는 감옥 환경 개선을 요구받았다.
(b) 토마스 오스본은 일주일 전에 오번 감옥에 머물길 원했다.
(c) 감옥 생활에 대한 토마스 오스본의 생각이 바뀌었다.
(d) 토마스 오스본은 죄수들과 교도관들을 두려워하지 않았다.

해법 토마스 오스본이 오번 감옥에서 일주일을 보낸 후 놀라고 화나게 하는 많은 것들을 발견했다고 했으므로 감옥 생활에 대한 기존의 생각이 바뀌었음을 추론할 수 있어 (c)가 정답이다. (b)는 지문이 쓰여진 시점을 확인할 수 없어 지문이 쓰여진 시점이 오번 감옥에서 일주일을 보낸 바로 직후 시점이라고 단정할 수 없다.

millionaire 백만장자 hail from (사람이) ~ 출신이다 mayor 시장 convict 죄수 crime 죄 governor 주지사 anger 화나게 하다

정답 (c)

When unidentified thieves took $4,000 worth of musical equipment from the Two Tones musical duo on Wednesday, the two performers were forced to cancel all their fall bookings—and plans for a December wedding. Joyce Benedict, 25, and Donald Jarvis, 27, both of Albany, were planning to help pay for their December 20 wedding with money earned from performances here over the next four days. The couple arrived at the Stagecoach Hotel in South Merrick about 3:00 P.M. Wednesday for their first appearance. When Jarvis went to their car at about 4:30 P.M., he found a broken window and their speakers, microphones, and other sound equipment missing. The equipment was not insured and there is little hope of recovering it.

Q: What can be inferred from the passage?
(a) The couple did not take their musical equipment into the hotel.
(b) The couple was supposed to get married at the end of December.
(c) The couple had their musical instruments stolen in the morning.
(d) The couple had to have part of the performances canceled.

번역 신원이 밝혀지지 않은 도둑이 수요일에 2인조 그룹인 투 톤즈 소유의 4천 달러 상당의 음악 장비를 훔쳐가자 두 사람은 가을 공연과 관련해서 예약된 모든 일정과 12월의 결혼 계획을 취소할 수밖에 없었다. 뉴욕 올버니 출신인 25세의 조이스 베네딕트와 27세의 도널드 자비스 두 사람은 앞으로 이곳에서 4일 동안 열릴 공연을 통해 번 돈으로 12월 20일로 잡혀 있는 결혼식 비용에 보태고자 했다. 커플은 첫 공연을 위해 수요일 오후 3시에 사우스 메릭에 있는 스테이지코치 호텔에 도착했다. 자비스가 4시 30분경에 그들의 차로 갔을 때 차창은 깨져 있었고 차 안에 둔 스피커, 마이크, 그리고 다른 사운드 장비들이 없어진 것을 발견했다. 장비들은 보험에 들어 있지 않았고 되찾을 가능성도 거의 없는 것으로 보인다.

(a) 커플은 그들 악기를 호텔 안으로 가져가지 않았다.
(b) 커플은 12월 말에 결혼할 예정이었다.
(c) 커플은 그들 악기를 아침에 도난당했다.
(d) 커플은 공연 일부를 취소해야만 했었다.

해법 첫 공연을 위해 수요일 오후 3시에 호텔에 도착했고 자비스가 4시 30분경에 그들의 차로 갔을 때 창문이 깨져 있고 장비들이 없어진 것을 발견했다고 했으므로 처음부터 호텔에 악기를 가지고 가지 않았다는 (a)가 정답이며, 내용상 오전에 도난당한 것이 아니기에 (c)는 오답이다.

unidentified 신원 미상의 duo 2인조 booking 출연 계약 performance 공연 insure 보험에 들다

정답 (a)

Dear Mr. Gupta,

It has come to our attention here at Oleander Ltd. that your magazine has been publishing unfavorable reviews of our products. We take pride in producing the best cosmetics and creams from all-natural products. Your assertion that we use "questionable production practices" to make our New You line of facial creams is unfounded. I assure you that we do not, as you reported, pay our workers in Southeast Asia "slave wages" but rather have them all on a rate that is higher than the local average. I invite you to investigate our company further and more thoroughly. You will find that we produce high-quality products with a heart.

Q: What can be inferred from the letter?
(a) Mr. Gupta will respond to the letter before he visits Oleander Ltd.
(b) Oleander Ltd. is doing business in Southeast Asia.
(c) Oleander Ltd. just began to produce a new line of facial creams.
(d) The employees of Oleander Ltd. can speak more than one language.

번역 귀하의 잡지가 저희 올리앤더 사 제품에 대해 부정적인 품평을 게재해 왔다는 사실을 알게 되었습니다. 저희는 순수 자연산 재료로 저희 화장품과 크림 제품을 생산해 낸다는 사실에 자부심을 갖습니다. 저희의 New You 안면 크림 제품 라인 생산에 '의심이 갈 만한 생산 공정'을 사용하고 있다는 귀 잡지 측의 주장은 사실무근한 내용입니다. 귀하의 잡지가 보도한 것처럼 저희는 동남아시아 직원들에게 '노예 임금'을 지불하지 않으며 오히려 그 지역의 평균 임금보다 높은 기준의 임금을 지불하고 있습니다. 저희 회사를 보다 더 깊고 세세하게 조사해 보시기 바랍니다. 저희 회사가 고품질의 제품들을 따뜻한 마음으로 생산한다는 것을 알게 될 것입니다.
(a) 굽타 씨는 올리앤더 사를 방문하기 전에 답장을 할 것이다.
(b) 올리앤더 사는 동남아시아에서 사업을 하고 있다.
(c) 올리앤더 사는 이제 막 새로운 안면 크림 제품 라인을 생산하기 시작했다.
(d) 올리앤더 사 직원들은 한 개 이상 언어를 구사한다.

해법 동남아시아의 올리앤더 사 직원들에게 노예 임금을 지불하지 않는다고 했으므로 동남아시아에서 사업을 하고 있다는 (b)가 정답이다. (a)는 단정할 수 없고, (c)는 지문의 our New You line of facial creams와 선택지의 a new line of facial creams는 의미가 다르다. 모든 직원들이 외국어를 할 수 있다는 (d)는 비약이다.

take pride in ~을 자랑스럽게 여기다 **cosmetics** 화장품 **assertion** 단언, 주장 **questionable** 의심스러운, 수상한 **unfounded** 근거 없는 **with a heart** 따뜻한 마음으로

정답 (b)

Play is an almost universal activity of higher animals but one that is hard to define. In essence, it consists of two main ingredients: activity for its own sake and experimentation with types of behavior that will subsequently be carried out in earnest. In animals, both of these kinds of play are carried out by the young and are clearly a part of the learning process. The former aids in familiarizing the young animal with its capabilities. The latter provides practical training in skills which may be utilized later in life. In humans, play is important for what it can reveal about society. Forms of sport reflect the nature of society, as do forms of art, theater, and literature.

Q: What can be inferred from the passage?
(a) Play can be a subject of study in sociology.
(b) Some forms of art are based on play.
(c) People use play differently.
(d) Animals can be taught to play.

번역 고등 동물들에게 있어서 놀이는 거의 공통적인 활동이긴 하지만 정의하기는 어려운 활동이기도 하다. 본질적으로 놀이는 두 가지 주요 요소로 구성되어 있는데, 하나는 놀이 자체를 위한 활동이고 다른 하나는 나중에 가서 진지한 자세로 임하게 될 행동과 유사한 행동을 실험하기 위한 것이 그것이다. 동물에게 있어서 이와 같은 두 종류의 놀이는 모두 새끼들에 의해 행해지며 배움의 한 과정인 것이 분명하다. 놀이의 첫 번째 요소는 새끼 동물들이 자신들의 능력을 알고 익숙해지도록 도와주며, 두 번째 요소는 훗날 실제 생활에서 활용할 수 있는 실용적인 기술 훈련을 제공한다는 것이다. 인간에게 있어서 놀이는 사회의 모습을 반영한다는 점에서 중요하다. 예술, 연극, 그리고 문학의 여러 형태가 그렇듯이 운동 경기의 형태 또한 사회의 성격을 보여준다.

(a) 놀이는 사회학의 연구 주제가 될 수 있다.
(b) 예술의 형태 중 일부는 놀이에 토대를 두고 있다.
(c) 사람마다 놀이를 다르게 이용한다.
(d) 동물들은 놀이를 하도록 교육받을 수 있다.

해법 인간에게 있어서 놀이는 사회에 대해 보여줄 수 있어 중요하다고 했으므로 놀이는 사회학의 연구 주제가 될 수 있다고 추론할 수 있어 (a)가 정답이다. (b), (c), (d)는 지문에서 확인할 수 없다.

in essence 본질적으로 **ingredient** 성분, 요소 **for one's sake** ~을 위해 **subsequently** 계속해서 **carry out** 행하다 **in earnest** 진지하게 **former** 전자 **familiarize A with B** A가 B에 익숙하게 하다 **capability** 능력 **latter** 후자 **reveal** 드러내다 **nature** 성격, 본질

정답 (a)

When we talk about development, we talk about human progress with its positive and negative consequences. On this occasion, we should not forget that development does not start with goods. Rather, as a scientist points out, it starts with people and their education, with organization, and with discipline. All these three require time and effort to succeed. However, even more important than development are the quality of life of the people and the strong social structure it provides. A good quality of life and a strong social structure, which depend as much on the spiritual as on the material, provide social welfare, the goal of every society. At the same time they provide the foundation on which to build as the society develops and prospers.

Q: What can be inferred from the passage?
(a) Quality of life is as important as a strong social structure.
(b) The goal of human progress is social welfare.
(c) The foundation of society is based on the quality of life.
(d) Human progress does not involve material development.

Gelufire announced Wednesday that their financial problems have gotten the best of them. (a) The hair and body care product manufacturer has seen profits fall into the red for the sixth month in a row and has declared bankruptcy. (b) There have been reports that Realmake has expressed interest in acquiring some parts of the company, but analysts expect that offer might only be extended to the profitable HairGlare line. (c) Realmake has indicated a desire to expand into hair care and this might be a good opportunity for them. (d) As yet, it is still unclear what will become of the company's facilities and employees.

번역 젤루파이어는 수요일에 회사의 재정 문제가 최악의 상황에 치달았다고 발표했다. (a) 헤어와 바디 제품 제조사인 젤루파이어는 지난 여섯 달 연속으로 적자를 내다가 결국 파산 선언을 했다. (b) 리얼메이크가 젤루파이어의 일부를 흡수하는 데 관심 표명을 했다는 보도들이 있었지만 리얼메이크의 이런 제안은 이익을 낼 만한 헤어글레어 제품 라인에만 해당될 가능성이 크다는 것이 전문가들이 내다보는 전망이다. (c) 리얼메이크는 헤어 제품 쪽으로도 사업을 확장하려는 의사를 표명해 왔고 이것이 그들에게는 좋은 기회가 될지도 모르는 일이다. (d) 아직은 회사 시설과 직원들의 처리 방법은 불분명한 상태다.

해법 지문에서 재정 상황이 최악인 Gelufire와 Gelufire 일부를 흡수하려는 Realmake라는 두 회사의 상황과 회사 시설과 직원들이 어떻게 될지는 아직 불분명하다는 (d)의 내용을 생각해보면 (d)는 Gelufire에 대한 내용이라고 보는 것이 자연스럽다. 따라서 (d)를 삭제하거나 (a) 뒤로 보내야 한다.

the red 적자 in a row 연속으로 declare bankruptcy 파산을 선언하다

정답 (d)

번역 발달에 대해 말할 때 우리는 긍정적인 결과와 부정적인 결과를 함께 가진 인간의 진전에 대해 이야기한다. 이런 경우에 있어서 발달은 물질에서 출발하지 않는다는 것을 잊어서는 안 된다. 오히려 어떤 과학자가 지적하듯이 사람과 교육, 조직, 그리고 규율로 시작된다. 이 세 가지 모두를 이루기 위해서는 시간과 노력이 요구된다. 그러나 발달보다 훨씬 더 중요한 것은 사람들의 삶의 질과 그것이 제공하는 튼튼한 사회 구조다. 질 높은 삶과 튼튼한 사회 구조는 물질만큼 정신적인 측면에 의해서도 결정되며, 이것은 모든 사회의 목표인 사회 복지를 제공하기도 한다. 그와 동시에 사회가 발달하고 번영함에 따라 구축할 기초도 제공한다.

(a) 삶의 질이 튼튼한 사회 구조만큼이나 중요하다.
(b) 인간 진보의 목표는 사회 복지다.
(c) 사회 기초는 삶의 질에 토대를 두고 있다.
(d) 인간 진보는 물질의 발달과 관련되지 않는다.

해법 질 높은 삶과 튼튼한 사회 구조가 사회 복지를 제공한다고 했고 사회가 발달하고 번영할 때 세워야 할 기초도 제공한다고 했으므로 사회의 기초가 삶의 질에 토대를 두고 있다고 추론할 수 있어 (c)가 정답이다. (d)는 인간 진보를 발달로 이야기할 때 물질로 시작하지 않는다는 것이지 물질과 관련되지 않는다는 것은 아니므로 맞지 않다.

consequence 결과 discipline 훈육, 규율 spiritual 정신적인 prosper 번영하다

정답 (c)

An accident at an air show in Colorado yesterday claimed the life of a pilot. (a) Captain Paul Morris was flying a Korean War era F-86 Saber Jet when he failed to pull out of a steep climb. (b) No one on the ground was hurt and investigators are blaming the crash on pilot error. (c) "The plane went straight up, did a loop, and then came straight down," said Jack Harvey, a spectator at the air show. (d) The crash was the first in the fifteen-year history of the Colorado Air Show.

번역 어제 콜로라도 에어쇼 도중에 발생한 사고로 조종사 한 명이 목숨을 잃었습니다. (a) 폴 모리스 대령이 몰던 6.25 전쟁 당시의 F-86 세이버 제트기가 급상승에서 벗어나지 못했습니다. (b) 지상에 있던 사람 중 부상자는 없었고 조사반은 추락 사고의 원인을 조종사 과실로 보고 있습니다. (c) "비행기가 똑바로 올라가서 공중 제비를 한 번 돌고는 바로 곤두박질쳤어요"라고 에어쇼 관객인 잭 하비가 말했습니다. (d) 이 사고는 15년 역사의 콜로라도 에어쇼에서 발생한 최초의 추락 사고였습니다.

해법 지상에 있던 사람 중 부상자가 없었다는 내용과 비행기가 똑바로 올라가다가 한 바퀴 돌고 곤두박질쳤다는 내용을 연계해 보면 (a)의 steep climb이 steep fall 정도로 바뀌어야 한다.

claim (병·재해 등이) 인명을 빼앗아 가다 **pull out of a steep climb** 급상승에서 벗어나다 **loop** 공중 제비 **spectator** 구경꾼, 방관자

정답 (a)

The basic things in life are the same no matter where you live. (a) A toothache feels just as miserable to an American in the United States as it does to a Korean in Korea. (b) Joy and pleasure are the same sensations whether their origin is in the Orient or on the other side of the world. (c) Then what is it that makes people who live in one part of the world so similar to people living in another part of the world? (d) They aren't really different at all, but the ways in which they express their sensations and sometimes the things from which they derive pleasure are different.

번역 삶의 기본은 사는 곳이 어디든지 똑같다. (a) 치통이 한국에 사는 한국인에게 괴로운 것이 듯 미국에 사는 미국인에게도 마찬가지이다. (b) 기쁨과 즐거움도 그 발생지가 동양이든 지구 반대편이든 상관없이 감정은 똑같다. (c) 그렇다면 세상 어느 한 곳에 사는 사람들을 다른 곳에서 사는 사람들과 그토록 비슷하게 만드는 것은 무엇인가? (d) 실제로 그들은 전혀 다르지 않고 감정을 표현하는 방식과 기쁨을 느끼게 하는 대상이 때로는 다를 뿐이다.

해법 사람 사는 곳이면 어디든 똑같다는 주제의 지문으로 (a)에서는 치통을 (b)에서는 기쁘고 즐거운 감정을 예로 들면서 이런 것들이 어떤 나라 사람이든지 똑같이 느낀다고 지문 주제를 뒷받침하는 내용과 연결되면서 (d)의 실제로는 전혀 다르지 않지만 감정을 표현하는 방식과 기쁨을 느끼게 하는 것들이 다르다는 내용과 연결되려면 (c)의 so similar with를 different from 등으로 고쳐야 한다.

toothache 치통 **miserable** 괴로운 **sensation** 감각, 기분 **derive** 이끌어내다, 얻다

정답 (c)

Actual Test 02

1 (a)	2 (c)	3 (b)	4 (b)	5 (d)	6 (d)	7 (c)	8 (a)	9 (b)	10 (d)
11 (d)	12 (a)	13 (c)	14 (c)	15 (c)	16 (a)	17 (d)	18 (c)	19 (c)	20 (d)
21 (a)	22 (b)	23 (d)	24 (c)	25 (a)	26 (d)	27 (c)	28 (b)	29 (b)	30 (d)
31 (b)	32 (b)	33 (b)	34 (b)	35 (d)	36 (a)	37 (c)	38 (a)	39 (a)	40 (d)

P122

The book, *Your Husband: Napoleon or Tsar Nicholas?* humorously compares spouses of various historical figures, emphasizing their negative and positive qualities. The author shows a good knowledge of history and provides interesting details of how each famous man got along with his wife. Unfortunately, the book offers the reader only vague sketches of each figure, and it becomes less and less funny as it gets longer. Ms. Francini seems to have either lost her focus or _____. I'm afraid I cannot recommend this book to buyers. My advice is that if you're really interested, wait for the paperback edition to come out in June.

(a) been the victim of poor editing
(b) seen her good days
(c) failed to apply her new writing style
(d) did not make more efforts than she had done before

번역 〈당신의 남편은 나폴레옹형인가요 니콜라스 황제형인가요?〉라는 책은 다양한 역사적 인물과 배우자를 해학적으로 비교한 내용으로 특히 그들의 부정적인 면과 긍정적인 면을 강조했다. 저자는 역사에 대해 해박한 지식을 보여주고 유명한 인물이 각각 아내와 어떻게 지냈는지를 재미있고 상세하게 기술한다. 그러나 안타깝게도 이 책은 각 인물들에 대한 막연한 묘사로 그치는 데다가 묘사가 길어질수록 점점 재미가 줄어드는 느낌을 독자들에게 준다. 프랜치니 씨가 글의 초점을 잃은 게 아니라면 잘못된 편집의 피해자인 것으로 생각된다. 유감스럽지만 나는 이 책을 독자들에게 권할 수 없다. 그래도 정말 읽고 싶다는 생각이 든다면 6월에 출간 예정인 문고판이 나올 때까지 기다리라고 권해주고 싶다.

(a) 잘못된 편집의 피해자인
(b) 전성기가 지나가서
(c) 그녀의 새로운 글쓰기 스타일을 적용하지 못해서
(d) 예전보다 많은 노력을 들이지 않아서

해법 정말 관심 있는 사람은 6월에 (값이 저렴한) 문고판이 나올 때까지 기다리라고 했으므로 지금 나온 책은 편집상의 문제가 있는 것 같다는 흐름이 자연스러워 (a)가 정답이다. 나머지는 빈칸이 있는 문장만 놓고 보면 그럴 듯하지만 지문에서 근거를 찾을 수 없다.

humorously 해학적으로 **compare** 비교하다 **spouse** 배우자
figure 인물 **emphasize** 강조하다 **quality** 특성 **vague** 막연한,
희미한 **paperback edition** 문고판

 정답 (a)

Being a female concierge at a hotel, I've become adept at politely rebuking approaches from male guests. One evening there was a heavy rainstorm, which resulted in a long line at the hotel taxi stand. A customer asked me how much a limo would cost. I told him that _____. He decided to check the taxi queue. Moments later he was back. "I don't need the car now. I've got a taxi." Then he smiled, and asked, "Could I have your phone number?" Rather embarrassed, I explained it was against hotel policy to be friendly with the guests. "Young lady," he said, "I want the number of this place in case I need to call for a limo to get back."

(a) I was afraid to tell him that the service was not available
(b) it would be decided by how far his final destination was
(c) it depended on whether it was a one-way or round-trip transfer
(d) I would ask the hotel manager about that and let him know

번역 호텔 여성 안내원으로서 나는 남자 손님들로부터의 접근을 정중하게 거절하는 것에 숙달되었다. 어느 날 저녁, 심한 폭풍우 때문에 호텔의 택시 대기소에 줄이 길게 늘어서 있었다. 한 고객이 나에게 리무진 비용이 얼마인지 물었다. 나는 편도인지 왕복인지에 따라 다르다고 말해줬다. 그는 택시 대기 행렬을 살펴보기로 마음먹었다. 잠시 후 내게로 돌아와서, "이제 리무진이 필요 없어요. 택시를 잡았거든요"라고 말했다. 그리고 나서 미소 지으며 "전화번호 좀 알려주겠어요?"라고 물었다. 약간 당황한 나는 손님들과 필요 이상으로 가까워지는 것은 호텔 정책에 위배된다고 설명했다. 그는 "아가씨, 나는 돌아올 때 혹시 리무진을 불러야 할 필요가 있을 경우에 대비해 여기 전화번호를 달라는 겁니다"라고 말했다.

(a) 유감스럽게도 리무진이 운행되지 않는다고
(b) 최종 목적지까지 거리가 얼마인지에 따라 결정된다고
(c) 편도인지 왕복인지에 따라 다르다고
(d) 호텔 지배인에게 물어보고 알려주겠다고

해법 호텔로 돌아오기 위해 리무진을 부를 때 호텔 전화번호를 알아야 한다는 말은 리무진이 편도가 있다는 것을 알고 나서 할 수 있는 말이므로 (c)가 정답이다.

 정답 (c)

Cystic fibrosis is a dangerous disease in which abnormally thick mucus builds up in many organs, including the lungs. The accumulation of mucus causes difficulty in breathing. Cystic fibrosis is caused by a wrong gene. In cystic fibrosis patients, the gene for making a protein that helps pump ions into and out of cells has the wrong instructions. Because the protein is not made correctly, the cells cannot pump ions into and out of cells. This eventually results in ions building up within cells. Like sponges, these cells soak up the surrounding water, _____.

(a) causing a diuretic effect on patients to make them dehydrate to death
(b) turning the fluid around the outside of the cells into thick mucus
(c) resulting in patients having difficulty in breathing
(d) mutating the gene responsible for producing a certain protein

You can hardly believe it, but within a few years, treating eye disease may be as simple as popping in a contact lens. Special contact lenses are being developed which _____. Today most eye medications are in the form of drops, but often they drain into the nose and enter the bloodstream and travel throughout the body. Only about five percent of the medication stays in the eye. But these amazing lenses will deliver the drug to where it's needed in a steady dose, and could potentially treat most eye disease, including glaucoma and many other eye infections.

(a) will be sold both online and offline to reach more buyers
(b) contain tiny particles of drugs that are slowly released into the eye
(c) eye doctors and patients have waited for to be available
(d) are different from other ophthalmics in many ways

번역 낭포성 섬유증은 폐를 포함한 여러 장기에 비정상적으로 두꺼운 점액이 축적되는 위험한 병이다. 점액의 축적은 호흡 곤란을 유발한다. 낭포성 섬유증은 잘못된 유전자에 의해 초래되는 것이다. 낭포성 섬유증 환자들은 세포 안팎으로 이온이 들락날락하도록 돕는 단백질을 만드는 유전자가 잘못된 지시를 받는다. 단백질 생성이 제대로 되지 않기 때문에 세포가 세포 안팎으로 이온을 주입하거나 배출하지 못한다. 이로 인해 결국 세포 내의 이온이 축적되는 결과를 초래한다. 스펀지처럼 이 세포들은 주변의 수분을 빨아들여 세포 밖 주변의 체액을 두꺼운 점액으로 변화시킨다.

(a) 이뇨 작용을 일으켜 환자가 탈수증으로 사망하게 한다
(b) 세포 밖 주변의 체액을 두꺼운 점액으로 변화시킨다
(c) 환자가 호흡 곤란을 일으키게 한다
(d) 특정한 단백질을 만드는 유전자를 변형시킨다

해법 낭포성 섬유증은 잘못된 유전자에 의해 유발되고, 세포 안팎으로 이온 공급을 돕는 단백질이 정확하게 만들어지지 않아 이온이 축적된다고 했으므로 점액질 축적으로 인한 내용이 자연스러워 (b)가 정답이다. (d)는 세포 안팎으로 이온 공급을 돕는 단백질을 만드는 유전자가 잘못된 지시를 받고 난 후의 내용이므로 맞지 않다.

cystic fibrosis 낭포성 섬유증 **abnormally** 비정상적으로 **mucus** 점액 **lung** 폐 **accumulation** 축적 **gene** 유전자 **soak up** 빨아들이다 **diuretic** 이뇨의 **dehydrate** 탈수 상태가 되다 **mutate** 변화시키다

정답 (b)

번역 믿기 어렵겠지만 몇 년 뒤에는 눈병 치료가 콘택트 렌즈를 끼는 것만큼 간단해질지도 모른다. 눈 속으로 천천히 배출되는 아주 작은 입자의 약물을 함유한 특수 콘택트 렌즈가 개발되고 있다. 오늘날 대부분의 눈 치료제는 액체를 방울로 떨어뜨려 넣는 형태지만 종종 코를 통해서 혈류로 들어가 몸 전체를 돌아다닌다. 약물의 5%만이 눈에 남는다. 그러나 이 놀라운 렌즈는 정해진 일정 분량만큼만 필요한 곳에 약을 전달해 녹내장을 비롯한 눈과 관련된 염증 대부분을 치료할 수 있을 것으로 보인다.

(a) 더 많은 소비자들에게 다가가기 위해 온라인과 오프라인 시장 모두에서 판매될
(b) 눈 속으로 천천히 배출하는 아주 작은 입자의 약물을 함유한
(c) 안과의사들과 환자들이 시중에서 구할 날만 손꼽아 기다려온
(d) 다른 안약들과 많은 면에서 다른

해법 새로 개발되는 렌즈 때문에 눈병 치료가 콘택트 렌즈를 끼는 것처럼 간단해질 것이고 정해진 1회 분량이 필요한 곳에 약을 전달해서 눈병과 감염을 치료할 것이라고 했으므로 눈에 천천히 조금씩 배출되는 약을 포함하고 있는 렌즈라고 해야 자연스럽다. 따라서 (b)가 정답이다. (c)는 지문 첫 문장과 연결되지 않고, (d)는 선택지의 many ways가 맞지 않다.

treat 치료하다 **pop in** 안에 넣다 **bloodstream** 혈류 **dose** 1회 복용량 **glaucoma** 녹내장 **ophthalmic** 안약

정답 (b)

According to museum officials, as many as 170,000 artifacts have been stolen. The cuneiform tablets of the Code of Hammurabi, one of the museum's most famous collections, are also missing. What were the U.S. troops doing? Instead of stopping the robbery, they seem to have sat back and watched it. Some people suspect that the United States may have had some bad political intention. The antiquities in the museum, which belong to one of the four major civilizations of mankind, are the property not only of the Iraqis but also of all people around the world. Therefore, _____.

(a) it is wrong to hold only the U.S. troops responsible for the robbery

(b) the Iraqi government should seek as much international help as possible

(c) we should let the Iraqi government know the whereabouts of the missing items

(d) the international community should focus their attention on restoring human civilization

번역 박물관 관계자들에 따르면 무려 17만여 점의 유물이 도난당했다고 한다. 박물관에서 가장 유명한 소장품들 중 하나인 함무라비 법전의 설형 문자판도 행방불명이다. 미군은 무엇을 하고 있었나? 그들은 도난을 막기는 커녕 그냥 방관만 하고 있었던 것으로 보인다. 어떤 사람들은 미국이 정치적으로 불순한 뜻을 가지고 있던 것이라고 의심한다. 박물관에 있는 유물들은 인류의 4대 문명 중 하나의 것으로 이라크 사람들뿐만 아니라 세상 모든 사람들의 공동 자산이다. 따라서 국제 사회 전체가 인류 문명을 되찾는 데 관심을 집중해야 한다.

(a) 미군에게만 도난 사건에 책임을 물려야 한다는 것은 잘못됐다

(b) 이라크 정부는 국제적인 도움을 가능한 한 많이 모색해야 한다

(c) 우리는 잃어버린 유물들의 행방을 이라크 정부에게 알려줘야 한다

(d) 국제 사회 전체가 인류 문명을 되찾는 데 관심을 집중해야 한다

해법 이라크 국립 박물관에 있는 유물들은 4대 인류 문명 중 하나로 이라크 사람들뿐만 아니라 세상 모든 사람들의 공동 자산이라고 했으므로 (d)가 정답이다. (a)는 빈칸 앞의 박물관 유물들이 세상 모든 사람들의 공동 자산이라는 내용과 연결되지 않는다. (c)는 선택지의 we가 이라크 사람들을 포함하는 내용이 아니므로 맞지 않다.

artifact 인공물, 문화유물 cuneiform 설형 문자의 tablet 서판 robbery 도난 suspect 의심하다 antiquity 유물 civilization 문명 mankind 인류

정답 (d)

The young minister was on the pulpit for the first time and he was a little nervous. He read the text; "Behold I come." The sermon was to follow immediately, but his mind went blank and he repeated the text; "Behold I come." hoping to remember the opening words of the sermon—but with no success. Trying to calm himself, he leaned forward _____. Under his weight the pulpit gave way and he landed in the lap of one of the elders. "I'm awfully sorry," he said, much embarrassed. "I really didn't expect this to happen." The man gave a kind smile and replied, "Oh, that's OK. I should have been prepared after your third warning."

(a) and lost his footing

(b) to reach for the glass of water on the pulpit

(c) to gain attention from the audience

(d) as he repeated the text for the third time

번역 젊은 목사가 처음으로 설교단에 서니 약간 긴장이 됐다. 그는 준비한 성경 구절을 읽었다. "보라, 내가 왔노라"라는 말에 이어 바로 설교가 이어져야 했지만 정신이 멍해져서 혹시라도 설교의 첫머리가 생각나길 바라며 "보라, 내가 왔노라"를 한 번 더 외쳐봤지만 소용이 없었다. 마음을 가라앉히려고 애쓰며 몸을 앞으로 기대면서 같은 성경 구절을 세 번째 되풀이했다. 설교단이 목사의 체중을 못 이겨 무너져 버렸고 목사는 장로 한 분의 무릎 위로 넘어졌다. "정말 죄송합니다" 당황해서 어찌할 바를 모르는 목사가 말했다. "이런 일이 있을 줄 정말 몰랐습니다" 장로는 자상한 미소를 지어 보이며 말했다. "아, 괜찮아요. 목사님이 세 번째 경고를 외쳤을 때 미리 준비를 했어야 했어요."

(a) 그리고 발을 헛디뎠다

(b) 단상 위의 물컵을 잡기 위해

(c) 청중의 관심을 끌기 위해

(d) 같은 성경 구절을 세 번째 되풀이하면서

해법 목사님이 세 번이나 경고했을 때 준비를 했어야 했다는 장로의 말까지 읽어보면 (d)가 정답이다. 나머지는 빈칸이 있는 문장만 보면 그럴듯하지만 지문에서 근거를 찾을 수 없어 오답이다.

minister 목사 pulpit 설교단 sermon 설교 one's mind goes blank 정신이 멍해지다 lean 기대다 give way 무너지다 elder 장로 embarrassed 당황스러운

정답 (d)

Dear Mr. Cooper,

Thank you for your recent photographic submissions to our publication. Your experiences in Colorado and Wyoming were obviously quite interesting, and your photographs are vast and impressive. Unfortunately, the material for our magazine is supplied solely by our staff photographers and writers, and we are presently unable to accept contributions from outside sources. Please _____. If you would like to apply for a staff position, please send a cover letter and résumé to our Human Resources Director, Mr. Mark Hanlan. He would be happy to review your work and application. Good luck in your future endeavors.

Sincerely,
T. Simon Sinclair
Editor-in-Chief

(a) learn about our contribution policy
(b) try again with better photographs and text
(c) find enclosed your submissions
(d) understand the difficulty we are going through

💬 번역　최근 저희 간행물에 보내주신 사진 고맙게 잘 받아 봤습니다. 콜로라도 주와 와이오밍 주에서의 체험담은 확실히 흥미로웠고 사진들도 대단히 인상적이었습니다. 그러나 안타깝게도 저희 잡지의 사진과 글은 모두 내부 사진가와 필진의 작품만으로 채워지기 때문에 지금으로서는 외부 기고물을 반영할 수 없음을 알려드립니다. 보내주신 사진과 원고를 동봉합니다. 혹시 저희 직원으로 지원할 생각이 있다면 업무 중심의 커버레터와 함께 이력서를 인사부장 마크 핸랜 씨 앞으로 보내주십시오. 귀하의 작품과 지원서를 기꺼이 검토해 주실 겁니다. 앞으로 하고자 하시는 모든 일이 잘 되길 바랍니다.

(a) 저희 기고 정책에 대해 알아보십시오
(b) 더 나은 사진과 글로 다시 시도해 보십시오
(c) 보내주신 사진과 원고를 동봉합니다
(d) 저희가 겪고 있는 어려움을 이해해 주십시오

☀ 해법　사내 사진가와 작가들의 작품만을 쓰기 때문에 외부에서 보낸 자료를 반영할 수 없다고 했으므로 받은 제출물(사진과 체험담)을 반송한다는 흐름이 자연스러워 (c)가 정답이다. (b)는 체험담도 재미있고 사진들도 훌륭하다고 했으므로 맞지 않고, (d)는 선택지의 the difficulty에 해당하는 내용이 지문에 없다.

submission 제출　**publication** 간행물　**vast** 광대한, 대단한　**contribution** 기고, 투고　**cover letter** 자기소개서　**résumé** 이력서　**review** 검토하다　**endeavor** 노력, 시도　**enclosed** 동봉된

 정답 (c)

People who want to work, to do something in the world, find an unfailing inspiration in Schubert. He is a continual example to get up and go on again. His little room was always littered with music manuscripts, much as a dressmaker's is with scraps after a busy project. He knew no rest; as soon as one thing was finished, he put it aside and began to work on another, as if this new work, be it song, or mass, or sonata, or opera, _____. It is idle to imagine what Schubert would have finally most excelled in had he lived to a good old age. He died when he was only thirty-one.

(a) were the only thing he had been born to do
(b) should be done as fast as possible
(c) couldn't be done anywhere but in his little room
(d) were something that he could do by himself

💬 번역　일을 하고 싶어 하는 사람, 이 세상에서 뭔가를 하고 싶어 하는 사람들은 슈베르트에게서 한결같은 영감을 얻는다. 그는 일어나서 다시 움직이는 끊임없는 전형이다. 그의 작은 방은 언제나 악보들이 흩어져 있어서, 마치 급한 작품을 마친 양장점에 천 조각이 여기저기 흩어져 있는 모습과 비슷했다. 그는 쉴 줄을 몰랐다. 한 가지 일을 끝내자마자 그 일은 옆으로 제쳐놓고 또 다른 작품에 몰두하기 시작했는데, 그것이 가곡이건 미사곡이건 소나타이건 오페라이건 간에 마치 그것만을 위해 자신이 태어난 것처럼 몰두했다. 만약 슈베르트가 상당한 고령까지 살았더라면 결국 그는 어떤 일에 가장 출중했을까 하고 상상하는 것은 헛된 일이다. 그는 불과 31세의 나이에 죽었다.

(a) ~만을 위해 태어난 것처럼
(b) 가능한 한 빨리 해야 하는 것처럼
(c) 그의 작은 방 말고 다른 곳에서는 할 수 없는 것처럼
(d) 혼자서 할 수 있는 일인 것처럼

☀ 해법　슈베르트가 끊임없이 다시 일어나서 전진하는 모범을 보여주고 휴식이 없었다는 것으로 보아 일에 대한 열정이나 집중력이 매우 뛰어났음을 알 수 있어 (a)가 지문 흐름에 가장 잘 어울린다. (c), (d)는 슈베르트가 일에 대한 열정이나 집중력이 매우 뛰어났다는 지문 흐름에 연결되지 않는다.

unfailing 한결같은, 언제나 변함없는　**inspiration** 영감　**litter** 어지럽히다　**music manuscript** 악보　**mass** 미사(곡)　**idle** 태만한, 헛된　**excel** 능가하다, 출중하다

✓ 정답 (a)

_____ over the past decades. This has, for many, been a sad occurrence in a land where the railroad was widely heralded as the key to expansion into the West, and where many cities achieved greatness as railroad hubs. Sadly gone are the days when the most famous neighborhood in Chicago was the Stockyards, made famous by the thousands of heads of cattle sent there daily for slaughter. Gone, too, are the days when a trip to California was a scenic ride on the rails. President Eisenhower's push to build the interstate highways system for national defense and the development of modern airliners rang the death bell for railroads.

(a) The operation of the railroad in the U.S. has become more expensive
(b) The decline of the railroad in the U.S. has been continual
(c) The development of the railroad in the U.S. has been slow
(d) The railroad in the U.S. has been replaced by other means of transportation

번역 미국 철도의 쇠퇴는 지난 수십 년 동안 계속되었다. 이것은 한때 철도가 서부 지역으로의 팽창의 핵심으로 각광받았고 많은 도시들이 철도 요충지로 눈부신 발전을 이룩한 땅에 살던 많은 사람들에게는 슬픈 일이었다. 도축을 위해 날마다 수천 마리의 소를 이송해서 유명해진 스톡야드가 시카고에서 가장 유명한 동네였던 시절은 이제는 슬프게도 가고 없다. 캘리포니아로 여행가는 길이 기차를 타고 경치를 감상할 수 있는 여행이었던 시절도 가버렸다. 국방을 위해 미국의 각 주를 잇는 고속 도로망을 건설하도록 한 아이젠하워 대통령의 노력과 신형 항공기 개발이 철도 산업의 임종을 알리는 종을 울렸다.

(a) 미국 철도 운영 비용이 올라갔다
(b) 미국 철도의 쇠퇴가 계속돼 왔다
(c) 미국 철도의 발달이 늦어 왔다
(d) 미국 철도가 다른 교통 수단으로 대체됐다

해법 많은 도시들이 철도 요충지로 발전했던 미국에서 많은 사람들에게 슬픈 일이라고 했고, 캘리포니아 여행이 기차를 타고 경치를 감상하는 여행이었던 시절도 가고 없다고 했으며, 고속 도로망을 건설하도록 한 아이젠하워 대통령의 조치와 신형 항공기의 발전이 철도 산업의 임종을 알리는 종을 울렸다고 했으므로 미국 철도의 쇠퇴가 계속돼 왔다는 내용이 적절하다. 따라서 (b)가 정답이다.

occurrence 일　**railroad** 철도　**herald** 알리다, 전달하다　**hub** 중심
slaughter 도살, 도축(하다)　**interstate** 각 주간의　**airliner** 여객기

 정답　(b)

Outside of the Unites States, _____. For instance, in certain countries, African Americans are shown only as athletes, or criminals. The citizens of these countries receive very little or no exposure to the majority of African Americans, who are neither athletes, nor criminals. The Arab has also often been portrayed as either a wealthy merchant or a terrorist. However, in the United States, there are now citizen organizations that condemn and, therefore, influence the media when a group has been wrongly represented. This reaction to ethnic and cultural stereotypes is positive and healthy.

(a) it is difficult to learn about the status of foreigners living in the U.S.
(b) African Americans are treated only as a minority group
(c) there are not enough support groups for the rights of minorities
(d) the mass media does not always fairly portray American minority groups

번역 미국 밖에서는 대중매체가 항상 미국 내 소수 민족 집단들을 공정하게 그려내지는 않는다. 예를 들어, 어떤 나라에서는 아프리카계 미국인들이 운동선수나 범죄자로만 비춰진다. 이런 나라의 시민들은 운동선수도 범죄자도 아닌 대다수의 아프리카계 미국인들을 거의 혹은 전혀 볼 기회가 없다. 아랍인들도 종종 부유한 상인이나 테러범으로 그려져 왔다. 그러나 이제 미국에는 어떤 집단이 잘못 묘사되는 상황을 비판하고 언론 매체에 영향을 미치는 시민 단체들이 생겨났다. 소수 민족과 문화의 고정 관념에 대한 이런 반응은 긍정적이고 건전한 현상이다.

(a) 미국에 사는 외국인들의 신분에 대해 알기 어렵다
(b) 아프리카계 미국인들이 소수 집단으로만 다뤄지고 있다
(c) 소수 민족의 권리들을 지지하는 집단이 충분하지 않다
(d) 대중매체는 미국 내 소수 민족 집단을 항상 공정하게 그려진다

해법 아프리카계 미국인들이 운동선수나 범죄자들로만 비춰지고 아랍인들도 부유한 상인이나 테러범으로 그려져 왔으나, 미국 내에 어떤 집단이 잘못 묘사되면 비난하고 언론 매체에 영향을 미치는 시민 조직들이 생겨났다고 했으므로 미국의 대중 매체가 미국 내 소수 민족 집단의 구성원들을 공정하게 그려지지 않는다는 (d)가 정답이다.

athlete 운동선수　**exposure to** ~에 대한 노출　**portray** 그리다, 묘사하다　**merchant** 상인　**condemn** 비난하다, ~에게 유죄 판결을 선고하다　**represent** 묘사하다　**stereotype** 고정 관념

 정답　(d)

During the summer of 1829, Mendelssohn took a vacation in Scotland. The excursion, including a visit to Edinburgh and a trip through the Highlands, lasted less than three weeks. It no doubt produced pleasant memories, as witnessed in his letters and a few drawings he made of the scenery, but otherwise the trip was relatively insignificant. The present book gathers together Mendelssohn's drawings, reprints the letters, and provides a kind of commentary to the trip along with additional drawings, maps, and photographs. Except for a brief biographical sketch of Mendelssohn and a totally superficial discussion of his Scottish Symphony, this _____.

(a) is a recommendation for those interested in Mendelssohn's taste in travel
(b) provides very little information about how Mendelssohn lived in Scotland
(c) is easy to read and can be purchased at all the bookstores in town
(d) is essentially a travel book of exceptionally limited value

We are entitled to reconsider Aristotle's notion of the tragic flaw, if we find it incompatible with his central idea of the nature of tragedy, the indispensable feature of the literary form we have been able to study for ourselves. What Aristotle called catharsis is still as available for examination as in the fourth century before Christ. The examination we have so far been able to make does not suggest that a tragic flaw is a precondition of the phenomenon. It is true, _____, that this phenomenon is more difficult to examine than an egg, and that we are bound to look for validation or objection of our findings with some care.

(a) as admitted earlier
(b) like established literary theories
(c) whereas looked at metaphysically
(d) although discounted by some scholars

🔤 번역 우리가 아리스토텔레스의 비극적 결함의 개념이, 비극의 본질에 대한 중심 사상 그리고 우리 스스로 연구 가능했던 문학 형식의 필수불가결한 특징과 양립할 수 없다는 것을 발견하게 된다면 우리에게 그것을 재고해 볼 자격이 주어진다. 아리스토텔레스가 카타르시스라고 부른 것은 기원전 4세기 때만큼이나 지금도 검토할 가치가 있는 명제이다. 지금까지 우리가 수행할 수 있었던 검토의 결과로 볼 때 비극적 결함이 카타르시스 현상의 전제 조건이라는 사실을 시사하지 않는다. 이미 인정한 일이지만 카타르시스 현상을 조사하는 것은 달걀을 조사하는 것보다 더 어려운 것이 사실이고, 우리는 상당히 조심스럽게 우리 연구 결과의 타당성과 이에 대한 반론 또한 찾으려 할 것이다.

(a) 이미 인정한 일이지만
(b) 확립된 문학 이론처럼
(c) 형이상학적으로 살펴본 반면
(d) 몇몇 학자들에 의해 무시당했지만

☀️ 해법 문학 형식이 갖추어야 할 빼놓을 수 없는 특징을 연구해 왔다는 내용과 아리스토텔레스의 카타르시스는 기원전 4세기 때만큼이나 지금도 검토할 가치가 있는 명제라는 내용, 그리고 지금까지 우리가 수행해온 검토의 결과는 비극적 결함이 카타르시스 현상의 전제 조건이라는 사실을 시사하고 있지는 않다는 내용 모두 시간의 흐름과 관련되므로 (a)가 정답이다.

be entitled to ~할 자격이 있다 **notion** 관념, 생각 **flaw** 결점, ~에 흠을 내다(mar) **incompatible with** ~와 맞지 않는 **nature** 자연, 본질 **indispensable** 없어서는 안 될 **catharsis** 정화, 카타르시스 **precondition** 전제 조건 **phenomenon** 현상 **be bound to** ~할 의무가 있다 **validation** 확인 **objection** 반대, 반론

 정답 (a)

🔤 번역 1829년 여름 동안 멘델스존은 스코틀랜드에서 휴가를 보냈다. 에든버러와 하이랜즈를 돌아본 것을 포함한 그 여행 기간은 3주가 채 못 된다. 그의 편지와 경치를 그린 몇 점의 그림에서 볼 수 있듯이 그 여행은 그에게 즐거운 추억을 낳은 것임에 틀림없으나, 그 외에는 그 여행은 비교적 무의미한 것이었다. 여기 있는 책은 멘델스존의 그림들을 모으고, 편지를 재인쇄하고, 그림, 지도, 사진을 추가로 첨부해 그 여행에 대한 일종의 논평을 제공한다. 멘델스존의 삶에 대해 간단하게 요약된 전기와 그의 스코틀랜드 교향곡에 대한 전적으로 피상적인 논고를 제외하면 이 책은 근본적으로 매우 한정된 가치밖에 없는 여행기이다.

(a) 멘델스존의 여행에 대한 취향에 관심 있는 사람들에게 추천한다
(b) 멘델스존이 스코틀랜드에서 어떻게 살았는지에 대한 정보를 거의 제공하지 않는다
(c) 읽기 쉽고 동네 모든 서점에서 구입할 수 있다
(d) 근본적으로 매우 한정된 가치밖에 없는 여행기이다

☀️ 해법 멘델스존의 스코틀랜드 여행은 그가 남긴 편지와 경치를 그린 몇 점의 그림들 외에는 비교적 무의미하다 했으므로 한정된 가치밖에 없는 기행문이라는 흐름이 자연스러워 (d)가 정답이다. (a)는 선택지의 a recommendation이 맞지 않고, (b)는 멘델스존이 스코틀랜드에서 휴가를 보낸 것이지 산 것은 아니다.

excursion 유람, 여행 **witness** 보다 **insignificant** 무의미한, 중요하지 않은 **commentary** 논평 **biographical** 전기의 **superficial** 피상적인 **taste** 취향

 정답 (d)

Bonfires haven't always been innocent fun. In the Middle Ages, many criminals were burned at the stake. Because their bones were the last body parts to burn, this form of execution became known as a "bone fire." When Henry VIII of England separated from the Roman Catholic Church in the 1530s, he ordered all materials connected with the church to be burned. The resultant blazes recalled the bone fires, and like them, they _____. Gradually, the name was shortened to bonfire, and large fires grew to be a festive part of some celebrations. Indeed, the only similarity between today's bonfires and the bone fires of old is that they are often at the center of onlookers.

(a) were not simply used to warm people
(b) burned things to be burned completely
(c) usually attracted a crowd of bystanders
(d) had much for historians to study

After the French Revolution, French people didn't want any remains of the tyranny. As a result, French playing cards underwent an interesting transformation. Before the Revolution, the French used cards that were the same as those used today. Each deck was divided into four suits, and each suit had three face cards representing the King, Queen, and Jack. After the Revolution, the royal figures disappeared from the cards. The Queen was replaced by symbols of liberty, the King became nature, and the Jack became virtue. However, the unusual French cards _____, although they were revolutionary.

(a) failed to spread gambling among the public
(b) were not as popular as expected
(c) only lasted for a short period
(d) did not help people forget the tyranny

 번역 모닥불을 항상 순수한 마음으로 즐기기만 했던 것은 아니었다. 중세에는 말뚝에 매여 화형에 처해진 범죄자가 많았다. 신체 부위 중에서 가장 마지막으로 타는 부위가 뼈였기 때문에 이런 형태의 처형이 '본파이어'로 알려졌다. 영국의 헨리 8세가 1530년대에 로마 가톨릭 교회로부터 분리되어 나오고 나서 교회와 관련된 모든 물건을 태우라는 지시를 내렸다. 그 결과로 발생된 불길은 본파이어를 연상시켰고, 그것과 마찬가지로 많은 구경꾼을 끌어들였다. 차차 그 이름은 본파이어로 축약되어 크게 놓은 불이 일부 경축 행사의 축제 분위기를 조성하기 위한 순서로 발전하게 되었다. 실로 오늘날의 모닥불과 옛날 본파이어의 유일한 공통점은 둘 다 주로 많은 구경꾼들 가운데에 놓인다는 점이다.

(a) 사람들을 따뜻하게 하기 위해서만 사용되지는 않았다
(b) 태울 것들을 완전히 다 태웠다
(c) 보통 많은 구경꾼들을 끌어들였다
(d) 역사가들이 연구할 내용이 많았다

해법 오늘날의 모닥불과 옛날 본파이어의 유사점이 많은 사람들의 중앙에 놓인다는 것이라고 했으므로 많은 구경꾼들을 끌어 모았다는 (c)가 정답이다. 나머지는 지문 마지막 문장과 연결되지 않거나 지문에 근거가 없다.

bonfire 모닥불 **stake** 말뚝 **execution** 처형 **resultant** 결과로서 생긴 **blaze** 불길 **onlooker** 구경꾼

정답 (c)

번역 프랑스 혁명 후에 프랑스인들은 전제 정치의 어떤 잔재도 원하지 않았다. 그 결과 프랑스의 놀이용 카드는 흥미로운 변화를 겪었다. 혁명이 있기 전에 프랑스인들은 오늘날 사용되는 카드와 같은 카드를 사용했다. 각 카드 한 벌은 네 개의 패로 나뉘었고, 각 패는 킹과 퀸, 잭을 나타내는 세 장의 그림패를 지녔다. 혁명 후에 왕족의 형상은 카드에서 사라졌다. 퀸은 자유의 상징물로 대체됐고, 킹은 자연, 그리고 잭은 미덕으로 대체되었다. 하지만 그 특이한 프랑스 카드는 혁명적이기는 했지만 짧은 기간 동안밖에 사용되지 않았다.

(a) 대중 사이에서 도박을 퍼트리지 못했다
(b) 기대했던 만큼 인기 있지 않았다
(c) 짧은 기간 동안밖에 사용되지 않았다
(d) 사람들이 전제 정치를 잊는 데 도움이 되지 않았다

해법 프랑스 혁명 후 프랑스 사람들이 전제 정치 잔재를 원치 않아 프랑스 놀이용 카드가 변화를 겪었고, 혁명이 있기 전에 프랑스인은 오늘날 사용되는 카드와 같은 카드를 사용했다고 했으므로 결국 변화된 카드가 다시 프랑스 혁명 전의 형태로 바뀌었음을 알 수 있다. 따라서 단기간 동안만 지속됐다는 (c)가 정답이다.

tyranny 전제 정치 **deck** 카드 한 벌 **suit** 카드 한 세트(pack) **virtue** 미덕

정답 (c)

"Surfacing Sadness," a collection of poems, essays, and short stories written by 37 Korean-American writers, is the first serious attempt to bring together the Korean-American literary experience. Most of the works in this volume are translations from the Korean language and there is no doubt that some of the original meaning and cadences have been lost in the process. _____, some of the translations are awkward enough to render the final product a piece to be endured rather than enjoyed. The editors acknowledge this shortcoming, but point out that despite the problems presented by translation, there must be jewels in the mud.

(a) Likewise
(b) In addition
(c) In fact
(d) Consequently

Scientists agree that we are at present treating the effects of drug abuse rather than the underlying psychological and social causes. Addicts often "come off" one type of drug, only to take up another type, and a recent study revealed that almost half the patients at various drug clinics continued in their use of "hard" drugs, even after treatment. _____, the situation is continually being made more complicated by the use of newer and newer drugs by the addicts, so that as methods are found to deal with one particular type, another one replaces it, and doctors must look forward to future problems with as yet undiscovered drugs.

(a) Thus
(b) For all that
(c) Particularly
(d) In the meantime

 번역 한국계 미국인 작가 37명이 쓴 시와 수필 그리고 단편 소설 모음인 〈드러나는 슬픔〉은 한국계 미국인들의 문학적 체험을 집대성하려는 최초의 중대한 시도이다. 이 책에 실린 대부분의 작품들은 한국어를 번역한 것이라 원작의 의미와 운율 일부가 번역 과정에서 퇴색됐음이 틀림없다. 사실 일부 번역은 최종 결과물을 즐기기보다는 인내해야 할 작품이 되게 할 만큼 어색하다. 편집자들도 이런 결점을 인정하지만 번역으로 야기되는 문제점에도 불구하고 틀림없이 진흙 속에 보석이 있으리라는 점을 지적한다.

(a) 마찬가지로
(b) 게다가
(c) 사실
(d) 결과적으로

해법 빈칸 뒤의 일부 번역이 어색하다는 내용은 의미와 운율 일부가 번역 과정에서 퇴색됐다는 빈칸 앞의 내용이 다소 강조된 것이므로 (c)가 정답이다. (b)는 번역 이외의 다른 문제가 제시돼야 한다. (d)는 번역의 문제로 인한 결과만 나와야 하는데 빈칸 뒤에 인내해야 할 단편이 됐다는 결과와 더불어 원인에 해당하는 일부 번역이 어색하다는 부분도 있어 맞지 않다.

surface 표면(의), 명백해지다 **cadence** 운율 **awkward** 어색한 **render A B** A를 B로 만들다 **shortcoming** 결점, 결핍

정답 (c)

 번역 과학자들은 우리가 현재 마약 남용의 기초를 이루는 심리적, 사회적 원인보다는 마약 남용이 주는 영향만을 다루고 있다는 것에 동의한다. 중독자들은 더러 한 가지 유형의 마약을 '끊다'가도 다시 다른 유형의 마약을 사용할 뿐더러, 최근의 한 연구는 여러 마약 치료소의 환자들 중 거의 절반이 치료 후에도 '중독성' 마약을 계속 사용한다는 사실을 밝혀냈다. 따라서 중독자들이 끊임없이 새로운 마약을 사용함에 따라 한 가지 특정 유형에 대한 치료법이 발견되면 또 다른 유형이 나타나는 등 사태는 더 복잡해지고 있고, 거기에 더해 의사들은 아직 발견되지 않은 마약으로 빚어질 장래의 문제들에도 대비해야 한다.

(a) 따라서
(b) 그럼에도 불구하고
(c) 특히
(d) 그 동안

해법 빈칸 앞의 마약을 끊거나 치료를 받아도 계속 사용한다는 내용과 빈칸 뒤의 중독자들이 계속 새로운 마약을 사용하기 때문에 새로운 치료법들이 요구되어 사태가 더 복잡해지고 있다고 했으므로 (a)가 정답이다. (c)는 빈칸 뒤에 마약을 끊거나 치료를 받아도 마약을 계속 사용하는 특정한 예 따위의 내용이 오지 않아 맞지 않다.

underlying 밑에 있는, 잠재적인 **come off** ~을 그만두다 **take up** 시작하다, 차지하다

정답 (a)

A Danish biotech company will use a genetically modified flower they have developed to find land mines. Currently, experts remove them by putting a stick into the ground to locate them, but it is very dangerous because they are still able to take away the life of the person who activates them. Despite their war purposes, many of the old mines are still influencing the lives of humans in negative ways. Thale Cress, a kind of flower, will be a less dangerous way to find explosives because it changes color when its roots are exposed to nitrogen-dioxide coming from explosives buried in the ground.

Q: What is the passage mainly about?
(a) The development of Danish biotechnology
(b) The purposes of land mines in the past and now
(c) Flowers that change color when in contact with nitrogen-dioxide
(d) A form of biotechnology application to detect underground explosives

 번역 　덴마크의 한 생명 공학 회사는 그들이 개발한 유전자 변형 꽃으로 지뢰를 찾을 예정이다. 현재는 전문가들이 지뢰의 위치를 알아내기 위해 땅속으로 막대기를 넣어 제거하는데 이 방법은 아직도 잘못하면 지뢰를 작동시켜 사람의 생명을 앗아갈 수 있기 때문에 매우 위험하다. 이렇듯 지뢰는 오래전 전시에 설치된 것임에도 오늘날까지 사람들의 생명에 악영향을 끼치고 있다. 꽃의 일종인 데일 크레스는 그 뿌리가 땅속으로 파고 들어가다 속에 묻혀 있는 폭발물에서 나오는 이산화질소에 노출되면 색깔이 바뀌므로, 폭발물을 찾아내는 덜 위험한 방식이 될 것이다.

(a) 덴마크 생명 공학의 발달
(b) 과거와 현재 지뢰의 목적
(c) 이산화질소와 접촉할 때 색이 바뀌는 꽃들
(d) 땅속 폭발물 감지를 위한 생명 공학 활용의 한 형태

해법 　덴마크의 한 생명 공학 회사가 생명 공학 활용의 한 형태로 그들이 개발한 유전자 변형 꽃을 사용해서 지뢰를 찾아낸다고 했으므로 (d)가 정답이다. (a)는 덴마크의 한 생명 공학 회사의 유전자 변형 꽃 개발이 반드시 덴마크의 생명 공학 발달을 의미하진 않아 맞지 않고, (b)는 선택지의 now가 맞지 않다.

genetically modified 유전자가 변형된　**land mine** 지뢰　**activate** 작동시키다　**nitrogen-dioxide** 이산화질소

정답 **(d)**

Long before the white men set foot on the American Continent, the Native Americans were living there. When the Europeans started to arrive in the 16th and 17th century, they were welcomed by the Native Americans. They introduced many of the foods that are common today: corn, pumpkins, beans, chili peppers, pecans, cranberries, maple syrup, etc. It was the Native Americans who taught the colonists how to gather and use them. By the end of the 20th century, more than one third of all food produced in the U.S. originated from Native American crops. Much of what we take for granted comes directly from Native Americans. Perhaps we should learn how to say the Apache word for "thank you."

Q: What is the main idea of the passage?
(a) The Native Americans lived peacefully and helped the Europeans with farming.
(b) The traditional Apache Indian language is gaining popularity in the U.S.
(c) The American Indians helped the settlers live on a variety of foods.
(d) The contributions that the Native Americans made are not appreciated enough.

 번역 　백인들이 미국 땅에 발을 내딛기 오래 전부터 미국 원주민들은 그곳에 살고 있었다. 유럽인들이 16세기와 17세기에 도착하기 시작했을 때 그들은 미국 원주민들의 환영을 받았다. 미국 원주민들은 오늘날에도 흔히 볼 수 있는 여러 종류의 식품을 소개했는데, 옥수수, 호박, 콩, 고추, 피칸, 크랜베리, 단풍나무 시럽 등이 그것이다. 이 식품들을 채집하고 사용하는 법을 이주민들에게 가르쳐 준 사람도 바로 미국 원주민들이었다. 20세기 말에 이르러서는 미국에서 생산되는 모든 식품의 3분 1 이상이 미국 원주민들의 농작물에서 비롯된 것이었다. 우리가 당연하게 여기는 많은 것들이 미국 원주민들로부터 직접 온 것이다. 아마도 우리는 아파치 인디언어로 "감사합니다"라는 말을 어떻게 하는지 배울 필요가 있을 것 같다.

(a) 미국 원주민들은 평화롭게 살았고 유럽인들의 농사를 도왔다.
(b) 아파치 인디언 전통 언어가 미국에서 인기를 끌고 있다.
(c) 미국 인디언은 정착민들이 다양한 음식을 먹고 살 수 있도록 도왔다.
(d) 미국 원주민들의 기여가 충분히 인정받고 있지 못하다.

해법 　미국 원주민들이 많은 식품을 채집하고 사용하는 법을 이주민들에게 가르쳐 준 것이 주요 내용으로, 미국 원주민들이 정착민들이 스스로 먹고 살 수 있도록 도와준 것이므로 (c)가 정답이다. (d)는 미국 원주민들이 이주민들을 도운 여러 면 중 식품을 소개한 것만 나왔으므로 선택지의 contributions가 맞지 않다.

continent 대륙　**maple** 단풍　**colonist** 식민지　**originate** 비롯하다　**take ... for granted** ~를 당연히 여기다　**popularity** 인기

정답 **(c)**

"No female can swim the English Channel," scoffed newspapers around the world. But Gertrude Ederle didn't pay any attention. On August 6, 1926, just over 14 hours after entering the waves off the coast of France, Ederle stepped onto the pages of sports history. The English Channel was to swimmers what Mount Everest was to climbers. Before Ederle's attempt, only five people had successfully crossed the Channel—all of them men. During her crossing, the waves were so violent that people on her guide boat were seasick. Fighting 20-foot waves, she sliced through the water with her brand new stroke, the crawl. Ederle not only became the first woman to swim the English Channel, but she also beat the men's record by almost two hours.

Q: What is the best title of the passage?
(a) World's Fastest Female Swimmer
(b) The Crawl, Ederle's New Stroke
(c) Ederle's Success against the Waves
(d) How Female Swimmers Have Changed

In 1947, the AK-47, the automatic machine gun, won a Soviet competition for a submachine gun for the Red Army. It has been the primary weapon in most wars, causing 300,000 annual combat deaths in the wars of the last decade. As it were, it is the most successful killing machine. Even so, the inventor Mikhail Kalashnikov is proud of his creation. He takes no responsibility for the deaths it has caused. "I made it a mission of my life to protect the motherland. The weapon has been used successfully to complete that mission. I am not to blame for the fact that people die because of it. It is not because of the designer, but because of politics."

Q: What is the main topic of the passage?
(a) Why Mikhail Kalashnikov created the AK-47
(b) Mikhail Kalashnikov's success in protecting his nation
(c) Who should take responsibility for the deaths in wars
(d) Different views on how the AK-47 is used

📖 **번역** "영국 해협을 헤엄쳐 건널 수 있는 여자는 없다"라고 전 세계의 신문은 비웃었다. 하지만 거트루드 에델리는 그 말에 주목하지 않았다. 1926년 8월 6일 프랑스 해변에서 바다로 뛰어든 지 14시간이 조금 넘어서 그녀는 스포츠 역사의 한 페이지를 장식했다. 수영을 할 줄 아는 사람들에게 영국 해협은 등산가들의 에베레스트 산과 같은 의미였다. 그녀의 시도 이전에 영국 해협을 성공적으로 건넌 사람은 단 5명에 불과했고, 모두 남자였다. 그녀가 바다를 건너는 동안 파도가 너무 격렬해서 가이드 보트를 타고 옆에서 따라가던 사람들 모두가 뱃멀미를 할 지경이었다. 20피트 높이의 파도와 싸우면서 그녀의 새로운 영법인 크롤 영법으로 파도를 헤쳐 나갔다. 에델리는 영국 해협을 건넌 최초의 여성이 되었을 뿐 아니라 두 시간 이상 차이로 남성들의 기록을 깼다.

(a) 세상에서 가장 빠른 여성 수영 선수
(b) 크롤, 에델리의 새로운 영법
(c) 파도를 헤친 에델리의 성공
(d) 여성 수영 선수들이 어떻게 변해왔는가

✳ **해법** 에델리가 결국 영국 해협을 헤엄쳐 건넜으므로 (c)가 정답이다. (a)는 수영 속도를 비교할 수 있는 다른 여성 선수들에 대한 내용이 지문에 없고, (b)는 지엽적이다. (d)는 에델리 이외의 여성 수영 선수에 대한 내용이 지문에 없다.

channel 해협 **scoff** 비웃다 **A is to B what C is to D** A가 B에 대한 것이 C가 D에 대한 것과 같다 **seasick** 뱃멀미 **stroke** 수영법

 정답 (c)

📖 **번역** 1947년 자동 기관총 AK-47이 소련 적군의 소형 경기관총 부분 경연 대회에서 우승했다. 이 총은 대부분의 전쟁에서 주요 무기로 사용되었고, 지난 10년간 전쟁에서 연간 30만 명의 죽음을 초래했다. 말하자면 살상 무기로는 가장 성공적이다. 그럼에도 불구하고 이것을 발명한 미하일 칼라쉬니코프는 자신의 발명품을 자랑스러워한다. 그는 그 총으로 인한 희생자에 대해서는 책임을 지지 않는다. 그는 "나는 조국을 보호하는 것을 내 인생의 사명으로 여겼다. 그 무기는 나의 사명을 완수하는 데 성공적으로 사용되었다. 나는 사람들이 죽는다는 사실 때문에 비난받을 일이 없다. 문제는 무기를 고안해낸 사람이 아니라 정치이다"라고 말했다.

(a) 미하일 칼라쉬니코프가 AK-47을 만든 이유
(b) 그의 조국을 지켜낸 미하일 칼라쉬니코프의 성공
(c) 전쟁으로 인한 죽음은 누가 책임져야 하나
(d) AK-47의 사용에 대한 다른 견해들

✳ **해법** 자동 기관총 AK-47에 대해 가장 성공한 살상 무기로서의 내용과 이와는 상반되는 총을 만든 미하일 칼라쉬니코프의 생각이 주요 내용이므로 (d)가 정답이다. (a), (b)는 지엽적이고, (c)는 자동 기관총 AK-47을 포함한 전쟁에서 발생한 죽음에 대한 내용으로 지문에 대한 주제로는 너무 넓다.

automatic machine gun 자동 기관총 **submachine gun** 소형 경기관총 **mission** 사명 **motherland** 조국

정답 (d)

The protein, calcium, and other vital minerals of milk are of great biological value for growing children, but they don't drink enough milk. How can parents persuade their children to drink such nutritious milk? Some scientists argue that making milk more like soda is the best way to get them to drink milk instead of soda. Soda is popular with so many of today's young people. Scientists in Illinois are mixing milk with carbon dioxide gas to make milk like soda. These scientists are even trying to add more flavors to milk. Perhaps within a few years, people will enjoy a bubbly glass of lemon- or orange-flavored milk on a hot summer day.

Q: What is the best title for the passage?
(a) Getting Children to Drink More Milk
(b) How to Make Milk More Popular
(c) Benefits of Soda Drinks
(d) Making Better Milk

번역 우유의 단백질, 칼슘 그리고 다른 필수 무기물들은 자라는 아이들에게 대단한 생물가를 지니지만 아이들은 충분한 양을 마시지 않는다. 어떻게 하면 부모가 아이들에게 이렇게 영양가 높은 우유를 마시도록 설득할 수 있을까? 일부 과학자는 우유를 탄산음료같이 만들어 아이들이 탄산음료 대신 우유를 마시게 하는 것이 가장 좋은 방법이라고 주장한다. 탄산음료는 오늘날 대다수의 젊은이들 사이에 인기가 있다. 일리노이 주의 과학자들은 우유를 탄산음료처럼 만들기 위해 우유에 탄산가스를 섞고 있다. 이 과학자들은 우유에 더 많은 맛을 첨가하려는 노력까지 하고 있다. 어쩌면 몇 년 안에 사람들은 더운 여름날 공기 방울 가득한 레몬 맛 혹은 오렌지 맛 우유 한 잔을 즐길지도 모른다.

(a) 아이들에게 우유를 더 많이 마시게 하기
(b) 우유를 더 인기 있게 만드는 법
(c) 탄산음료의 장점
(d) 더 좋은 우유 만들기

해법 영양가 많은 우유를 아이들이 더 마실 수 있는 방법들을 다룬 지문으로 (a)가 정답이다. (b), (d)는 아이들이 우유를 더 마실 수 있는 방법들이 주요 내용이란 점을 볼 때 주제로는 너무 넓고, (c)는 지문에 구체적인 내용이 없다.

protein 단백질 calcium 칼슘 mineral 무기물 biological value 생물가 nutritious 영양가가 높은 carbon dioxide gas 탄산가스

정답 (a)

Some medical researchers in the U.S. are developing a clear gel that can immediately stop a cut or wound from bleeding. The gel creates a barrier of peptides when it is placed on a wound. And this has proved to be helpful in facilitating faster blood clotting in tests in monkeys. The medical industry is saying that if it works on humans, it could prove to be a significant advance for ordinary people as well as surgeons. Although surgeons have devised ways to stop it, excessive bleeding remains a serious challenge during surgery. The researchers have announced that the miraculous gel will be released to the market in about three years.

Q: Which of the following best summarizes the passage?
(a) Monkeys are used to test the most advanced medical products.
(b) The gel has yet to prove to be a breakthrough for its purpose.
(c) The product will facilitate the secretion of peptides in the human body.
(d) The gel will not be used for medical operations in the near future.

번역 미국 의료계의 몇몇 연구원들은 베이거나 상처 난 곳에서 피가 나는 것을 즉시 멈추게 해줄 투명한 젤을 개발하고 있다. 이 젤은 상처에 발랐을 때 펩티드 막을 형성한다. 원숭이 실험에서는 빠른 혈액 응고를 가능하게 하는 것으로 드러났다. 의학계는 만약 이것이 인간에게도 효과가 있다면 이 제품이 외과의사들뿐만 아니라 일반인들에게도 중요한 진보로 입증될 수 있을 것이라 말하고 있다. 비록 외과의사가 출혈을 멈추는 방법을 이미 고안하긴 했지만 수술 중 과도한 출혈은 의사들에게 여전히 난제로 남아 있다. 연구원들은 그 기적적인 젤이 약 3년 내에 시중에 나올 것이라고 발표했다.

(a) 가장 진보된 의료 제품 실험에 원숭이들이 사용된다.
(b) 아직 정해진 목적대로 이 젤이 획기적인 제품이라는 것이 증명되지 않았다.
(c) 이 제품은 인체에서 펩티드 분비가 용이하게 할 것이다.
(d) 이 젤은 가까운 장래에 의료 수술에 쓰이지 않을 것이다.

해법 인간에게 효과가 있다면 외과의사와 일반인 둘 다에게 중요한 진보로 판명될 수 있을 거라고 했으므로 (b)가 정답이다. (a)는 선택지의 the most advanced medical products에 해당하는 것으로 지문에는 gel밖에 나오지 않았고, (c)는 인간에게 효과가 있는지 아직 밝혀지지 않았다. (d)는 지엽적인 내용이며 아직 결론이 안 났다.

wound 상처 peptide 펩티드 facilitate 촉진하다, 용이하게 하다 clot 응고하다, 응고시키다 surgeon 외과 전문의

정답 (b)

John Barnes, manufacturer of ball bearings, agrees to supply Vitesse Automobile Company with 100 boxes of custom-designed ball bearings (Model CX-123) by March 31, 2012. If the ball bearings are delivered on or before 3/31/2012, Vitesse will pay Mr. Barnes $1,000 per box, or $100,000 for the order requested, plus a bonus of $5,000 for prompt delivery. However, for every day the order is past 3/31/2012, Mr. Barnes will pay Vitesse $2,000 per day as penalty. Also, because Vitesse designed and tested Model CX-123, Mr. Barnes must let Vitesse know that appropriate security measures will be offered to protect the design from being stolen. If both parties agree to the points, the contract will go into effect on January 1, 2012.

Q: Which of the following is correct according to the passage?
(a) Vitesse will pay $98,000 to John Barnes if the delivery is made before April 1, 2012.
(b) It will take about 3 months for John Barnes to make the ball bearings.
(c) John Barnes and Vitesse have to conclude the contract before January 1, 2012.
(d) Vitesse specified the type of ball bearings that they wanted for their products.

Each December, the World Elephant Polo Association tournament is held in Nepal. Elephant polo is quite similar to horse polo. Players wear traditional polo hats and use a polo ball. There are four players on each side. The largest elephant is always given to the referee because it gives him an excellent vantage point from which to watch the game. There are some special rules for this sport. Because one team trained a baby elephant to dribble the ball with its front foot, elephants are no longer allowed to touch the ball with their trunk or hind feet. Another team trained an elephant to lie down in front of the goal, which now draws a penalty.

Q: Which of the following is correct about Elephant polo?
(a) Its rules have changed recently.
(b) It is held every year with horse polo.
(c) Every match starts with nine elephants.
(d) Elephants will not be trained in front of the goal.

번역 매년 12월, 세계 코끼리 폴로 협회 시합이 네팔에서 열린다. 코끼리 폴로는 말을 타고 하는 폴로와 매우 비슷하다. 선수들은 전통적인 폴로 모자를 쓰고 폴로 공을 사용한다. 각 진영에는 4명의 선수가 경기를 한다. 경기를 보기에 가장 유리한 위치에 있도록 심판에게 가장 큰 코끼리가 주어진다. 이 경기에는 특별한 규칙이 몇 가지 있다. 한 팀에서 어린 코끼리를 앞발로 공을 드리블하는 훈련을 시켰기 때문에 코끼리가 더 이상 코나 뒷발로 공을 건드릴 수 없도록 했다. 또 다른 팀은 코끼리가 골 문 앞에 눕도록 훈련을 시켜서 이제 이러한 행위를 하면 벌칙을 받게 되었다.

(a) 최근에 규칙이 바뀌었다.
(b) 말 폴로와 함께 매년 열린다.
(c) 매 시합이 코끼리 9마리로 시작한다.
(d) 코끼리들이 골 문 앞에서 훈련받지 않을 것이다.

해법 각 진영에는 4명의 선수, 즉 코끼리 8마리가 경기한다고 했고, 가장 큰 코끼리가 심판에게 주어진다고 했으므로 매 시합마다 9마리의 코끼리로 시작하는 셈이므로 (c)가 정답이다. (a)는 선택지의 Its rules가 Some of its rules 정도가 돼야 하고 recently에 대한 근거 역시 지문에 없다.

polo 말 따위를 타고 스틱을 이용해서 공을 차는 경기 **referee** 심판 **vantage** 우월, 유리한 위치 **trunk** 나무줄기, 코끼리 코 **hind** 뒤의, 후방의 **draw** 초래하다

정답 (c)

번역 볼베어링 제조사인 존 반즈는 주문 설계된 볼베어링(Model CX-123) 100박스를 비테스 자동차 회사에 2012년 3월 31일까지 공급하기로 동의한다. 볼베어링이 2012년 3월 31일이나 그 전에 도착하면 비테스는 반즈 씨에게 상자당 1,000달러, 즉 주문량 전체에 대해 100,000달러, 그에 더해 조기 납품에 대해 5,000달러의 보너스를 지급하기로 한다. 그러나 물건이 납기일인 2012년 3월 31일을 넘어서 도착할 경우, 하루 초과할 때마다 2,000달러씩의 벌금을 반즈 씨가 비테스에 지급하기로 한다. 또한 Model CX-123의 설계와 시험을 비테스가 했으므로 볼베어링의 디자인이 도용되는 것을 방지하기 위해 적절한 보안 조치를 취하겠다는 사실을 알릴 의무가 있다. 이 조건에 양 당사자가 동의하면 본 계약 내용은 2012년 1월 1일부터 효력이 발생한다.

(a) 2012년 4월 1일 전에 배달이 되면 비테스는 존 반즈에게 98,000달러를 지불할 것이다.
(b) 존 반즈가 볼베어링을 만드는 데 3개월이 걸릴 것이다.
(c) 존 반즈와 비테스는 2012년 1월 1일 전에 계약을 마쳐야 한다.
(d) 비테스는 그들의 제품으로 사용할 볼베어링의 구체적인 사양을 명시했다.

해법 볼베어링 제조사인 존 반즈가 주문 설계된 볼베어링을 비테스 자동차 회사에 공급하기로 했으므로 비테스 자동차 회사는 그들이 원하는 볼베어링의 사양을 구체화했음을 알 수 있어 (d)가 정답이다. (a)는 물건값 $100,000와 보너스 $5,000가 추가되므로 $98,000은 $105,000이 돼야 한다. (c)는 동의하지 않을 수도 있으므로 맞지 않다.

custom-designed 주문 설계된 **go into effect** 효력이 발생하다

정답 (d)

A blind boy is the subject of an unusual psychological experiment designed to speed up the learning process in blind children. Through the use of a sonar-type electronic device on his head, Dennis Daughters is learning to identify objects in the world around him by means of echoes. A transmitter emits an ultrasonic pulse that creates an 80-degree cone of sound at six feet. Echoes from objects within the cone are changed into audible signals fed into each ear. The signals vary in sound and pitch with the size and distance of the object. What remains to be determined is how well the device will help children as they venture further into their environment and must cope with more complicated surroundings.

Q: Which of the following is correct according to the passage?
(a) The echoes are changed into sound electronically.
(b) The device is not fully functional at the moment.
(c) The transmitter of the device imitates a cone of sound.
(d) The closer an object is, the louder the sound becomes.

번역 눈이 안 보이는 한 소년은 맹아들의 학습 과정을 촉진시키고자 고안된 이례적인 심리 실험 대상이다. 데니스 도터스는 머리에 쓰는 수중 음파 탐지기 형태의 전자 장치를 통해 그의 주변 세계의 물체들을 메아리로 식별하는 방법을 배우고 있다. 송신기가 초음파 파동을 방출하면 이 파동이 6피트 거리에 80도 각도의 소리 원추를 형성한다. 이 원추 내에 들어 있는 물체로부터 발생하는 메아리는 청각을 이용하여 감지할 수 있는 신호로 바뀌어 두 귀로 흘러 들어간다. 이 신호들은 물체의 크기와 거리에 따라 소리와 소리의 높낮이가 달라진다. 앞으로 규명해야 할 문제는 아이들이 자신의 주변 환경을 넓혀나가 보다 복잡한 주위 상황에 대처해야 할 때 이 장치가 얼마나 도움이 될 것인가 하는 것이다.

(a) 전자적인 방식으로 메아리가 소리로 바뀐다.
(b) 이 장치는 현재 완전히 작동되고 있지 않다.
(c) 이 장치의 송신기가 소리 원추를 형성한다.
(d) 물체가 가까울수록 소리가 더 커진다.

해법 메아리들이 청각적 신호로 바뀐다는 내용과 수중 음파 탐지기 형태의 전자 장치라는 내용을 연계해 보면 (a)가 정답이다. (b)는 아이들이 그들의 환경을 보다 멀리 개척해나가고, 보다 복잡한 주변 상황에 대처해야만 할 때 얼마나 도움이 될지를 규명해야 할 것이라는 지문 내용과 다르고, (c)는 초음파 파동이 소리 원추를 형성하므로 맞지 않다.

sonar 수중 음파 탐지기 **by means of** ∼에 의해 **ultrasonic** 초음파의 **cope with** 대처하다, 극복하다

정답 (a)

Dear Tucker,

Enclosed are some cases involving sewer rate increases. They are relevant to our case and for your reading interest. The scheduling hearing on August 9 affirmed the final hearing date for October 4 in the De Kalb County Magistrate Court and confirmed the need for a pre-trial order. Further, I need to provide opposing counsel and the court with a list of witnesses within the week. Since the hearing will only last a couple of hours, our witnesses should be limited to three to four, one being Mr. Greenwood. Do you also wish to spend money on finding an accountant who specializes in utility rates? If so, we must contact that person immediately.

Sincerely yours,
Ronald Glen Thomas
Enclosures

Q: Which of the following is correct according to the letter?
(a) The date for the final hearing was set in the magistrate court.
(b) Tucker and Ronald will contact an accountant before October 4.
(c) Tucker asked for cases regarding sewer rate increases.
(d) Mr. Greenwood will defend for Tucker.

번역 수도 요금 인상과 관련된 몇몇 사건 내용을 담은 서류를 동봉합니다. 저희 사건과 관련 있는 내용이며 읽어볼 만합니다. 일정을 정하기 위해 8월 9일에 열린 공청회에서, 최종 공청회는 드 캘브 카운티 치안 판사 법원에서 10월 4일에 열기로 했고 공판 전 명령서가 있어야 한다고 했습니다. 게다가 상대편 변호사와 법원에 이번 주 내로 증인 목록을 제출해야 합니다. 공청회는 불과 두어 시간 정도밖에 진행되지 않을 것이므로 우리 측 증인은 3∼4명으로 제한해야 하며 이 중 한 명은 그린우드 씨입니다. 시설 관리비 사용 요금률을 전문으로 하는 회계사 또한 고용하길 원하십니까? 그렇다면 그런 사람에게 당장 연락을 취해야 합니다.

(a) 최종 공청회 날짜가 치안 판사 법원에서 정해졌다.
(b) 터커와 로널드는 10월 4일 전에 회계사에게 연락할 것이다.
(c) 터커가 하수도 요금 인상과 관련된 사건 내용들을 요청했다.
(d) 그린우드 씨가 터커 씨를 옹호할 것이다.

해법 하수도 요금 인상 건에 대한 공청회를 앞둔 터커 씨에게 그를 돕는 로널드(변호사)가 보낸 편지로, 그린우드 씨가 터커 씨 쪽 증인으로 나서게 됐으므로 (d)가 정답이다. (a)는 최종 공청회 날짜가 드 캘브 카운티 치안 판사 법원에서 정해진 것은 아니다.

sewer 하수구, 하수도 **affirm** 확언하다, 단정하다 **hearing** 공청회

정답 (d)

Without fruit bats, baobabs would be unable to get fruit and would die out as a species. Yet, fruit bats are detested by mango growers in East Africa who consider them to be crop pests. Mango growers set fire to the concentrated fruit bat colonies found in the few caves in the area, and threaten the species with extinction. Yet, fruit bats only eat ripe fruit, which is never picked by mango growers, who ship green fruit to market to prevent spoilage. Ripe mangos, when uneaten by fruit bats, usually fall to the ground and host fruit fly larvae. East African mango growers are risking not only their mango crops but the delicate balance of East African ecology.

Q: Which of the following is correct according to the passage?
(a) Baobabs are in danger of extinction because of fruit flies.
(b) Baobabs are dependent on fruit bats for pollination.
(c) Fruit bats do not eat ripe mangos fallen to the ground.
(d) Fruit bats in East Africa are almost extinct.

The seyah ythak is a beautiful ostrich-like creature which lives in the Sinai Peninsula, Israel, and on across into central India. They prefer semi-desert and desert regions and can withstand the high temperatures and low water availability which characterize these areas. As an adult, it stands approximately 75-80cm and weighs about 15-23kg. It has light, sandy colored feathers on its back and creamy white belly plumage. Its face is handsome, with the brown color running along its nose and the creamy white coloration along its cheeks. Peculiar among birds, it has horns which are about 10cm in length and protrude upward in a somewhat V-like shape, curving to the center as they terminate.

Q: Which of the following is correct about the seyah ythak?
(a) The length of its horns is equal to its height.
(b) It appears colorful.
(c) It can live without water.
(d) An adult standing about 80cm weighs about 23kg.

번역 큰 박쥐들이 없다면 바오밥 나무는 열매를 맺지 못해 멸종할 것이다. 그러나 동아프리카의 망고 재배자들은 큰 박쥐를 작물에 피해를 주는 해충으로 생각해 몹시 싫어한다. 망고 재배자들은 지역 내의 새로운 동굴에서 발견되는 큰 박쥐 집단 서식지에 불을 놓아서 종의 보존을 위협한다. 그러나 망고 재배자들은 과일의 손상을 막기 위해 새파란 열매만 수확해서 시장으로 내다 팔며, 큰 박쥐는 이들이 따지 않고 나무에 남겨둔 익은 열매만을 먹는다. 나무에서 익은 망고들을 큰 박쥐가 먹지 않으면 땅에 떨어져 보통 과일 파리 유충들의 숙주가 된다. 동아프리카의 망고 재배자들은 그들의 망고 농사를 위태롭게 하고 있을 뿐 아니라 동아프리카 생태의 정교한 균형까지 위태롭게 만들고 있다.

(a) 바오밥 나무는 과일 파리로 인해 멸종 위기에 처해 있다.
(b) 바오밥 나무는 큰 박쥐에 의존해서 수분한다.
(c) 큰 박쥐들은 땅에 떨어진 익은 망고들을 먹지 않는다.
(d) 동아프리카의 큰 박쥐들은 거의 멸종했다.

해법 나무에서 익은 망고를 큰 박쥐가 먹지 않으면 땅에 떨어져 과일 파리 유충들의 숙주가 된다고 했으므로 땅에 떨어진 망고들은 큰 박쥐가 먹지 않음을 알 수 있어 (c)가 정답이다. (a)는 망고 재배자들이 망고 농사를 위태롭게 하고 있을 뿐 아니라 동아프리카 생태의 미묘한 균형까지 위태롭게 만들고 있다고 했으므로 맞지 않다.

fruit bat 큰 박쥐 **species** 종 **detest** 몹시 싫어하다, 혐오하다 **spoilage** 손상 **larvae** 유충(larva의 복수형) **delicate** 섬세한, 민감한 **ecology** 생태학, 생태(계) **pollination** 수분

정답 (c)

번역 세야 이타크는 이스라엘의 시나이 반도와 중부 인도 내륙에서 서식하는 타조를 닮은 아름다운 동물이다. 이들은 반사막이나 사막 지역을 좋아하며 이런 지역들의 특징인 고온건조 현상을 이겨낼 수 있다. 이 동물은 다 성장했을 때 대략 키가 75~80cm, 몸무게가 약 15~23kg이다. 등은 모래 색깔의 가벼운 깃털로 덮여 있고 가슴은 크림빛 흰 털로 덮여 있다. 얼굴은 잘 생겨서 코를 따라 갈색을 띠고 양쪽 볼을 따라 미색을 띤다. 새 중에서 이 새는 특이하게 뿔이 있는데 길이는 10cm 가량으로 V자 모양으로 위로 솟아 있고 끝 부분이 가운데로 굽어져 있다.

(a) 뿔의 길이가 키와 동일하다.
(b) 외모가 화려하다.
(c) 물 없이도 살 수 있다.
(d) 키가 80cm정도 되는 다 큰 것은 몸무게가 23kg 정도이다.

해법 등은 모래 색깔의 가벼운 깃털로 덮여 있고, 가슴은 크림빛 흰 털로 덮여 있으며, 얼굴은 코를 따라 갈색을 띠고 있고, 양쪽 볼을 따라 크림빛 흰 색깔을 띠고 있다고 했으므로 (b)가 정답이다. (d)는 지문 내용이 이 동물이 다 컸을 때 키가 75~80cm 정도가 되고 몸무게는 15~23kg 정도라는 것이지, 키가 80cm가 됐다고 해서 몸무게가 반드시 23kg이라는 객관적 내용이 지문에 없다.

ostrich 타조 **withstand** 견디다 **plumage** 깃털 **cheek** 볼, 뺨 **peculiar** 독특한, 별난 **protrude** 내밀다 **terminate** 끝내다

정답 (b)

Dear Kim,

Thank you for your participation in HUG's REFLECTIONS. The unique mirror that you are designing will be displayed for auction at the HUGS benefit, which will be held on Friday, June 2, from 7:00 -10:00 P.M. at the home of Bob and Lori Bergman, 1620 Forest Park Boulevard. In appreciation of the generous donation of your time and talents to this project, HUGS would like to invite you to be our guest at the gala. You may order additional reservations by sending $75.00 per guest, with a check made out to Friends of HUGS. You may claim $30.00 as a tax deduction for each person.

We hope to see you at our fantastic REFLECTIONS.

Sincerely,
Camilla

Q: Which of the following is correct according to the letter?
(a) Camilla will be at a private residence this Friday.
(b) Kim showed his interest in HUG's REFLECTIONS.
(c) Bob and Lori Bergman want to invite Kim as a guest.
(d) Kim will get a $30.00 tax reduction.

Go did not become a genuinely popular game with everyone until the twentieth century. At first it was played only by the aristocracy and then gradually spread to the warrior class and the Buddhist clergy, these being the educated classes. There was some improvement in the game at this time, but perhaps the most significant development occurred in the 14th or 15th century, when the traditional practice of placing two white stones and two black stones on the corner star points prior to the game was abandoned. Up to that time fighting ability was most important, but without corner stones players began to develop opening strategies as well.

Q: Which of the following claims is made about the passage?
(a) Most of the changes to go were made in the 14th or 15th century.
(b) Go was not popular among the learned people for about 550 years.
(c) There were four corner star points on the original go board.
(d) A major go improvement involved the omission of pairs of stones.

번역 허그스 리플렉션즈에 참여해 주셔서 감사합니다. 귀하가 디자인하고 있는 독특한 거울은 허그스 자선 행사의 경매를 위해 전시될 것입니다. 이 행사는 포리스트 파크 가 1620번지에 있는 밥, 로리 버그만 부부 집에서 6월 2일 금요일 저녁 7시부터 10시까지 열릴 예정입니다. 이번 행사에 대한 귀하의 시간과 재능의 아낌없는 후원에 감사하는 뜻으로 허그스는 이번 행사의 손님으로 귀하를 초대하고자 합니다. 손님 한 명당 75달러 수표를 프렌즈 오브 허그스 앞으로 보내주시면 추가 예약을 하실 수 있습니다. 그 중 30달러씩은 세금 공제 요청도 하실 수 있습니다.
저희 환상적인 리플렉션즈에서 귀하를 만나기를 희망합니다.

(a) 이번 금요일에 카밀라가 개인 가정집에 있을 것이다.
(b) 김 씨가 허그스 리플렉션즈에 관심을 보였다.
(c) 밥, 로리 버그만 부부가 김 씨를 손님으로 초대하길 원한다.
(d) 김 씨는 30달러 세금 공제를 받을 것이다.

해법 카밀라가 김 씨에게 보낸 편지로 허그스 리플렉션즈에 참여해 주셔서 감사하다고 했으므로 (b)가 정답이다. (a)는 6월 2일 금요일이 이번 요일이라고 할 만한 객관적인 근거가 지문에 없고, (d)는 김 씨가 다른 손님을 데리고 오지 않으면 해당되는 내용이 아니다.

auction 경매(하다) **boulevard** 큰 길가, 대로 **tax deduction** 세금 공제

 정답 (b)

번역 20세기가 되고 나서야 바둑은 모든 사람에게 진정으로 인기 있는 게임이 되었다. 처음에 이것은 귀족들 사이에서만 즐기던 것이었고, 점차 교육받은 계급들인 전사 계급과 불교 승려들에게 퍼져나갔다. 당시에 이 게임에 다소 개선이 있었으나 아마도 가장 중요한 발전은 14세기 혹은 15세기에 이뤄졌다. 그때 게임에 앞서 귀퉁이 별점에 두 개의 흰 돌과 두 개의 검은 돌을 놓던 전통적 관행이 폐지됐다. 그때까지는 싸움 능력이 가장 중요했으나 귀퉁이 돌들이 없어지자 게임을 하는 사람들은 초장 전략들을 개발하기 시작했다.

(a) 바둑에 대한 대부분의 변화들은 14세기 혹은 15세기에 이루어졌다.
(b) 바둑은 약 550년 동안 지식인들 사이에서 인기가 없었다.
(c) 최초의 바둑판에는 4개의 귀퉁이 별점들이 있었다.
(d) 바둑의 가장 큰 발전은 바둑돌을 색상별로 한 쌍씩 두는 규정을 없앤 것과 관련이 있다.

해법 가장 중요한 발전은 14세기 혹은 15세기에 이뤄졌다는 내용과 게임에 앞서 귀퉁이가 별점에 두 개의 흰 돌과 검은 돌을 놓던 전통적 관행이 폐지됐다는 내용을 연계하면 (d)가 정답이다. (a)는 14세기 혹은 15세기에 가장 중요한 발전이 있었다는 지문 내용과 다르고, (b)는 선택지의 for about 550 years에 대한 근거가 지문에 없다.

go 바둑 **genuinely** 진정으로 **aristocracy** 귀족정치 **clergy** 성직자 **abandon** 버리다, 포기하다 **opening strategy** 초장 전략

 정답 (d)

The world's first subway system was put forward for London in 1843. After years of discussion, Parliament gave approval and work began in 1860. The line was open in 1863, using coal-burning steam locomotives and, in spite of the sulfurous fumes, it was a success from its inception. In 1886 the city started excavations for a tube railway. Two twin tunnels were driven deep in the London clay and consequently neither support of buildings nor disruption of traffic was required. The original plan called for the use of steel cables to haul the trains, but before the tunnels were completed electricity was substituted. In 1890, the London underground was opened, becoming the first underground electric railway.

Q: Which of the following claims is made about the passage?
(a) It took more than half a century to complete the London underground.
(b) The plan to build the world's first subway system went through a change.
(c) British people first became interested in a subway system in 1843.
(d) Coal-burning steam locomotives were replaced by underground trains in 1890.

After the birth of the baby rhino Athena last fall, the zoo's attendance soared to more than a million visitors for the seventh time in history. The number of zoo visitors jumped to 1,013,990—up 35,943 from the previous year. The all time attendance record of 1,211,100 was set in 1963, the year Trumpet the elephant was born. The zoo keeps having the highest attendance of all paid tourist attractions in Kansas. Only Pioneer Lodge and Muddy Falls, which are free tourist attractions, attract more yearly visitors. Attendance could jump to the record high once again this year thanks to the koala exhibit running through October, and the new Metropolitan rail station.

Q: Which of the following is supported by the passage?
(a) The zoo's attendance has reached one million seven times since 1963.
(b) Less than one million people visited the zoo two years ago.
(c) It is expected that 1963's attendance record will be broken this year.
(d) The zoo has the largest number of newborn animals of any in Kansas.

번역 1843년 런던에 세계 최초의 지하철을 만들자는 의견이 제안됐다. 수년 동안의 논의 끝에 의회는 이 제안을 승인하고 1860년에 공사가 시작됐다. 석탄을 사용하는 증기 기관차를 투입한 지하철이 1863년 개통됐는데 열차가 계속 유황 연기를 내뿜는데도 불구하고 시작부터 성공적이었다. 1886년 런던시 당국은 튜브형 지하철 건설을 위해 굴착 작업을 시작했다. 쌍둥이 땅굴이 런던 지하 깊숙이 뚫렸고 결과적으로 건물들을 버텨줄 필요도 없었고 교통 혼란도 일지 않았다. 원래 계획으로는 강철 케이블을 사용해서 열차를 예인하는 방식을 채택했으나 땅굴이 완성되기도 전에 전기로 움직이는 열차인 전철로 바뀌었다. 1890년 런던 지하철이 개통되었고 이것이 최초의 지하 전동 열차인 지하철이 되었다.

(a) 런던 지하철 공사를 완공하는 데 반 세기 이상 걸렸다.
(b) 세계 최초의 지하철을 만들 계획이 한 가지 변화를 겪었다.
(c) 1843년에 영국 사람들이 지하철에 처음으로 관심을 가지게 되었다.
(d) 1890년에 석탄을 사용하는 증기 기관차들이 지하철로 교체됐다.

해법 원래 계획은 강철 케이블로 열차를 예인하는 방식이었으나 땅굴이 완성되기 전에 전철로 대체됐다고 했으므로 한 가지 변화를 겪었다는 (b)가 정답이다. (a)는 선택지의 more than a century가 맞지 않고, (c)는 1843년 런던에 세계 최초의 지하철을 만들자는 의견이 제안된 것이지 지하철에 처음 관심을 가졌다는 것은 아니다.

parliament 의회   steam locomotive 증기 기관차   sulfurous fumes 유황 연기   excavation 굴착, 발굴   call for 요구하다   haul 끌어당기다   substitute A for B B 대신 A를 쓰다

✔ 정답 (b)

번역 지난 가을 아기 코뿔소 아테네의 탄생 이후 동물원의 관람객 수가 역사상 일곱 번째로 백만 명 이상을 기록했다. 동물원 관람객 수는 전년도보다 3만 5,943명이 늘어난 101만 3,990명이었다. 121만 1,100명이라는 동물원 사상 최고의 관람객 동원 기록은 코끼리인 트럼펫이 태어난 1963년에 수립된 것이다. 이 동물원은 캔자스 주의 유료 관광소로는 최다 관람객 수를 유지하고 있다. 단지 무료로 운영되는 파이오니어 롯지와 머디 폴즈만이 이곳보다 연간 관광객 수가 더 많다. 10월까지 운영될 코알라 전시와 새로 개통된 도시 철도역 덕분에 올해 관람객 수가 다시 한번 기록을 갱신할지도 모른다.

(a) 이 동물원의 관람객 수는 1963년 이래로 백만 명을 7번 기록했다.
(b) 2년 전에 백만 명이 못 되는 사람들이 이 동물원을 방문했다.
(c) 1963년의 관람객 수 기록이 올해 깨질 것으로 전망하고 있다.
(d) 이 동물원은 캔자스의 모든 동물원들 중에서 새로 태어난 동물들이 가장 많다.

해법 지난 가을 아기 코뿔소 아테네의 탄생으로 백만 명 이상의 관람객이 동물원을 찾았고, 관람객 수가 전년도보다 3만 5,943명 늘어난 101만 3,990명에 달했다고 했으므로 재작년에는 관람객 수가 백만에 미치지 못했으므로 (b)가 정답이다. (a)는 one million이 아니라 over 1 million 정도가 돼야 하고, (c)는 지문 내용이 1963년 기록이 올해 깨진다는 것은 아니다.

rhino 코뿔소   attendance 관객 수   soar 치솟다   metropolitan 대도시의

✔ 정답 (b)

A glacier, simply put, is a slow-motion river of ice. It runs from high mountaintops through rough valleys, carrying off frozen snow that compacted over many years into a hard, slowly flowing ice stream. This ice is driven by gravity and the constantly mounting snows behind it and into an area called the accumulation zone. In Alaska only a few glaciers reach the sea, pushing out across the floor of a bay or seacoast. Several factors affect the actions of these great cascades of mountain-born ice, among them long-term atmospheric warming or sustained changes in precipitation patterns.

Q: What can be inferred from the passage?
(a) Only a few glaciers in Alaska melt away.
(b) There are many accumulation zones in Alaska.
(c) Four factors are involved in moving glaciers.
(d) Glaciers react slowly to environmental changes.

번역 간단히 말하자면, 빙하는 천천히 움직이는 얼음 강이다. 여러 해에 걸쳐 굳어져 단단해진 녹지 않은 눈이 높은 산꼭대기로부터 거친 계곡을 따라서 아주 천천히 흐르는 언 개울로 흘러 내려가 형성된 것이다. 이 얼음은 중력과 그 위에 계속 얹히는 눈에 의해 조금씩 밀려 내려가 퇴적 지대라 불리는 층에 도달한다. 알래스카의 경우 소수의 빙하만이 만이나 해안의 하상을 가로질러 바다로 빠져나간다. 이렇게 산에서 비롯된 거대한 폭포의 움직임에 영향을 미치는 요소에는 몇 가지가 있는데, 그 중 장기적인 요소로 대기 온도의 상승이나 꾸준히 일어나는 강설 패턴의 변화를 들 수 있다.

(a) 알래스카의 오직 몇몇 빙하만 녹아 없어진다.
(b) 알래스카에 많은 퇴적 지대가 있다.
(c) 빙하를 움직이는 데 4가지 요소들이 관련되어 있다.
(d) 빙하는 환경 변화에 천천히 반응한다.

해법 얼음이 중력과 그 얼음 뒤에 계속 얹히는 눈에 의해 움직여 퇴적 지대라 불리는 지대에 도달한다는 내용과 알래스카의 경우 오직 소수의 빙하만이 만이나 해안의 하상을 가로질러 바다로 빠져 나간다는 내용을 연계해 보면 알래스카에는 퇴적 지대가 많음을 추론할 수 있어 (b)가 정답이다. (d)는 지문 내용만으로는 알 수 없다.

glacier 빙하 simply put 간단히 말해 compact 빽빽하게 찬, 밀집한 accumulation 축적 cascade 폭포, 폭포처럼 떨어뜨리다 sustain 지속하다, 양육하다 precipitation 낙하, 강수량

정답 (b)

NFL officials announced today that they would begin random drug testing in all league training camps beginning this summer. This is in response to the recent wave of incidents involving some of the league's most well-known players. Owners were not available for comment on the league's action, but many players have expressed their displeasure with the announcement. In the past the player's union has opposed such tests on the grounds that they were often unreliable and that even players taking prescription medicines could test positive initially. Union officials have stated they might seek a court order that would delay putting this into effect until further studies could be done.

Q: What can be inferred from the passage?
(a) The NFL feels its announcement has been misunderstood.
(b) Players are considering suing NFL officials to nullify the decision.
(c) Drug testing has been done to players regularly.
(d) The NFL has developed a more reliable drug test.

번역 NFL 관리들은 올 여름부터 모든 연맹 훈련 캠프에서 무작위 약물 검사를 시작할 것이라고 오늘 발표했다. 이는 이 연맹의 가장 잘 알려진 선수들 중 일부가 관련된 최근 일련의 사건들로 빚어진 소동에 응하여 취해진 조치이다. 이 연맹의 조치에 관해 논평을 해줄 구단주는 만날 수 없었으나 많은 선수들은 이 발표에 불쾌감을 표했다. 과거에는 선수 조합이 이런 검사가 더러 신빙성이 없으며 처방약을 복용한 선수들도 초기에는 양성 반응을 보일 수 있다는 이유를 들어 이런 검사를 반대해왔다. 조합 관리들은 보다 확실한 연구 결과가 나올 때까지 이의 시행을 보류하는 법원 명령을 청구할지도 모른다고 말했다.

(a) NFL 측은 그들의 발표가 곡해된 것 같다고 생각한다.
(b) 선수들은 NFL의 결정을 무효화하기 위해 NFL 관리들을 고소할 것을 고려 중이다.
(c) 선수들을 대상으로 한 약물 검사가 규칙적으로 행해져 왔다.
(d) NFL이 신뢰성이 높아진 약물 검사를 개발했다.

해법 조합 관리들은 보다 확실한 연구 결과가 나올 때까지 이의 시행을 보류하는 법원 명령을 청구할지도 모른다고 했으므로 (b)가 정답이다. 나머지는 각각 선택지의 misunderstood, regularly, more reliable에 대한 근거가 지문에 없다.

in response to ~에 응하여 on the grounds (that) ~라는 근거로 prescription 처방 positive 확신하는, 긍정적인 court order 법원 명령 put ... into effect ~을 시행하다

정답 (b)

해설 및 정답 Actual Test 02

What caused slavery? One factor that contributed to the rise of this social evil was Eli Whitney's invention of the cotton gin in 1793. The cotton gin was designed to separate the cotton plant's fibers from its seeds. Done by hand, this was a time-consuming task that made cotton farming costly, and as a result, not widely practiced. After the invention of the gin, however, cotton farming suddenly began to make economic sense, and legions of plantation owners quickly began to grow the crop. The need for hands to pick the cotton increased rapidly, and the best source of cheap labor, as far as the owners were concerned, was the slaves.

Q: What can be inferred from the passage?
(a) Eli Whitney was one of those who supported slavery.
(b) Cotton had not been picked by hand before the cotton gin.
(c) Cotton farming needed more slaves than any other industry did.
(d) Eli Whitney did a lot of business with plantation owners.

Guatemala's Indian tribes are as of yet an unassimilated group. The country has two cultures sharing the same land but not sharing the same cultural values. The Indian has distanced himself from Guatemalan society as is reflected in the differences in traditions, languages, dress, and attitudes toward social obligation. Some feel that Indians combine outward docility with an inward refusal to accept European ways, thus creating an environment in which they could be exploited by a social order that they elect not to join. For a country with such formidable social problems and separate cultures to achieve success as a nation will be a difficult task and a tough problem for Guatemala's fledgling democracy.

Q: What can be inferred from the passage?
(a) Indians do not comprise the entire population of Guatemala.
(b) Indians in Guatemala have lost their own ruling system.
(c) Guatemala's Indian tribes have to accept European ways.
(d) There is not an official language in Guatemala.

번역　노예 제도는 왜 생겨났는가? 이런 사회악의 발생에 기여한 가지는 엘리 휘트니가 1793년에 조면기를 발명한 것이라 할 수 있다. 조면기는 면섬유를 씨앗으로부터 분리하기 위해 고안됐다. 손으로 작업했을 때는 시간이 많이 소모되어 목화 농사에 많은 비용이 들었다. 그 결과 목화 재배는 널리 확산되지 않았다. 그러나 이 조면기 발명 후에는 목화 농사가 갑자기 경제적으로 수지가 맞는 사업이 되어 농장 주인들이 서둘러 목화를 재배하기 시작했다. 이에 따라 목화를 딸 일손이 급격히 증가했으며 농장 주인 입장에서는 값싼 노동의 가장 훌륭한 자원은 노예였던 것이다.

(a) 엘리 휘트니는 노예 제도를 지지한 사람들 중 하나였다.
(b) 조면기 이전에는 목화를 손으로 따지 않았다.
(c) 목화 농사는 다른 산업보다 많은 노예들을 필요로 했다.
(d) 엘리 휘트니는 농장 주인들과 사업을 많이 했다.

해법　엘리 휘트니가 조면기를 발명했다는 내용과 조면기 발명으로 목화 농사가 경제적으로 수지가 맞게 됐다는 내용, 그리고 많은 농장 주인들이 목화를 재배하기 시작했다는 내용을 연계해 보면 엘리 휘트니가 농장 주인들에게 조면기를 팔면서 사업을 많이 했음을 추론할 수 있어 (d)가 정답이다. (c)는 목화 농사와 비교되는 산업이 지문에 없다.

slavery 노예 제도　**factor** 요소　**contribute to** ~에 공헌하다
cotton gin 조면기　**seed** 씨(앗), 열매　**costly** 비싼, 비용이 많이 드는
practice 행하다, (법률, 의술 따위에) 종사하다　**legion** 다수

 정답　(d)

번역　과테말라 인디언 부족들은 현재 하나로 동화되지 않은 집단이다. 이 나라는 땅은 공유하지만 문화적 가치는 공유하지 않는 두 개의 문화를 갖고 있다. 인디언들은 스스로 과테말라 사회로부터 거리를 두어 왔으며 이와 같은 현상은 전통, 언어, 의상, 사회적 의무에 대한 태도 등의 차이에 반영되어 있다. 일부 사람들은 인디언들이 외적인 순종을 유럽 방식에 대한 내적 거부와 결합시켜 그들이 참여하지 않기로 선택한 사회 질서에 의해 이용될 수 있는 환경을 조성하고 있다고 느낀다. 이와 같은 엄청난 사회적 문제와 이분화된 문화를 가진 나라가 국가로서 성공을 거둔다는 것은 초보 민주주의 국가인 과테말라로서는 어려운 과업이며 골치 아픈 문제일 것이다.

(a) 인디언들은 과테말라의 전체 인구를 구성하지 않는다.
(b) 과테말라 인디언들은 그들 고유의 통치 체제를 잃었다.
(c) 과테말라 인디언 부족들은 유럽 방식을 받아들여만 한다.
(d) 과테말라에는 공식 언어가 없다.

해법　인디언들은 스스로 과테말라 사회로부터 거리를 두어 왔다고 했으므로 과테말라 인구가 인디언들로만 구성되지 않음을 추론할 수 있어 (a)가 정답이다. (c)는 인디언들은 외적인 순종을 유럽 방식에 대한 내적 거부와 결합시켜, 참여하지 않기로 선택한 사회 질서에 의해 이용될 수 있는 환경을 조성하고 있다는 것은 이미 유럽 방식을 받아들인 것이므로 맞지 않다.

unassimilated 동화되지 않은　**obligation** 의무　**docility** 순종, 유순함
exploit 개발하다, 채굴하다　**formidable** 무서운, 광장한　**fledgling** 초보자

정답　(a)

Many students study English as if they were jumping through hoops. They practice grammar exercises and memorize rules. They believe that when they learn all the rules, they have learned English. But English is more than a list of rules. English is a tool for thinking and communicating. In English-speaking countries, English classes do not emphasize grammar and language rules. These things are helpful, but they are secondary. The emphasis is on thinking and communicating. Students learn to organize ideas and information; build cogent arguments; tell the narratives of life and work; distill and interpret written materials; and communicate their thoughts, insights, and feelings to their readers.

Q: Which of the following would the writer most likely agree with?

(a) English rules can be ignored as long as speakers understand each other.

(b) Most students study English only when told to do so.

(c) Sharing outside classroom experience is part of learning English.

(d) Learning English is all about making oneself understood.

Norbert Rillieux was born in the United States; however he received his education in Paris, France. (a) At 24, he was teaching applied engineering at the Ecole Centrale; however, his interest in chemistry and steam engineering led him to a process that almost revolutionized the sugar industry. (b) In 1846, Rillieux made use of the reduced boiling point of a liquid under a vacuum evaporator. (c) This process produced a cheaper, better, and more automated method of crystallizing sugar. (d) The same concept is now used in the manufacture of condensed milk, soap, and glue.

  노버트 릴리유는 미국에서 태어났으나 프랑스 파리에서 교육을 받았다. (a) 24세에 그는 에콜 상트랄에서 응용 공학을 가르치고 있었지만 화학과 증기 공학에 대한 그의 관심은 설탕 제조 산업에 혁신을 일으키는 공정을 거의 개발할 뻔하게 했다. (b) 1846년 그는 진공 기화기 안에서 액체의 끓는점이 줄어드는 점을 이용했다. (c) 이 공정은 더 자동화된 설탕 정제법을 통해서 보다 저렴한 비용으로 양질의 설탕을 만들어내는 것을 가능하게 했다. (d) 현재는 동일한 원리가 농축 우유와 비누, 접착제를 제조하는 데에도 적용되고 있다.

해법 1846년 진공 기화기 안에서 액체의 끓는점이 줄어드는 점을 이용했고, 이 공정은 더 자동화된 설탕 정제법을 통해서 보다 저렴한 비용으로 양질의 설탕을 만들어내는 것을 가능하게 했으며, 동일한 원리가 현재 농축 우유와 비누, 접착제를 제조하는 데에 이용되고 있다는 내용을 볼 때 (a)의 almost revolutionized에서 almost가 없어야 지문 흐름에 어울린다.

applied engineering 응용 공학 **vacuum evaporator** 진공 기화기 **crystallize** 결정화시키다 **condensed** 농축된 **glue** 접착제

✓ 정답 (a)

번역 많은 학생들은 영어 공부를 지나치게 어렵게 한다. 그들은 문법을 공부하고 규칙을 암기한다. 규칙을 모두 익히고 나면 영어를 배웠다고 믿는다. 그러나 영어는 규칙 그 이상이다. 영어는 생각하고 의사소통을 하기 위한 하나의 도구이다. 영어를 사용하는 나라에서는 영어 수업 시간에 문법이나 언어 규칙을 강조하지 않는다. 그런 것이 도움이 되긴 하지만 부차적이다. 중점은 생각과 의사소통에 있다. 따라서 학생들은 생각과 정보를 정리하는 법, 설득력 있는 논쟁을 벌이는 법, 인생과 일에 대해 묘사하는 법, 글을 읽고 걸러서 이해하는 법, 그리고 그들의 생각, 통찰력, 느낌을 전달하는 글을 쓰는 법을 배운다.

(a) 영어의 규칙은 화자들끼리 알아들을 수만 있다면 무시될 수 있다.

(b) 대부분 학생들은 남들이 시킬 때만 영어 공부를 한다.

(c) 교실 밖 경험을 나누는 것이 영어 학습의 일부분이다.

(d) 영어 학습은 자기 말을 남에게 이해시키는 것이 전부이다.

해법 영어를 사용하는 나라들의 영어 수업 시간에 문법이나 언어 규칙보다 생각하는 것과 의사소통하는 것이 중요하고, 따라서 인생과 일에 대해 묘사해서 말하는 것을 배운다고 했으므로 (c)가 정답이다. (d)는 읽을거리들의 의미를 순화하고 뜻을 헤아리는 것도 배우므로, 영어를 배우는 것은 남들이 이해할 수 있는 표현을 하는 것이 전부라는 선택지의 all about making oneself understood가 맞지 않아 오답이다.

jump through hoops[a hoop] (결과를 얻기 위해) 어려운 과정을 겪다 **cogent** 설득력 있는 **distill** 증류하다, 다듬다

✓ 정답 (c)

There is no doubt that there are many tourist attractions in Prague. (a) But some visitors have complained of there not being enough light for them to walk around the streets at night. (b) Recently, the magnificent 600-year-old Prague Castle was equipped with a new lighting system, so it could be seen better at night. (c) The high-tech system was financed by the British rock group the Rolling Stones, and set up by the engineer who designs the lighting for their own rock performances. (d) The Rolling Stones' gift to Prague resulted from their friendship with the Czech President, but they made all the arrangements without his knowing of the plan.

번역 프라하에 많은 관광 명소들이 있다는 것에는 의심의 여지가 없다. (a) 그러나 일부 방문객은 밤에 거리를 걸어 다니기에 충분한 불빛이 없다는 것에 대해 불평해 왔다. (b) 최근에 600년 된 웅장한 프라하 성에 새로운 조명 시설이 설치되어 야간에도 더 잘 보이게 되었다. (c) 설치 공사에 들어간 첨단 조명 시설에 필요한 자금은 영국의 록 그룹인 롤링 스톤즈가 제공했고, 평소 그들의 록 공연장에 조명 설계를 담당하는 기술자가 설치를 담당했다. (d) 롤링 스톤즈가 프라하를 위해 준비한 이 선물은 이들의 체코 대통령과의 우정 때문이었지만 정작 대통령은 그 계획을 모르게 한 채 모든 준비를 했다.

해법 프라하에 많은 관광 명소들이 있고, 최근에 600년 된 웅장한 프라하 성에 새로운 조명 시설이 설치되어 밤에 더 잘 볼 수 있게 됐다고 했으므로 (a)의 walk around the streets at night이 admire the buildings at night 정도가 돼야 한다.

magnificent 장엄한, 훌륭한

정답 (a)

The movie *X-Men* is a powerful reminder that many of us still abhor the idea of differences and hold strong bonds to things that are similar. (a) If we see *X-Men* only as entertainment, we miss so many precious messages in it. (b) W. H. Auden once said, "Many misunderstandings arise over a failure to recognize certain attitudes we all take, according to our upbringing, in such a way that we cannot imagine anybody taking any other one." (c) Yet, we are still avoiding the unfamiliar, out of groundless fear and prejudice. (d) This is why the movie is regarded as one of the best by psychologists.

번역 영화 〈엑스맨〉은 우리들 중 많은 사람들이 여전히 본인과 다른 생각을 몹시 싫어하고 유사한 것들에 대해 강한 유대를 느끼고 있음을 강력히 시사한다. (a) 만약 〈엑스맨〉을 그저 오락으로만 본다면 영화에 담겨 있는 소중한 메시지를 상당히 많이 놓치는 것이다. (b) W. H. 오든은 "사람은 모두 자신이 자라면서 받아온 교육에 따라 각자의 관점을 취하는데, 누군가 본인과 다른 관점을 취할 수 있다는 것을 상상하지 못하는 수준일 수 있음을 깨닫지 못하는 데서 많은 오해가 빚어진다"라고 말했다. (c) 그러나 우리는 아직도 근거 없는 공포나 편견으로 인하여 낯선 대상을 피하고 있다. (d) 이런 이유로 이 영화가 심리학자들로부터 최고의 영화 중 하나로 여겨진다.

해법 영화 〈엑스맨〉이 나오는 다른 생각을 싫어하고 유사한 것들을 좇는 많은 사람들의 일반적인 성향을 보여주고 왜 이런 성향이 나타나는지 설명하는 지문의 주요 내용과 동떨어진 (d)의 This is why에 해당하는 내용이 (c)에 없어 (d)가 흐름에 어울리지 않는다.

reminder 생각나게 하는 것 **abhor** 몹시 싫어하다, 혐오하다 **precious** 귀중한 **upbringing** 양육, 가정교육 **groundless** 근거 없는 **prejudice** 편견 **psychologist** 심리학자

정답 (d)

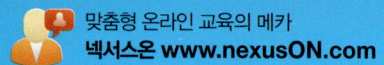

How to TEPS 시크릿 독해편

텝스 독해 유형 탄탄 훈련 코스

Reading Drills
비교적 짧고 간단한 지문으로 본격적인 텝스 독해를 위한 워밍업

Model Test
전체 지문 이해를 위한 토픽 제시, 텝스 독해 브리지 기능

TEPS Reading Practice
본격적인 고득점을 위한 고난도 텝스 독해

Actual Test
시험 직전 마무리 점검용으로 출제 비밀 100% 반영

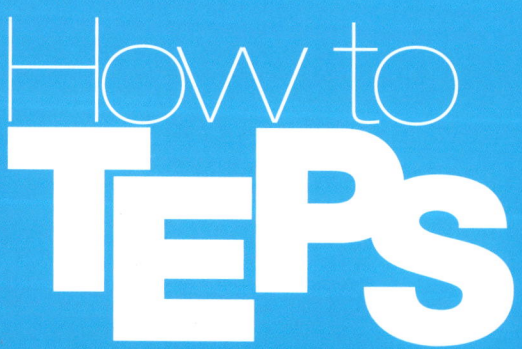

서울대 텝스 관리위원회 최신기출 스피킹·라이팅 | 서울대학교 TEPS관리위원회 문제 제공·유경하 해설 | 340쪽 | 28,000원
서울대 텝스 관리위원회 최신기출 i-TEPS | 서울대학교 TEPS관리위원회 문제 제공·넥서스 TEPS연구소 해설 | 296쪽 | 19,800원

독해 · 청해

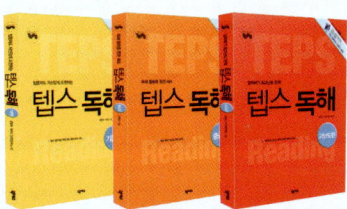

How to 텝스 독해 기본편 | 양준희·넥서스 TEPS연구소 지음 | 312쪽 | 17,500원
How to 텝스 독해 중급편 | 장우리 지음 | 360쪽 | 17,500원
How to 텝스 독해 고난도편 | 넥서스 TEPS연구소 지음 | 324쪽 | 17,500원
How to 텝스 청해 중급편 | 양준희 지음 | 276쪽 | 18,500원

How to TEPS 실전력 500·600·700·800·900 | 넥서스 TEPS연구소 지음 | 308쪽 | 실전력 500~800: 16,500원, 실전력 900: 18,000원
서울대 텝스 관리위원회 속성 실전테스트 | 서울대학교 TEPS관리위원회 문제 제공 | 164쪽 | 9,800원
텝스 기출모의 5회분 | 김학수·넥서스 TEPS연구소 지음 | 364쪽 | 14,500원

어휘

How to TEPS VOCA 2nd Edition | 김무룡·넥서스 TEPS연구소 지음 | 320쪽 | 12,800원
How to TEPS 넥서스 텝스 보카 | 이기헌 지음 | 536쪽 | 15,000원
How to 텝스 어휘 기본편 | 고명희·넥서스 TEPS연구소 지음 | 304쪽 | 15,500원
How to 텝스 어휘 고난도편 | 김무룡·넥서스 TEPS연구소 지음 | 296쪽 | 17,000원

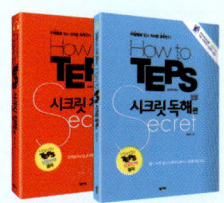

How to TEPS 시크릿 청해편·독해편 | 유니스 정(청해), 정성수(독해) 지음 | 청해: 22,500원, 독해: 14,500원
텝스, 어려운 파트만 콕콕 찍어 점수 따기 | 이성희·전종삼 지음 | 176쪽 | 13,000원

고급 (800점 이상)

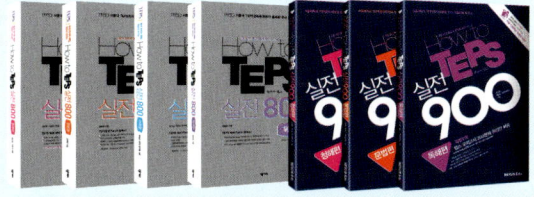

How to TEPS 실전 800 청해편·문법편·어휘편·독해편 | 강소영·서인석(청해), 김태희(문법), 넥서스 TEPS연구소(어휘), 한정림(독해) 지음 | 청해: 22,000원, 문법: 15,000원, 어휘: 12,800원, 독해: 22,000원
How to TEPS 실전 900 청해편·문법편·독해편 | 김철용(청해), 이용재(문법), 김철용(독해) 지음 | 청해: 17,000원, 문법: 16,500원, 독해: 17,500원

How to TEPS L/C | 이성희 지음 | 400쪽 | 19,800원
How to TEPS R/C | 이정은·넥서스 TEPS연구소 지음 | 396쪽 | 19,800원

How to TEPS Expert L | 박영주 지음 | 340쪽 | 21,000원
How to TEPS Expert GVR | 박영주 지음 | 520쪽 | 28,000원
How to TEPS Expert 고난도 실전 모의고사 | 넥서스 TEPS연구소 지음 | 388쪽 | 21,500원